The Notion of Employer in the Era of the Fissured Workplace

Bulletin of Comparative Labour Relations

VOLUME 95

Editor

The series started in 1970 under the dynamic editorship of Professor Roger Blanpain (Belgium), former President of the International Industrial Relations Association. Professor Blanpain, currently Professor Emeritus of Labour Law, Universities of Leuven and Tilburg, is also General Editor of the International Encyclopedia of Laws (with more than 1,600 collaborators worldwide) and President of the Association of Educative and Scientific Authors.

In 2015 Frank Hendrickx, Professor of labour law at the Faculty of Law of the University of Leuven (Belgium) joined as a co-Editor. Frank Hendrickx has published numerous articles and books and regularly advises governments, international institutions and private organisations in the area of labour law as well as in sports law. He is the Editor-in-Chief of the European Labour Law Journal and General Editor of the International Encyclopaedia of Laws together with Professor Roger Blanpain.

Introduction

The Bulletins constitute a unique source of information and thought-provoking discussion, laying the groundwork for studies of employment relations in the 21st century, involving among much else the effects of globalization, new technologies, migration, and the greying of the population.

Contents/Subjects

Amongst other subjects the Bulletins frequently include the proceedings of international or regional conferences; reports from comparative projects devoted to salient issues in industrial relations, human resources management, and/or labour law; and specific issues underlying the multicultural aspects of our industrial societies.

Objective

The Bulletins offer a platform of expression and discussion on labour relations to scholars and practitioners worldwide, often featuring special guest editors.

The titles published in this series are listed at the end of this volume.

BULLETIN OF COMPARATIVE LABOUR RELATIONS – 95

The Notion of Employer in the Era of the Fissured Workplace

Should Labour Law Responsibilities Exceed the Boundary of the Legal Entity?

Editors

Roger Blanpain

Frank Hendrickx

Guest Editors

Hiroya Nakakubo
Takashi Araki

Contributors

Diego Álvarez Alonso
Takashi Araki
Matthew W. Finkin
Tess Hardy
Sylvaine Laulom
Shih-Hao Liu
Hiroya Nakakubo
Jeremias Prassl
Bernd Waas
Aelim Yun
Qi Zhong
Mimi Zou

Wolters Kluwer

Published by:
Kluwer Law International B.V.
PO Box 316
2400 AH Alphen aan den Rijn
The Netherlands
Website: www.wklawbusiness.com

Sold and distributed in North, Central and South America by:
Wolters Kluwer Legal & Regulatory U.S.
7201 McKinney Circle
Frederick, MD 21704
United States of America
Email: customer.service@wolterskluwer.com

Sold and distributed in all other countries by:
Turpin Distribution Services Ltd
Stratton Business Park
Pegasus Drive, Biggleswade
Bedfordshire SG18 8TQ
United Kingdom
Email: kluwerlaw@turpin-distribution.com

Printed on acid-free paper.

ISBN 978-90-411-8470-2

e-Book: ISBN 978-90-411-8471-9
web-PDF: ISBN 978-90-411-8472-6

Printed in the United Kingdom.

Notes on Contributors

Diego Álvarez Alonso, Lecturer of Labour Law and Social Security Law, University of Oviedo.

Takashi Araki, Professor, the University of Tokyo, Senior Research Fellow, JILPT.

Matthew W. Finkin, Professor of Law, the University of Illinois.

Tess Hardy, Lecturer in Law, University of Melbourne.

Sylvaine Laulom, Professor, Head of the Institute of Labour Studies of Lyon, University Lumière Lyon 2.

Shih-Hao Liu, Professor, Law School, Ming-Chuan University.

Hiroya Nakakubo, Professor, Hitotsubashi University, Senior Research Fellow, JILPT.

Jeremias Prassl, Associate Professor in the Faculty of Law, Fellow of Magdalen College, University of Oxford.

Bernd Waas, Professor of Law, Faculty of Law, Goethe University of Frankfurt.

Aelim Yun, Professor of Law and Social Security Law, Korea National Open University.

Qi Zhong, Researcher, Japan Institute for Labor Policy and Training.

Mimi Zou, Assistant Professor, Faculty of Law, Chinese University of Hong Kong.

Summary of Contents

Table of Contents

Introduction

Hiroya Nakakubo[*] & *Takashi Araki*[**]

THE TOPIC AND ITS BACKGROUND

The Japan Institute for Labor Policy and Training (JILPT) hosted its 13th Comparative Labor Law Seminar (the Tokyo Seminar) on February 29 and March 1, 2016.[1] The seminar addressed the topic *Reconsidering the Notion of "Employer" in the Era of the Fissured Workplace: Should Labor Law Responsibilities Exceed the Boundary of the Legal Entity?* which was on consultation with Prof. Kazuo Sugeno, President of the JILPT. As the organizers of the seminar, it was our pleasure to invite distinguished scholars from Australia, China, France, Germany, Japan, the Republic of Korea, Spain, Taiwan, the United Kingdom and the United States (U.S.) to participate in the project. The following memo was sent to the participating scholars to elaborate on the topic:

> "The fissured workplace" is the term used by David Weil in his recent book, "The Fissured Workplace: Why Work Became So Bad for So Many and What Can Be Done to Improve It" (Harvard University Press, 2014). Weil describes the phenomenon of "fissuring" as follows (pp. 8-9):
>
> During much of the twentieth century, the critical employment relationship was between large businesses and workers. ... However, most no longer directly employ legions of workers to make products or deliver services. Employment has been actively shed by these market leaders and transferred to a complicated network of smaller business units. Lower-level businesses operate in more highly competitive markets than those of the firms that shifted employment to them.

* Hitotsubashi University.

** University of Tokyo.

1. The JILPT Tokyo Seminar was originally organized by Professor Kazuo Sugeno (Professor Emeritus, the University of Tokyo, Honorary President of the International Society for Labour and Social Security Law, President of JILPT) and Professor Yasuo Suwa (Professor Emeritus, Hosei University, Chairman, Central Labor Relations Commission) in 1991. The papers submitted to the previous JILPT Tokyo Seminars were published in the Bulletin of Comparative Labour Relations No. 30 (1995), No. 34 (1999), No. 38 (2000), No. 47 (2003), No. 53 (2005), No. 61 (2007), No. 68 (2008), No. 76 (2010), No. 81 (2012), and No.88 (2014).

> Consequently, [w]age setting and supervision shift from core businesses to a myriad of organizations, each operating under the rigorous standards of lead businesses but facing fierce competitive pressures. Although lead businesses set demanding goals and standards, and often detailed work practice requirements for subsidiary companies, the actual liability, oversight, and supervision of the workforce become the problem of one or more other organizations. And by replacing a direct employment relationship with a fissured workplace, employment itself becomes more precarious, with risk shifted onto smaller employers and individual workers, who are often cast in the role of independent businesses in their own right.
>
> As the fissured workplace has deepened and spread across the economy, work that once provided middle-class wages and benefits has declined. Jobs that once resided inside lead businesses providing decent earnings and stability now reside with employers who set wages under far more competitive conditions. Where lead companies once shared gains with their internal workforce, fissuring leads to growing inequality in how the value created in the economy is distributed.
>
> Traditionally, labor and employment law has imposed various obligations on "employers." Legal responsibilities usually stop at the boundary of the legal entity, even though there are some exceptions reflecting the nature of the subject. However, Weil's argument of the "fissured workplace" vividly shows that there has been a fundamental change in the structure of businesses. It is no longer sufficient to discuss the responsibility of the person directly hiring workers. Law should squarely grasp and tackle this new reality. But how far can the current labor law go in questioning the responsibility of persons who have no direct contractual relationship with the workers? Can we develop effective theories under the existing legal framework? Or do we need a new set of legislation? Do other measures such as soft law or reputation mechanisms in the market deal with the undesirable consequences of the fissurization more properly? Inspired by Weil's excellent analysis, we would like to discuss these challenges facing our labor law today.

SUGGESTED FOCUS AND OUTLINE

Fissurization may take various forms, such as multi-layered subcontracting, outsourcing, franchising, and supply-chains. These measures are aimed at, or result in, "externalization" of the employment relationship, which brings about many problematic phenomena.

From the legal point of view, it seems there are two types of employment externalization. First, by outsourcing, contracting out, or utilizing supply-chain mechanisms, the lead companies may be relieved of employment-related responsibilities in multi-layered contractual relationships even though they wield considerable influence on the fate of the actual workers. This is the issue of the notion of "employer," or who should bear the legal responsibility as the employer. Second, in the process of fissurization, traditional workers or employees tend to be converted into, or sometimes misclassified as, self-employed or independent contractors. This is the issue of the notion of "employee."

While the second issue is of course important, it has already been discussed rather extensively. We therefore decided to place the focus of the 13th Tokyo Seminar on the first issue.

After explaining the aforementioned focus of the discussion, we offered the following points to the participants as a general guideline for the country papers, with a note that they were free to depart from them given that the situation and legal responses might differ in their respective countries:

1. **Introduction**
   - General observation about the topic before going into the analysis.
2. **Current situation of fissurization**
   - How far has the overall phenomenon conceptualized as "fissurization of the workplace" developed in your country, and why (if not, why so)?
     A. What are the individual phenomena composing such "fissurization of the workplace" (such as subcontracting, supply chain, franchising and others). Please describe them somewhat concretely. Are they new phenomena or rather conventional practices?
     B. What are managerial motives and socioeconomic backgrounds which give rise to such "fissurization of the workplace" (such as cost-cutting and evasion of labor-law responsibilities under intensified global competition)?
     C. Please give an overview of the labor law issues (both interpretative and legislative) contained in "fissurization of the workplace."
3. **Current legislative and interpretative responses**
   - Measures to protect workers by going beyond the boundary of the legal entity should be described both in individual employment relations and collective labor relations.

   3.1 Individual labor relations
   - Please describe the current legislation in your country, if any, to protect workers in a multi-layered contractual relationship or indirect employment relationship, for instance:
     - Site owner's responsibilities concerning health and safety regulations in the construction site
     - User's responsibilities in a temporary agency work relationship
     - Parent or holding company's responsibilities to the daughter company's workers concerning wages, work-related injuries, dismissal regulations, and other duties arising from employment.
     - Have these regulations existed for a long time, or were they newly adopted to deal with fissurization?
     - Please describe the interpretative responses to protect workers in a multi-layered contractual relationship or indirect employment relationship, such as expanding the notion of "employer" (single employer, joint employer, etc.), and piercing the corporate veil.
     - Have these theories existed for a long time, or were they newly adopted to deal with fissurization?

   3.2 Collective labor relations
   - Please describe the current legislative and interpretative responses to fissurization in collective labor relations, for instance:
     - Does a parent or holding company bear the duty to bargain with, consult with, or give information to, representatives of the workers (such as labor unions or works councils) of its daughter or subsidiary company?
     - Does your country have special regulations on behalf of those who are not directly employed by the company concerning matters such as works council elections or other procedures in workers' involvement schemes?
     - Have social partners (labor unions and employers' organizations) set up special mechanisms addressing fissurization?

4. **Evaluation and future prospects**
   - How do you evaluate the current legal situation? Has your country's current legal system successfully dealt with the issue of "employer"? If not, what are the problems of the current system? What is under discussion? What should be done for the future?

PRELIMINARY OBSERVATIONS

At the seminar, the participating scholars delivered presentations based on their country papers and lively discussions followed. It was unfortunate that the German representative became unable to attend shortly beforehand, but his paper was also shared with and appreciated by the participants. The ten papers are contained in the following chapters, with some revisions to reflect the discussions. It is impossible to summarize their rich contents here, but we would like to make several remarks as preliminary observations in the hope that they will provide readers with some kind of analytical guidance when going through this volume.

First, various forms of fissurization are in fact progressing in these countries – although there are indications that the large integrated enterprises before such fissurization were only dominant for a particular phase of industrialization – and employment relationships are being shed from the lead company off to external contractors. Thus, it is becoming all the more important to go beyond the formal boundary of the legal entity.

Second, generally speaking, the notion of "employer" has been addressed very little in comparison with that of "employee." While there is a presumption of a unitary employer entering into a contract with the employee, the function of the employer may be assumed by, or distributed among, multiple entities. There are legal techniques to deal with such reality, such as the doctrine of joint employer or co-employer, or the ultimate method of "piercing the corporate veil."

Third, we can identify legislative attempts from various aspects. As regards the safety and health of workers, a special legal scheme is often adopted to involve the principal contractor or other person that is not the employer in the narrow sense. Wage payment is another area where such a scheme tends to develop. Some countries regulate the use of subcontracting though special legislation, the most aggressive being that of Spain. Franchising is also subjected to special regulation in some countries.

Fourth, the notion of "employer" is also being reconsidered in the sphere of collective labor law, especially in relation to the employer's duty to bargain in the U.S. and some other countries with a similar legal framework. Meanwhile, the European countries have a mechanism of worker representation covering multiple, related employers. It is also notable that a broader range of citizens and groups may support workers' activities from the outside.

Finally, temporary work or "worker dispatching" arrangements form an important part of fissurization. Legal regulation of such triangular relationships varies from country to country and has rightfully inspired a significant amount of research by labor law scholars. It would be helpful to look at the regulation of such relationships alongside the other aspects of fissurization in the papers. Perhaps we could find in it a model for legally implicating a non-employer who wields substantial influence on the fate of the worker.

David Weil's book provided a clear viewpoint from which we can analyze the fragmentation and externalization of employment, trends that have become increasingly severe in the last couple of decades. Law cannot solve all the problems, but it undoubtedly remains a major tool for addressing the latter part of the book's subtitle – *Why Work Became So Bad for So Many and What Can Be Done to Improve It?* This volume is designed to contribute to such efforts, which we expect will be taken up by many other scholars around the world.[2]

2. For an earlier comparative study that was inspired by Weil's *The Fissured Workplace*, *see* Volume 37, Number 1 (Fall, 2015) of the Comparative Labor Law & Policy Journal.

CHAPTER 1

The Legal Ambiguity of Fissured Work in the United States

Matthew W. Finkin[*]

§1.01 INTRODUCTION

For more than a generation, students of the American economy have drawn attention to the growing segmentation of the work force, to the resulting deterioration in labor standards and to the lag in the law's response.[1] The situation has been dealt with comprehensively by David Weil, who captured the process in what he termed "fissurization:"

> During much of the twentieth century, the critical employment relationship was between large businesses and workers. Large businesses with national and international reputations operating at the top of their industries..... ["*Lead businesses*"] continue to focus on delivering value to their customers and investors. However, most no longer directly employ legions of workers to make products or deliver services. Employment has been actively shed by these market leaders and transferred to a complicated network of smaller business units ....

* Professor of Law, the University of Illinois. The author would like to thank Sanford Jacoby and Wilma Liebman for comment on a previous draft. Thanks are also due to the comments of the participants in the Tokyo Seminar and to Fellows of the Institute of Advanced Studies, Nantes, France, for their comments on the revised paper presented to them for discussion on May 9, 2016.

1. The body of literature is substantial. Attention to the former was drawn early on by David Gordon, Richard Edwards, & Michael Reich, SEGMENTED WORK, DIVIDED WORKERS: THE HISTORICAL TRANSFORMATION OF LABOR IN THE UNITED STATES (1982). Attention to the latter was drawn most insightfully in the U.K. by Hugh Collins, *Independent Contractors and the Challenge of Vertical Disintegration to Employment Protection Laws*, 10 Oxford J. Legal Studies 353 (1990) and in the U.S. by Craig Becker, *Labor Law Outside the Employment Relationship*, 74 Tex. L. Rev. 1527 (1996).

> This creates downward pressure on wages and benefits, *murkiness about who bears responsibility for work conditions*, and increased likelihood that basic labor standards will be violated. In many cases, fissuring leads simultaneously to a rise in profitability for the lead companies who operate at the top of industries and increasingly precarious working conditions for workers at lower levels.[2]

Two features of the scene Weil describes bear emphasis at the outset. First, fissurization takes diverse forms: contracting with individual workers on terms designed to have them regarded as independent contractors, not employees, and so ineligible for the protections accorded employees under labor law; contracting with businesses in systems of franchising, and sub-franchising, that require these companies to adhere to intense oversight by the franchisor to maintain the attributes of its brand identification even as the franchisees retain managerial discretion over employment; contracting for goods and services down chains of supply, sometimes quite long, that competitively pit these smaller business entities against one another resulting in a race to the bottom on labor standards and the creation of strong incentives for wage theft and unlawful union avoidance.

The resort to individual independent contractors, currently subject to increasing litigation and state "misclassification" law, has a well-developed set of tests to distinguish one from another.[3] That aspect of fissurization will not be addressed here; not directly, that is. The latter two contracting models engage the theme of business structure; they will be addressed. Here, the law's approach in the United States (U.S.) probes whether the relationship of the lead company, as it will be called, to the contracting company below is such as to make them joint employers of the affected employees. Even so, the law of joint employment often echoes the law of individual classification and, to that extent, will be reflected in the discussion.

2. David Weil, The Fissured Workplace: Why Work Became So Bad for So Many and What Can Be Done to Improve It 8 (2014) (italics added).
3. Most states apply a multi-pronged test of economic reality under their wage and hour laws that echo the federal Fair Labor Standards Act. *See* e.g., *Slayman v. FedEx Ground Package Sys., Inc.*, 765 F.3d 1033 (9th Cir. 2014) (applying Oregon law); *Alexander v. FedEx Ground Package Sys., Inc.*, 765 F.3d 981 (9th Cir. 2014) (applying California law); 863 To Go, *Inc. v. Dept. of Labor*, 99 A.3d 629 (Vt. 2014). New Jersey has adopted a three-part "ABC" test which presumes the worker is an employee unless all of three conditions are met:

   (A) Such individual has been and will continue to be free from control or direction over the performance of such service, both under his contract of service and in fact.
   (B) Such service is either outside the usual course of the business for which such service is performed, or that such service is performed outside of all the places of business of the enterprise for which such service is performed.
   (C) Such individual is customarily engaged in an independently established trade, occupation, profession or business.

   Hargrove v. Sleepy's, LLC, 106 A.3d 449 (N.J. 2015). Kansas, in contrast, has adopted a twenty-part test that mixes elements of both "right to control" and "economic reality." *Craig v. FedEx Ground Package Sup., Inc.*, 355 P.3d 66 (Kan. 2014). The National Labor Relations Act adopts a "right of control" test under which, however, the National Labor Relations Board, in disagreement with a federal Court of Appeals, held FedEx drivers to be employees. The court assigned the individual's opportunity to engage in entrepreneurial activity heightened weight. The Board has disagreed. FedEx Home Delivery, 361 NLRB No. 55 (2014). The matter awaits judicial resolution.

Second, the relevant body of law in the U.S. was enacted on the tacit and sometimes, not so tacit assumption that it was concerned with workers employed in large, vertically integrated companies; that is, with American business structure at a certain moment of historical development. That structure was not characteristic of American businesses in the run-up to integration and is disintegrating today. Whence the legally vexing nature of fissurization, the law's time boundedness, its historical disconnect with what is presented today.

What follows explores the "murkiness about who bears [legal] responsibility" for wages, hours, and working conditions in this fissured world. The state of affairs will be examined through the three sets of the protective law most implicated: wage and hour law, collective bargaining law, and employment discrimination law, with a sidelong glance at social security and unemployment compensation.[4] However, the focus throughout is only partly on legal tests and outcomes. The primary focus is on the fact that these laws were fashioned at a moment in time that is not characteristic of antecedent business structures and well before what is happening now. Consequently, the thrust of this chapter is to summon attention anew to the legal protections working people need in a world of fissured work.

§1.02 THE ARC OF BUSINESS SIZE AND STRUCTURE

Most manufacture in antebellum America was done in small workshops, even in the home, as it had long been in Western Europe. There were exceptions where production demanded high energy consumption and substantial capital outlays for technology – iron manufacture, for example.[5] But even in textile manufacture, one of the earliest to assemble large numbers of machine operators under a single roof, work was often "put out," as it had been in Europe from the sixteenth century. The European merchant-capitalists of that time:

> coordinated great numbers of cottage workers at different stages in the production process, such as combers, spinners, weavers, bleachers, and dyers, and they frequently used middlemen to conclude and enforce contracts with individual

4. This essay will not take up responsibility under workplace safety and health law as it is too complex for summary treatment. The law is a mixture of federal law, which has an exacting set of detailed rules governing multi-employer workplaces, and state law, both legislative and judge-made. Federal law deals extensively with the obligations of contractors to their subcontractors' workers who work on the lead company's premises. OSHA Instruction CPL 02-00-124 (Dec. 10, 1999). State law is more variegated. *Compare Halterman v. Radisson Hotel Corp.*, 523 S.E.2d 823 (Va. 2000) (hotel not negligent under state law in failing to inform dispatched workman of exposure to hazardous chemicals, nor would liability be imposed under federal "multi-employer workplace" rule as this required only that the receiving employer inform the dispatching employer, not the dispatched employee, of the hazard) *with Afoa v. Port of Seattle*, 296 P.3d 800 (Wash. 2013) (airport authority would be liable for workplace injury to employee of its contractor's contractor despite lack of privity of contract between the airport and the subcontractor, depending on the degree of control the airport exercised over the manner and instrumentalities of the subcontractor's employee's work).
5. Anne Knowles, Mastering Iron: The Struggle to Modernize an American Industry, 1800-1868 (2013).

> workers (*Verlagssystem*, or putting-out system). The activities of merchant-manufacturers or master-manufacturers thus came fairly close to what Alchian and Demsetz have defined as the entrepreneur in a modern firm. They monitored the use of inputs in the team production of a complex good; they measured output performance; they acted as a central party at least for contracts relating to individual stages of production; they were able to alter the structure of their workforce at short notice; and they were residual claimants, that is, they earned a profit from their efforts at co-ordinating and supervising production processes.[6]

These contracts could be made with individuals; but, more often, they were made with the heads of workshops employing journeymen and apprentices, i.e., with contracting firms. The putting out of work in antebellum America was simpler, usually involving only individual home workers; but it continued as a business model well into the twentieth century and continues afresh today where cognitive work is bid on and performed electronically by individuals working away from a common work site.[7]

The putting-out system had advantages over centralized production: the merchant-capitalist, or "lead business," did not have to invest in real estate and technology; the work did not require close supervision by the lead business; the lead company had considerable flexibility in responding to market demand; and, as it contracted at a piece rate, the problem of labor cost and control was the contractor's. In addition, by dispersing the work the contractor reduced the prospect of collective action by the workers.

However, this business model was ill suited to the needs of mass production toward which America moved from the last third of the nineteenth century into the first third of the twentieth and at breakneck speed.[8] Mass production required the use of large amounts of energy at a single location; heavy investment in real estate and technology; and the close coordination and supervision of a complex of interrelated tasks by an on-site workforce. A number of companies, especially those producing products composed of interchangeable parts – firearms, sewing machines, farm implements, machine tools – used "inside contractors" for the production of work requiring a high degree of technical knowledge and skill.[9] The system had been used in

6. Ulrich Pfister, *Craft Guilds, the Theory of the Firm, and Early Modern Proto-Industry* in Guilds, Innovation and the European Economy, 1400-1800, 25, 31-32 (S.R. Epstein & Maarten Prak eds. 2009) (reference omitted).
7. This is discussed by Matthew Finkin, *Beclouded Work in Historical Perspective*, 37 Comp. Lab. L. & Pol'y J. – (2016) (in press).
8. Daniel Rodgers, The Work Ethic in Industrial America 1850-1920, 22-25 (1978):

> By 1916, the McCormick plant had grown to 15,000 workers; and in that year, the payroll at the Ford Motor Company works at Highland Park reached 33,000. Workshops of the size that had characterized the antebellum economy, employing a handful or a score of workers, persisted amid these immense establishments. But they employed a smaller and smaller fraction of the workers. By 1919, in the Northern states between the Mississippi River and the Atlantic Ocean, three-fourths of all wage earners in manufacturing worked in factories of more than 100 employees, and 30% of the giants of more than 1,000.

9. John Buttrick, *The Inside Contract System*, 12 J. Econ. Hist. 205 (1952).

the Venetian arsenal for the production ships in the sixteenth century[10] and in some early American textile factories.[11] It entailed a contract between the company and a master craftsman. The:

> factory owner agreed to provide a fixed piece rate to the contractor in exchange for completed product components. Components collected from the contractors were usually assembled by owner-employed workers under the supervision of owner-employed foremen. Three key elements, when combined, made this arrangement different from ordinary contracts: (1) the contractor hired, fired, and set the wages for his own helpers (employees); (2) the owner provided the contractor with machinery (although the contractor could make changes in the production techniques), raw materials, and working capital; and (3) production took place inside the owner's factory rather than in the contractor's workshop.[12]

The system was popular with companies because it kept costs low. The system also stimulated innovation and careful management by the contractors who often pocketed the fruits of both. A consequence, as with contemporary fissurization, was that the men who worked for the contractor "often bore the brunt of the downward 'alignment' of the contractor's price when the manufacturer decided that his [the contractor's] profits were too high."[13]

The inside contract system was eventually abandoned, the inside contractor replaced by company foremen. Various reasons have been given for the change: management's perceived need for greater control over cost and production; its concomitant desire to acquire the cost information as well as the technical knowledge hoarded by its contractors; even as a response to the challenge, the system posed to

10. Robert Davis, Ship Builders of the Venetian Arsenal 54-55 (1991). *See also* Frederick Lane, Venetian Ships and Shipbuilders of the Renaissance 200-201 (1934); Frederic Lane, Venice: A Maritime Republic 364 (1973) ("For occasions when galleys were needed in a hurry and a large labor force had to be made to work more efficiently, the Lords of the Arsenal devised a system of 'inside contracts,' much like that employed by American gun manufacturers in the nineteenth century. Using materials and equipment supplied by the management, shipwrights bid for contracts to make specified numbers of hulls. The lowest bidder received the contract and hired other shipwrights to work for him under his supervision. The Senate felt that work done by inside contracting was not of top quality. It forbade caulking to be done in that way, and permitted it for construction of hulls only in emergencies.").

11. For example, in Samuel Riddle's mill in Rockdale, Pennsylvania, in the 1830s where the "mule spinner":

> was treated as a subcontractor (and in census returns, even as late as 1850, might be referred to as a "cotton manufacturer"), paying his creel attender and piecer out of his own wages. As Samuel Riddle said, "The mule spinners are paid by the quantity they do, and they employ their own help." Although the spinners did not own their own mules.

Anthony F.C. Wallace, Rockdale 177 (1980) (reference omitted).

12. Ernest Englander, *The Inside Contract System of Production and Organization: A Neglected Aspect of the History of the Firm*, 28 Labor Hist. 429, 436 (1987).

13. Daniel Nelson, Managers and Workers: Origins of the New Factory System in the United States 1880-1920, 37 (1975).

managerial hierarchy.[14] Whatever the reason, or reasons, the abandonment of inside contracting coincided with a period of intense business integration – forward into distribution and marketing, backward into the supply of parts and raw materials. "Although nonexistent at the end of the 1870s, these integrated enterprises came to dominate many of the nation's most vital industries within less than three decades."[15]

The drive toward vertical integration responded to the imperatives of continuous mass production: to be assured of the consistency of the supply, cost, and quality of materials entering the plant; to schedule and coordinate the flow of materials in production; to get products efficiently into distribution. "[M]eat packing, brewing, cotton, oil, and sugar companies, owned their own ships, fleets of railing cars, and transportation equipment."[16] American Chicle owned 3 million acres in Mexico to grow its raw materials.[17] As late as the 1990s, a subsidiary of Monsanto, a chemical company, owned one of California's largest strawberry producers.[18]

Archetypical instances of integration are found in the production of steel and electricity and in railroad transportation, all of which depended on a reliable supply of coal at a predictable cost. Many of these companies acquired what came to be called "captive mines." As a result, these coal consumers placed themselves in the position of mining employers subject to unionization, upward pressure on wages, and work stoppages.[19]

Some companies, aware of those consequences, strove to find alternative means of securing reliable supplies of specified quality at predictable prices without actually owning and operating the supplying companies. Perhaps the most prominent example, foreshadowing contemporary fissurization, is Campbell Soup. It was a forwardly integrating company – it replaced the purchase of tin cans by making them – and one of the most innovative. It manufactured demand for its product, condensed soup, a product that had not been a feature of the American diet, by the aggressive and creative use of advertising.[20] But it needed a reliable supply of fresh vegetables, especially suitable for its condensing process at a low and predictable cost.

---

14. Dan Clawson, Bureaucracy and the Labor Process: The Transformation of U.S. Industry, 1860-1920 Ch. 3 (1980) (from a Marxist perspective). Inside contractors sometimes earned more than their superiors. A cartoon of the period depicts an inside contractor "as a cunning, wealthy, well-dressed mechanic who put his own interests before his company's." David Hounshell, From the American System to Mass Production Fig. 2.26 at p. 111 (1984).
15. Alfred Chandler, The Visible Hand: The Managerial Revolution in American Business 285 (1977).
16. *Ibid.* at 352.
17. *Ibid.* at 341.
18. Nano Riley, Florida's Farm Workers in the Twenty-First Century 64 (2002).
19. The owners of captive mines were also less able to resist union demands for higher wages in times of high demand. Their agreement to better wages put pressure on commercial mining operators. As a student of the industry explains:

> Several times since World War II the union has succeeded in splitting the captives away from the rest of the bituminous industry, has achieved much of its demands, and has then imposed the settlement on the commercial operators. That this procedure has stirred the helpless wrath of the latter is well indicated by the angry statement that "the steel industry or someone else is going to write the contract."

Morton Baratz, The Union and the Coal Industry 38 (1955) (reference omitted).

20. Douglas Collins, America's Favorite Food: The Story of Campbell Soup Company (1994).

Unlike American Chicle, Campbell Soup did not decide to grow its own raw materials. Instead, it contracted with about two thousand farmers in trucking distance of its major plant in Camden, New Jersey, and, later, with farmers in northern Ohio for its plant there. These standardized contracts dictated the specific breed of vegetables to be grown – in fact, Campbell developed and supplied the seeds of a tomato that met its needs – and allowed Campbell to oversee production: "Company inspectors visited contractors' farms throughout the growing season to ensure that farmers were supplying the proper amounts of fertilizer."[21] These contracts specified the condition of the product on delivery and the price; they also set tonnage limits per acre of production. They even forbade the growers from selling the product to anyone other than Campbell without Campbell's permission, but allowed Campbell to refuse to accept purchase, a practice so sharp that it was eventually held unenforceable.[22]

In the wake of efforts by farm workers to unionize, the company required its growers to harvest tomatoes mechanically.[23] Mechanical harvesting could incur a loss of production as well as a reduction in quality, but a student of the company concludes that mechanization was imposed on the growers to eliminate the "uncertainties and expense of employing human labor to harvest tomatoes and other crops."[24] However, when those farm workers sought collectively to bargain with Campbell, Campbell rebuffed them on the ground that it was not their employer.[25] Campbell's approach thus adumbrates the modern fissurized world, and strongly; but, at the time, it stood apart from the general integrative trend.

§1.03 THE CONUNDRUM OF VICARIOUS LIABILITY

The drive toward mass production fueled an intense, decades-long debate on "the labor question": how a country rooted in the small farm and workshop, whose employment law reflected those roots, would deal with the social problems thrust upon it by the

21. Daniel Sidorick, CONDENSED CAPITALISM: CAMPBELL SOUP AND THE PURSUIT OF CHEAP PRODUCTION 36 (2009).
22. The "sum total" of these provisions were held to drive "too hard a bargain for a court of conscience to assist." *Campbell Soup Co. v. Wentz*, 172 F.2d 80, 84 (3rd Cir. 1948) (refusing to enforce that part of the contract as "unconscionable." The combination of a provision that allowed Campbell to reject the produce while prohibiting its resale was said to be "carrying a good joke too far," *ibid.* at 83).
23. Sidorick, *supra* n. 21 at 160.
24. *Ibid.*
25. W.K. Barger & Ernesto Reza, THE FARM LABOR MOVEMENT IN THE MIDWEST 65 (1994) (italics in original):

> The company [Campbell] had claimed that it had no direct relations with farmworkers in its operations. It had also said that it could not intervene in the internal operations of its growers. Yet, the mandate to mechanize ... made clear that the large food-processing corporations *were* directly involved in determining farmworkers' conditions and could mandate how the growers ran their operations.

As the National Labor Relations Act excludes agricultural workers, whatever control Campbell exercised over its growers employees was irrelevant as federal law could not compel Campbell to bargain with them.

concentration of wealth and power in the hands of industrialists and the emergence of an industrial working class, often restive and subject to exploitation. It was a period of enormous legal as well as social flux.

The inadequacy of the law of tort to deal with mutilation and death on an industrial scale was an early subject of public concern and legislative address.[26] So, too, were other questions of responsibility and liability that had not emerged theretofore, not, at least, on the scale of modern mass production. Most of the response was and would be legislative.[27] Some states, for example, made railroads liable for the wages of construction workers engaged by the railroads' contractors which, in one case, was held to render the railroad liable for the wages owed an employee of the subcontractor of a subcontractor of a subcontractor of the railroad's contractor:

> It is common knowledge that contracts for building railroads are nearly always taken in the first instance by construction companies or syndicates, who then let out the entire work in various divisions to subcontractors, without themselves directly employing any laborers. The most if not all the work of building the railroad is thus done by laborers directly employed by subcontractors. If these should be excluded from the statute by interpretation, its evident purpose would be defeated.[28]

As an aside, that approach has been taken anew in California; it imposes joint liability on a lead company that uses workers supplied by a contractor for those workers' wages and worker compensation coverage.[29]

Part of the response was judge-made, notably in attending to an employer's liability to third parties for the negligence of its employees, an issue exacerbated by the expansion of mass industrial employment. It was taken up by the American Law Institute (ALI) in an effort to simplify and modernize the law. The ALI's *Restatement of Agency* appeared in 1933. It distinguished employees, for whose negligence their employer would be liable when they acted within the scope of their employment, from independent contractors, for whose employees' negligence the lead company would not be liable. It did so by crafting criteria to determine who is an employee (a "servant"

26. John Fabian Witt, THE ACCIDENTAL REPUBLIC: CRIPPLED WORKINGMEN, DESTITUTE WIDOWS, AND THE REMAKING OF AMERICAN LAW (2004); Donald Rogers, MAKING CAPITALISM SAFE: WORK, SAFETY, AND HEALTH REGULATION IN AMERICA, 1880-1940 (2009).
27. At about the century's turn a number of states enacted "wage payment" laws, modeled on the British "Truck Act" of 1831, requiring that workers be paid in U.S. currency and on a regular periodic basis. The field of contestation over these laws was constitutional; of whether these laws wrongfully abridged "freedom of contract," not their coverage, of who is a worker. *See generally*, Robert Patterson, WAGE PAYMENT LEGISLATION IN THE UNITED STATES (1918). That question had arisen under the British law, however. The Truck Act, 1 & 2 Will. 4, c. 37 (1831), applied to "artificers," understood to be workers. It was held that a worker had to perform the work personally in order to be protected; he could not be only a contractor. But, if he employed others to work with him he was a worker entitled to statutory protection even as he was also a contractor. The texture of British law is laid out in 5 C.B. Labatt, COMMENTARIES ON THE LAW OF MASTER AND SERVANT § 1973b at pp. 6136-6137 (1913).
28. *George v. Washington County Rr. Co.*, 44 Atl. 377, 377-378 (Me. 1899) (citing authority to the same effect from Massachusetts and New York).
29. Cal. Labor Code § 2810.3 (2014).

in the anachronistic usage at the time) as distinct from an independent contractor.[30] The manner in which the distinction was drawn was to influence analysis under federal labor protective law legislated later in the decade, albeit for different purposes.[31] In other words, the determination of those who could secure the coverage of labor protective law was made to turn on whether their negligence could be attributed to a third party that had utilized their service.

It is important to note that the ALI's engagement proceeded against a background of intense engagement with the issue at the turn of the century; that is, during the period of the most socially unsettling drive toward industrialization and integration. American courts had looked to British precedent, but that drew on the law of a domestic relationship, of "master and servant," the assumptions and contours of which did not map easily on to an amorphous, anonymous industrial work force.[32] And even

30. Restatement of Agency § 220 (1933):

> (1) A servant is a person employed to perform service for another in his affairs and who, with respect to his physical conduct in the performance of the service, is subject to the other's control or right of control.
> (2) In determining whether one acting for another is a servant or an independent contractor, the following matters of fact, among others, are considered:
> (a) the extent of control which, by the agreement, the master may exercise over the details of the work;
> (b) whether or not the one employed is engaged in a distinct occupation or business;
> (c) the kind of occupation, with reference to whether, in the locality, the work is usually done under the direction of the employer or by a specialist without supervision;
> (d) the skill required in the particular occupation;
> (e) Whether the employer or the workman supplies the instrumentalities, tools, and the place of work for the person doing the work;
> (f) the length of time for which the person is employed;
> (g) the method of payment, whether by the time or by the job;
> (h) whether or not the work is a part of the regular business of the employer; and
> (i) whether or not the parties believe they are creating the relationship of master and servant.

31. Fleming James, a noted torts scholar, called this "cross-pollinization." Fleming James, *Vicarious Liability*, 28 Tulane L. Rev. 161, n. 176 at 202 (1954); *see also* Gerald Stevens, *The Test of the Employment Relation*, 38 Mich. L. Rev 188 (1939), focusing on the effect of the distinction on labor legislation.

32. Compare the majority and dissenting opinions in *Payne v. Western & Atl. Ry*, 81 Tenn. 507 (1884), wherein the orders of a railroad superintendent to its entire workforce, forbidding them to shop at a certain store, was likened to the order a father could give a child, a master could give a maid; the dissenters argued that an industrial employer was not a father.

American courts came to distinguish industrial workers from children, apprentices, and household servants in applying the common law rule allowing a master to use corporal punishment on a servant. 1 C.B. Labatt, *supra* n. 29, § 242b at pp. 740-741. The Louisiana Code of 1838 allowed a master to "correct his indentured servant or apprentice for negligence or other misbehavior, provided he does it with moderation, and provided he does not make use of the whip." La. Civil Code § 167. In 1888, the section was amended to provide, "but he can not exercise such rights with those who only let their services."

the British had not had an easy time of it in deciding who should be liable to whom for what.[33] In fact, British law had been subjected to withering fire at the time.[34]

The contemporary context for the controversy was noted by no less a figure than Oliver Wendell Holmes, Jr., who attacked the very idea of vicarious liability: the doctrine was, he said, "the resultant of a conflict between logic and good sense" the "most flagrant" rules of which "now-a-days often present ... [themselves] as a seemingly wholesome check on the indifference and negligence of great corporations ...."[35] On the distinction between an independent contractor and a "servant," Holmes prefaced his analysis thusly:

> [I]t may be urged that when you have admitted that an agency may exist outside the family relations, the question arises where you are to stop, and why, if a man who is working for another in one case is called his servant, he should not be called so in all. And it might be said that the only limit is found, not in theory, but in common-sense, which steps in and declares that *if the employment is well recognized as very distinct*, and all the circumstances are such as to show that it would be mere folly to pretend that the employer could exercise control in any practical sense, then the fiction is at an end.[36]

Contemporary fissurization places that common sense assumption at issue: when is the relationship one so "very distinct" that liability will not be imputed when the work done by the contractor's workers becomes woven into, as an intrinsic part of the lead company's process or product?

The issue was taken up afresh by Harold Laski in 1916.[37] Three grounds had been offered for an employer's liability for the wrongful act of its employee: (1) as a moral consequence of a person's failing to do his own work; (2) as a logical consequence of setting in motion the chain of events that resulted in the loss; (3) as the practical consequence of the need to have employers select employees with care and to exercise care in their supervision. Only the latter speaks to the employee-independent contractor distinction; but, on close examination, none of it held up.

---

33. A 1799 case, repudiated fifty years later, but which found some sympathy in American courts, held a property owner liable for injury to a traveler under these facts: The defendant property owner's house lay along a road. He hired a contractor to repair the house. The contractor subcontracted the work. The subcontractor contracted with a supplier of materials whose employee left materials on the road causing the traveler's carriage to overturn. *Bush v. Steinman*, 1B & P 404 (1799) *overruled Reedie v. London & North Wales Ry.*, 4 Ex. 256 (1849). The sense of it was that as the sub-subcontractor was set upon the property owner's work, the property owner should be liable for the consequences. *Bush v. Steinman* was cited as authority in *Inhabitants of Lowell v. The Boston & Lowell Rr. Corp.*, 40 Mass. 24 (1839) and *Stone v. Cheshire Rr. Corp.*, 19 N.H. 427 (1849).
34. T. Baty, VICARIOUS LIABILITY (1916).
35. Oliver Wendell Holmes, Jr., *Agency II*, 5 Harv. L. Rev. 1, 14 (1891).
36. *Ibid.* at 15 (italics added).
37. Harrold Laski, *The Basis of Vicarious Liability*, 26 Yale L.J. 105 (1916). Laski, who rose to international prominence in the 1930s, has faded from view today. *See generally*, Jeffrey O'Connell & Thomas O'Connell, *Book Review: The Rise and Fall (and Rise Again?) of Harold Laski*, 55 Md. L. Rev. ,1384 (1996). As the issue of the vicarious liability of fissured-lead companies has come to the fore, Laski's thoughts under circumstances obtaining a century ago against which fissurization resonates repays attention.

The assumption of the first – which Laski attributed to "the unctuous Bacon"[38] – is obviously untenable in an industrial society. The second moves along rather strained causal grounds, that he whose work results in an injury must be responsible for it; but, there actually was precedent for something akin to it.[39] The third ignores the fact that a duty of care in the selection and control of employees can and has been imposed, but that an employer's vicarious liability obtains no matter how careful the employer has been in employee selection and supervision. Moreover, categories of "non-delegable duties" and of contracting for "inherently dangerous" undertakings were later added that do render lead companies liable for the acts of the employees of their contractors.[40] The distinction rests on rather shaky grounds.

Laski took all this in and concluded that, at bottom, the question is one of public policy, the resolution of which had to draw from the realities of mass industrial employment and the need to give meaningful effect to labor legislation:

> It is only by enforcing vicarious liability that we can hope to make effective those labor laws intended to promote the welfare of the workers; for it is too frequently the corporation that evades the statute or attempts to discredit it.[41]

To sum up so far, when the laws about to be addressed – wage and hour law, collective bargaining law, social security and unemployment compensation law and even antidiscrimination law – were enacted, the legislature confronted what it saw to be the situation of a helpless industrial working class in the hands of large mass production enterprises.[42] It was not concerned with such a company's relationship to a contractor's employees. By then, the inside contractor system had become a thing of

---

38. Bacon's belief in the individual's duty to work as a religious obligation is discussed by Keith Thomas, *Work and Leisure in Pre-Industrial Society*, 29 Past & Present 50, 59 (1964).
39. *Bush v. Steinman*, discussed *supra* n. 33.
40. Today, the issue would be more likely addressed in economic terms, as resting on the determination of who the superior risk-bearer is. Alan Sykes, *The Economics of Vicarious Liability*, 93 Yale L.J. 1231 (1984).
41. Harold Laski, *The Basis of Vicarious Liability*, *supra* n. 37 at 124 (references omitted):

> [I]f we admit that the state has the right, on grounds of public policy, to condition the industrial process, it becomes apparent that the basis of the vicarious liability is not tortious at all; nor, since it is withdrawn from the area of agreement, is it contractual. It is simply a statutory protection the state chooses to offer its workers.

Ibid. at 130.

42. The "public policy" of the United States was declared in the Norris-LaGuardia Act of 1932:

> Whereas under prevailing economic conditions, developed with the aid of governmental authority for owners of property to organize in the corporate and other forms of ownership association, the individual unorganized worker is commonly helpless to exercise actual liberty of contract and to protect his freedom of labor, and thereby to obtain acceptable terms and conditions of employment.

29 U.S.C. § 102. The National Labor Relations Act echoed "inequality of bargaining power" as a basis for the law. 29 U.S.C. § 151. The Fair Labor Standards Act rested upon a legislative finding of "labor conditions detrimental to the minimum standards of living" necessary for worker health and well-being in industry. 29 U.S.C. § 202. The later extension of civil rights in the employment setting, especially in laws prohibiting discrimination, was limited to employers exceeding a certain number of employees.

the past. And by then, the word "employee" had taken on a gloss of meaning that distinguished that person from an independent contractor, albeit for the purpose of vicarious liability for negligence. Even then, however, the distinction refused to defer automatically to contractual determination; that is, it disallowed the superior party the power to declare the relationship to be such as to avoid responsibility.[43] Consequently, the matter of labor protective coverage in today's fissurized world moves across legal terrain on which the sign posts are, for the most part, absent, ambiguous, or unresponsive.

§1.04 THE LEGISLATIVE TERRAIN

The Fair Labor Standards Act (FLSA), requiring payment of a minimum wage and time and a half for overtime, defined an employee, circularly, as a person employed, and defined employment as being "suffered or permitted" work.[44] The National Labor Relations Act (NLRA) was equally circular, defining an "employee" as "any employee."[45] Title VII of the Civil Rights Act and cognate federal and state antidiscrimination law – the Americans with Disabilities Act (ADA) or Californian fair employment law – similarly apply to "employees" without further elaboration.[46] The Social Security Act (which also authorized state participation in the unemployment compensation system) only said that the term "'employee' includes an officer of a corporation."[47] These would seem to give the agencies administering these laws and the courts construing them ample room to craft the scope of coverage to deal with business structures or practices that would otherwise defeat the statutory ends. As, indeed, they did; but, there's more to the story.

In 1944, the U.S. Supreme Court held in *Hearst Publications* that newspaper distributors, euphemistically called "newsboys," were employees entitled to bargain collectively with the newspaper under the NLRA even though they would be considered independent contractors at common law: "Congress had in mind a wider field than the narrow technical legal relation of 'master and servant,' as the common law

43. Note that the RESTATEMENT OF AGENCY, *supra* n. 30, does not list an express contractual term between the parties as a factor to be considered let alone to be given dispositive effect. It lists instead what the parties "believe" the relationship to be and that only as one among eight other factors. The blackletter rule today is the parties' agreement is to be considered, but it is not dispositive. So well entrenched is this principle that even where a contract between a lead company and a contractor designated them as joint employers a court undertook the further examination of the relationship to see if that was actually so. *Childress v. Ozark Delivery of Mo.* LLC, 95 F.Supp.3d 1130, 1140 (W.D. Mo. 2015).
44. 29 U.S.C. § 203(g) (1938).
45. 29 U.S.C. § 152(3) (1935). An earlier draft of the law defined an "employee" as an individual working under a contract of hire "including any contract entered into by any helper or assistant of any individual, whether paid by him or his employer" – that is, to define employees of inside contractors as employees of the lead employer. Matthew Finkin, *Legal Craftsmanship?The Drafting of the Wagner Act* in PROCEEDINGS OF THE FORTY-EIGHTH ANNUAL MEETING OF THE INDUSTRIAL RELATIONS RESEARCH ASSOCIATION 381, 383 (Paula Voos ed. 1996). This requirement was omitted as "employee" was defined to extend beyond a proximate employer relationship.
46. Title VII provides that an "employee" is an "individual employed by an employer." 42 U.S.C. § 2000e(f); as does the ADA, 42 U.S.C. § 1211(4); *see also* Cal. Gov. Code § 12926(c).
47. Internal Revenue Code § 110(a)(6) (1935).

had worked this out in all its variations ...."[48] The determination would be driven by whether those seeking the law's protection were "as a matter of economic fact"[49] within the compass of what the law sought to effect. In 1947, the Court took the same approach with respect to the FLSA: the test is "'economic reality' rather than 'technical concepts'."[50] And it did so as well with the Social Security Act, echoing *Hearst*, that the word employee must be "construed 'in light of the mischief to be corrected and the end attained'."[51]

In that year, however, a conservative Congress clipped two of these laws' wings. Over President Truman's veto, it legislated against *Hearst*, amending the NLRA to exclude independent contractors, importing the common law test that the Court had rejected as too technical and as having scant bearing on the problem the law addressed.[52] Also in that year, the Treasury Department proposed a regulation to redefine an "employee" under the Social Security Act as: "an individual in a service relationship who is dependent as a matter of economic reality upon the business to which he renders service and not upon his own business as an independent contractor." Though this seems to remove only authentic contractors, those who run their own businesses, the proposal provoked an uproar in the Republican-controlled Congress resulting in a resolution legislating against it. This, too, was enacted over President Truman's veto.[53] The Social Security Act as amended now defines employees as individuals who are employees "under the usual common law rules."[54]

The Supreme Court took heed of these legislative reversals in the *Darden* decision in 1992 when confronted with the scope of coverage, of who is an "employee" under federal pension protection law, and engaged in a strategic withdrawal.[55] The Court made clear that it had abandoned the principle that it would construe the statute "in light of the mischief to be corrected and the end to be attained."[56] As a critic pointed out, the Court thus enshrined purposelessness as a guiding principle of statutory construction.[57] This assessment is unassailable. Nevertheless, at the same time, the Court reiterated its long-standing approach to the FLSA: that law, it opined, "stretches the meaning of 'employee' to cover some parties who might not qualify as such under a strict application of traditional agency law principles."[58] Following *Darden*, the scope of control or, sometimes, a hybrid test conjoining control with the idea of economic dependence, has been applied to the reach of antidiscrimination law generally.[59]

48. *National Labor Relations Board v. Hearst Pub.*, 322 U.S. 111, 124 (1944).
49. *Ibid.* at 127.
50. *Rutherford Food Corp. v. McComb*, 331 U.S. 722 (1947), *reiterated in Goldberg v. Whitaker House Cooperative, Inc.*, 336 U.S. 28, 33 (1961).
51. *United States v. Silk*, 331 U.S. 704, 713 (1947) (reference omitted).
52. 29 U.S.C. § 152(3).
53. 62 Stat. 438 (1948). The legislative history is set out in 2 U.S. Code & Cong. News 1752 (1948).
54. 42 U.S.C. § 401(j)(2).
55. *Nationwide Mut. Ins. Co. v. Darden*, 503 U.S. 318 (1992) (references omitted).
56. *Ibid.* at 325.
57. Marc Linder, *Dependent and Independent Contractors in Recent U.S. Labor Law; An Ambiguous Dichotomy Rooted in Simulated Statutory Purposelessness*, 21 Comp. Lab. L. &Pol'y J. 187 (1999).
58. *Nationwide Mut. Ins. Co. v. Darden*, *supra* n. 55at 326.
59. *See* the text accompanying notes 76-80, *infra*.

In sum, the statutory tools to deal with fissurization have become fissured. Under the three statutory systems about to be taken up, a notion of joint employment has been developed that extends to a lead company vis-à-vis its contractors employees; but, the contours differ significantly, the doctrine's reach is in a state of flux.

[A] Wage and Hour Law

The test of whether the lead contractor would be liable for a subcontractor's wage and hour obligations, as a joint employer with the contractor, is governed by the "economic reality" of the relationship. But, in applying it the courts have uniformly looked to the power the lead company exercises, not over the contractor's business, but over the contractor's employees. Commonly, a four-part test or some variation of it is applied, as, for example, in the case of the franchisor of a pizzeria:

> Under the economic reality test, we evaluate "whether the alleged employer: (1) possessed the power to hire and fire the employees, (2) supervised and controlled employee work schedules or conditions of employment, (3) determined the rate and method of payment, and (4) maintained employment records." ... "The dominant theme in the case law is that those who have operating control *over employees* within companies may be individually liable for FLSA violations committed by the companies."[60]

This approach has been widely followed. To mention only some recent cases, it has been applied to the franchisor of a janitorial service (and to the lead company that retained the franchisor) with respect to an employee of its franchisee,[61] to a hotel with respect to employees of a temporary staffing agency,[62] and by a trial court a case involving a jobber in the garment industry.[63] However, in that case, *Zheng v. Liberty Apparel Co. Inc*,[64] the Court of Appeals considered the test applied by the lower court - which it termed one of "formal control" - to be a sufficient condition to find joint employer status, but not a necessary one. If relied on exclusively, the test might fail to capture the essence of the relationship. The appeals court adopted a six-part test, of "functional control," as conducing toward a better grasp of the "totality of circumstances":

(1) whether the lead company's premises and equipment were used by the workers;
(2) whether the subcontractor had a business that could or did shift the workers as a unit to work from one lead contractor to another;
(3) the extent to which the work was a discrete job (a "line job") integral to the lead company's process of production;

60. *Orozco v. Plackis*, 757 F.3d 445, 448 (5th Cir. 2014) (reference omitted) (italics added).
61. *Becerra v. Expert Janitorial*, LLC, 332 P.3d 415 (Wash. 2014).
62. *Tolentino v. Starwood Hotels & Resorts Worldwide, Inc.*, 437 S.W.2d 754 (Mo. 2014) (en banc).
63. *Ling Nan Zheng v. Liberty Apparel Co.*, 2002 U.S. Dist. LEXIS 4226 (S.D. N.Y. May 12, 2002).
64. 355 F.3d 61 (2d. Cir. 2003) *jury verdict aff'd* 617 F.3d 183 (2d Cir. 2010), *followed and explained Barfield v. N.Y.C. Health & Hosps. Corp.*, 537 F.3d 132, 145 (2d Cir. 2008).

(4) whether responsibility to fill the contract could shift under the contract from one contractor to another;
(5) the degree to which the lead company supervised the workers; and
(6) whether the workers worked exclusively or predominantly for the lead company.[65]

Only one of these, supervision of the contractor's workers by the lead company, goes to the relationship between the lead company and the contractor's employees. The others concern the relationship of the lead company to the work done by the contractor's workers for the lead company. One of the nine factors the *Restatement of Agency* put into the mix was whether the work the person did was a part of the company's "regular business." The functional control test converts that factor into the almost singular focus of attention – not only that the contractor's work is part of the regular business but also how deeply integrated the contractor's work is with the lead company – and it infuses that focus into five of the elements of analysis. When these "indicate that an entity has functional control over workers even in the absence of the formal control measured by the [four-part test]" it will be jointly responsible.[66]

The difference between formal and functional control could have important consequences in a fissured relationship. Take the archetypical instance anticipating modern fissurization – Campbell Soup. Under a test that attends only to formal control, Campbell Soup could not be a joint employer of its growers' workers and would bear no responsibility to assure compliance with the wage and hour provisions of the FLSA governing them. But, under a test of functional control, it is at least arguable that Campbell would bear joint responsibility: although the farm workers do not work in the Campbell plant, the growing field is their workplace, and are not directly supervised by Campbell's supervisors, though their work is subject to Campbell's inspection in the field, they cannot be shifted by their growers to non-Campbell work; their work is integral to Campbell's production; their growers' contracts cannot be shifted to another (though Campbell can refuse the product, the growers could even dispose of it

65. *Zheng, supra* n. 64 at 72.
66. *Ibid. Olivera v. Bareburger Group*, LLC, 73 F.Supp.3d 201 (SDNY 2014), concerned a franchisor's liability for its franchisees' wage and hour violations. The complaint alleged that the franchisor:

> (1) guided franchisees on "how to hire and train employees"; (2) set and enforced requirements for the operation of franchises; (3) monitored employee performance; (4) specified the methods and procedures used by those employees to prepare customer orders; (5) exercised control, directly or indirectly, over the work of employees; (6) required franchises to "employ recordkeeping" of operations, including "systems for tracking hours and wages and for retaining payroll records"; and (7) exercised control over their franchises' timekeeping and payroll practices. The [complaint] also alleges that the franchisor defendants had the right to inspect the facilities and operations of franchises, to audit any franchise's financial records, and to terminate the franchise agreement and the operations of any restaurant that violated the FLSA.

Ibid. at 207. Note that the controls the franchisor reserved were largely over the franchisee's practices, not over the franchisee's workers save for monitoring (3) and a general assertion of "indirect" control. Nevertheless, these allegations raised enough questions of material fact to preclude a grant of summary judgment for the franchisor.

elsewhere without Campbell's approval); and their work is not only predominantly but exclusively done for Campbell, the lead company. In other words, by deploying exclusive supply contracts dictating quantity, quality, and price, deploying inspectors to monitor production, and dictating the manner of production – leaving the contractor's room for profit to be grounded significantly, perhaps predominantly, in keeping its labor costs low[67] – the lead company might not be able to avoid responsibility for its contractors' wage and hour violations.[68]

It remains to be seen whether "functional control" test is only a straw in the wind.[69] But, it holds open the possibility of the application of wage and hour law to lead companies operating in exactingly fissurized frameworks.

[B] Collective Bargaining Law

The National Labor Relations Board has long held, with judicial approval, that two or more enterprises can be joint employers of the same employees for the purposes of collective bargaining; but, the test of joint employment has echoed the requirements of "formal control" taken under the FLSA.[70] For example, the U.S. Court of Appeals for the Second Circuit, the same court that was later to decide the *Zheng* case, affirmed the NLRB's conclusion that the purchaser of a building was not a joint employer of the janitors who worked for a janitorial company with which the owners had contracted for janitorial services:

> "[A]n essential element" of any joint employer determination is "sufficient evidence of *immediate* control over the employees," ... namely, "whether the alleged joint employer (1) did the hiring and firing; (2) *directly* administered any disciplinary procedures; (3) maintained records of hours, handled the payroll, or

67. *See* the discussion of agriculture by David Weil, The Fissured Workplace, *supra* n. 2 at 259-260.
68. In *Depiantiv. Jan-Pro Franchising, Int'l, Inc.*, 990 N.E.2d 1054 (Mass. 2013), the Massachusetts Supreme Court addresses two questions certified to it by a federal court under the following business model. Jan-Pro was a national franchisor of janitorial services. It contracted with Bradley Mtg. Enterprises, Inc., to be Jan-Pro's regional master franchisee. Booking and billing for janitorial services were made by Bradley. Bradley takes its fees, remits Jan-Pro its fee (or royalty) and pays Depianti. Bradley treats Depianti as an independent contractor thereby avoiding state wage law and other employment benefits. Depianti sued Jan-Pro as being vicariously liable for Bradley's misclassification of him and as being directly liable under the state's independent contractor misclassification law. The federal court posed two questions of state law to the state's highest court: (1) could Jan-Pro be vicariously liable? The court held it could not unless it had the right to control the specific policy or practice resulting in the injury. (2) Could it be liable for Bradley's misclassification when it, Jan-Pro, had no contract with Depianti? It held it could. Such would be a direct violation of the statute, not a matter of vicarious liability. One Justice dissented in the latter on the ground that the lack of privity of contract between Jan-Pro and Depianti was dispositive.
69. The Third Circuit, for example, applied the "formal control" test to the parent company of a car rental system noting *Zheng's* endorsement of it without mention of that court's additional embrace of functional control actually operative in the decision. In Re Enterprise Rent-A-Car Wage and Hour Employment Practices Litigation, 683 F.3d 462 (3d Cir. 2013).
70. *NLRB v. Browning-Ferris Indus. of Pennsylvania*, 691 F.3d 1117 (3d Cir. 1982).

provided insurance; (4) *directly* supervised the employees; or (5) participated in the collective bargaining process".[71]

However, in 2015, the NLRB, by vote of three to two (along political lines) opined that that standard was "increasingly out of step with ... recent dramatic growth in contingent employment relationships."[72] In that case, the lead company, Browning-Ferris (BFI), owned and operated a recycling plant. It contracted with Leadpoint Business Services (Leadpoint) who provided sorters, screen cleaners and housekeepers. Leadpoint workers were hired by Leadpoint, subject to BFI's standards including drug and background testing. Leadpoint had sole contractual authority to discipline these workers, but BFI had the authority to discontinue any of Leadpoint's workers by denying them access to the plant. The contract specified the amount BFI would pay Leadpoint for each worker's wage. Although it reserved to Leadpoint the sole determination of pay rates, BFI's approval was required for any payment in excess of the usual rate for the job. Leadpoint's workers were entitled only to Leadpoint's benefits. BFI set the shift schedule including overtime, but that was calculated by Leadpoint's on-site supervisor. BFI determined the number of Leadpoint workers assigned to each material stream, but Leadpoint assigned the specific workers to them. BFI solely set production standards, including the speed of the material streams and any adjustments to them. Any employee problems identified by BFI are referred to Leadpoint. The contract requires Leadpoint's workers to comply with BFI's safety policies, which BFI reserved the right to enforce; however, most, but not all safety training was done by Leadpoint.

The Board's Regional Director found BFI not to be a joint employer under extant law for the want of the sort of immediate and direct control of these workers by BFI that the Board had required. The Board disagreed, modifying its approach. The Board majority opined that prior to the 1980s, the Board's focus was on the right to control the employees' work and conditions, not with the actual exercise of that power. "The Board had never looked to the common law to justify the requirements that a putative joint employer's control be exercised and that the exercise be direct and immediate, not 'limited and routine'."[73] Accordingly, it recalibrated the standard. First, the putative joint employer's relationship to the worker must be that of a common law employment relationship - so much is a statutory requirement. Second, the Board retained the requirement that the putative joint employer "share or co-determine" those matters

---

71. Service Employees Int'l Union, *Local 32BJ v. NLRB*, 647 F.3d 435, 442-443 (2d Cir. 2011) (italics added) (references omitted). A joint employer can be required to bargain collectively with the other joint employer with a union designated or selected by their joint employees all of which is subject to rather complicated rules involving multi-employer bargaining structures. *See generally*, Robert Gorman & Matthew Finkin, Labor Law: Analysis and Advocacy § 6.7 (2013). However, a joint employer is liable for only those acts of anti-union discrimination which it either knew or should have known and acquiesced in by failing to protest or to have exercised the right of control it possessed. Capitol EMI Music, Inc., 311 NLRB 997 (1993) *enf'd* 23 F.3d 399 (4th Cir. 1994).
72. Browning-Ferris Indus., 362 NLRB No. 186 (2015) (slip opinion at 1). It noted that in 2014, 2.87 million workers, about 2% of the workforce, were contingent employees supplied by temporary help agencies. *Ibid.* at p. 11.
73. *Ibid.* at 13.

governing "essential terms and conditions of employment"; but, it pointed to what those essentials might be matter other than hiring, firing, discipline, and supervision – that is, wages and hours, "the number of workers to be supplied; ... scheduling, seniority, and overtime, and assigning work and determining the manner and method of work performance."[74](By footnote, the Board also observed that authority need not be reserved over all of them, but could well be apportioned between the joint employers.[75]) Third, it abandoned the requirement that actual exercise beyond the possession of power to act will be required.[76]

The Board's newly announced standard is a variation on a test of "formal control." Even as it broadens the areas of shared or co-determined subjects – the number of workers, the scheduling of their work, and the manner in which it is to be performed – and relaxes any requirement of "direct and immediate" control over them, it is not a test of "functional control." The focus remains on the lead company's relationship to the contractor's employees, not to its business. Nevertheless, the decision, if judicially sustained, could open the door a bit wider for employees of contractors to compel the lead company to bargain with them.

[C] Antidiscrimination Law

Laws prohibiting discrimination in employment on a variety of invidious grounds – race, sex, disability, and the like – and forbidding the creation of workplaces hostile to employees on such grounds create, in essence, statutory torts.[77] Employers are liable for the wrongful actions of their managers and supervisors and liable as well for those other actions, for example, by coworkers, which they know about and could have remedied.

74. *Ibid.* at p. 15. The dissenters contested the degree of control the lead company possessed at every point. On control of the hours and monitoring of production, they argued that a contractor does not become an employer of its subcontractor's employees because the subcontractor is required to fit its work around the lead company's schedule: if one hires a roofing company to repair one's roof, the property owner does not become the employer of the roofer's workers by requiring the work to be done while he is at home. The analogy is inapt. BFI set the speed by which the sorting would be done by Leadpoint's workers. The speed of work is a mandatory bargaining subject; the "speed up" has long been a bone of labor contention, so contentious that some collective bargaining agreements reserved a right to strike over it. R. Herding, Job Control and Union Structure 29 (1972). If Leadpoint's workers can bargain only with Leadpoint, how can their demands over a speed up be bargained about?

75. *Ibid.* n. 80 at p. 15.

76. The new, or, in the Board majority's view, resurrected standard will most likely be tested in the courts i.e., Browning-Ferris Indus., 363 NLRB No. 95 (2016), the actual order to bargain, can be subject to judicial review. Even if affirmed, its reach remains to be seen. A pending complaint brought by the Board's General Counsel against a national franchisor, McDonald's USA, for alleged unfair labor practices jointly with several of its franchisees might provide more definitive guidance. Meanwhile, the decision provoked a response on the right to legislate against it. Lawrence Dubé, *Senate Panel Reviews Joint Employer Bill Intended to 'Pull Back' Labor Board Ruling*, 193 DLR (Oct. 6, 2015) at A-1.

77. *Staub v. Proctor Hosp.*, 131 S.Ct. 1186, 1187 (2010) (terming Title VII of the Civil Rights Act a "federal tort"). The goodness of fit has been much debated. *See generally*, The Symposium: *Torts and Civil Rights Law: Migration and Conflict*, 75 Ohio St. L. Rev. 1021-1412 (2014) (and the sources cited therein).

Accordingly, whether by a test of "economic reality"[78] or "hybrid economic realities/common law right of control,"[79] or the *Darden* test of "common-law agency,"[80] or the Equal Employment Opportunity Commission's recommended fifteen question test of formal control,[81] the courts attend closely to the degree of control the lead contractor exercises in the matter or could have exercised consistent with the contractual apportionment of responsibilities between the lead company and contractor. Inasmuch as a multi-factor balancing test is involved, much turns on what those who do the balancing see – as an undue extension of liability[82] or a better realization of the statutory end even when the action challenged was taken by the lead company vis-à-vis a contractor's worker.[83]

The issue was taken up under California law by that state's Supreme Court addressing a fast food franchisor's liability under state law for an alleged pattern of sexual harassment by its franchisee.[84] The court closely parsed the details of the franchise agreement and, by vote of four to three, upheld the grant of summary judgment for the franchisor. The court noted the "profound" economic effects a contrary result would have on the "business format" model of franchising, a model that did not begin to take root until the 1950s:[85]

---

78. *Love v. JP Cullen & Sons, Inc.* 779 F.3d 697 (7th Cir. 2015).
79. *Burton v. Freescale Semiconductor, Inc.*, 798 F.3d 222 (5th Cir. 2015).
80. *Fusch v. Tuesday Morning, Inc.*, 808 F.3d 208 (3d Cir. 2015).
81. *Casey v. Dept. of Health and Human Servs.*, 807 F.3d 395 (1st Cir. 2015).
82. The Seventh Circuit opined, in the context of a lead construction contractor's relationship to the employees of sub-subcontractor, that a five-part test applied by the lower court was not inconsistent with – merely gave more concrete expression to – the test of "economic reality." *Viz:*

> (1) the extent of the employer's control and supervision over the employee; (2) the kind of occupation and nature of skill required, including whether skills were acquired on the job; (3) the employer's responsibility for the costs of operation; (4) the method and form of payment and benefits; and (5) the length of the job commitment.

Love v. JP Cullen & Sons, Inc., *supra* n. 78 at 702. However, even though the contractor had reserved the right to control the presence of any worker on the job site and had allegedly ordered the worker off the job site for racial reasons, it was held incapable of being responsible because it did not control the subcontractor's dismissal of the worker; his dismissal was due to the fact that the subcontractor had no other work for the worker to do after the lead contractor ordered him off the site. *Accord Knitter v. Corvais Military Living*, LLC, 758 F.3d 1214 (10th Cir. 2014). *But see Burton v. Freescale Semiconductor, Inc., supra* n. 79, where the contractor's exercise of its right to demand a labor contractor's removal of a worker from assignment to it, allegedly on grounds of violation of the Americans with Disabilities Act, was held to be capable of rendering it liable under that law.

83. *Fausch v. Tuesday Morning, Inc., supra* n. 80, concerned the subjection of a supplied worker to an atmosphere of racial hostility and eventual removal from work at the lead company by its request. The lead company supervised the workers and had ultimate control on whether the supplied workers would be permitted to work at the location. Though other factors were to the contrary, the court took the "broad remedial policies" supporting antidiscrimination law to allow the case to proceed to trial.
84. *Patterson v. Domino's Pizza*, LLC, 333 P.3d 723 (Cal. 2014).
85. *Ibid.* at 733. The court explains the "business format" thusly. The franchisor's business plan:

> requires the franchisee to follow a system of standards and procedures. A long list of marketing, production, operational, and administrative areas is typically involved ....

> [T]here are sound and legitimate reasons for business format contracts like the present one to allocate local personnel issues almost exclusively to the franchisee. As we have explained, franchisees are owner-operators who hold a personal and financial stake in the business. A major incentive is the franchisee's right to hire the people who work for him, and to oversee their performance each day. A franchisor enters this arena, and becomes potentially liable for actions of the franchisee's employees, only if it has retained or assumed a general right of control over factors such as hiring, direction, supervision, discipline, discharge, and relevant day-to-day aspects of the workplace behavior of the franchisee's employees. Any other guiding principle would disrupt the franchise relationship.[86]

In other words, in deciding the scope of responsibility, the court was persuaded that casting too broad a net would result in lead companies' exertion of greater direct control over its franchisees which, in turn, would deter future investment by those who choose to be entrepreneurs, not corporate managers. Thus extending responsibility to the lead company would be contrary to the entrepreneurial interests of franchisees. The next question, of how those interests should weigh against the effective realization of their employees' rights, was begged.

The dissenters criticized the majority for placing too much weight on the terms of the franchise agreement and too little on how the franchisor actually behaved which, to them, presented triable issues of fact. They addressed the policy issue as well. The judicial function, they opined:

> Is not to give effect to private contracts intended to shift or avoid liability, nor is it to promote the use of franchising as a business model or to avoid "disrupt[ing] the franchise relationship." ... Instead, our duty is to vindicate the Legislature's "fundamental *public* interest in a workplace free from the pernicious influence of sexism."[87]

The legal obstacle for the dissent, and so for the employees of fissured employers, is the tort-focus of antidiscrimination law. Analysis focuses on corrective justice for acts of individual fault, not on enterprise compliance with regulatory norms.[88] The approach to discrimination, and especially sexual harassment, as a matter of formal

---

> The franchisor's system can take the form of printed manuals, training programs, advertising services, and managerial support, among other things .... The business format arrangement allows the franchisor to raise capital and grow its business, while shifting the burden of running local stores to the franchisee ... The systemwide standards and controls provide a means of protecting the trademarked brand at great distances .... The goal—which benefits both parties to the contract—is to build and keep customer trust by ensuring consistency and uniformity in the quality of goods and services, the dress of franchise employees, and the design of the stores themselves.

Ibid. (references omitted). An example is echoed in the complaint in *Olivera v. Bareburger Group, LLC, supra* n. 66 which was held sufficient to deny the franchisor's motion for summary judgment under the FLSA.

86. *Ibid.* at 739.
87. *Patterson v. Domino's Pizza*, LLC, *supra* n. 84 at 745 (Werdegar, J. dissenting) (italics in original).
88. *See generally*, Martha Chamallas, *Two Very Different Stories: Vicarious Liability Under Tort and Title VII Law*, 75 Ohio St. L. Rev. 1315 (2014). *See also* William Corbett, *What Is Troubling About the Tortification of Employment Discrimination Law*, 75 Ohio St. L. Rev. 1027, 1049 (2014).

control, stands in contrast to that at least potentially available to secure compliance with wage and hour law. In that setting, the business format model of franchising can generate incentives to cheat: franchisees are far more likely to violate wage and hour law than are company-owned outlets, even adjusting for other factors that might explain these differences,[89] and the differences are dramatic.[90] It remains to be seen if there is an analogous pattern of practice by franchisees violative of antidiscrimination law.

[D] A Sidelong Glance at Social Security and Unemployment Compensation

The Social Security Act of 1935 established a public system of old age pensions and created a state-participative system of unemployment compensation. The law embraces a test of common law agency.[91] Consequently, as Judge Learned Hand put it: "the servant of a servant may be the master's servant, but the servant of an 'independent contractor' is not."[92]

Questions of coverage have tended most frequently to arise when a payer asserted that the persons for whom the Internal Revenue Service had had taxes withheld was not an employee, but an independent contractor, and sought the return of those sums. Consequently, there is scant texture to the law's reach to what, under the FLSA or NLRA, would be a relationship of joint employment: either the taxpayer was the employer or not. But another early case hints at another possibility, if ever so slightly.

This much appears from the opinion. Mr Concello was the head of a family troupe, of trapeze performers, "the Flying Concellos." He signed a contract with the Ringling Brothers-Barnum and Bailey Combined Shows, "the circus," for the performances of his troupe. The contract was for a season of seven months. It could be renewed and had been for many years. The circus paid Mr Concello a fixed sum per week; he, in turn, paid the members of his company. From what appears, what he paid them was for him to decide. The troupe supplied their own costumes and equipment; they controlled their safety. The circus covered transportation costs, meals, and the like. The contract required them to perform wherever the circus did. The lower court

89. David Weil, The Fissured Workplace, *supra* n. 2 at 124-131.
90. *Ibid.* at 131 (footnote omitted):

> The probability of noncompliance is about 24% higher among franchisee-owned outlets than among otherwise similar company-owned outlets. Total back wages owed workers who were paid in violation were on average 50% higher for franchisees, and overall back wages found per investigation were close to 60% higher.

91. The Treasury Regulation of the time was set out in *Texas Co. v. Higgins*, *infra* n. 92 at 637. It has been refined into a twenty-question test echoing the basic thrust of the "right of control" test. Avram Sacks, 2006 Social Security Explained 138-139 (2006).
92. *Texas Co. v. Higgins*, 118 F.2d 636, 638 (2d Cir. 1941).

held the troupe to be employees of the circus. The Court of Appeals agreed, albeit over a strong dissent.[93]

At the threshold, the court dealt with the "right of control" test which extends not only to the result of the work, but to the means of achieving it. The court had little difficulty with that, given the nature of the work: The circus "would hardly be expected to direct the manner and means by which a human cannon ball should be shot from a gun."[94]

The more difficult problem arose from the fact that the court had earlier confronted the status of individual vaudevillians and held that they were independent contractors, the degree of control being exercised by the putative employer, the Radio City Music Hall, amounting to little more than the sort of scheduling at a contracting party's convenience that one might for any independent contractor.[95] Thus, the question was whether there was a difference between the two. The majority thought there was, endorsing the trial court's reasoning:

> The performers were an integral part of plaintiff's business of offering entertainment to the public. They were molded into one integrated show, 'the circus.' It was not a loose collection of individual acts like a vaudeville show. The individuality of the performers was subordinated to the primary purpose of enhancing the reputation of the plaintiff and of producing one integrated show that would entertain the public.[96]

The court took it that the circus had contracted individually with each of the performers; they were its employees, not independent contractors, and that was enough. But, the relationship could be looked at differently – as a contract made with a contractor, Mr Concello, who, in turn, hired and paid those whom he supplied to perform under his direction. This relationship would beakin to that with an "inside contractor" in the previous century, save for the inconsequential difference that the work was performed for the lead company on the premises of third parties. By that reasoning, the performers could still be the lead company's employees because of their complete integration into its work despite the lead company's privity of contract only with Mr Concello and its lack of any direct control over his workers. In that sense, the case foreshadows the "functional control" approach taken under the FLSA: it looks to the extent of integration of the contractor's workers into the lead company's business.

§1.05 THE CHALLENGE OF FISSURIZATION

A half century ago, Fleming James observed that businesses:

> commonly farm out many tasks which may well be regarded as normal incidents to their enterprises .... Where the entrepreneur uses familiar existing patterns, questions seldom arise .... Questions arise mainly where an enterprise makes

93. *Ringling Bros.-Barnum & Bailey Combined Shows, Inc. v. Higgins*, 189 F.2d 865 (2d Cir. 1951).
94. *Ibid.* at 870.
95. *Radio City Music Hall Corp. v. U.S.*, 135 F.2d 715 (2d Cir. 1943). This decision was relied on by the dissenting NLRB members in Browning-Ferris, *supra* n. 72.
96. *Ringling Bros.-Barnum & Bailey Combined Shows, Inc. v. Higgins*, *supra* n. 93 at 870.

> regular use of ... units that would *ordinarily* be regarded as subordinate to it ... in order to get something done which would *ordinarily* be regarded as a part of its enterprise.[97]

Fissurization has shifted the bounds of the ordinary. What makes that possible is the "glue," as David Weil has termed it, that often solves the problems of informational transparency and coordination that bedeviled inside contracting; the availability of sophisticated information technology. Companies abandoned inside contracting because it was a "*disintegrated* system."[98] Companies sought to get control of the process and product, the knowledge secreted by the contractor and his employees, and the only way they could do that is by having the work done by their own employees supervised by their own supervisors.

In contrast, Campbell Soup, anticipating contemporary fissurization, was able to achieve the benefits of vertical integration by imposing a system of business accountability so oppressive of its suppliers as to be held unconscionable[99] even as it structured the relationship to avoid any responsibility to the farm workers so critically affected by it.

Today, a lead company can require its contractors and franchisees to be subject to continuous and intense business mentoring and monitoring even as it abjures any role in the contractor's management of its workforce. Outside contractors can be brought "in," virtually; but, unlike the inside contractors of a century ago, the lead company has no resulting problem of informational asymmetry or loss of product or cost control. The technology allows the lead company to treat its contractors much as Campbell Soup treated its growers, but with greater immediacy, constancy, and efficiency, all the while avoiding any responsibility for foreseeable, perhaps inevitable negative consequences for the subcontractor's workers.

The contemporary legal conundrum derives from the fact that the laws obviated by these means were not drafted with this business structure in prospect. They were fashioned when business was driving toward ever more extensive integration, well before the business format model of franchising and well before the development of sophisticated information technology. Consequently, these laws do not focus on what power the lead company *could have* reserved, but rather on the power it did. As Judge Learned Hand opined, in a case concerning whether an oil company was liable for the social security taxes of its distributor's employees, of a gas station, "The character of the relation was determined by the rights and obligations assumed, and it is no answer

---

97. Fleming James, *Vicarious Viability*, 37 Tulane L. Rev. 161, 200 (1954) (emphasis added). Even as the court fashioned the "functional control" test of a lead company's responsibility under the FLSA, the Second Circuit was cognizant of the role of "buy" instead of "make" decisions in business: "manufacturers of relatively sophisticated products that require multiple components, may choose to outsource the production of some of those components in order to increase efficiency" without the law making them responsible for their contractors' observance of labor protective law. *Zheng v. Liberty Apparel Co. Inc.*, *supra* n. 63 at 73.

98. David Hounshell, *The* System: *Theory and Practice* in YANKEE ENTERPRISE: THE RISE OF THE AMERICAN SYSTEM OF MANUFACTURES, 127, 147 (Otto Mayr & Robert C. Post eds. 1981) (italics in original).

99. *Campbell Soup Co., v. Wentz*, *supra* n. 22.

that the plaintiff [the lead company] could force a change in these by threatening to terminate the agency."[100]

Campbell Soup, for example, could have bargained with its growers' employees. In fact, eventually Campbell did bargain with them in the wake of a national campaign mounted against it.[101] But, insofar as its contracts kept Campbell at arms-length from the farm workers' wages, and hours – from their hiring, firing, and working conditions – collective bargaining was the result not of its business model (putting aside the lack of agricultural worker coverage under the Labor Act), but of social and economic pressure to change it.

The distinction is less obvious than first appears, however. The common law justified vicarious liability instrumentally, i.e., as a means of encouraging employers to exercise control over their employees. That would make sense if employers were otherwise disinclined to impose controls, as employees might balk to the point of terminating the relationship if they thought the control imposed to be excessive. Truck drivers, for example, might refuse to accept continuous electronic sensory monitoring of their driving,[102] and employers might be loathe to assert such control or might even assure employees expressly of a degree of autonomy as part of the contract of employment. The law, not parties' agreement, implies an employer's authority to require employees to submit to control on pain of terminating that agency relationship and places limits as well on the scope of that control.[103] Reliance on the contract thus begs the question of whether the law should imply an analogous power on the part of the lead company in the governance of this agency relationship irrespective of contractual terms.

Moreover, the contract focus of the joint employer doctrine – exacting under a test of "formal control," slightly less exacting under a test of "economic reality," and more cognizant still of the reality of the circumstances under a test of "functional control" – tends to shy away from engaging with the role that might or could be played by the principle that public policy cannot be contracted away or around; or, less strongly, that efforts to do so should be viewed skeptically.[104] The principle was raised by the dissenting judges of the California Supreme Court in *Patterson v. Dominos Pizza LLC;*[105] but, the majority, singularly concerned not to disturb the business format of franchising, declined to engage with it.[106]

---

100. *Texas Co. v. Higgins*, 118 F.2d 636, 638 (2d Cir. 1941). The "gas station" cases posed a recurring problem under *responde at superior* akin to franchisor liability today. Annot., 116 ALR 457 (1938) and 83 ALR 2d 1282 (1962).
101. Daniel Sidorick, CONDENSED CAPITALISM *supra* n. 23 at 222-224. The struggle, which took almost a decade, is described by Barger and Reza, THE FARM LABOR MOVEMENT IN THE MIDWEST, *supra* n. 25 at 60-84. There are more recent examples, e.g., by the Coalition of Immokalee Workers. *See* Steven Greenhouse, *In Florida Tomato Fields, a Penny Buys Progress*, N.Y. Times, Apr. 24, 2014. *See generally*, Nano Riley, FLORIDA'S FARMWORKERS, *supra* n. 18 at 60. This is discussed as well by David Weil, THE FISSURED WORKPLACE, *supra* n. 2 at 260-262.
102. Matthew Finkin, PRIVACY IN EMPLOYMENT LAW 450 (4th ed. 2013) (on just such systems).
103. *See supra* n. 32.
104. *See Fauschv. Tuesday Morning, Inc.*, *supra* n. 80.
105. *Supra* n. 83.
106. One might expect that there would be *some* empirical evidence or even experience to draw on that would address both these concerns.

§1.06 CLOVEN WORK, CLOVEN WORKERS

There is a rather awkward technical term in linguistics – a mouthful: enantiosemia.[107] It designates a category of words that simultaneously bear opposite meanings. The verb "to cleave" is an example. It means "to join together," perhaps quite intricately, even intimately, as in marriage. But it also means "to separate," sharply, even violently, as by an axe. Fissurization gives rise to cloven employers with cloven workforces. Employers down the contractual chain cleave to the lead company through webs of contractual obligation, instruction, and technological oversight. They are cogs engineered by the lead company into its working machinery. But, the employees of these companies, who actually do the work, are cloven from the lead employer by the same design.

The question for law, unlike language, is whether lead companies can have it both ways; can they reap the benefits of fissurization without bearing responsibility for the consequences. The doctrine of employer vicarious liability took full form in the wake of industrialization. It imposed liability for negligence on companies as a matter of social policy, but only for its employees, not its contractors – and certainly not for its contractor's employees. Where the lines were drawn a century ago – even then understood to be grounded in pragmatism, not principle – live with us today, despite radical change in business models and practices. Consequently, the question put at the time by Harold Laski echoes anew: without some form of vicarious liability can labor protective legislation be effective?[108]

107. *See* Jordan Finkin, *Enantiodrama: Enantosemia in Arabic and Beyond*, 68 Bull. School of Oriental & African Studies 369 (2005), to whom I am indebted for educating me.
108. Harold Laski, *The Basis of Vicarious Liability*, *supra* n. 37 at 130.

CHAPTER 2

Fissurization in Japan: Overview and Analysis from a Legal Perspective

Qi Zhong[*]

§2.01 INTRODUCTION

In recent years, vast quantities of capital have been concentrated in fund management companies, and the businesses in which they invest are expected to "produce more profit in less time." In response to this, "cutting off divisions not directly related to core competency" has emerged as a corporate strategy. Innovations in methods of communication technology as well as the management and monitoring of workers have made it possible to direct and supervise workers remotely, and a byzantine variety of contractual and relational arrangements have been used between business entities and their workforces within the same workplace. This phenomenon, known as "the fissured workplace," has been comprehensively analyzed from the angles of sociology, legal studies, and economics in David Weil's *The Fissured Workplace*.

In *The Fissured Workplace*, the above-mentioned changes in corporate strategy and innovation in worker management technologies lead to the involvement of multiple business entities as participants in labor relations, which in turn leads to uncertainty vis-à-vis the applicability of labor laws and the identity of actors that must bear responsibility as employers. Such circumstances cover changes not only in the "workplace" or the "establishment" but also in the entire organization engaged in business itself; therefore, the phenomenon could also be called "the fissured business organization." However, this kind of "fissuring" of the workplace or business organization has been apparent in Japan for many years. This chapter first attempts to overview fissured workplace phenomena in Japan by presenting a time sequence-based look at such phenomena identified as problems in labor legislation and judicial

* Japan Institute for Labor Policy and Training.

precedent. The author then focuses on the judicial and legislative extension of employer's responsibility in the fissured workplace context to ascertain to what extent Japanese labor law has been addressing fissurization phenomena by coping with the boundary of legal entities.

[A] Overview of Fissurization Phenomena Dealt within Legislation and Case Law

Japan's labor legislation after the Second World War is built around the labor contract relationship. In principle, protection provisions in labor laws are applied only to the parties of labor contract relationships. Therefore, in general, the provisions in current labor laws are not applied to parties in a "contracting relationship."

However, historically speaking, whether the parties are connected by a labor contract relationship or not is not the sole criterion for determining the scope of application of the provisions of labor laws. Under the Factory Act enacted before the Second World War, as long as workers were involved in operations at a "factory," the Factory Act was deemed to be applicable regardless of whether they worked under an "employment relationship" or "contracting relationship."

The following will explain a system under the Factory Act called the "foreman contracting system" to provide a historical background. It will then introduce contract formats such as subcontracting, worker dispatch, and franchising, with their development and legal treatment in Japan, as workplace fissurization phenomena that have occurred under the modern labor law system built around the labor contract relationship.

[1] The Foreman Contracting System

Under current labor laws, even if both relationships involve the use of manpower, "employment relationship" and "contracting relationship" are clearly distinguished as a relationship involving the provision of labor under instructions and orders and a relationship that is focused solely on the "results" of labor. However, a look at the actual circumstances of plant labor prior to the Second World War shows that employment and contracting were intertwined under an employment format called the "foreman contracting system." Accordingly, the dichotomy did not have practical viability, as the foremen who undertook work from a factory owner distributed it to factory workers under the control of them. Those workers were all factory workers deployed by the factory owner, and their work was based on contracting relationships rather than employment relationships. In light of such practices, under the Factory Act,[1] Japan's first full-scale labor legislation prior to the Second World War, if a person was engaged in labor at a factory and his operations were, by nature, the work of a factory worker, the worker would be handled as a factory worker employed by the factory owner, regardless of whether a direct employment relationship existed between

1. Promulgated in 1911 and executed in 1916.

the factory owner and the factory worker or a foreman (contractor) existed in between the two sides.[2] Thus, restrictions on the employment of minors, restrictions on the working hours of minors and women, and obligation on the part of the business operator to provide compensation to workers or survivors with regard to work-related accidents were administered to be applicable regardless of whether workers worked under a contract for labor or under a contracting relationship so long as those workers were involved in operations at a factory.[3]

After the Second World War, the Factory Act was fundamentally reformed to a Labor Standards Act to be applied to all industries and all business categories, including manufacturing plants. Under this new legislation, whether or not a person could be described as a "worker" under an employment contract became established as a determining criteria when making judgments concerning the applicability of labor standards.

[2] Multilayered Subcontracting Relationships in the Construction Industry, Etc.

In the construction industry, even since before the Second World War, several subcontracting businesses had been cooperating with each other by dividing up the work of a single construction site in a multilayered fashion. Thus, the Workers' Compensation Act of 1931 imposed responsibility for workers' accident compensation on the prime contractor, which stood at the top of such multilayered subcontracting framework. This responsibility applied even to industrial accidents suffered by subcontractors' workers when accidents occurred at the prime contractor's construction site. This stipulation was succeeded by Article 87 of the Labor Standards Act after the Second World War, and continues to be applied to the construction sites.

Also under the industrial safety and health regulation, it has long been the responsibility of the prime contractor of a construction project to take safety measures to prevent industrial accidents when engaging in operations in which the prime contractor and subcontractors work together at the same worksite. Such special regulation will be discussed in II-2.

[3] Business Process Contracting in the Workplaces of Ordering Companies (In-House Subcontracting)

The practice by which a company, in order to execute its business, contracts another business operator to handle a portion of its processes (i.e., outsourcing) has been commonly used for many years. In such business process contracting, the contractor itself frequently supplies the labor; however, it is also often the case that the contractor

2. This case is a kind of "fissuring of the workplace phenomenon" because the worker is in an employment relationship with a contractor who has entered into a subcontracting contract with the business operator.
3. For more on this topic, *see* Minoru Oka, "*KōjōHō Ron*" (*Theory of the Factory Act*) [3rd Edition] (Yuhikaku, 1917) p. 287 and thereafter.

hires employees to engage in the performance of the work. Thus "business process contracting" – whereby ordering companies and contracting companies enter into a business process contracting agreement and then workers employed by the contracting company execute the contracted process under the instructions and orders of the contracting company at the work site of the ordering company – falls under a typical contract of "subcontracting" on the Civil Code. So long as business process contracting is practiced in line with the manner stated in the agreement, responsibility as the employer rests solely with the contracting company in terms of the labor contract as well as the Labor Standards Act. In principal, no employer obligations are attributed to the ordering company.

However, in Japan, labor supply undertakings that have workers engage in labor under the instructions and orders of another person based on a supply contract had been strictly regulated under the Employment Placement Act from before the Second World War. Later it became completely prohibited by the newly enacted Employment Security Act of 1947 amid reforms for democratization following the war.[4] Accordingly, business process contracting became subject to Article 4 of the Ordinance for the Enforcement of the Employment Security Act, which stipulates that a person who supplies a worker to work for another person based on a contracting-out agreement is regarded as being engaged in a labor supply undertaking prohibited by the Act, unless all of the following four requirements are satisfied:

(1) The person assumes all responsibilities and liabilities, both financially and legally as a business operator.
(2) The person gives directions to and provides supervision of the worker.
(3) The person bears all employer's responsibilities provided by law.
(4) The work contracted out does not merely involve the execution of physical labor.

If the business process contracting meets all four of these requirements, no employer obligations were attributed to the ordering company. However, even in such cases, if the contracting company exclusively undertakes work for a particular ordering company, and if all wages of workers employed by the contracting company are covered by contract fees provided by the ordering company, the contracting company and its employees are, in actuality, placed in an extremely weak position in their negotiations with the ordering company, and it is particularly so in the case of in-house subcontracting, where contracted work is executed in the workplace of the ordering company. In this case, the ordering company may lower the subcontract price and even cancel its order with the subcontracting company, when another business that will accept work at a lower price exists. If such a case occurs, the workers of the subcontracting company (or their union) may request negotiations with the ordering company asking for consideration vis-à-vis the subcontract price or continuation of the

4. Article 44 or the Employment Security Act. It should be noted that worker dispatch was established as being outside the scope of labor supply when worker dispatch was made legal by the 1985 Act to be mentioned later.

order. In such cases, the question arises whether or not ordering companies cannot be deemed as an employer which is obligated to engage in collective bargaining under Article 7 of the Labor Union Act with the union of subcontracted workers. Such a question has frequently been discussed in Labour Relations Commission (LRC) orders and judicial precedents. This will be discussed in II-5.

[4] Worker Dispatch

Until the Worker Dispatching Act was enacted in 1985, worker dispatching by temporary employment agencies was uniformly prohibited under Article 44 the Employment Security Act as one form of labor supply business prohibited by the article. In practice, however, there was a sharp increase in worker dispatch businesses from the mid-1970s into the 1980s after the first Oil Crisis of 1973. This increase occurred in the operation of information equipment, cleaning and maintenance of buildings and other services requiring special skills, amid increasing demands, on the part of companies, to enhance outsourcing to reduce payroll costs and, on the part of female workers, to seek employment opportunities compatible with their family responsibilities.

Although worker dispatching before the 1985 Act was mostly conducted in the form of business process subcontracting, ordering companies which received dispatched workers in their undertakings tended to make certain directions or supervisions on those workers in the execution of subcontracted work. Thus, questions arose frequently regarding whether or not such worker dispatching practices violated the ban on labor supply businesses. Moreover, there was the problem of uncertainty regarding where legal responsibility under labor protective laws should rest, since the receiving companies that actually used the labor were not employers in terms of labor contracts.

The Worker Dispatching Act of 1985 was enacted, accordingly, under the principle of revising the policy of uniformly banning labor supply business and of permitting worker dispatch businesses for limited types of work (jobs) while at the same time placing those newly permitted businesses under appropriate regulation. On the one hand, the Act placed strict regulations on "temporary employment-type" dispatch businesses whereby each time a business operator dispatches workers who are registered as desiring dispatch employment, the operator hires those workers for the required dispatch period only and then dispatches them to other companies. In light of the instability of dispatch employment under this type, the Act required such type of dispatch businesses to obtain a "license" from the Minister of Labour (currently the Minister of Health, Labour and Welfare) enumerating reasons for disqualification of business operators (Article 6 of the Worker Dispatching Act). On the other hand, in the case of "stable employment-type" dispatching whereby only workers employed under non-fixed-term contracts or for periods in excess of one year are dispatched, dispatch business operators are merely obligated to notify the Minister of Health, Labour and Welfare to engage in such type of dispatch business.

Thus, although worker dispatch is, in terms of its characteristics, the supply of workers to another, it was expressly excluded from "labor supply," which is banned by the Employment Security Act, in terms of its definition. On the other hand, purposefully, repeatedly, and continuously having a person under one's own control provide manpower for a third party under the instructions and orders of that party in a form that does not fall under the definition of "worker dispatch" and, therefore, continued to be prohibited as "labor supply business."

The Worker Dispatching Act initially adopted a "positive list" method, whereby the types of work for which dispatch is permitted were specifically listed. However, the types of work were in principle liberalized with progressing deregulation in the 1990s, and a 1999 revision of the act shifted to a "negative list method" whereby only prohibited types were listed. Moreover, manufacturing industries, which had been suffering from competition with their Asian counterparts using less expensive manpower demanded that manufacturing dispatching, a practice that had been banned, be allowed. Their demand became reality in 2003. Such deregulation led to a dramatic increase in the use of dispatching; however, it was those dispatched workers who were hit first by employment adjustment in the wake of the global recession that was sparked by Lehman Brothers' collapse in the autumn of 2008. At that time, enterprises using dispatched workers first cancelled their worker dispatch contracts with dispatching firms and removed dispatched workers from their production sites. Many dispatched workers were then dismissed by the dispatching firms and became unemployed, even though their labor contracts with those firms had not yet concluded. Such actions – known as *haken-giri* ("Cutting off dispatched workers") – were widely reported in the media. Coupled with the criticism against the increase in the practice of day worker dispatching, claims that deregulation had gone too far mounted in the media. As a result, the Worker Dispatching Act was revised in 2012 to tighten regulation in the following respects:

- Dispatches on a daily basis or for periods of less than two months (so-called day worker dispatching) are prohibited.
- Dispatching of workers inside group enterprise shall not exceed 80% of dispatches performed by a particular dispatch operator.
- In cases of illegal dispatch, it shall be deemed that the firm receiving the dispatched worker offered direct employment to the dispatched worker under the labor conditions having been provided by the dispatching firm.[5]

A further revision of the Worker Dispatching Act was made on September 30, 2015 to strengthen protection of dispatched workers in the following respects:

- All worker dispatching undertakings are placed under the license system, regardless if they engage in temporary employment-type or stable employment-type dispatching.
- The period during which a worker can be dispatched to the same establishment is redefined to three years, in principle.

5. The regulation concerning the deeming of illegal dispatch as an offer of direct employment was executed on October 1, 2015; the other revisions were executed on October 1, 2012.

- Dispatching firms must see to it that dispatched workers are directly employed by the recipient firm or continue employment with the dispatching firm as a dispatched worker after the dispatch to the firm concludes due to the expiration of the three year limitation stated above ("employment security measures").
- Dispatching firms are obligated to execute career development measures, such as provision of education and training and career consulting, to the dispatched workers they employ.
- Dispatching firms and firms receiving dispatched workers must see to it that dispatched workers receive working conditions in balance with those of workers who engage in similar work at the receiving firm.

As will be discussed in II-5(2), it should be noted that several judicial precedents and Central Labour Relations Commission (CLRC) orders of recent years have recognized employer status under the Labor Union Act for firms that receive dispatched workers.

[5] Individual Contracting

Since the Labor Standards Act was enacted in 1947, it has always been contested whether workers such as foremen individually participating in construction projects or truck drivers engaged in transport operations for a specific company using his or her own truckfall under "workers" to be protected by the Act since they tended to be under the arrangements of independent contractors. Labor inspection offices and the court have been dealing with the cases by examining the substance of work relationships, and there are two Supreme Court precedents both of which denied worker status for a truck driver[6] and a foreman carpenter[7] in the context of the cases.

In recent years, use of individual contractors has increased for services associated with companies' core competencies, giving rise to the cases in Labour Relations Commissions regarding the refusal of collective bargaining by an ordering firm vis-à-vis a union organizing such contractors. Disputed were the status of "worker" under the Trade Union Act in regard to technicians that engage in repair work on household water-use equipment in kitchens, bathrooms and toilets;[8] workers that provide express courier service by bicycle or motorbike;[9] and technicians that visit sites to repair audio equipment.[10]

6. Chief of Yokohama Minami Labor Standards Office Case, First Petty Bench 11/28/1996, *Rohan* No. 714, p. 14.
7. Chief of Fujisawa Labor Standards Office Case, First Petty Bench 6/28/2007, *Rohan* No. 940, p. 11.
8. The State and CLRC (INAX Maintenance) Case, Third Petty Bench 4/12/2011, *Rohan* No. 1026, p. 27.
9. Sokuhai Case, Tokyo District Court 4/28/2010, *Rohan* No. 1010, p. 25.
10. The State and CLRC (Victor) Case, Third Petty Bench 2/21/2012, *Minshū* Vol. 66 No. 3, p. 955.

Three rulings by the Supreme Court in 2011 and 2012[11] may be cited to provide a framework for the actual scope of workers under the Labor Union Act. According to these rulings, basic elements for judgment are (1) whether the persons are incorporated, as a labor force, in a business organization of the enterprise for which they are supplying labor; (2) whether they are subject to unilateral and routine decisions on the contents of contractual relations; and (3) whether remuneration for their services has the aspect of compensation for their labor. Supplementary elements for judgment are (4) whether they are in practice obligated to respond to work requests, and (5) whether they provide labor under direction and supervision in the broad sense, and whether and to what extent they are under constraints in the location and time of work. A final element that works negatively on worker status is (6) the existence of entrepreneurship aspects such as the ownership of machines and other equipment, and the discretion to make profits or losses of their own.[12] In the cases of individual contractors mentioned above, the "worker" status was recognized by the Labour Relations Commissions, of which decisions were supported by the Supreme Court in the above-stated rulings.

Contracting has been used for many years mainly as a means to avoid employer's responsibilities under protective labor law and social security systems. However, the active use of individual contractors for services that concern companies' core competencies appears to be a very recent phenomenon which may be understood in the following context.

When a task in which a labor is to be engaged is closer to a company's core operations, that labor must possess a higher work standard and maintain tighter collaboration with the company. However, because providing direction and supervision in the contractor's execution of the work from a remote location in real time was difficult, which thus also made it difficult to ensure a high work standard, entrusting core tasks to contractors was virtually impossible. However, recent advancements in information and communication technologies and the preparation of detailed work processing manuals have made it possible to control workers in remote locations in real time and, by extension, to utilize contractors for core tasks.

[6] Franchising

In Japan, the franchise industry has largely shown continuous strong growth as a new form of business since the 1990s. The growth of convenience stores is receiving particular attention within this trend.

In the case of the United States (U.S.), inferiority of the labor conditions of workers employed by franchisees to those of workers in directly managed stores is seen as a problem. On the other hand, in Japan, those that are hired based on the authority

11. The State and CLRC (New National Theatre Foundation) Case, Third Petty Bench 4/12/2011, *Minshū* Vol. 65 No.3 p. 943; the State and CLRC (INAX Maintenance) Case, Third Petty Bench 4/12/2011, *RōdōHanrei* No.1026 p. 27; and the State and CLRC (Victor) Case, Third Petty Bench 2/21/2012, *Minshū* Vol. 66 No.3 p. 955.

12. *See* Ministry of Health, Labour and Welfare, "Labor Relations Research Group Report (On the Criteria for Judging Worker Status under the Labor Union Act)" (http://www.mhlw.go.jp/stf/houdou/2r9852000001juuf-att/2r9852000001jx2l.pdf), p. 10 ff.

of the store manager are ordinarily part-time workers, regardless of whether the store is a directly -managed store or franchisee operating one. Given this, the problem of lower labor conditions for peripheral workers under the organizational format of "franchising" is largely seen as a problem of part-time workers. Additionally, because regulations that guarantee labor conditions, including the minimum wages, extend to workers who are employed by franchisees, the problem of lower labor conditions based on the specific circumstance of "franchising" has not been viewed as one of great importance.

However, the labor conditions of convenience store managers who are given contractual status of "franchisees" have recently come into the spotlight. The reason for this is that convenience store managers are told by their companies that they are not "workers" because they signed a service agreement, despite the fact that in reality they work in the same way as ordinary workers. As a result, there are many cases in which managers are made to work under harsh conditions. Against this backdrop, there has been a trend whereby such convenience store managers join small local unions in their regions to demand better conditions. On March 20, 2014, a Labour Relations Commission order was issued stating that convenience store managers are workers in terms of the Labor Union Act.[13] Relying on the criteria established by the Central Labour Relations Commission and Supreme Court, specifically, the Commission studied the following elements individually and in detail, and ruled that despite being business operators in a location separate from the company, member store managers have weak bargaining power that should be protected under collective bargaining laws and accordingly correspond to "workers" under the Labor Union Act.

Incorporation into a business organization:

(1) Standardized content of contractual relations unilaterally decided by the franchiser (inequality in bargaining power).
(2) Nature of remuneration as compensation for labor.
(3) Obligation to respond to work requests.
(4) Provision of labor under direction and supervision in the broad sense, and the existence of certain constraints in the location and time of work.
(5) The lack of clear entrepreneurship aspects.

Compared to individual and multilayered subcontracting, franchising appears to be a relatively new form of business. The reason for this is that maintaining a brand's overall image makes it necessary to maintain a working standard among workers who work under franchisees. The creation of detailed work training manuals to achieve this as well as the preparation of agreements that spell out responsibilities if a problem occurs require a high level of technical capability. Meeting such requirements has only become possible recently.

In relation to franchising, in Japan, there is another type of commercial arrangements by which multiple retail stores do business within the same store building. Such

13. Okayama Prefecture Labour Relations Commission 2010 (Fu) No.2 Unfair Labor Practice Relief Petition Case Order, http://www.pref.okayama.jp/uploaded/attachment/182426.pdf.

a facility is called a "cooperative department store." Maintaining brand image is an important consideration in the franchise industry; however, in the case of a cooperative department store, the companies that open stores have their brands and the department store providing the place and facilities also has its own brand. In such cases, the workers who work at the stores are obligated to abide by the regulations of both the company that operates the store and the department store, and there are times when the assignment of worker status and employer's responsibility becomes problematic. To illustrate as an example, say Brand C store opens stores in Brand A department store and Brand B department store. However, the Brand A department store declares that it will open for business on January 1, while the Brand B department store says it will begin sales on January 3. In this case, despite working for the same Brand C store, workers assigned to the Brand A department will be obligated to work beginning on January 1, while those assigned to the Brand B department store will begin work on January 3. In this sense, cooperative department stores can decide, even if only partially, the labor conditions of workers who are employed by the stores that do business in them.

[7] Subcontracting Alliance ("Keiretsu") and Offshoring

As was mentioned previously, subcontracting has been used in Japan since before the Second World War, and it has served as a buffer during a great number of international economic fluctuations. Particularly in the case of manufacturing, it has been pointed out that an important characteristic of Japan's manufacturing industry is the lowness of its ratio of in-house production compared to that of the US.[14]

In a number of manufacturing sectors, of which the automobile manufacturing industry is representative, a division of labor-based approach through subcontracting relationships extending over multiple stages and levels was used for the production and processing of components and fittings that are not made in-house. Specifically, production and processing tasks are divided up among subcontractors at the primary, secondary, tertiary, and even quaternary levels. The large enterprise standing at the top of this subcontracting system mainly devotes itself to final assembly.

Within this kind of subcontracting system, some large enterprises standing at the top of the division of labor have become oligopolistic. They engage in long-term business with a number of small and medium-sized subcontractors (exclusive subcontractors) that mainly make their parts, thus creating a relationship resembling a "one-to-many" pyramid. While doing business with several subcontractors that make the same parts, lead companies have constantly reorganized their subcontracting in order to reinforce their own competitiveness. Among other steps, this has involved strengthening their relationship (building an alliance) with prominent subcontractors and cutting ties with subcontractors that have difficulty with responding.

This "*Keiretsu*" or subcontracting alliance system has advantages for parent companies in that it conserves fixed capital and labor, makes it possible to procure

14. Solow, M. and John C. Scott, *Made in America* (Cambridge, Mass., MIT Press, 1989).

parts below the external labor market price, and allows flexible adjustment of the internal-external manufacturing ratio. For subcontractors, however, it exposes them to fierce competition with other subcontractors, and pressure from the parent company to engage in in-house production, and it requires that they be as flexible as possible in responding to various demands from the parent company so that they may continue doing business with the parent company. Consequently, companies nearer to the bottom of this layered subcontracted production structure pay lower wages. This produces a structure of hierarchal wage disparities.

The mechanism that moderated wage disparities between large enterprises and subcontractors had been the spring wage negotiations ("*Shunto*") that take place between March and April of each year. Although actual wage negations themselves take place at the employer-company union level, these negotiations have been coordinated and linked across industries through the setting of wage- increase targets within an industry or throughout all industries by industrial union federations or trade union national centers as well as the setting of negotiation schedules within or among industries on the union side, and through the coordinated setting of negotiation schedules between or among industries on the management side. Additionally, the wages paid by major enterprises within each industry made their influence felt in company wage negotiations through the industry hierarchy. The *Shunto* wage-increase patterns thus spread to small and medium-sized enterprises to a significant extent coupled with the assistance of shortage of labor in overall national economy.

The *Shunto* system was extremely successful as a mechanism for extending wage increases across industries and firms during Japan's period of high economic growth. However, following the collapse of the "bubble economy" and the intensified globalized competition, the mechanism's effectiveness to spread wage increases across firms and industries weakened significantly due to the differences between winning and losing firms as well as deterioration of the labor market for job-seekers.

In recent years, much of the production and processing of components and fittings that traditionally took place in Japan has moved to overseas manufacturing bases as Japanese manufacturing expands internationally. As a result, the supply chain for Japan's industry now crosses international borders. Many subcontractors that became exposed to fierce competition with overseas rivals as a result now do business with multiple parent companies to secure the volume of orders they need. Consequently, rather than manufacturing narrowly defined parts mainly for a single company, they now provide specialized technical assistance to end-product manufacturers to meet a variety of purposes. Subcontracting companies that successfully made this switch in roles have become "specialized processing companies" possessing a number of clients and gained the ability to do business with large enterprises on an equal footing. At the same time, the corporate relationship between specialized processing companies and client companies has also shifted from a pyramid-type relationship with large enterprises at the top to a network-type industrial organization with horizontal and equal links. As a result, the subordinate relationships that subcontracting companies had with large enterprises are weakening, and new interdependent relationships as equal business partners are emerging.[15]

As companies move low-added-value parts manufacturing and assembly offshore to low-wage developing countries, the labor conditions of workers working at overseas production sites that are now part of the supply chain have also become a matter of concern. However, unless there are exceptional circumstances, Japanese labor laws are not applicable to labor issues in foreign countries. As an example, there was a case in which the union of an overseas local subsidiary of a Japanese company joined an industrial union in Japan in connection with a labor dispute in the office of that subsidiary. The industrial union then approached the Japanese headquarter company with a request to engage in collective bargaining to settle the dispute but was refused. The industrial union responded by filing a complaint against the Japanese company claiming that its refusal to engage in collective bargaining constituted an unfair labor practice. However, the CLRC ruled that the case essentially concerned labor relations in a foreign country in which Japan's Labor Union Act did not apply and, therefore, that the case was outside of the CLRC's jurisdiction.[16] The ruling was subsequently endorsed by the court in its judicial review.[17]

[B] Extension of Employer's Responsibility in the Fissured Workplace Context

As described above, the main problems within the fissuring of workplaces phenomenon in Japan were the concept of "worker," the concept of "employer," and the extension of employer's responsibilities in the area of industrial health and safety. Leaving explanation of the problems concerning extension of employer's responsibilities in the area of industrial health and safety and the concept of "worker" to that provided above, the following will present the concept of "employer" in terms of labor contracts and in terms of the Labor Union Act, with emphasis on the concept and its extension in line with the problems and concerns addressed by this seminar. It will then present legal principles for expanding employer's responsibilities beyond the scope of judicial personality.

[1] The Issue of Extending Employer's Responsibility under Individual Labor Relations

The most basic concept of the "employer" under individual labor relations law is that of the employer under a labor contract. The definition given in Article 2 paragraph 2 of

15. For more on this topic, *see* GendaiKigyoKenkyukai (ed.), "*Nihon no Kigyo-kanKankei: SonoRiron to Jittai*" (inter-corporate relations in Japan: theory and reality) (Chuokeizai-sha, 1994) p. 175 and thereafter; and Kenichi Imai and Ryutaro Komiya, "*Nihon no Kigyo*" (Japanese Enterprises) (University of Tokyo Press, 1989) p. 163 and thereafter.
16. Toyota Philippines Case, CLRC 12/6/2006, *Meireishu* 136, p. 1258.
17. Tokyo High Court 12/26/2007, *Rokeisoku* No. 2063, p. 3.

the Labor Contract Act is that "The term 'employer' as used in this Act means a person who pays wages to the workers he/she employs."

In this regard, the employer status of someone who is not formally one of the parties to a contract sometimes causes problems. Specifically, these include cases of tripartite labor relationships such as the acceptance of dispatched workers or subcontracting relationships, in which a third party to the labor contract appears to be exhibiting employer-like functions but escaping from employer's responsibilities. Similarly, there are cases where, as in a parent-subsidiary relationship, the subsidiary company as a direct contractual employer is controlled by another corporation, thus influencing the subsidiary's labor relations.

[2] Statutory Extension of Employer's Responsibility under Individual Labor Relations

It should first be mentioned that there have been a few statutory responses to the need to extend employer's responsibility under the labor contract to the employer-like third party.

The first is the imposition of quasi-employer responsibilities under the Industrial Safety and Health Act. The Labor Standards Act originally included provisions in Chapter 5 "Safety and Health," imposing several obligations and systems of safety and health management on employers. In the process of high-level economic growth from 1955 onwards, however, major changes occurred in the labor environment, in terms of the innovation of machinery and equipment, intensification of work, and handling of new hazardous substances. This led to an increase in both the risk of industrial accidents and accident victims. To address this situation, the Industrial Safety and Health Act was enacted in 1972 as a comprehensive law aimed at preventing work-related accidents. Characteristic among the provisions of the new Act is that the obligation to take certain measures to prevent accidents or health impairment from occurring in the workplace is imposed not only on employers under labor contracts, but also on the manufacturers, orderers and leasers of hazardous machines or equipment, or harmful materials. Especially remarkable in the fissured workplace context is the special regulation to prevent hazards in the workplace involving multilayered subcontracting. Namely, the prime contractor must give necessary guidance so that related subcontractors do not violate the Industrial Health and Safety Act. The prime contractor in construction and shipbuilding projects, in particular, must take various measures to prevent industrial accidents from occurring as a result of workers of the prime contractor and subcontractors working together in the same workplace (Articles 29-34 of said Act).[18]

The second is the special arrangement concerning the employer's responsibility for industrial accident compensation in construction projects. Article 87 of the Labor

18. Such measures include the establishment and administration of consultative organization carrying out liaison and adjustment between related operations, conducting inspection tours of places of operation, and providing guidance and assistance regarding education conducted by related subcontractors for the safety and health of workers.

Standards Act prescribes that, in construction projects executed with multilayered subcontracting, the prime contractor shall be deemed the employer responsible for compensating for work-related accidents occurring during a project. The Act further states that the prime contractor may conclude a written agreement with one of the subcontractors to assume responsibility for compensation. In such a case, the Act stipulates that both the prime contractor and the subcontractor assume joint responsibility for compensation.

The third is a partial extension of the employer's responsibilities under protective labor legislation to recipient firms in a worker dispatch setting. As previously explained, under the Worker Dispatch Act, the dispatching firm in principle assumes the employer's responsibilities under the Labor Standards Act, the Industrial Safety and Health Act, and others in relation to the dispatched workers. The reason is, of course, that it is not the recipient firm but the dispatching firm that is the employer under the labor contract with dispatched workers. Nevertheless, the Act imposes certain regulations in the Labor Standards Act and others solely or cumulatively on the accepting firm, as responsibilities in actually using the manpower of dispatched workers under its direction and supervision. For example, the employer's responsibilities to abide by the limit of daily and weekly working hours and to provide daily rest periods and weekly rest days are imposed solely on the recipient enterprise. The responsibilities to give equal treatment to workers in terms of working conditions, irrespective of their nationality, religion, creed and social origin, and to men and women in terms of wages are imposed on both the dispatching and recipient enterprises.

[3] Extension of Employer's Responsibility under the Doctrine of Denying the Legal Entity of the Direct Employer

In the triangular settings of business process contracting or parent-subsidiary relationships, there are cases in which the business management and labor relations of the contractor or subsidiary company are so greatly dominated by the client or parent company that the contractor or subsidiary company appears to be part of the corporate organization of the client or parent company. In such a situation, one can argue for the doctrine of denying the legal entity of the contractor or subsidiary company vis-à-vis the client or parent company, thereby deeming workers employed by the former company to be those employed by the latter company.

More concretely, in parent-subsidiary relationships, there are cases in which the parent company completely dominates the decisions of the subsidiary company and comprehensively controls its operations. In this context, the employment relationships and working conditions of workers in the subsidiary would be completely dominated by the parent company. In such a situation, if the workers of the subsidiary find that the subsidiary, as their direct employer, has been dissolved by the parent company, that wages for work already done are not yet paid and workers are subjected to economic dismissal, they may wish to pursue liability for unpaid wages or unfair dismissal against the parent company.

According to established case law of the Supreme Court, the status of a corporation as an independent legal entity can be denied when the substance of the corporate organization is a mere shell as a legal entity, or when the corporate organization is abusing the legal entity for unlawful purposes. Applying this general doctrine, where a subsidiary corporation is placed under the parent corporation's comprehensive and complete control through the latter's holding all of the subsidiary's shares, dispatching of officers to run the subsidiary, and exclusive business relationship with the subsidiary, and the parent exercises tight control over the subsidiary's decisions on wages, working conditions and other personnel matters, the employees may argue that the legal entity of the subsidiary company is a mere shell vis-à-vis the parent company, and, therefore, that the subsidiary company should be deemed to be a business branch of the parent company. By so arguing, they can contend that they should legally be deemed to be in a labor contract relationship with the parent company. They may thus be able to claim unpaid wages against or employment relations with the parent corporation.

In the setting of business process contracting, on the other hand, there are also cases in which a contractor company is wholly dependent on the client company as its exclusive contractor. The contractor company is doing nothing but the businesses contracted out by the client company, solely within the facilities of the latter company. Contractual conditions are unilaterally decided by the client company, which frequently puts pressure on the contractor company to reduce its workers' wages and thus save the cost of contracting. The client company can also make contracting workers perform their work together with its own employees, and can issue directions to the contracting workers. In such a situation, if the client company decides to replace the contractor company with another firm proposing less expensive and more efficient contracting, the workers may lose their jobs due to the termination of business process contracting. The workers of the contractor company may claim labor contract relations with the client company by relying on the doctrine of denying legal entity. Generally speaking, however, it is difficult to apply the doctrine to contractual relations unless the client company is at the same time the parent company of the contractor company.

[4] Extension of Employer's Responsibility under the Theory of the Implied Labor Contract

The next theory that is useful for extending the employer's responsibility under a labor contract is the theory of implied labor contracts. According to case law, implied labor contract relations can be recognized between an enterprise and a worker who are not in an explicit labor contract relationship, but are in fact in a relationship in which the worker is providing labor for the enterprise and the enterprise is paying wages to the worker as remuneration to that labor. To ascertain an implied labor contract relationship, it is not sufficient that a worker is providing labor under the direction and supervision of an enterprise, according to case law. The worker has to identify the enterprise directing and supervising his/her labor as the employer who is paying wages in return for that labor.

In parent-subsidiary relations, for example, this theory can be workable in cases when there is almost no independence of the subsidiary in business operations as well as in personnel management, and, accordingly, the subsidiary could be recognized merely as a part of the parent's business organization. In such cases, the workers of the subsidiary may consider that they are actually working for the parent company and that the wages they are receiving are paid by the parent company as remuneration for their work for the parent company. These are also cases in which one can rely on the doctrine of denying the legal entity of the subsidiary company. In the parent-subsidiary setting, workers of the subsidiary more often resort to the doctrine of denying legal entity than the theory of implied labor contract relations.

The theory of implied labor contract relations is also referred to in cases of worker dispatch and business process contracting. Namely, when dispatched workers lose their jobs due to the termination of worker dispatch agreements between dispatching and recipient enterprises, they may criticize the callous attitude of the recipient enterprise and may even claim the existence of labor contract relations with the recipient company. Such an attempt will not be successful unless the dispatching company can be regarded in fact not as an independent business entity but as a mere manpower office of the recipient company performing recruitment of workers on its behalf.

The above-mentioned workers of a contractor company who lose their jobs due to the termination of an exclusive contractual relationship between the client (recipient) company and the contractor company may also contend that real labor contract relations can be found between them and the client company, in accordance with the theory of implied labor contract. Here again, such a contention will not be persuasive unless the contractor company could be recognized not as an independent business entity but as a mere client company's branch office performing personnel management on its behalf.

[5] Extension of Employer's Responsibilities under the Labor Union Act

[a] Extension in the Cases of Parent-Subsidiary and Subcontracting Rrelations

Article 7 of the Labor Union Act prohibits certain acts by employers which are not permissible in collective labor relations institutionalized by the Act; these acts are known as unfair labor practices. When a violation occurs, an administrative committee called a Labour Relations Commission issues an administrative relief order, the aim being to restore and secure proper order in collective labor relations.

Article 7 mentioned above prescribes that the "employer shall not commit" the listed unfair labor practices. Here, the problem lies in what "the employer" refers to as the actor of unfair labor practices. It goes without saying that the employer should be identified with one party to a labor contract who receives the labor of and pays wages to the other party, but here, we shall question whether some legal entity other than this employer based on a labor contract could be regarded as an employer.

The combined efforts of labor law academics and the courts have established a doctrine of extending employer status to the third party in a labor contract who dominates and controls the working conditions of workers in the labor contract. This doctrine has been formed with regard to cases of parent-subsidiary relations and subcontracting relations in the following way.

If a parent company controls a subsidiary company's operations and the treatment of the latter's workers, this could work towards affirming the employer status of the parent company pursuant to Article 7 of the Labor Union Act. Thus, if the parent company, through its stock ownership, dispatch of officials, subcontracting relations and the like, places the subsidiary company under its control, and has actual and concrete managerial authority with respect to the working conditions of the latter's employees, the parent will have employer status in collective bargaining, along with the subsidiary, with regard to those employees' working conditions.[19]

Also, when an enterprise subcontracts some of its work to another enterprise and provides its own employees to that other enterprise, the recipient enterprise may acquire the status of an "employer" for purposes of Article 7 towards those employees of the subcontractor enterprise. Thus, where the recipient company has actual and concrete control over the working conditions and treatment of such workers working in its place of business, it is deemed to possess the status of the employer towards the workers. According to a Supreme Court precedent,[20] even where the recipient company does not control working conditions in the contractor company comprehensively, it should still be deemed "a partial employer" if it has "substantial and concrete domination" over partial but significant working conditions in the latter company.[21]

[b] Extension of the Employer in the Fissured Workplace Context

Applying the theories explained above, a typical legal issue arising in multilayered subcontracting relationships is whether a client company that contracts out part of its work to a subcontractor should be viewed as an employer under the Labor Union Law, vis-à-vis the workers employed by the bottom level subcontractor and received in the place of business of the contracting-out company. According to the theory of extending employer status mentioned above, the basic criterion is the extent to which the client (recipient) company has "substantial and concrete domination" over the working conditions of the subcontractor's workers.

19. Kazuo Sugeno, *Japanese Employment and Labor Law* (North Carolina Academic Press 2002) p. 699.
20. Asahi HōsōCase, Supreme Court 3rd Petty Bench Decision, February 28, 1995.
21. Sugeno 2002, p. 700.

Figure. 2.1 Extension of Employer Status in Multilayered Subcontracting Relationship

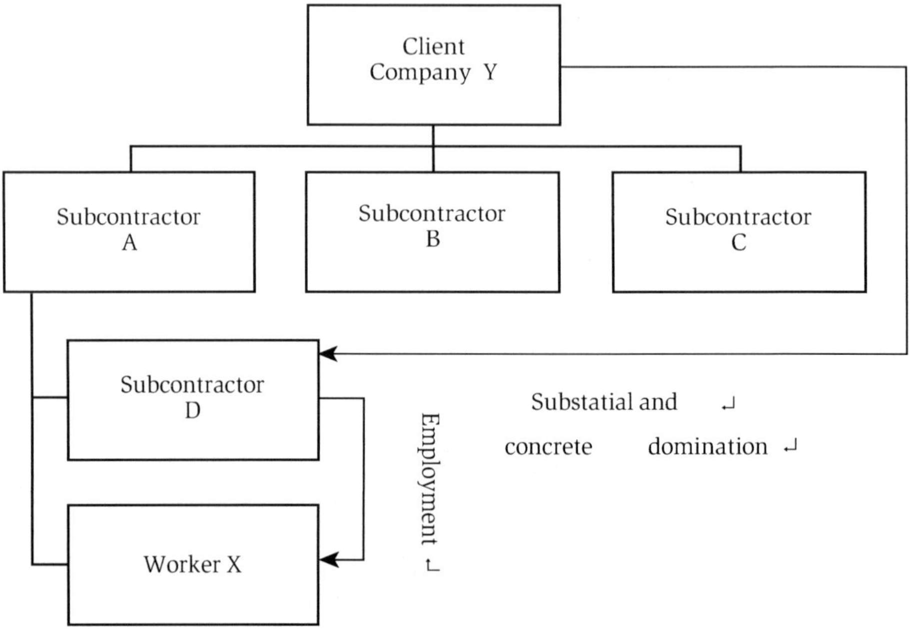

As shown in Figure 2.1, let us assume that Company D is one of Company A's subcontractor companies, and that Company A is a subcontractor company of Company Y. If Company Y has substantial and concrete domination over Company D not only in its business operation but also in partial yet substantial working conditions of Company D's Worker X, who is engaged in the subcontracted work, Company Y would be viewed as the employer of Worker X, even though the worker is directly employed by Subcontractor D.

The same approach is used when the Labour Relations Commissions ascertain the existence or non-existence of employer status on the part of firms which receive workers dispatched by temporary agencies within their establishments and, in practice, direct and supervise them.

Figure. 2.2 Extension of Employer Status in Parent-Subsidiary Relationship

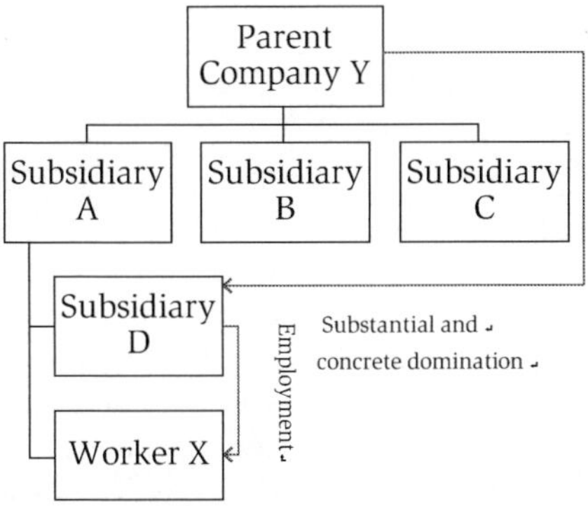

A similar extension of employer status could be applied to the multilayered parent-subsidiary relationship. For example, as shown in Figure 2.2, let us assume that Company D is a subsidiary company of Company A, and Company A is a subsidiary company of Company Y. If Company Y has substantial and concrete domination over Company D not only in its business operation but also in the management of partial yet significant working conditions, Company Y would be viewed as the employer of Worker X, even though the worker is directly employed by Subsidiary D. The point is that the doctrine of extending employer status under the Labor Union Act can be applied to tripartite business relations such as the parent, subsidiary and subsidiary's employees, or the subcontractor, subcontractor's employees and recipient, whether these be simple tripartite relations or more complex multilayered tripartite relations. It should be added that the doctrine would be usable even for other tripartite relations such as that of the franchiser, franchisee and franchisee's employees, or the dispatcher, dispatcher's employees and recipient, whether these be simple or a multilayered relations.

§2.02 CONCLUSION

The "fissured workplace" in the USA is described by David Weil as a new form of fundamental restructuring of business organizations which is making work so bad for so many. Being such a new phenomenon proceeding against the backgrounds of globalization and new information technology, there seems yet to be no definite answer on the question of what can be done from the viewpoint of legal studies. One finds the significance of comparative studies, which started in the Amsterdam Conference and the Fall 2015 issue of Comparative Labor Law and Policy Issue Journal under the leadership of Matthew Finkin. One could at least confirm that it is also a phenomenon occurring across national borders generating similar policy issues in labor relations.

The author found in this chapter that Japan had rather been experiencing several components of "fissured workplace" in its modern history, and that labor law had been making certain responses against the problems arising therein. On the other hand, there are certainly new phenomena such as franchising, offshoring, and active use of individual contractors under globalization and new information technology, but legal responses are made by using conventional tools of labor law having been developed in relation to conventional phenomena of fissurization. For example, recent advancements in information and communication technologies and the preparation of detailed work processing manuals have made it possible to control workers in remote locations in real time, without any limitations placed on the workplace, and to receive the results of labor of a certain level of quality simply by having workers get in compliance with a work training manual, without having to provide supervision in the labor provision process. With these changes, people who do not correspond to the traditional employer concept are able to make use of the manpower of workers. Therefore, whether or not we need to modify the current concept of employer and whether we should introduce a fundamental reform of labor law are issues we are starting to discuss in this international seminar.

CHAPTER 3

Reconsidering the Notion of 'Employer' in the Era of the Fissured Workplace: Traversing the Legislative Landscape in Australia

Tess Hardy[*]

§3.01 INTRODUCTION

The concept of the employer has been receiving renewed attention in Australia following a raft of media and government investigations into the working conditions of temporary foreign workers in the past twelve months.[1] In particular, these recent inquiries have highlighted that certain sectors of the Australian labour market – most notably the horticulture and food processing industries,[2] and the convenience store franchise sector[3]– may be 'riddled with exploitation'.[4] While it is generally now accepted that employer non-compliance with work place laws is a pressing problem in

* University of Melbourne.

1. These investigations have prompted a number of ongoing government inquiries at both federal and state levels. *See*, e.g., Australian Government, Senate Education and Employment References Committee, Inquiry into the Impact of Australia's Temporary Work Visa Programs on the Australian Labour Market and on the Temporary Work Visa Holders (Final Report, March 2016); Victorian Government, Inquiry into Labour Hire and Insecure Work (due to report by 31 July 2016); South Australian Government, Economic and Finance Committee, Inquiry into Labour Hire Industry (established on 11 June 2015, submissions closed on 27 July 2015).
2. Caro Meldrum-Hanna and Ali Russell, 'Slaving Away', Four Corners, 4 May 2015 (available at http://www.abc.net.au/4corners/stories/2015/05/04/4227055.htm; accessed on 14 September 2015).
3. Adele Ferguson and Klaus Toft, '7-Eleven: The Price of Convenience', Four Corners, 31 August 2015, (available at http://www.abc.net.au/4corners/stories/2015/08/30/4301164.htm; accessed on 16 September 2015).
4. Meldrum-Hanna and Russell, *supra* n. 2.

Australia, there is far less consensus about what can be done and who should be held responsible. These issues are undeniably complicated by the 'fissuring' of work described by David Weil.[5]

Indeed, the labour market in Australia reflects many of the structural shifts which have occurred in the United States (US) and elsewhere.[6] Like many advanced economies, Australia has also witnessed a move away from manufacturing towards services, a decline in trade unionism, greater competition in capital and product markets, and increased commercialisation of work relationships. Particular management techniques and organisational forms – such as subcontracting, outsourcing and franchising – have grown in popularity.[7] Combined, these developments have generally promoted forms of work that are more insecure and precarious.[8]

This chapter begins by exploring the available evidence on the extent to which Australian workplaces have become fissured. This chapter then provides an overview of the central statutory responses in the respective regulatory spheres of labour, work health and safety, and competition and consumer protection. In reviewing this legislative landscape, this chapter reveals that while Australian statutes are innovative and inclusive in some respects, critical regulatory gaps remain. This can be linked, at least in part, to the way in which these statutory regimes conceptualise the principal subject and object of the relevant regulation.

First, the *Fair Work Act 2009* (Cth) (*FW Act*) continues to reflect the binary notion of employment and the unitary conception of the 'employer'.[9] While this statute prescribes a comprehensive 'safety net' for employees making it less appealing for lead firms to shed direct employment, ultimately it is the employer, as identified at common law, who is positioned as the primary wrongdoer. This underlying premise makes it more difficult for regulators and others to hold lead firms responsible for workplace contraventions taking place in their supply chain or franchise network.

Second, and in stark contrast to the FW Act, the harmonised work health and safety legislation 'no longer normalises the employment relationship as a starting point of regulation'.[10] Rather, it seeks to protect all workers (regardless of employment

5. David Weil, *The Fissured Workplace: Why Work Became So Bad for So Many and What Can Be Done to Improve It* (Harvard University Press, 2014).
6. Judy Fudge, 'Blurring Legal Boundaries: Regulating for Decent Work' in Judy Fudge, Shae McCrystal and Kamala Sankaran, *Challenging the Legal Boundaries of Work Regulation* (Hart Publishing, 2012).
7. Richard Johnstone, Shae McCrystal, Igor Nossar, Michael Quinlan, Michael Rawling and Joellen Riley, *Beyond Employment: The Legal Regulation of Work Relationships* (Federation Press, 2012).
8. The term 'insecure work' has been defined by the Australian Council of Trade Unions as 'poor quality work that provides workers with little economic security and little control over their working lives'. *See* Brian Howe et al., *Lives on Hold: Unlocking the Potential of Australia's Workforce* (The Report of the Independent Inquiry into Insecure Work in Australia, 2012) at 14.
9. *See*, generally, Mark Freedland, *The Personal Employment Contract* (Oxford University Press, 2003); Jeremias Prassl, *The Concept of the Employer* (Oxford University Press, 2015).
10. Johnstone et al., *supra* n. 7, at 5.

status) by placing the primary duty on a 'person conducting a business or undertaking'.[11] The broader scope of this legislation makes it far more amenable to addressing the problems presented by fragmented work arrangements, albeit the full potential of this regulation may not yet have been realised.

Third, and finally, this chapter considers recent reforms under the competition and consumer regulation which are principally designed to safeguard small businesses – including independent contractors and franchisees – from abuses of market power by larger firms. These statutory reforms are relevant to the notion of the employer to the extent that contracting and franchising relationships bridge the traditional boundaries between employment and commercial law.[12]

In the final section, this chapter considers the extent to which these statutory schemes either adhere to, or depart from, the dominant employment paradigm and evaluates the implications this may have for affected workers. This analysis is principally conducted by examining two separate, high-profile cases involving the Baiada Group (*Baiada*), the largest poultry processing corporate group in Australia,[13] and the Australian arm of the 7-Eleven convenience store franchise (*7-Eleven*).[14] These cases lie at the heart of the current debate taking place in Australia and illustrate both the challenges and potential of the present regulatory regime.

§3.02 TO WHAT EXTENT ARE AUSTRALIAN WORKPLACES 'FISSURED' AND WHAT ARE THE POSSIBLE EFFECTS?

[A] Available Data on Fissured Forms of Work

While there is a large degree of variation in working patterns and employment arrangements, there does appear to be some evidence to suggest that fissured work arrangements are an increasing feature of the Australian labour market. In the absence of detailed empirical research, however, it is far more difficult to precisely assess the prevalence of fragmented work forms in Australia and the relevant consequences of such, including the extent to which it perpetuates non-compliance with minimum employment standards and work health and safety obligations. As will be discussed

11. *See* ss 19(1)-(2) of each of the harmonised Work Health and Safety Acts (WHS Acts).
12. Joellen Riley, 'A Blurred Boundary between Entrepreneurship and Servitude: Regulating Business Format Franchising in Australia' in Judy Fudge, Shae McCrystal and Kamala Sankaran, *Challenging the Legal Boundaries of Work Regulation* (Hart Publishing, 2012) at 104.
13. The Baiada Group – which includes Baiada Poultry Pty Limited and Bartter Enterprises Pty Limited – supplies many of its chickens to leading supermarkets and fast food chains. Fair Work Ombudsman, *A Report on the Fair Work Ombudsman's Inquiry into the Labour Procurement Arrangements of the Baiada Group in New South Wales* (FWO Baiada Inquiry, June 2015).
14. In Australia, 7-Eleven Stores Pty Ltd – a private, family-owned company – has a licence to operate and franchise 7-Eleven stores. The 7-Eleven franchise has been operating for almost forty years and currently operates over 600 stores within Australia. While the international head office of 7-Eleven is currently located in Dallas, Texas – the brand is currently owned by a Japanese corporation, Seven & I Holdings Co Ltd. Japan now has more 7-Eleven locations than anywhere else in the world.

below, even the available data on the incidence and extent of independent contracting, labour hire, franchising and supply chains in the Australian labour market is somewhat uncertain.

For instance, the most recent data on forms of employment suggests that of the 11.6 million persons in paid work in Australia, 8.6% (or just over 1 million) were independent contractors.[15] Yet, this same data also suggests that this segment of the workforce displays many of the typical hallmarks of employees. For instance, 63% of independent contractors did not have authority over their own work; 43% were not able to subcontract their own work; and 87.2% had been with their current 'client' for more than twelve months.[16] This data, along with other research, suggests that many workers may be misclassified as independent contractors rather than employees.[17] What this data does not show is the extent to which self-employed franchisees and labour hire workers perceive themselves either as 'independent contractors' (predominantly providing their own labour), or alternatively, as 'other business operators' (operating a business which generates income not principally derived from providing their own labour).[18] As discussed in section §3.06[B] below, the distinction between those contractors/franchisees which are self-employed and those contractors/franchisees, which are themselves employers, can have important implications for the way in which competition and consumer regulation applies to these businesses and the employees that work for them.

The data on labour hire is also somewhat ill defined. For example, depending on the methodology, data source and time period which is selected, the proportion of labour hire workers in the Australian workforce appears to vary from between 1.8%[19] to 5.2%.[20] According to official data, labour hire work appears to be most prevalent in the IT and telecommunications, construction and trades, health care and medical sectors.[21] However, it is less clear to what extent marginal labour hire businesses operating in highly competitive sectors, such as cleaning, security, horticulture and

15. In this context, the term 'independent contractor' is defined to include people operating their own business and who are contracted to provide 'labor type services' without having the legal status of employee.
16. Australian Bureau of Statistics, *Characteristics of Employment* (Cat No 6333.0, 2015).
17. Research undertaken in the construction industry found that around 13% of all workers who had self-identified as independent contractors were 'possibly misclassified' and may well be employees at common law. *See*, e.g., Office of the Australian Building and Construction Commission, Sham Contracting Inquiry Report (2011); TNS Social Research, Working Arrangements in the Building and Construction Industry: Further Research Resulting from the 2011 Sham Contracting Inquiry (2012). *See also* Fair Work Ombudsman, *Sham Contracting and the Misclassification of Workers in the Cleaning Services, Hair and Beauty and Call Centre Industries* (Report on the Preliminary Outcomes of the Fair Work Ombudsman Sham Contracting Operational Intervention, November 2011).
18. 'Other business operators' is defined as persons who operate businesses which principally generate income through managing their own workers, or providing goods and services to the public, rather than by providing their own labour services (as is the case of independent contractors). ABS, *supra* n. 16.
19. Australian Government, *Workplace Relations Framework – Productivity Commission Inquiry Report* (30 November 2015) at 5.
20. *Ibid.*
21. IBIS World Industry Report N7212, *Temporary Staff Services in Australia* (July 2015) at 15.

food processing, formally identify their business as such. There is certainly anecdotal evidence that labour hire is a prominent way to source labour in these sectors.[22]

Similarly, the lack of any official registration requirements on franchisors makes it impossible to accurately identify the population. The data which is available estimates that in Australia there are currently 1,160 franchisors, 79,000 franchising units employing around 460,000 people.[23] Indeed, there is evidence to suggest that franchising is more prevalent in Australia than in the US – the home of the franchise model.[24] While franchising spans an increasingly wide variety of sectors from hotels to hospitality to hairdressers, franchises are especially prominent in service industries, such as retail and food services.[25]

It is even more difficult to pin down the numbers of domestic workers in national and/or transnational supply chains.[26] However, supply chains appear to be a common organisational form in a wide range of industries in Australia, including transport (by road, rail, air or sea), manufacturing (such as textile, clothing and leather goods and food processing), construction, hospitality, horticulture, nursing and homecare, cleaning, information technology and waste disposal.[27] While concrete data is sparse, it is now accepted that workers in supply chains in the textile, clothing and footwear and the road transport industries are often vulnerable and in need of additional legislative protection. In the last decade, there have been a number of statutory reforms designed to address worker exploitation arising in these specific types of supply chains. For example, in 2012, the FW Act was amended to include sector-specific regulation of the textile, clothing and footwear industry. These statutory provisions are deliberately designed to provide workers – regardless of their formal employment status or their specific working arrangements – with basic workplace entitlements, such as minimum rates of pay and penalty rates for overtime work.[28] It also expands the workers' rights of recovery by allowing them to bring claims against third-party firms higher in the

22. *See*, e.g., *Fair Work Ombudsman v. Eastern Colour Pty Ltd (No 2)* [2014] FCA 55; *Fair Work Ombudsman v. Jooine (Investment) Pty Ltd & Anor* [2013] FCCA 2144.
23. Lorelle Frazer, Scott Weaven and Anthony Grace, *Franchising Australia Survey 2014* (Asia-Pacific Centre for Franchising Excellence, Griffith University, 2014) (Franchising Survey).
24. *See* Riley (2012), *supra* n. 12. Further, the Australian franchise sector operates over 50% more units than in Britain. *See* British Franchise Association, NatWest/British Franchise Association Survey (2011).
25. In particular, 27% of franchisors are in retail trade and 18% of franchisors are in accommodation and food services, including fast food. *See* Franchising Survey, *supra* n. 23. For analysis of franchising behaviour in the café sector, *see*, e.g., AshleaKellner, David Peetz, Keith Townsend and Adrian Wilkinson, '"We are Very Focused on the Muffins": Regulation of and Compliance with Industrial Relations in Franchises' (2016) 58(1) *Journal of Industrial Relations* 25.
26. Supply chains are defined broadly in this chapter as an interconnected series of contracts or business transactions organised to provide goods or services to organisations at the apex of contractual chains for profit. The organisations at the apex of these chains – so-called lead firms – are contractually separated from the workers that produce the goods or provide the services by a series of contracts with and between intermediate parties. Michael Quinlan, *Supply Chains and Networks* (Safe Work Australia, Canberra, 2011).
27. *Ibid.* at 8.
28. For further discussion, *see* Igor Nossar, Richard Johnstone, Anna Macklin and Michael Rawling, 'Protective Legal Regulation for Home-Based Workers in Australian Textile, Clothing and Footwear Supply Chains' (2015) 57(4) *Journal of Industrial Relations* 585.

supply chain.[29] While these types of initiatives may be instructive to some extent, they are limited in other respects – not least by the fact that they are restricted to narrowly confined sectors.[30]

[B] Possible Effects of Fissured Work

The relationship between fissured forms of work (such as subcontracting, labour hire and franchising) and insecure work arrangements (including casual and fixed term work) is not straightforward. For example, casual work[31] is particularly prevalent in Australia making up around 23.5% of the paid workforce.[32] While casual work may be characterised as inherently insecure, these arrangements do not necessarily represent a 'fissured' form of employment where the worker continues to be directly employed by the lead firm.[33] That said, there does appear to be some link between fissured forms of work and employment insecurity. For example, when compared to the labour market overall, casual work not only appears to be more concentrated in franchising,[34] its incidence in the franchise sector continues to increase whereas the concentration of casual work has largely plateaued in other parts of the Australian economy.[35] It has been similarly observed that the outsourcing or subcontracting of work in supply chains typically involves the use of contingent workers, including self-employed subcontractors, home-workers, labour hire and casual employees.[36]

While this data suggests that there are greater levels of insecure work in supply chains and franchises than in other parts of the economy, this does not, of itself, mean that there are necessarily higher rates of employer non-compliance. Indeed, it is difficult to make a firm link between these two trends because there is no conclusive data on the rate of workplace contraventions available in Australia – either by sector, employment arrangement, organisational form or more generally. While there is no

29. There have been numerous statutory initiatives in the road transport industry, including the enactment of the Heavy Vehicle National Law and the establishment of the Road Safety Remuneration Tribunal. *See* Igor Nossar and Michael Rawling, 'Regulating Supply Chains to Protect Road Transport Workers: An Early Assessment of the Road Safety Remuneration Tribunal' (2015) 43(3) *Federal Law Review* 397.
30. For further discussion of alternative regulatory models, including the TCF scheme, *see* Tess Hardy, 'Who Should Be Held Liable for Workplace Contraventions and On What Basis?' (2016) *Australian Journal of Labour Law* (forthcoming).
31. While casual employees have no entitlement to regular hours of work or other benefits accruing to permanent employees, such as paid leave, notice of termination or redundancy pay, they are generally entitled to be paid a loading on their base rate of pay by way of compensation.
32. Australian Bureau of Statistics, *Forms of Employment, Australia* (Cat No 6359.0, 2013).
33. Richard Johnstone and Andrew Stewart, 'Swimming Against the Tide? Australian Labour Regulation and the Fissured Workplace' (2015) 37 *Comparative Labor Law & Policy Journal* 55, at 59.
34. The latest estimates suggest that approximately 82% of all workers were employed as casuals in company-owned franchised units and around 57% were engaged on a casual basis in independent franchised units. Franchising Survey, *supra* n. 23.
35. It has been argued that self-employed workers are also more common in the franchise sector. *See* Riley (2012), *supra* n. 12, at102.
36. Quinlan, *supra* n. 26, at 8.

definitive data on compliance rates, there is certainly anecdotal evidence that underpayment of employees 'has become a kind of norm amongst many small businesses in Australia'.[37]

Ultimately, the incidence of workplace contraventions are likely to turn on a range of other factors such as: the nature and terms of the contract between the lead organisation and the employing company, the size and assets of the putative employer, the extent to which the employer entity has a viable business that is independent of the lead organisation, the competitiveness of the relevant sector and the vulnerability (or otherwise) of the workers.[38] These various issues are highlighted by the two case studies examined in section §3.06 below.

§3.03 REGULATORY RESPONSES IN THE LABOUR SPHERE

This section examines the central provisions of the FW Act: the statutory cornerstone of the federal workplace relations system.[39] It provides an overview of critical employee rights and protections, before considering the way in which provisions relating to accessorial liability and sham contracting may serve to address some of the issues compliance and enforcement challenges raised by the vertical disintegration of firms and work.

Many of the protections and entitlements under the FW Act apply only to employees[40] as defined at common law.[41] Classifying a work contract as one of employment therefore has significant regulatory consequences. Similar in many ways to the tests adopted in other common law countries, the question of whether a particular individual is an employee or an independent contractor requires the balancing of multiple indicia taking into account the totality of the relationship.[42] While

37. Evidence to Senate Inquiry into the Impact of Australia's Temporary Work Visa Programs on the Australian Labour Market and on the Temporary Work Visa Holders, Parliament of Australia, Melbourne, 5 February 2016, 20 (Michal Smith, 7-Eleven Australia Pty Ltd). This is confirmed by the results of a number of recent industry campaigns carried out by the Fair Work Ombudsman, which found that employer non-compliance was greater than 50% (*see*, e.g., Fair Work Ombudsman, *National Hospitality Industry Campaign: Restaurants, Cafes and Catering – Report* (June 2015)).
38. Johnstone and Stewart, *supra* n. 33, at 4.
39. The distinction between employees and independent contractors is also relevant in relation to a range of other legislation regulating matters, such as long service leave, workers' compensation and superannuation/pension entitlements, amongst others.
40. This legislative framework generally applies to all employees regardless of visa, residential or citizenship status and are therefore critical in protecting foreign-born workers from workplace exploitation.
41. There is no statutory definition of employment. For constitutional reasons which are not relevant for present purposes, particular parts of the FW Act – including the provisions dealing with the National Employment Standards, modern awards, enterprise agreements, minimum wages and other terms and conditions of employment – apply only to a 'national system employer' and a 'national system employee': FW Act, ss 13, 14. Other parts of the FW Act – including the provisions dealing with parental leave and notice of termination – apply to all employers and employees as ordinarily defined (i.e., as defined at common law): FW Act, s. 11.
42. These indicia include, amongst other factors, whether the hirer has the right to control the way work is performed, whether the worker is integrated into the hirer's business, whether the worker is exposed to financial risk or potential profits from the running of a business and

this broad list of indicia usefully captures a wide range of circumstances, the application of this general test is not necessarily settled. Indeed, some recent decisions of the Full Court of the Federal Court place a different emphasis on different factors.[43] In the past, these nuanced distinctions were perhaps less consequential given that the boundaries of the firm were more concrete. However, as Weil points out, the 'more the workplace has fissured, the more the subtleties raised by definitions of employment matter'.[44]

The fragmented work structures referred to above – subcontracting, labour hire and franchise arrangements – have generally been accepted by the courts as being both genuine and legitimate. In particular, when assessing the lawfulness (or otherwise) of labour hire and subcontracting arrangements, the courts have typically been reluctant to treat on-hired workers as employees of the 'client' or 'host' business.[45] There has been even less judicial enthusiasm for regarding the labour hire agency and the host business as joint employers.[46] There have, however, been instances where the courts have been willing to dismiss labour hire arrangements as a 'sham', where a business is clearly seeking to avoid its employment obligations by contracting labour through a corporate intermediary, particularly where this occurs as part of a company group.[47]

Similarly, in cases involving employment contraventions in franchises, courts have generally confirmed the validity of franchise arrangements and commonly accepted that an independently owned and operated franchisee company is the relevant employer entity.[48] So far, and with the exception of company-owned franchisees,[49] there have been no cases where the courts have been willing to pierce the corporate veil in order to find that the franchisor is the relevant employer of the affected employees – either on a sole or joint basis.[50]

---

whether the worker has the power to delegate or subcontract the work to another: *Hollis v. Vabu Pty Ltd* (2001) 207 CLR 21; *Stevens v. Brodribb Sawmilling Co Pty Ltd* (1986) 160 CLR 16.

43. In particular, the proper weight to be placed on the terms of the written employment contract, the receipt of paid leave and the deduction of employment-related taxes and other entitlements is somewhat contentious. *See On Call Interpreters and Translators Agency Pty Ltd v. Federal Commissioner of Taxation (No 3)* (2011) 214 FCR 82; *ACE Insurance Ltd v. Trifunovski* (2013) 209 FCR 146; *Fair Work Ombudsman v. Quest South Perth Holdings Pty Ltd* [2015] FCAFC 37; Cf. Jessup J in *Tattsbet Ltd v. Morrow* [2015] FCAFC 62.
44. Weil (2014), *supra* n. 5, at185-6.
45. *See*, e.g., *Mason & Cox Pty Ltd v. McCann* (1999) 74 ASASR 438; *Wilton v. Coal & Allied Operations Pty Ltd* (2007) 161 FCR 300.
46. *See*, e.g., *FP Group Pty Ltd v. Tooheys Pty Ltd* (2013) 238 IR 239.
47. *See*, e.g., *Fair Work Ombudsman v. Eastern Colour Pty Ltd (No 2)* [2014] FCA 55; *Fair Work Ombudsman v. Ramsey Food Processing Pty Ltd* [2011] FCA 1176.
48. *See*, e.g., *Fair Work Ombudsman v. Zillion Zenith International Pty Ltd* [2014] FCCA 433 and *Fair Work Ombudsman v. Haider Pty Ltd & Anor*[2015] FCCA 2113. In both these cases, an independently owned franchisee was found to have underpaid its workers and was subsequently fined under the FW Act.
49. *See*, e.g., *Fair Work Ombudsman v. Ultra Tune Australia Pty Ltd* [2012] FMCA 560 and *Brobbel v. Darrell Lea Chocolate Shops Pty Ltd* [2008] FMCA 714. In both these cases, the franchisee store or outlet was owned and operated by the franchisor – accordingly, it was the franchisor company which was penalised as a result of employment contraventions which took place.
50. There has been at least one case where the director of the franchisor was found to be 'involved in' contraventions of one of its franchisees and held liable as an 'accessory' under s. 550 of the

Many of the issues arising under common law - such as the contention surrounding the legal classification of workers and the judicial reluctance to lift the corporate veil - reflects some of the key trends in other jurisdictions. However, there are a number of features of the Australian workplace relations framework which distinguish it from systems elsewhere. These regulatory distinctions may mean that lead firms have fewer incentives to use fissured work arrangements in that they have less to gain from sourcing labour from smaller, separate businesses. While subcontracting or outsourcing may not allow a lead firm to source labour more cheaply, it may deliver a number of other benefits, including greater access to a flexible workforce, an avenue for minimising union influence and a way in which to limit the lead firm's risk and responsibilities towards those that work in their organisation, supply chain or franchise network.[51]

[A] Minimum Employment Standards as Prescribed by Statute and Modern Awards

While many of the key protections in the FW Act - such as the National Employment Standards[52] and modern awards[53]- only apply to employees and do not typically extend to independent contractors,[54] these 'safety net' provisions generally apply across the spectrum of employment arrangements and business settings.[55] This means, for example, that a labour hire employee will commonly be covered by the modern award which applies on the basis of the type of work they are undertaking.[56] The employer entity which has engaged the worker or the union which is entitled to represent them is not determinative in this respect.[57]

FW Act: *see United Voice v. MDBR123 Pty Ltd* [2014] FCA 1344 and *United Voice v. MDBR123 Pty Ltd (No 2)* [2015] FCA 1344. The accessorial liability provisions are discussed in more detail in s. 3.4 below.

51. Johnstone et al., *supra* n. 7, at 101.
52. The National Employment Standards statutorily prescribes ten minimum employment conditions, including working hours, various leave entitlements, notice of termination, redundancy pay and other matters. While all these standards apply to ongoing employees (including full-time and part-time employees), only a select number apply to casual employees.
53. Modern awards are instruments which operate with the force of legislation and are designed to supplement the National Employment Standards. Modern awards generally prescribe industry or occupational wage rates across different work classifications, loadings, penalty rates and allowances. Awards also generally regulate scheduling of working hours, consultation over change initiatives and dispute resolution procedures. The coverage of awards does not normally extend to managerial, supervisory or professional workers.
54. Outworkers in the textile, clothing and footwear industries are a notable exception. *See* s. 2.1 for further discussion of this sector-specific regulation.
55. This is also true of superannuation/pension entitlements which are regulated by legislation administered by the Australian Tax Office. Under this legislative scheme, all employers are required to contribute a percentage of each employee's earnings (presently set at 9.5%) to a pension fund.
56. The modern award may be displaced, however, if the labour hire employee is covered by an enterprise agreement.
57. For example, a cleaner employed by a labour hire agency and supplied to clean offices of the host business will generally be covered by the Cleaning Services Award 2010 (Modern Award).

In addition, and in more confined ways, the FW Act provides some level of protection for independent contractors. In particular, employees *and* independent contractors may be able to make a claim under provisions dealing with workplace bullying,[58] as well as an array of prohibitions – known as 'general protections' – which are broadly designed to protect workers from a range of discriminatory or wrongful treatment.[59]

[B] Enterprise Agreements

Enterprise agreements are instruments which are negotiated between employers and their employees (often, but not always, with the involvement of a union).These agreements generally deal with wages and other employment conditions as they apply to a specific enterprise – albeit 'enterprise' is defined broadly in this context to mean any kind of business, activity, project or undertaking.[60] Indeed, there are a number of ways in which enterprise agreements may apply to workers beyond the boundaries of a single firm.

First, a registered enterprise agreement covers any employers and employees which come within its scope.[61] This not only includes employees who are engaged by the relevant employer entity after the agreement was made and registered, it may also encompass labour hire employees engaged by a separate entity altogether. Although enterprise agreements cannot prohibit firms from using labour hire employees, it can include terms which effectively extend their coverage to any employees of a labour hire company performing work with the host organisation. In some instances, enterprise agreements may contain so-called site rates provisions which require that any externally engaged workers receive pay and conditions at least as favourable as the host organisation's direct employees.[62] That said, there is no requirement to include such a term, and it is quite possible for a labour hire employee and a direct employee to work alongside one another at a host organisation and be covered by entirely different industrial instruments prescribing distinctive terms and conditions of employment.[63]

Second, the FW Act contains provisions designed to protect employees in a transfer of business. The definition of 'transfer of business' generally captures situations where an employee has transferred from one employer to another and the work they are performing with the new employer is substantially the same as that which they

58. FW Act, Pt. 6-4B.
59. FW Act, Pt. 3-1. In addition, independent contractors may avail themselves of protections under various anti-discrimination statutes that apply at both federal and state levels in Australia.
60. FW Act, s. 12.
61. FW Act, s. 53.
62. The Productivity Commission has recently recommended that these types of matters (extensions to, and restrictions on, use of labour hire) should be prohibited from inclusion in enterprise agreements. *See* Australian Government, *Workplace Relations Framework – Productivity Commission Inquiry Report* (30 November 2015) at 686.
63. *See* Johnstone et al., *supra* n. 7, at 101.

did for the old employer.[64] A transfer of business will not only arise in circumstances where there has been a commercial transfer of ownership or use of assets from the old employer to the new employer or where the new and old employers are associated entities,[65] it also includes situations where the work has been outsourced from the old employer to the new employer.[66] If a transfer of business has occurred, and in the absence of any tribunal order to the contrary,[67] any enterprise agreement that previously covered an employee at the old employer will transmit to cover that employee at the new employer (to the exclusion of any award or enterprise agreement that may otherwise apply to the transferring employee).[68] These provisions are principally designed to prevent employers who have made enterprise agreements from simply avoiding the obligations set out in these agreements by shifting the employees to a separate entity.

Combined, these two sets of provisions - the wide coverage of enterprise agreements and the obligations that come with transferring employees - may serve to inhibit a lead firm from outsourcing various functions to a labour hire firm or subcontracting if it is doing so solely on cost grounds.

Finally, under the FW Act, there are a number of different types of agreements available, including single- and multi-enterprise agreements, which may be especially relevant in relation to franchises. While a single-enterprise agreement can be made by a single employer,[69] it can also be made with two or more employers where they are related corporations, or conduct a joint venture or common enterprise, or have obtained a 'single interest employer authorisation' from the federal tribunal.[70] The wide definition of what constitutes a 'single enterprise' means that a group of franchisees operating separate businesses under the same brand can apply for a single interest authorisation and make an agreement which applies to workers throughout the franchise. In comparison, a multi-enterprise agreement is an agreement made by two or more employers that cannot meet the 'single interest' requirement noted above. There is no need to obtain prior authorisation before making a multi-enterprise agreement, no capacity for protected industrial action to be taken in support of such an agreement and no enforceable obligation to bargain in good faith in relation to a

64. *See* Breen Creighton and Elizabeth Shi, 'The Transfer of Business Provisions of the Fair Work Act in National and International Context' (2009) 23 *Australian Journal of Labour Law* 39.
65. Corporations Act 2001 (Cth), s. 50AAA.
66. The fourth way in which a transfer of business may occur for the purposes of the FW Act is where work which has previously been outsourced from the new employer to the old employer, is being transferred back (sometimes referred to as 'insourced').
67. Such orders will generally only be made where the Fair Work Commission is satisfied that the transferring employees will not be disadvantaged by varying the terms of the transferring agreement or exempting the new employer from any obligation to comply with the enterprise agreement with the old employer. *Communication, Electric, Electronic, Energy, Information, Postal, Plumbing and Allied Services Union of Australia v. CSIRO* [2010] FWA 1171.
68. FW Act, s. 313.
69. There may also be more than one single-enterprise agreements within a single employer. This is particularly common where there are multiple unions representing workers within the employer's business or where the employer has multiple sites at different locations.
70. FW Act, s. 172(2), (5).

multi-enterprise agreement. The major drawback of a multi-enterprise agreement (as compared to a single-enterprise agreement) relates to the procedures for employee approval.[71]

In some respects, the potential flexibility and breadth of these enterprise agreements represent important developments in light of the fact that it has been 'very difficult for employees in small franchise outlets to organise and bargain effectively for wages and working conditions'.[72] So far, however, there have been very few agreements made of this nature.[73] Indeed, as will be discussed in section §3.06 below, removing legal hurdles to bargaining across a franchise does not necessarily address the many practical obstacles facing workers and their unions in this sector, not least of which is ensuring sustainable compliance with minimum employment standards.[74]

[C] Sham Contracting

As eluded to earlier, another common way in which employers have sought to avoid the application of protective employment legislation, such as the FW Act,[75] is through the misclassification of workers as 'independent contractors'. Under the sham contracting provisions of the FW Act, employers are prohibited from misrepresenting an actual or proposed employment relationship as an independent contracting arrangement.[76] If the sham contracting provisions are enlivened, the 'real' or 'actual' employer may be liable not only for employment-related entitlements, but may also be exposed to a range of civil remedies, including pecuniary penalties.

While the sham contracting provisions are designed to deter misclassification of workers either directly or via triangular labour hire agency arrangements,[77] they have not been used extensively. One of the obstacles to their wider application is that, as noted earlier, the distinction between employees and independent contractors is not clear-cut under the common law in Australia. This inherent uncertainty has meant that employers have routinely been able to rely on the relatively generous defence available

71. A multi-enterprise agreement will only be valid if there is majority approval in at least one enterprise. Where such approval is not given by employees at any given enterprise, that enterprise will not be bound by the multi-enterprise agreement. In comparison, a single-enterprise agreement must be approved by a majority of employees across the relevant enterprise casting a valid vote: FW Act, s. 182. Another potential disadvantage of multi-enterprise agreements is that at any time an employer who is covered by such an agreement may choose to enter into a single-enterprise agreement of its own. If this occurs, the single-enterprise agreement effectively overrides the multi-enterprise agreement. FW Act, s. 58(3).
72. Riley (2012), *supra* n. 12, at 107.
73. But *see* McDonald's Australia Pty Ltd [2010] FWAFC 4602 (21 July 2010).
74. Riley (2012), *supra* n. 12, at 107.
75. In addition to the FW Act, a whole raft of other regulation ordinarily applies to employment relationships, including workers' compensation, superannuation and payroll tax.
76. *See* FW Act, s. 357. Sections 358 and 359 of the FW Act respectively prohibit a person: from dismissing or threatening to dismiss an employee in order to engage them to perform substantially the same work as an independent contractor; and from making what they know to be false statements to induce a current or former employee to agree to such an engagement. *See* generally FW Act, Pt. 3-1, Div. 6.
77. *Fair Work Ombudsman v. Quest South Perth* [2015] HCA 45.

under these provisions.[78] In particular, a number of defendants have successfully pleaded that they should not be held liable because at the time they made the representation they did not know, and were not reckless to, the true nature of the working relationship.[79] Further, the sham contracting provisions themselves have proved 'very complex'[80] – which has meant that some actions have been unsuccessful partly because of the way in which they have been pleaded.[81]

Another important conceptual limitation is that, unlike the accessorial liability provisions outlined below, the sham contracting provisions do not have the effect of extending liability to third parties that display only some (if any) employer characteristics.[82] Rather, the sham contracting provisions reflect and uphold key concepts underpinning the binary employment relationship, albeit a greater emphasis is placed on the economic realities of the relevant arrangements, rather than technical corporate forms. While there are some obvious limitations, the sham contracting provisions have proved useful where companies have sought to convert employees into independent contractors or transfer them into labour hire companies in order to avoid statutory workplace relations protections.[83]

[D] Accessorial Liability

If a person contravenes a civil remedy provision of the FW Act, including a failure to comply with the National Employment Standards, a term of a modern award or enterprise agreement or the sham contracting provisions, the person may be liable for a range of civil remedies, including a pecuniary penalty and compensation orders.[84]

To a large extent, the civil remedy regime established under the FW Act reflects traditional presumptions about employment arrangements – that is, primary responsibility and liability for contraventions of employment standards regulation is ordinarily ascribed to the relevant employer at common law. However, under the

---

78. An employer who engages a worker purportedly under an independent contractor arrangement, which the court subsequently finds should be more properly classified as an employment contract, may avoid liability under s. 357 on the basis of the 'recklessness' defence available under s. 357(2) of the FW Act. For further discussion, *see* Andrew Stewart and Cameron Roles, 'The Reach of Labour Regulation: Tackling Sham Contracting' (2012) 25 *Australian Journal of Labour Law* 258. Various inquiries have recommended that s. 357(2) be modified so that the 'recklessness' defence is replaced with a 'reasonableness' defence. *See*, e.g., Australian Government, *Workplace Relations Framework – Productivity Commission Inquiry Report* (30 November 2015), Recommendation 25.1.
79. *See*, e.g., *Construction, Forestry, Mining and Energy Union v. Nubrick Pty Ltd* (2009) 190 IR 175.
80. Johnstone and Stewart, *supra* n. 33.
81. *See*, e.g., *Wells v. Fair Work Ombudsman* [2013] FCAFC 47.
82. Guy Davidov, 'Indirect Employment: Should Lead Companies be Liable?' (2015) 37 *Comparative Labor Law & Policy Journal* 5.
83. *See*, e.g., Enforceable Undertaking between the Office of the Fair Work Ombudsman and Telco Services Pty Ltd (24 December 2013).
84. Under s. 545 of the FW Act, the courts have a broad power to 'make any order the court considers appropriate' where it is satisfied that a person has contravened a civil remedy provision. The maximum civil penalty which is currently available under the FW Act is AUD 54,000 for a corporation and AUD 10,800 for a natural person.

accessorial liability provisions, there is some capacity for liability to extend beyond the legal employer to other persons found to be 'involved in' a contravention of the Act.[85]

Broadly speaking, a person will be taken to be 'involved in' a contravention under section 550 of the FW Act if they have:

(a) aided or abetted the contravention;
(b) procured or induced the contravention (whether by threats or promises or otherwise);
(c) conspired with others to bring about the contravention; or
(d) been in any way, by act or omission, 'knowingly concerned' in the contravention.

These provisions have proven particularly valuable where the direct employer is insolvent or no longer in existence and the FWO has routinely used the accessorial liability provisions to bring enforcement proceedings against the individual directors of failed companies.[86] On occasion, the FWO has brought enforcement proceedings against advisors, such as HR managers, who may have the necessary knowledge of the essential matters making up the contravention.[87] There have only been a handful of cases in which the FWO has sought to use section 550 against a separate corporation which is said to be 'involved in' a contravention of the direct employer. One of the most significant and novel examples of the accessorial liability provisions involves the Australian supermarket retailer, Coles Supermarkets Australia Pty Ltd (*Coles*).[88]

In this particular case, the FWO alleged that at least ten trolley collectors working at several Coles' sites were underpaid approximately AUD 200,000. The affected trolley collectors were engaged through a series of separate contracts with individual businesses. None of the underpaid workers was actually employed by Coles. Further, there was no direct contract between Coles and the relevant employers. Notwithstanding the legal obstacles presented by these disaggregated arrangements, the FWO alleged that the supermarket chain should be held liable as an accessory under the FW Act on the basis that it was 'involved in' the contraventions. Although the case against Coles was settled prior to being heard,[89] it remains significant – both in symbolic and practical terms.[90] This proceeding is of less value, however, when it comes to clarifying the way

85. FW Act, s. 550.
86. This is essentially what occurred in the case *Fair Work Ombudsman v. Haider Pty Ltd & Anor* [2015] FCCA 2113, discussed in s. 6.1 below.
87. *Fair Work Ombudsman v. Centennial Financial Services &Ors* [2011] FMCA 459. For further discussion of the liability of advisors and other 'gatekeepers', *see* Tess Hardy and John Howe 'Gatekeepers in Labour Law' (Paper presented at the Australian Labour Law Association National Conference, Sydney, Australia, 14-15 November 2014); and Helen Anderson and Linda Haller, 'Phoenix Activity and the Liability of the Advisor' (2014) 36 *Sydney Law Review* 471.
88. *See*, e.g., *Fair Work Ombudsman v. Al-Hilfi&Ors*[2012] FCA 1166 (26 October 2012); and *Fair Work Ombudsman v. Al-Hilfi&Ors (No 2)* [2013] FCA 16 (17 January 2013).
89. *Fair Work Ombudsman v. Al Hilfi*[2016] FCA 193.
90. For further discussion of this case and the relevant outcomes, *see* Tess Hardy and John Howe, 'Chain Reaction: A Strategic Approach to Addressing Employment Non-Compliance in Complex

in which accessorial liability provisions may apply to complex supply chains, as well as labour hire and franchise arrangements. Indeed, while there have been a number of proceedings since the *Coles* case which have reached final determination,[91] there are a number of critical issues which are yet to be authoritatively determined. For example, in respect of corporate accessories, it is not entirely clear whether it is possible to aggregate the knowledge of various employees and thereby prove that the corporation itself had requisite knowledge of the contravention.[92]

These previous and pending test cases are critical in clarifying whether the accessorial liability provisions have the capacity to successfully cut through contracting chains and trespass traditional legal boundaries so as to ensure that lead firms are not able 'to have it both ways'.[93] The experience so far underlines the value of targeting principal contractors, supply chain heads and franchisors. First, these third-party corporations are often better resourced than the direct employer and are less likely to wind up the relevant corporate entity in order to avoid the consequences of any relevant court orders. This not only means that affected workers are fully compensated, but that the imposition of penalties is more than a token exercise.[94] Second, and perhaps most critically, the threat of legal liability (and the possibility of significant brand damage) may be enough to prompt voluntary and far-reaching measures amongst lead firms – a trend which will be further explored in section §3.06[B] below.

§3.04 REGULATORY RESPONSES IN THE WORK HEALTH AND SAFETY SPHERE

The harmonised Work Health and Safety Acts (*WHS Acts*) evidence a deliberate and drastic move away from the traditional employment paradigm.[95] Under the WHS Acts, 'primary' responsibility is placed on 'a person conducting a business or undertaking' to ensure, so far as is reasonably practicable, the health and safety of 'workers' and 'other persons'.[96] The definition of a 'person conducting a business or undertaking' – colloquially referred to as a PCBU – includes not just employers, but also principal

Supply Chains' (2015) 57(4) *Journal of Industrial Relations* 563; *See also* Coles Supermarkets Australia Pty Ltd, *Annual Report Pursuant to the Enforceable Undertaking between the FWO and Coles* (3 November 2015).

91. *See*, e.g., *Fair Work Ombudsman v. Al Hilfi*[2016] FCA 193; and *Fair Work Ombudsman v. South Jin Pty Ltd* [2015] FCA 1456.
92. *See* Ingmar Taylor and Larissa Andelman, 'Accessorial Liability under the *Fair Work Act*' (Paper presented at the Australian Labour Law Association, Manly, 14-15 November 2014).
93. Weil (2014), *supra* n. 5, at 14.
94. In the *Coles* case, key subcontractors, such as Starlink Operations, had gone into liquidation in the course of the proceeding. However, under the enforceable undertaking between the FWO and Coles, the supermarket retailer agreed to rectify any relevant underpayments.
95. *See*, e.g., *Baiada Poultry Pty Ltd v. The* Queen [2012] HCA 14. For detailed discussion of these Acts, *see* Richard Johnstone, Elizabeth Bluff and Alan Clayton, *Work Health and Safety Law and Policy* (3rd ed., 2012). The Model Work Health and Safety Act adopted in 2011 has been enacted in all Australian jurisdictions, except for Victoria and Western Australia.
96. WHS Acts, s. 19(1)-(2).

contractors, head contractors, franchisors and the Crown.[97] Similarly, the term 'worker' is exceptionally wide (especially in comparison to the definition of 'employee' under the FW Act). In particular, this term is defined under the work health and safety legislation as including any person who carries out 'work in any capacity for' a PCBU, including work as: a contractor; a sub-contractor; an employee of a labour hire company; an outworker; and a volunteer.[98]

Importantly, the WHS Acts contain provisions which are designed to address what is sometimes referred to as 'counterproductive liability avoidance'[99] – that is, where firms seek to recalibrate their contracting relationships to avoid being defined as an employer or further reduce the extent to which they monitor suppliers' production or franchisee's practices. Rather, the work health and safety legislation is crafted in a way that seeks to encourage firms to respond with the 'right kind of liability avoidance',[100] that is, by taking additional, voluntary measures to minimise the relevant legal risks, including closer monitoring of contractors, increased investment in training and skills or reintegrating the work back into the core organisation.[101] To achieve this objective, the legislation provides that:

(a) the relevant duties cannot be delegated;[102]
(b) that one person can owe a number of duties;[103]
(c) that more than one person can hold a duty and that each person must comply with the duty even though it might be also owed by others.[104]

A related aspect of the WHS Acts is the way in which it imposes a horizontal duty on all PCBUs to consult, cooperate and coordinate with other PCBUs.[105] Again, this provision is specifically designed to address the 'problem of hazards arising from fractured, complex and disorganised work processes.'[106] Finally, the WHS Acts place a 'positive and proactive duty'[107] on all officers of a PCBU 'to exercise due diligence' to ensure that the PCBU complies with all relevant duties and obligations arising under

97. WHS Acts, s. 5 of WHS Acts *See also* Explanatory Memorandum, Work Health and Safety Bill 2011 (Cth), [23].
98. WHS Acts, s. 7.
99. Cynthia Estlund, 'Who Mops the Floor at the Fortune 500? Corporate Self-Regulation and the Low Wage Workplace' (2008) 12(3) *Lewis & Clark Law Review* 671, at 692.
100. *Ibid.*
101. *Ibid.*
102. WHS Acts, s. 14.
103. WHS Acts, s. 15.
104. WHS Acts, s. 16.
105. WHS Acts, s. 46. PCBUs are also under a vertical duty to consult all of the 'workers' who carry out work in any capacity for the PCBU and who are 'likely to be directed affected by a matter relating to' health and safety. WHS Acts, ss 47-49.
106. Johnstone and Stewart, *supra* n. 33, 28.
107. *Ibid.*

the Act. An officer can be prosecuted for a failure to exercise proper due diligence,[108] even if the PCBU itself is not breaching its own duties.[109]

The novelty of these provisions, together with the fact that they are still relatively new, means that it is not entirely clear how these provisions will play out, and how liability will be ascribed, when applied to the various corporate structures and employment arrangements described earlier.[110]

§3.05 REGULATORY RESPONSES IN THE COMPETITION AND CONSUMER SPHERE

As noted in the introduction, there are a number of statutes which potentially influence the notion of the firms and their relevant responsibilities to workers, but which lie somewhat beyond the world of workplace relations – at least as far as this regulatory sphere is conventionally conceived. While the regulation of commercial exchange was once the domain of contract law and equitable doctrines, these common law rules have been increasingly supplemented by statutes, such as the *Independent Contractors Act 2006* (Cth) (*IC Act*) and the *Competition and Consumer Act 2010* (Cth) (*CC Act*). The IC Act represented an important development at the time of its enactment in that it enabled, for the first time at a federal level, a party to a 'services contract' to challenge the 'fairness' of the contract before a court.[111] However, it is likely that this legislation may be soon superseded by some of the more far-reaching reforms of the federal competition and consumer regulation summarised below.

The first way in which the CC Act affects work contracts is by way of the unfair contract terms provisions of the Australian Consumer Law.[112] While these protections are currently confined to consumer contracts, from November 2016, the provisions will be extended to small business contracts.[113]

---

108. Section 27(5) of each of the WHS Acts defines 'due diligence' to include taking 'reasonable steps' to do the following, amongst other things: to acquire and keep up-to-date knowledge of work health and safety matters; to gain an understanding of the nature of the PCBU's operations and generally of the hazards and risks associated with these operations; and to ensure that the PCBU has, and implements, processes for complying with any duty or obligation under the Act.
109. WHS Acts, s. 27(4).
110. While key provisions have changed under the WHS Acts, some of the prosecutions brought under predecessor legislation are likely to provide the courts with some guidance on how to appropriately ascribe liability in respect of certain organisational forms, such as franchising. For example, in *WorkCover Authority of New South Wales v. McDonald's Australia Ltd* (2000) 95 IR 383, both the franchisor and the franchisee were convicted on the basis that they had, as was required under the previous legislation, 'to any extent, control of' the premises. For further discussion of these issues, *see* Andrew Terry and Joseph Huan, 'Franchisor Liability for Franchisee Conduct' (2012) 39(2) *Monash University Law Review* 388.
111. IC Act, ss 7(2), 11(1)(a). However, very few successful cases brought under these statutory provisions in the decade since it came into operation: But *see Keldote Pty Ltd v. Riteway Transport Pty Ltd* (2008) 176 IR 316.
112. The Australian Consumer Law is set out in Schedule 2 of the Competition and Consumer Act 2010 (Cth).
113. 'Small business contracts' are defined to include contracts where: at least one party is a business that employs less than twenty people; the upfront price payable under the contract is

Under these statutory provisions, a party to a small business contract can seek a declaration that unfair contract terms be declared void, amongst other remedies.[114] In determining whether a term is unfair, the court must consider whether the term:

(a) causes a significant imbalance in the parties' rights and obligations;
(b) is reasonably necessary to protect the legitimate interests of the benefited party; and
(c) causes detriment (financial or otherwise) to the other party.[115]

The types of terms which are likely to be subject to the most scrutiny are terms that enable one party (but not the other): to vary the contract; to terminate the contract; to impose penalties for breaching the contract; or to limit liability.

The extension of unfair contract term protections to small business contracts may place critical restrictions on the principal contractor and/or the franchisor. For example, in a franchising context, it is likely that a provision in a franchise agreement which allows the franchisor to terminate the agreement at any time without cause and without providing any compensation to the franchisee is likely to be characterised as 'unfair' and therefore void. Further, if the franchise agreement expressly incorporates the franchisor's operations manual, then it is possible that the provisions of the manual may also be subject to the unfair contract terms law. Another important limitation is on the variation rights of the franchisor. This is critical given that franchising relationship is often one where 'franchisors assume an entitlement to dictate rather than negotiate with franchisees'.[116]

The second, significant way in which the CC Act potentially shapes work relationships is via industry-specific codes of regulation,[117] including the Franchising Code of Conduct[118] and the Food and Grocery Code of Conduct.[119] The Franchising Code – a mandatory code which applies to all franchising relationships in Australia – was introduced on the basis of a growing awareness of the way in which the

AUD 300,000 or less (or AUD 1,000,000 or less if the contract is for more than twelve months); and the contract is a standard form contract.

114. Proceedings may also be brought by the relevant regulator, the Australian Competition and Consumer Commission under these provisions.

115. In determining this matter, the court may take into account the contract as a whole and the extent to which the term is transparent.

116. Riley (2012), *supra* n. 12, at 115.

117. Section 51AD of the federal Competition and Consumer Act 2010 (Cth) requires corporations to comply with industry codes and enables access to the remedial provisions of the Act, including rights to seek declarations, compensatory damages, injunctions and pecuniary penalties.

118. The Franchising Code is set out in Schedule 1 to the Competition and Consumer (Industry Codes—Franchising) Regulation 2014 (Cth).

119. The Food and Grocery Code of Conduct – which operates on a voluntary basis and came into effect from 2015 – governs certain conduct by grocery retailers and wholesalers in their dealings with suppliers, including with respect to disclosure, termination of agreements and dispute resolution. This Code is especially relevant to the *Baiada* case referred to below.

'asymmetric power dynamic within franchise agreements [had the] potential to lead to abuse of power'.[120]

In summary, the Franchising Code requires the franchisor to disclose critical and comprehensive information to existing and prospective franchisees before entering into a franchise agreement, and on an annual basis thereafter.[121] In addition, the Franchising Code restricts the termination rights of the franchisor in a number of different ways. Summary termination of a franchise agreement is only permitted in very confined circumstances.[122] Even where there is a breach by the franchisee, a franchisor is only permitted to terminate a franchise agreement, where it has given notice of the breach to the franchisee and the franchisee has failed to remedy the breach within the specified timeframe.[123] If the franchisee successfully rectifies the breach, the franchisor may not terminate the agreement for that breach. Further, the Code also now expressly requires franchisors to deal with franchisees in good faith.[124] While the obligation to act in good faith does not prevent parties acting on the basis of their legitimate commercial interests, it may serve to prevent the capricious and opportunistic exercise of contractual rights – particularly those that afford the franchisor a high level of discretion. In many ways, the good faith obligation may supplement the unfair contract terms law, especially in relation to rights of variation. It also potentially complements the statutory prohibition on unconscionable conduct generally available under the Australian Consumer Law.[125]

The third and final way in which the CC Act affects the rights, power and position of workplace actors is via its regulation of collective action. Although independent contractors and franchisees have a right to freely associate,[126] they have no access to the statutory collective bargaining framework under the FW Act or otherwise. It is therefore unclear what actions (if any) contractors and franchisees may legitimately take in pursuit of their freedom of association.[127] In addition to a number of common law obstacles, the CC Act further restricts the rights of independent contractors and

120. *See* Parliamentary Joint Committee on Corporations and Financial Services, Opportunity Not Opportunism: Improving Conduct in Australian Franchising (Commonwealth of Australia, December 2008) at 6.
121. Franchising Code, Pt. 2.
122. The franchisor may only terminate the franchise agreement without notice where the franchisee: no longer holds the necessary licence to carry on the franchised business; becomes bankrupt, insolvent or the company is deregistered; abandons the franchise; is convicted of a serious offence; operates the franchised business in a way that endangers public health or safety; or acts fraudulently. Franchising Code, cl. 29.
123. Franchising Code, cl. 27-28.
124. Franchising Code, cl. 6.
125. Australian Consumer Law, s. 22. This prohibition generally applies to situations where one person has supplied or acquired goods or services to or from another, albeit there are some exclusions in relation to listed public companies.
126. The federal Fair Work (Registered Organisations) Act 2009 (Cth) allows the registration of employee associations that have independent contractors as members, but there is a level of uncertainty as to whether an association can be registered under this Act where its members consist solely of independent contractors. In comparison, cl. 33 of the Franchising Code of Conduct expressly protects the right of franchisees (or prospective franchisees) to form an association. *See* Johnstone et al., *supra* n. 7, at 134-5.
127. Riley (2012), *supra* n. 12, at 113.

franchisees to take collective action as such conduct is generally perceived as contravening the anti-competitive provisions.[128] While it is possible to seek an exemption from these provisions by application to the ACCC, such an exemption has been sought and granted only sparingly.[129]

§3.06 EVALUATION AND FUTURE PROSPECTS

As noted in the introduction, the capacity of these separate regulatory schemes will be assessed by reference to the recent controversies surrounding the workplace rights and responsibilities of various actors in the Baiada supply chain and the 7-Eleven franchise network. Before engaging in this evaluative discussion, however, it is necessary to briefly provide some background on each of these cases.

[A] Background

In the *Baiada* case, it has been found that plant workers – many of whom were on working holiday visas and sourced through a complex chain of contractors – were being routinely underpaid, forced to work long and arduous hours in poultry processing factories and compelled to pay inflated rent amounts for substandard accommodation. There was also evidence of discrimination and misclassification of employees as independent contractors.

A comprehensive inquiry undertaken by the FWO in 2015 revealed that Baiada principally sourced labour through six contractors and paid these contractors on the basis of the kilogram of poultry processed rather than hours worked. These contractors then sub-contracted to second- and third-tier entities, involving up to thirty-four entities in total. There were no written agreements between any of the entities. The FWO Inquiry also found that over half of Baiada's products were purchased by supermarkets and that '[i]ntensive discounting undertaken by the major supermarkets [may] have placed downward pressure on profit margins in the industry which has led to diminished profits at the processing level.'[130] Since the conclusion of the FWO's Inquiry, Baiada has taken a range of measures designed to address these issues. The relevant outcomes will be discussed in further detail shortly.

In addition, and more recently, the 7-Eleven franchise in Australia has been grappling with allegations of widespread underpayment of international student

128. In particular, the CC Act prohibits: contracts, arrangements or understandings that have the purpose, or would likely have the effect, of substantially lessening competition; collective refusals to deal with other parties; and cartel behaviour by way of price fixing. *See* CC Act, ss 44ZRD, 44ZRF, 45(2). For further discussion, *see* Shae McCrystal, 'Collective Bargaining by Independent Contractors: Challenges from Labour Law' (2007) 20 *Australian Journal of Labour Law* 1.
129. The ACCC is authorised to grant an exemption where the proposed collective bargaining conduct produces sufficient 'public benefit' (so as to outweigh any public detriment). Johnstone et al., *supra* n. 7, at 145.
130. Ryan Lin, *Poultry Processing in Australia*, IBIS World Pty Ltd, February 2014, cited in the FWO Baiada Inquiry, *supra* n. 13.

workers by franchisee employers.[131] In particular, there is evidence to suggest that franchisee employers across the convenience store chain have deliberately sought to evade the law by adopting a number of illegitimate strategies, including the so-called half-pay scam[132] and the cash-back scam.[133] The main outcome of both these arrangements was that 7-Eleven employees were frequently receiving only half of what they were actually entitled to under the relevant workplace laws and industrial instruments.[134] While investigations continue, it is estimated that thousands of employees have been underpaid and the total back-pay claim across the franchise may ultimately exceed AUD 30 million.[135] It has been argued that this poor compliance behaviour may have been driven, at least in part, by the relevant business model. Indeed, there is growing evidence to suggest that while the Australian head office of the 7-Eleven franchise continued to reap significant profits, many independent franchisees were struggling to survive.[136] Professor Allan Fels – the former head of the ACCC – has noted that, in his view, the 7-Eleven 'business model will only work for the franchisee if they underpay or overwork employees'.[137]

Despite the fact that both cases revealed serious and systemic non-compliance with workplace laws, there has been overwhelming evidence showing that the affected

131. Documents which were reviewed as part of the Fairfax/*Four Corners* investigation revealed that 69% of stores had payroll compliance issues. *See* Adele Ferguson, Sarah Danckert and Klaus Toft, '7-Eleven: A Sweatshop on Every Corner', *The Age*, 29 August 2015.
132. Under the half-pay scam, employment records were deliberately manipulated in a way that disguised the real number of hours worked. In general, half the number of actual hours worked were formally recorded, but in some instances, only a third of the actual hours worked were recorded in the payroll system. Evidence to Senate Inquiry into the Impact of Australia's Temporary Work Visa Programs on the Australian Labour Market and on the Temporary Work Visa Holders, Parliament of Australia, Melbourne, 5 February 2016, 28 (Professor Allan Fels, Fels Wage Fairness Panel).
133. Under the cash-back scam, the employees were paid the full amounts owing to them under workplace laws, and the correct amounts were reflected on formal employment records and payslips. However, the employees were then forced or coerced to repay to their employer half of that amount in cash. *Ibid*. At 29.
134. The more recent allegations reflect previous evidence of serious underpayments and deliberate falsification of employment records in the 7-Eleven franchise: *see*, e.g., *Fair Work Ombudsman v. Bosen Pty Ltd & Anor* [2011] VMC 81; Enforceable Undertaking between the Commonwealth of Australia (as represented by the Office of the Fair Work Ombudsman) and PSP International Trading Pty Ltd and Kumar Sundarakumar (13 March 2015). *See also* Fair Work Ombudsman, 'More 7-Eleven Store Operators to Face Court for Allegedly Short-Changing Employees', Media Release, 14 January 2016.
135. Sarah Danckert, '7-Eleven Workers who Helped Expose Wage Fraud Get Paid', *Sydney Morning Herald*, 14 February 2016.
136. In an internal document uncovered as part of the Fairfax/*Four Corners* investigation, it was revealed that 228 stores, which represents approximately one-third of all stores in the network, delivered a total income to the franchisee of AUD 350,000 or less for the year to June 2015. More specifically, it shows that one store earned less than AUD 150,000, thirty-eight stores generated an income of less than AUD 200,000 and 84 stores had an income ranging between AUD 200,000 and AUD 250,000. Labour costs for one casual employee amounted to around AUD 230,000 and generally represented the most expensive item for franchisees given that they are required to be open twenty-four hours per day, seven days per week. *See* Adele Ferguson, Sarah Danckert and Klaus Toft, '7-Eleven Stores in Strife', *The Age*, 31 August 2015.
137. Adele Ferguson, Sarah Danckert and Klaus Toft, '7-Eleven: Allan Fels says Model Dooms Franchisees and Workers', *The Age*, 31 August 2015.

employees – who were predominantly temporary migrant workers – were unlikely to complain to government authorities out of fear, ignorance or both.[138] Further, in both cases, more proactive methods of detection were foiled by the fact that employment records were either completely absent or deliberately falsified.[139] Enforcement activities were not only compromised by problems of proof, but were further undermined by illegal 'phoenix' behaviour.[140] For instance, last year, the former operator of a 7-Eleven store in Queensland was fined AUD 6,970 after it was found that a temporary foreign worker – an international student from Nepal – had been underpaid more than AUD 21,000. The corporate employer was not fined because it had been wound up prior to final determination of the matter and the action against it was stayed.[141] As a result, the former owner was liable for a much reduced penalty amount and the former employee was left substantially out of pocket.[142] Similarly, during the course of the FWO's Inquiry into Baiada, a large number of entities identified in the supply chain ceased trading.[143] The effect of this systematic company collapse was to make the relevant employer entities immune to the imposition of compensatory orders and pecuniary penalties.[144]

Another issue at play in these cases – and that underlined in Weil's work – is that punishment of the putative employer (i.e., the contractor or the franchisee) may do little to address the underlying drivers of poor compliance behaviour, namely the attitude and activities of the lead firm. For example, in the *Baiada* case, the FWO found that Baiada's principal operating model was to 'transfer costs and risks associated with the engagement of labour to an extensive supply chain of contractors responsible for

---

138. Professor Allan Fels recently gave evidence that some 7-Eleven franchise workers were reluctant to make a claim to the independent panel for fear that the immigration authorities would take action against them for breaching working conditions. Others may be subject to threats from franchisees if they put in a claim. Fels observed that 'there is a strong, powerful and quite widespread campaign of deception, fear mongering, intimidation and even more physical actions of intimidation by franchisees.' Evidence to Senate Inquiry into the Impact of Australia's Temporary Work Visa Programs on the Australian Labour Market and on the Temporary Work Visa Holders, Parliament of Australia, Melbourne, 5 February 2016, 30 (Professor Allan Fels, Fels Wage Fairness Panel).
139. *See*, e.g., FWO Baiada Inquiry, *supra* n. 13.
140. Illegal phoenix activity has been described as occurring where there is a deliberate liquidation of a company with unpaid debts and the assets of the original company are transferred to a newly created company for undervalue. The outcome of this transfer is to deprive employees and unsecured creditors of any remedy against the original company. *See* Helen Anderson, 'Phoenix Activity and the Recovery of Unpaid Employee Entitlements - 10 Years On' (2011) 24 *Australian Journal of Labour Law* 141.
141. *See Fair Work Ombudsman v. Haider Pty Ltd & Anor* [2015] FCCA 2113 (30 July 2015).
142. Under the FW Act, natural persons are liable for a maximum penalty which is one-fifth of the penalty set for corporations.
143. In particular, four of the six key contractors and seventeen of the other sub-contractors ceased trading. FWO Baiada Inquiry, *supra* n. 13.
144. However, eligible employees may be able to recover their outstanding wages and other entitlements through a federal government scheme, where the employee has lost their employment due to the liquidation or bankruptcy of their employer. *See* Fair Entitlements Guarantee Act 2012 (Cth); Helen Anderson, *The Protection of Employee Entitlements in Insolvency: An Australian Perspective* (University of Melbourne Press, 2012).

sourcing and providing labour.'[145] Further, Baiada's competitive procurement processes and poor governance arrangements were also viewed as creating an environment ripe for worker exploitation. However, as Baiada was not the direct employer of the affected employees, there was some hesitation about how to prompt Baiada – one of the lead firms in this case – to make a firm commitment to improve workplace relations compliance throughout its contracting chain. There was even less certainty on what could be done to encourage supermarkets and fast food chains to revise their contracting practices.

Similar challenges have confronted the FWO with respect to the 7-Eleven franchise network. While the regulator had been very active in bringing litigation against 7-Eleven franchisees over a span of some years, the franchisor has generally sought to distance itself from the unlawful behaviour of so-called rogue franchisee employers. It was not until the high-profile media investigation late last year, the revelation of the breadth and gravity of the non-compliance and the incurrence of significant brand damage, that the franchisor was ultimately prepared to accept a level of responsibility for the underpayments,[146] revise the relevant monitoring practices and make sweeping changes to the existing business model.[147]

[B] Strengths and Weaknesses of Current Statutory Responses

Most of the underpaid workers in the *Baiada* and *7-Eleven* cases – many of whom were foreign nationals – were legally classified as employees. This meant that they were covered by many of the statutory safeguards available under the FW Act, including the National Employment Standards, modern awards and enterprise agreements. However, these two cases reveal that these formal protections were somewhat futile in the face of systemic non-compliance occurring in complex contracting chains and franchise networks. As noted above, one of the main drawbacks of the FW Act is the way in which it adheres to, and upholds, traditional notions of employment. While the affected employees had rights to bring claims against their employer – these rights were

145. FWO Baiada Inquiry, *supra* n. 13, at 2.
146. In particular, the head office has established an independent panel – chaired by Professor Allan Fels – to receive, process and determine any claims from employees of its franchisees. *See* Adele Ferguson and Sarah Danckert, '7-Eleven: Allan Fels to Lead Wage Scandal Inquiry', *Sydney Morning Herald*, 4 September 2015.
147. While it has continued to dispute the assertion that the franchise system is not financially viable, the Australian franchisor of 7-Eleven has agreed that it will, for any existing franchisee who wishes to exit the franchise system, refund the franchise fee that has been paid and help sell any store where a goodwill payment has been made. Subsequently, in December 2015, the Australian franchisor of 7-Eleven entered into a variation agreement with over 97% of all franchisees whereby it was agreed that the existing financial arrangements between the franchisor and franchisees would be adjusted in favour of franchisees. Under this variation agreement, franchisees are projected to earn an additional AUD 150 million over three years. Evidence to Senate Inquiry into the Impact of Australia's Temporary Work Visa Programs on the Australian Labour Market and on the Temporary Work Visa Holders, Parliament of Australia, Melbourne, 5 February 2016, 18 (Robert Baily, Chief Executive Officer, 7-Eleven Stores Pty Ltd).

thwarted by the fact that the putative employer was often evasive and frequently no longer in existence. Although the accessorial liability provisions of the FW Act provide a possible avenue for redress, and a legal mechanism to pursue the relevant lead firms, their application to third-party corporations remains somewhat experimental.

The limitations of the current legal framework, combined with a growing appreciation of Weil's strategic model of enforcement, have prompted the FWO to experiment with a whole raft of voluntary initiatives.[148] While these interventions are distinct in substance, they are linked by a common appreciation of the fact that the FWO's compliance and enforcement activities should serve to:

> create awareness among large organisations that it is not acceptable to be indifferent regarding the treatment of people that work for, and within, their organisations just because it does not directly employ them.[149]

The FWO inquiries present one of the most recent manifestations of this principle. These formal, long-term inquiries generally involve the federal regulatory agency undertaking a detailed examination – though site visits, interviews and payroll audits – of the drivers of compliance behaviour in an industry, region, supply chain or labour market. Particular focus is placed on the role of lead firms. At the conclusion of an inquiry, a written report is made publicly available which sets out the findings, the regulator's recommendations and the actions taken. Ten comprehensive inquiries were active during 2014-2015, including the Baiada Inquiry referred to above, as well as an ongoing inquiry into the workplace practices of 7-Eleven franchise stores.[150]

The Baiada Inquiry – which was concluded in June 2015 – demonstrates the power of informal sanctions, such as disapproval and adverse publicity. In the past, Baiada has fiercely resisted taking responsibility for workplace contraventions which have occurred at its sites.[151] However, as a result of the FWO Inquiry, the threat of accessorial liability and the public airing of some of its practices, Baiada has now entered into a 'proactive compliance deed' with the regulator.[152] Under this voluntary, common law agreement, the Baiada Group expressly acknowledged that:

148. For further discussion of these various initiatives, *see* Hardy and Howe, *supra* n. 90; Tess Hardy and John Howe, 'Too Soft or Too Severe? Enforceable Undertakings and the Regulatory Dilemma Facing the Fair Work Ombudsman' (2013) 41 *Federal Law Review* 1; and Tess Hardy, 'Brandishing the Brand: Enhancing Employer Compliance through the Regulatory Enrolment of Franchisors' (Paper presented at the Labour Law Research Network Conference, Amsterdam, 25-27 June 2015).
149. Fair Work Ombudsman, 'Push to End Exploitation of Trolley Collectors', Media Release, 29 August 2014.
150. Fair Work Ombudsman, Annual Report 2014-15, at 31. The Australian franchisor of 7-Eleven has indicated that they intend to enter into a 'compliance partnership' with the FWO. Evidence to Senate Inquiry into the Impact of Australia's Temporary Work Visa Programs on the Australian Labour Market and on the Temporary Work Visa Holders, Parliament of Australia, Melbourne, 5 February 2016, 6 (Michael Smith, Chairman, 7-Eleven Australia Pty Ltd).
151. *See*, e.g., *Baiada Poultry Pty Ltd v. The* Queen [2012] HCA 14.
152. For further discussion of proactive compliance deeds, *see* Hardy and Howe (2015), *supra* n. 90.

> it has a moral and ethical responsibility to require standards of conduct from all entities and individuals involved in its enterprise that ... meet Australian community and social expectations to provide equal, fair and safe work opportunities for all workers at all of its sites.[153]

In addition, the Baiada Group agreed to a number of practical measures designed to stamp out worker exploitation at its factories, such as improving the transparency and documentation of contractor arrangements, arranging for a third-party professional to conduct periodic audits of all contractors and subcontractors supplying labour to its sites, introducing electronic timekeeping and ensuring that all workers are informed of the relevant employing entity and their employment rights.[154] Subsequently, and outside of the formal terms of the deed, it appears that Baiada has also simplified its contracting arrangements so that it now engages labour through a much 'flatter' structure.[155]

While the Baiada proactive compliance deed may be seen as a positive outcome in many respects, especially for the workers immediately affected, the broader implications of this approach are not as clear-cut. Indeed, while these 'light-touch' regulatory techniques may mitigate some of the underlying problems that plague conventional compliance and enforcement tools, there are some potential obstacles to this approach. For a start, the legal status of proactive compliance deeds is not entirely clear given that it is made under the general law rather than statute.[156] Further, it is not certain to what extent (if at all) firms would be willing to adopt voluntary compliance mechanisms in the absence of consumer pressure, regulatory scrutiny and/or the credible threat of liability. These issues are particularly pertinent in relation to the 'other' lead firms involved in the food processing industry, namely supermarket retailers and fast food chains, which have predominantly adopted and relied on self-regulatory measures, such as ethical sourcing policies. There is evidence to suggest that supermarkets have limited oversight as to whether firms actually comply with such policies. Further, it appears that they have little inclination to change their monitoring practices in the absence of sufficient positive or negative incentives to do so: that is, where there is no real prospect of legal liability.[157] While policy measures are valuable, the importance of an adaptable legislative scheme cannot be overstated.

153. Proactive Compliance Deed between the Office of the Fair Work Ombudsman and Baiada Poultry Pty Ltd and Bartter Enterprises Pty Ltd dated 23 October 2015.
154. *Ibid.*
155. Evidence to Senate Inquiry into the Impact of Australia's Temporary Work Visa Programs on the Australian Labour Market and on the Temporary Work Visa Holders, Parliament of Australia, Melbourne, 5 February 2016, at 45 (Michael Campbell, Deputy Fair Work Ombudsman, Operations, Fair Work Ombudsman).
156. In comparison, enforceable undertakings made under the FW Act have statutory force and can be enforced in a court. *See* Hardy and Howe (2013), *supra* n. 90.
157. Evidence to Senate Inquiry into the Impact of Australia's Temporary Work Visa Programs on the Australian Labour Market and on the Temporary Work Visa Holders, Parliament of Australia, Melbourne, 18 May 2015, at 4 (ArminehMardirossian, Group Manager, Corporate Responsibility, Community and Sustainability, Woolworths Limited).

In comparison to the FW Act, the WHS Acts present a broad and flexible regulatory regime which reflects many of the core principles of the strategic enforcement model – that is, it allows regulators to traverse traditional legal boundaries in order to better address work health and safety issues arising in complex supply chains, labour hire arrangements, company groups and franchise networks. It is explicitly designed to deter actors from interposing corporate entities in a bid to avoid liability – rather it encourages direct employers, as well as third-party firms situated above them, to take proactive steps to ensure their respective compliance with work health and safety obligations. The horizontal duties imposed under this statutory scheme are especially helpful where there may be more than one 'lead firm' – one of the issues identified in the *Baiada* case. In particular, the fact that all PCBUs along a supply chain have a separate and concurrent duty to consult, cooperate and coordinate with other PCBUs – would mean that the Baiada Group, as well as the major buyers of processed poultry, would be obliged to take steps to reduce risks to health and safety.[158] Further, in comparison to the uncertainty associated with the scope of the accessorial liability provisions and their application to franchise arrangements, there is little doubt that the franchisor and the franchisee in the *7-Eleven* case are both responsible for minimising health and safety risks amongst franchise workers.

While the work health and safety legislation holds much potential in terms of addressing some of the adverse consequences arising from fragmented work arrangements, it is not yet clear how rigorously the regulatory agencies and judiciary will enforce these novel provisions. Indeed, in contrast to the FWO which has been very active and innovative in crafting-policy mechanisms that effectively harness market power and reputational concerns, the work health and safety inspectorates have generally taken a more conventional approach to achieving sustainable compliance – at least historically.

Finally, it is necessary to examine the regulatory constraints and capabilities of the competition and consumer regulation to counter some of the problems identified in the *Baiada* and *7-Eleven* cases. While some of these reforms may address a number of issues raised by fissured work in ancillary ways, they do not directly confront the difficult situation that arose in these cases – that is, where small businesses operated not only as autonomous employer businesses, but were simultaneously vulnerable contracting parties. It is arguable that the failure to fully address this apparent tension appears to have led, in some cases, to adverse consequences for workers labouring at the foundations of these supply chains and franchise networks.

While there are clearly some limitations under the CC Act, there are also some notable benefits. The unfair contract terms law and the good faith obligations of the prescribed industry codes may provide small businesses with greater capacity to challenge the commercial decisions and bureaucratic power of lead firms. For instance, the duty of good faith may require franchisors and major buyers, such as supermarkets and fast food heads, to engage in negotiations in a more measured way. Further, the

158. WHS Acts, s. 46. PCBUs are also under a vertical duty to consult all of the 'workers' who carry out work in any capacity for the PCBU and who are 'likely to be directed affected by a matter relating to' health and safety. WHS Acts, ss 47-49.

unfair contract terms protections allow contractors and franchisees the opportunity to have one-sided contractual clauses struck out.[159] That said, it is somewhat doubtful as to whether contractors or franchisees may be able to use these statutory provisions (i.e., the unfair contract terms law and the good faith obligations) to effectively challenge the amounts paid or payable under their contractual arrangements with larger firms.[160] This is a significant limitation given that there appears to be a link between the unsustainable business practices adopted by the lead firm and the poor compliance behaviour of independent contractors or franchisees further down the supply chain.

Further, the fact that the CC Act restricts the taking of any collective action by contractors and franchisees means that there are limited points of leverage by which to compel lead firms to revise the relevant contract price, discounting strategy or business model. Indeed, in the absence of over whelming public pressure, it is highly questionable whether the franchisor of 7-Eleven would have acceded to the demands of its franchisees to vary the relevant profit-sharing arrangements.

One of the most troubling consequences of the CC Act is the way in which the protection of small businesses interests may come at the expense of workers in commercial contracting or franchising relationships. For example, the relevant lead firms in the *Baiada* and *7-Eleven* cases have suggested that the restrictions imposed under the relevant industry codes prevent them from using critical commercial sanctions, such as termination of the relevant supply contract or franchise agreement, even in the face of egregious breaches of workplace laws by their suppliers and/or franchisees.[161] These termination restrictions potentially obstruct effective implementation of Weil's strategic enforcement model which is premised on the idea that harnessing the regulatory resources of lead firms is often far more powerful than legal penalties in terms of driving long-term behavioural change among potentially wayward franchisees or contractors. Circumscribing the rights of lead firms in this way, potentially allows contractors and franchisees repeated opportunities to correct their concerning compliance behaviour which may ultimately lead to the continuation, rather than the curbing, of exploitative employer behaviour.

---

159. In relation to Baiada, it is important to note that the unfair contract terms law is unlikely to offer much assistance to the employer entities in this case given that the arrangements between the second and third-tier contractors and the Baiada Group were not formalised in writing.
160. In particular, the good faith obligations do not prevent the larger firm acting in their own legitimate commercial interests. Further, the unfair contract terms law does not apply to terms which set the 'upfront price payable'. This term refers to any payments (including any contingent payments) to be provided for the supply, sale or grant under the contract where such payments are disclosed at or before the time the commencement date of the relevant contract.
161. *See*, e.g., Evidence to Senate Inquiry into the Impact of Australia's Temporary Work Visa Programs on the Australian Labour Market and on the Temporary Work Visa Holders, Parliament of Australia, Melbourne, 5 February 2016, at 12 (Robert Baily, Chief Executive Officer, 7-Eleven Stores Pty Ltd).

§3.07 CONCLUSION

Outsourcing, subcontracting and franchising have grown in popularity in Australia, and all have been accepted as common and lawful business strategies. Yet, there is mounting evidence and increasing appreciation of the way in which these arrangements can create difficulties for both regulators and unions seeking to uphold minimum employment standards. This chapter has canvassed some of the core regulatory responses in labour, work health and safety, and competition and consumer regulation and assessed the extent to which they are able to effectively tackle the problems raised by fissured work arrangements. While there is a growing consensus that harnessing the power, position and resources of lead firms is critical, and although there have been some important legislative and policy developments in this direction, analysis of the *Baiada* and *7-Eleven* cases has revealed a gap between law and practice. The question remains whether the current regulatory frameworks are capable of bridging this divide. While the work health and safety legislation holds much promise, the FW Act is potentially limited by its implicit adherence to the dominant employment paradigm. It is arguable that focusing on the commercial regulation of fragmented work may be more fruitful. To this extent, it is crucial that greater attention is paid to the complex interplay between workplace and competition and consumer regulation so as to better ensure that all firms are clear as to their relevant legal responsibilities and all workers enjoy the benefit of the relevant statutory protections.

CHAPTER 4

Reconsidering the Notion of 'Employer' in the Era of the Fissured Workplace in the UK: Should Labour Law Responsibilities Exceed the Boundary of the Legal Entity?

Jeremias Prassl[*]

§4.01 INTRODUCTION

This chapter explores David Weil's concept of the 'fissured workplace'[1] in the context of United Kingdom (UK) employment and labour law,[2] arguing that regulation cannot keep up with fragmenting employment relationships because our concept of the employer is still very much fixated on a unitary concept, i.e., a single entity as the employer, reminiscent of the master of old. It answers the seminar question, *viz*

* Associate Professor in the Faculty of Law, Fellow of Magdalen College, and Research Fellow in the Institute of European and Comparative Law, University of Oxford; Associate Research Scholar, Yale Law School. This chapter draws on research funded by the UK Arts and Humanities Research Council (AH/I012826/1) and supervised by Prof Mark FreedlandQC (hon) FBA, now published as J Prassl, The Concept of the Employer (OUP 2015). For questions and discussion, please contact me at jeremias.prassl@law.ox.ac.uk

1. For present purposes, the two terms will be used interchangeably. The same is true for 'English' and 'UK' law in this context: whilst there are generally considerable differences between the different legal systems found within the United Kingdom, in particular between the law of England and Wales, and the law of Scotland, large parts of Employment law are an important exception to this rule, insofar as they apply across Great Britain: Trade Union and Labour Relations (Consolidation) Act 1992 (hereinafter, 'TULRCA') s. 301(1); A Bradley and K Ewing, *Constitutional and Administrative Law* (15th ed, Pearson 2011) 40. For an important earlier discussion on point, *see* W Njoya, 'Corporate Governance and the Employment Relationship: The Fissured Workplace in Canada and the United Kingdom' (2015-16) 37 Comparative Labour Law & Policy Journal 121.
2. D Weil, *The Fissured Workplace: Why Work Became So Bad for So Many and What Can Be Done to Improve It* (Harvard University Press 2014).

whether labour law responsibilities should exceed the boundary of the legal entity, with an emphatic 'yes, but ...': it is only through the careful adoption of a functional concept of the employer that the law will be able to adapt to the increasing fissurisation of workplaces whilst ensuring theoretical coherence.

In order to develop this argument, the chapter is structured as follows. Following this Introduction, section §4.02 looks at the difficulty of identifying the employer in English law, in terms of both the absence of case law directly on point, and the competing notions which emerge upon closer inspection. Section §4.03 then turns to fissured work in the UK today, looking at three specific examples (agency work, private equity groups, and crowdwork) and the potentially dramatic legal implications for the scope of employment law. Section §4.04 turns to legislative and judicial responses, both in individual and collective employment law, and their varying degrees of effectiveness in overcoming the problems identified. Section §4.05 then introduces the proposed future development, *viz* a functional concept of the employer; a brief Conclusion demonstrates how its adoption could restore regulatory coherence in a world of fissured employment.

Before turning to that discussion, an important preliminary remark should be made: the concept of the employer in UK (and to a lesser extent in European Union (EU)) law has been the subject of my recent book, *The Concept of the Employer* (OUP 2015).[3] Given present space limitations, this chapter can only set out a very limited summary of my broader research in this area. In order to guide the interested reader, a brief appendix identifies the relevant chapters or passages of the book on which each section draws.

§4.02 IDENTIFYING THE EMPLOYER

At first glance, there is little case law discussing the concept of the employer in the UK: this section explains how information may nonetheless be gleaned indirectly, before setting out the two competing strands of the concept of the employer which emerge upon detailed scrutiny: a unitary, and a multi-functional one.

[A] Identifying the Relevant Case Law

It is a striking feature of English law that outside pockets such as triangular employment relationships, there are comparatively few decided cases on the question of the nature of the employer, as opposed to an abundance of decisions on the definition of employees, workers and dependent labour more generally. Cases disposing of questions as diverse as obtaining particulars of employment,[4] health and safety provisions,[5]

3. J Prassl, *The Concept of the Employer* (OUP 2015): https://global.oup.com/academic/product/the-concept-of-the-employer-9780198735533.
4. *Carmichael v. National Power Plc* [1999] 1 WLR 2042 (HL).
5. *Ferguson v. John Dawson Ltd* [1976] 1 WLR 1213 (CA); Construction (Working Places) Regulations 1966, SI 1966/94, reg 28(1).

and collective representation rights[6] have to address the issue of the claimant's status as an initial hurdle. The definition of an individual's legal position, however, traditionally takes place in a rather circular line of enquiry, where two analytically distinct questions become intertwined: that as to the existence and definition of a contract of service and that as to the definition of its parties. On the one hand, both employee and employer could be seen as parties to a contract of service. On the other, a contract of service can only come into existence if both parties to it show the necessary features of employer and employee. Whilst puzzling in some analytical contexts, the resulting conundrum is a useful basis for present purposes: it facilitates deduction of information about the concept of the employer from pronouncements on the concept of the employee. The decisions are, after all, also on the question of the existence of a contract - and thus in turn on the nature of both, rather than merely one, of the parties to it.

[B] Competing Strands of the Concept of the Employer

Viewed thus, an analysis of decided cases identifies two contradictory conceptions: a unitary conception, first, assumes that the employer must always be a single entity: the counterparty to the employee in the contract of employment. A multi-functional conception, on the other hand, defines the employer by reference to the exercise of various functions or roles. A particular 'function' of being an employer in this sense is one of the actions employers are entitled or obliged to take within the open-ended scope of the contract of employment.

[1] A Unitary Strand

With discipline and hierarchy embodied in the very idea of *the master*, to be found in the common law long before a contract of service evolved,[7] a personified unitary concept of the employer is undoubtedly a historically accurate starting point. Two main factors can be identified as carrying over that function until today: the role of contract as key organising device of the employment relationship, and the company as a predominant legal form of the employer.

In 1967, Lord Wedderburn famously referred to contract as the 'fundamental legal institution' of Labour Law.[8] Whilst Simon Deakin has successfully challenged the traditional assumption that a common law system of employment law, based on freedom of contract, predated the welfare state,[9] the institution of the contract and its connected doctrines have nonetheless had a fundamental effect on the perception of the employment relationship in general, and the employer as work-taking counterparty to a contract of service in particular. By looking at the vast majority of personal work relationships through the contractual prism, a unitary view of the employing entity is

6. *O'Kelly v. Trusthouse Forte Plc* [1984] QB 90 (CA).
7. A Merritt, 'Control v. Economic Reality: Defining the Contract of Employment' (1982) Australian Business Law Review 105.
8. K Wedderburn, *Cases and Materials on Labour Law* (CUP 1967) 1.
9. S Deakin and F Wilkinson, *The Law of the Labour Market* (OUP 2005).

bound to emerge: if the exchange of wage and work is characterised as a bilateral contractual relationship, emphasis shifts onto a single work-taking counterparty at the non-employee end. When used as the central category of personal work relationships, the contract of employment has a strong normative function. In substantive terms, the most significant influence of a contractual analysis in the Employment context is its inherent emphasis on *bilateral* relationships between two individual parties. The nature of the implied contract under consideration in *James* illustrates this fundamental attachment to the concept of unilateral relationships: even clearly multilateral scenarios are tackled through several bilateral contracts.[10]

The perception of companies as anthropomorphic individual units as a result of separate legal personality is a further factor contributing to the historical assumption that the employer must be a singular entity, substantively identical across all different domains of employment law. Despite a multitude of actors, from employees and management to a board of directors and shareholders, it has become a singular focal point for a unitary conception of the corporate entity, with powers and responsibilities perceived in anthropomorphic terms; a concept to which employment relationships then fasten. In economic theory, the conception of the firm as a singular unit is built on two factors: the firm as internalising what would otherwise be cost-inefficient market transactions between factors of production,[11] and the firm as concentrating management powers in the hands of a small group, thus taking them away from the shareholders of the company.[12]

Company law developed against this background, setting the legal boundaries of the company not at the economic remit of all those involved, but on a far narrower basis, shaped by two closely related doctrines: separate legal personality, and limited liability.[13] The potential for abuse of the limited liability form is rarely doubted; the courts have nonetheless provided clear affirmation of the 'right [...] inherent in our corporate law'[14] to rely on the principles expounded in *Salomon* in deliberately structuring corporate groups to parcel out liability. In the employment context, Davies and Freedland have therefore suggested that limited liability applies within corporate groups:

> even though the managerial structure of the group (or part of it) itself ignores the division of the group into separate legal entities. [...] The fact that the business organisation of the group ignores the separate legal entities of the group companies

10. *James v. London Borough of Greenwich* [2008] EWCA Civ 34, [2008] ICR 577 [5] (Mummery LJ). Despite dicta to the contrary in *Stephenson v. Delphi Diesel Systems Ltd* [2003] ICR 471 (EAT)[53], the potential of multiparty contracts is not entirely barred: *Dacas v. Brook Street Bureau (UK) Ltd* [2004] EWCA Civ 217, [2004] ICR 1437[20], [78]; *Cable & Wireless Plc v. Muscat* [2006] EWCA Civ 220, [2006] ICR 975[41].
11. R Coase, 'The Nature of the Firm' (1937) 4 Economica 386, 388. Today, centralised management exercises the entrepreneur's role.
12. A Berle and G Means, *The Modern Corporation and Private Property* (The Macmillan Company 1939) 119.
13. *Salomon v. Salomon & Co Ltd* [1897] AC 22 (HL).Though the rules for incorporation are found in statute. The Companies Act 2006, s. 3(1)-(3) defines limited liability companies, and Part II of the Act sets out the incorporation process.
14. *Adams v. Cape Industries Plc* [1990] Ch. 433 (CA)544 D-E.

will not enable the employee to go behind or beyond his or her employing company.[15]

As the following subsection will show, however, this unitary view is rather different from the conception of the employer borne out in another context: the common law tests through which the concept of the employee as party to the contract of employment has evolved.

[2] A Multi-Functional Strand

A 'function' of being an employer here is one of the various actions employers are entitled or obliged to take as part of the bundle of rights and duties falling within the scope of the open-ended contract of service. In trawling the established common law tests of employment status such as control, economic reality or mutuality of obligation for these employer functions, there are endless possible mutations of different fact scenarios, rendering categorisation purely on the basis of past decisions of limited assistance. The result of this analysis of concepts underlying different fact patterns, rather than the actual results on a case-by-case basis, is the following set of functions, with the presence or absence of individual factors becoming less relevant than the specific role they play in any given context. Individual elements can vary from situation to situation, as long as they fulfil the same function when looked at as a whole.[16] Key to this concept of the employer being a *multi-functional* one is the fact that no one function mentioned above is relevant in and of itself. Rather, it is the *ensemble* of the five functions that matters: each of them covers one of the facets necessary to create, maintain and commercially exploit employment relationships, thus coming together to make up the legal concept of employing workers or acting as an employer.

The *five main functions* and their functional underpinning of the employer are discussed below.[17]

[a] Inception and Termination of the Contract of Employment

This category includes all powers of the employer over the very existence of its relationship with the employee, from the 'power of selection',[18] to the right to dismiss.[19]

15. P Davies and M Freedland, 'The Employment Relationship in British Labour Law' in C Barnard, S Deakin and G Morris (eds), *The Future of Labour Law: Liber Amicorum for Sir Bob Hepple QC* (Hart 2004) 137.
16. The 'equipollency principle' (Äquivalenzprinzip): L Nogler, 'Die Typologisch-Funktionale Methode am Beispiel des Arbeitnehmerbegriffs' (2009) 10 ZESAR 459, 463.
17. For earlier lists *see* e.g., M Freedland, *The Personal Employment Contract* (OUP 2003) 40.
18. *Short v. J&W Henderson Ltd* 1945 SC 155 (CS).
19. *Narich Pty v. Commissioner of Payroll Tax* [1984] ICR 286 (EAT)295E.

[b] *Receiving Labour and Its Fruits*

Duties owed by the employee to the employer, specifically to provide his or her labour and the results thereof,[20] as well as rights incidental to it.[21]

[c] *Providing Work and Pay*

The employer's obligations towards its employees, such as, for example, the payment of wages.[22]

[d] *Managing the Enterprise-Internal Market*

Coordination through control over all factors of production, up to and including the power to require both how and what is to be done.[23]

[e] *Managing the Enterprise-External Market*

Undertaking economic activity in return for potential profit,[24] whilst also being exposed to any losses that may result from the enterprise.[25]

As the following section will show, in the context of fissured work, the multi-functional conceptualisation of the employer poses a direct challenge to the unitary concept, reconcilable only in a small set of paradigm cases. On the other hand, in situations where different functions may be exercised from more than one *locus* of control,[26] the tension quickly comes to the fore. The practical implications of this conflict are considerable, from regulatory obligations placed on unsuitable entities to a complete breakdown of employment law coverage.

§4.03 FISSURISED WORK IN THE UK TODAY

The UK labour market is amongst the most flexible and deregulated in the world.[27] It is therefore perhaps unsurprising that fissurised work has long been an important issue

20. *WHPT Housing Association v. Secretary of State for Social Services* [1981] ICR 737 (HC).
21. *Stevenson Jordan & Harrison v. McDonnell & Evans* [1952] 1 TLR 101 (CA) 111; *Initial Services v. Putterill* [1968] 1 QB 396 (CA).
22. *Cassidyv Ministry of Health*[1951] 2 KB 343 (CA) 360.
23. *Simmons v. Heath Laundry Co* [1910] 1 KB 543 (CA) (Hilbery J).
24. *Ready Mixed Concrete Ltd v. Minister of Pensions* [1968] 2 QB 497 (HC) 522.
25. *Market Investigations Ltd v. Minister of Social Security* [1969] 2 QB 173 (HC).
26. The term '*locus*' of control is designed to avoid additional complexities arising out of the fact, noted *inter al* by Freedland (n. 17) 45-47, that even in traditional companies without external influence management control is often exercised by more than one person amongst a group of relatively senior executives.
27. MP Jo Swinson, *Employment Law 2013: Progress on reform* (BIS, March 2013) Foreword. It is interesting to note in this connection that Njoya has argued, convincingly, that there is a particularly strong link between public and private capital markets: (n. 1) 133 ff.

in litigation and academic discussions. This section begins by focussing in detail on perhaps the two most challenging phenomena - agency work and corporate groups, relying as a particularly stark example on those driven by financial investors such as Private Equity funds. For each of these models, the relevant subsection briefly explains the managerial motives and socio-economic background behind the relevant business models, and how they lead to a fissurisation of work. Following a brief account of a currently emerging challenge - digital crowdwork - a final subsection sets out the significant impact fissured work has had on the scope of employment law- from incomplete and incoherent coverage to a complete breakdown of protective mechanisms.

[A] Specific Phenomena

Whilst both scenarios under discussion have been the subject of academic scrutiny, different labels have traditionally been applied. On the one hand, agency work can be placed in what Fudge has referred to as the 'commercialisation' of employment.[28] The Private Equity model to be discussed, on the other hand, can be placed in the context of discussions about the disintegration of the enterprise,[29] where '[t]he boundaries of the firm have proved to be quite porous, "making it difficult to know where the firm ends and where the market or another firm begins"'.[30] Both examples are brought together for present purposes, however, as they are stark illustrations of the fissurisation of the workplace.

[1] Agency Work

A report commissioned in 2014 by the Recruitment & Employment Confederation, an industry representative body, suggested that '24% of the British population [have] worked as a temporary agency worker at some point in their working life',[31] and an international comparison published in the same year put the number at 1.13 million.[32] Relative to the overall size of the labour market, the agency industry is therefore larger in the UK than anywhere else in the EU.[33] Industry figures from 2014 suggest that there

28. J Fudge, S McCrystal and K Sankaran, *Challenging the Legal Boundaries of Work Regulation* (Oñati International Series in Law and Society, Hart 2012) 10 (footnotes omitted).
29. H Collins, 'Independent Contractors and the Challenge of Vertical Disintegration to Employment Protection Laws' (1990) 10 Oxford Journal of Legal Studies 353.
30. Fudge, McCrystal and Sankaran (n. 28) 11, citing also W Powell, 'The Capitalist Firm in the Twenty-First Century: Emerging Patterns in Western Enterprise' in P DiMaggio (ed), *The Twenty-First Century Firm: Changing Economic Organization in International Perspective* (Princeton University Press 2003) 58.
31. REC, *Flex Appeal: Why Freelancers, Contractors and Agency Workers Choose to Work This Way* (Recruitment & Employment Confederation 2014) 5.
32. F van Haasteren, A Muntz and D Pennel, *Economic Report: 2014 Edition* (CIET 2014) 15, 17.
33. E Berkhout, C Dustmann and P Emmder, *Mind the Gap* (International Database on Employment and Adaptable Labour 2007); van Haasteren, Muntz and Pennel (n. 32) 19.

are approximately 18,000 agencies operating across the UK, employing a workforce of approximately 93,360 internal staff to match agency workers with assignments.[34]

When enquiring into the use of agency work,[35] different studies have uncovered a wide range of potential motivations, with considerable divergence between the answers offered by end users and agencies. Users' arguments range from numerical flexibility to meet peaks and troughs in demand to obtaining specific skills or ensuring temporary leave and maternity cover.[36] Markova and McKay summarise these reasons under a series of categories.[37] Flexibility is considered to be of prime importance, though it is not always clear to what extent this is limited to complementarity, i.e., the use of agency workers in situations where required staff numbers rise temporarily, or whether there is an increasing move towards substitution of permanent employees and the long-term hiring of a workforce through agencies. Cost savings are a second factor frequently identified, though a considerable number of end users suggest that there are little, if any, overall savings. Legal factors, finally, also loom large. Some studies suggest that employers' primary motivation is not the avoidance of employment law regulation as such, but rather the possibility of shifting liability for immigration law violations, with the agency in charge of organising work permits, checking workers' documents and ensuring ongoing compliance.[38] Other studies, however, have found that up to a quarter of end user firms rely on agency labour specifically in order to avoid incurring employment law obligations.[39]

The set-up of triangular employment relationships is well rehearsed in employment law literature. An agency, in essence, contracts with individuals to supply their labour to end user clients. For present purposes, the key factor is the resulting shared exercise of employer functions between the day-to-day employer (the client) and the agency. Drawing on a series of recent qualitative field studies, the extremely 'varied

34. F van Haasteren, A Muntz and D Pennel, *Economic Report: 2014 Edition* (CIET 2014) 29; D Winchester, *Thematic Feature: Temporary Agency Work in the UK* (National Report 2007; available through the EIR Online database at <www.eurofound.europa.eu> accessed 28 August 2014; J Arrowsmith, *Temporary Agency Work in an Enlarged European Union* (Office for Official Publications of the European Communities, Luxemburg 2006).
35. *See also* S McKay, 'Employer Motivations for Using Agency Labour' (2008) 37 Industrial Law Journal 296.
36. EMAR, *Agency Working in the UK: A Review of the Evidence* (Employment Relations Research Series No. 93, BERR 2008) Table 1.1, drawing on survey of Recruitment Agencies in 2007, Table 4.1.
37. E Markova and S McKay, *Agency and Migrant Workers: Literature Review* (TUC Commission on Vulnerable Employment 2008) 19 ff, drawing on L Gramm and J Schnell, 'The Use of Flexible Staffing Arrangements in Core Production Jobs' 2001 (54) Industrial and Labour Relations Review 245; K Hakansson and T Isidorsson, 'Flexibility, Stability and Agency Work: A Comparison of the Use of Agency Work in Sweden and the UK' in B Furaker, K Hakansson and J. Karlsson, *Flexibility and Stability in Working Life* (Palgrave 2007) 123; P Allan, 'The Contingent Workforce; Challenges and New Directions' (2002) American Business Review 103.
38. Markova and McKay, *Understanding the Operation and Management of Employment Agencies in the UK Labour Market* (n. 43) 24-25.
39. Equality and Human Rights Commission, 'Inquiry into Recruitment and Employment in the Meat and Poultry Processing Sector' (EHRC 2010) 22.

and variable'[40] arrangements between different *loci* of employer functions can be illustrated using two of the functions set out, above.

[a] Inception and Termination of the Contract of Employment

As regards the first function, this will usually be the primary task of the employment agency: a worker is taken on its books, and contracted out to end users at the agency's discretion.[41] Agencies can also shortlist and select candidates on the end user's behalf,[42] and be in charge of organising work permits and checking other qualifications and documents.[43] End users are however also sometimes involved in the selection of individual workers, and there are reports of instances where they do so for illegal purposes, for example by specifying a particular race or nationality of the agency worker to be supplied.[44] Termination and replacement is likewise via the agency itself,[45] usually upon the end user's request,[46] and without significant notice periods.[47] Some clients, however, may retain a direct right to dismiss the employee,[48] again with several reports of this function being exercised for inappropriate reasons, such as dismissing a female line worker.[49]

[b] Providing Work and Pay

The division of this third employer function is amongst the more difficult to analyse, as it varies drastically across different scenarios. Looking first at the obligation to provide work, the agency will normally not be under any obligation to do so.[50] The situation of the end user is less clear. While an obligation to provide work is rarely found on the facts,[51] there have been decisions to the contrary, especially where the employee was deeply integrated in the end user's undertaking, up to and including managerial control over the end user's permanent employees.[52] Whilst the provision of day-to-day work is therefore clearly a role of the end user, for example in choosing the allocation of

40. P Leighton and M Wynn, Temporary Agency Working: Is the Law on the Turn? (Company Lawyer 2008) 7, 8.
41. E Markova and S McKay, *Agency and Migrant Workers: Literature Review* (TUC Commission on Vulnerable Employment 2008) 39 ff.
42. *Ibid.* 20; citing C Stanworth and J Druker, 'Human resource solutions? Dimensions of Employers' Use of Temporary Agency Labour in the UK (2006) 35 Personnel Review 175.
43. E Markova and S McKay, *Understanding the Operation and Management of Employment Agencies in the UK Labour Market* (TUC Commission on Vulnerable Employment, London 2008) 24-25.
44. Equality and Human Rights Commission (EHRC), *Inquiry into Recruitment and Employment in the Meat and Poultry Processing Sector* (EHRC 2010) 8.
45. M Aziz et al., *Hard Work, Hidden Lives: The Full Report* (TUC Commission on Vulnerable Employment 2008) 189.
46. Leighton and Wynn (n. 40) 9.
47. E McGaughey, *Should Agency Workers be Treated Differently?* (LSE Working Papers 07/2010) 2.
48. *Muschett v. HM Prison Service* [2010] EWCA Civ 25, [2010] IRLR 451, 14.
49. EHRC (n. 39) 11-12.
50. Leighton and Wynn (n. 40) 12.
51. *See* e.g., James (n. 10).
52. *Tilson v. Alstom Transport* [2010] EWCA Civ 1308, [2011] IRLR 169.

particular jobs,[53] such findings will be rare. In reality, workers will frequently turn up at an end user's site in the morning only to find that on that particular day no work is available.[54]

The provision of pay, on the other hand, is usually a function exercised by the agency, together with general payroll and tax services. Suggestions that an employment agency merely acts as the end user's agent in this regard no longer seems to feature in the most recent case law.[55] While wages are nearly always paid to workers by their agency or a payroll company associated with it,[56] the question as to who actually determines the levels of remuneration yields a much more mixed response, as a recent report for ACAS shows.[57]

[2] Private Equity

A second, and rather different, example of fissurised or multi-entity employer function exercise can be found in the Private Equity (PE) industry. As the traditional model of dispersed shareholdings has increasingly come under pressure,[58] industry analysts have noticed a strong trend towards concentrated ownership, from block holdings to outright subsidiary ownership. Private Equity funds are a prime example of this shift towards relational, or 'insider',[59] systems of corporate governance. Concentrated share ownership is particularly challenging in the employment context, as it leads to multiple parties potentially exercising traditional employer functions. Once the majority, or at least a significant proportion of, voting rights are vested in a single shareholder, it will be able to exert considerable power over management.

In the mid-2000s, the UK Private Equity industry, along with the rest of Europe (and indeed the world), enjoyed extremely benign economic and regulatory conditions, leading to record investments in 2006.[60] The demise of this rapidly maturing industry has been predicted by economic and academic commentators,[61] and current statistics do show a contraction of the Private Equity sector in line with the retreat of global financial markets during the recession:[62] overall, BVCA members' investment in

53. EHRC (n. 39) 10.
54. Aziz (n. 45) 14 (John's story).
55. Though cf. Munby J's dissent in *Cable & Wireless Plc v. Muscat*[2006] EWCA Civ 220, [2006] ICR 975.
56. EHRC (n. 39) 16.
57. C Forde and G Slater, *The Role of Employment Agencies in Pay Setting* (ACAS Research Paper 05/2011) 19.
58. H Gospel and A Pendleton, 'Markets and Relationships: Finance, Governance, and Labour in the United Kingdom' in H Gospel and A Pendleton (eds), *Corporate Governance and Labour Management: An International Comparison* (OUP 2005) 71.
59. *Ibid.* 62.
60. K Raade and C Dantas Machado, 'Recent Developments in the European Private Equity Markets' 319 European Commission Economic Papers 27.
61. For example, B Cheffins and J Armour, 'The Eclipse of Private Equity' (2008) 33 The Delaware Journal of Corporate Law 1.
62. E Appelbaum and R Batt, *Private Equity at Work—When Wall Street Manages Main Street* (Russell Sage Foundation 2014) Ch. 4 (The Effects of the Financial Crisis).

the UK fell from GBP 12 billion in 2007 to GBP 8.2 billion in 2008.[63] Figures for total global investment of UK-based firms show an even more drastic decline, from GBP 20 billion in 2008[64] to GBP 12.6 billion in 2009.[65] By 2012, these numbers had begun to stabilise, with BVCA member investing GBP 5.7 billion and GBP 12.2 billion, respectively.[66] The industry's significance is unlikely to diminish in future: a key forward-looking measure – the amount of new funds raised – showed a significant upturn during 2012 with GBP 5.9 billion in fresh capital committed to Private Equity (and venture capital) funds.[67]

The underlying economic rationale of this industry can be summarised in three main strands. The first of these rejects traditional models of firms built on managerial discretion and shareholder deference to professional managers,[68] focussing on the agency costs that arise from a misalignment of owners' and managers' interests.[69] Second, a clearly defined and closely monitored obligation to service creditors[70] settles what could otherwise be a constant struggle between owners and managers over the allocation of free cash flow;[71] thus removing further inefficiencies that are said to result from the public corporation's split between ownership and control. Finally, the much more detailed and regular provision of information about the company to investors considerably reduces the price of financing operations by overcoming the 'lemons market' problem, where uncertainty about the true quality of a product impedes otherwise beneficial market transactions.[72]

Management control is thus the unique selling point of the Private Equity industry: in order to ensure the success of their investments, General Partners must carefully work with and oversee entrepreneurs and portfolio companies.[73] Their PE management company thus becomes a second entity with the potential to exercise employer functions, up to and including control over the supposedly singular counterparty to the contract of employment itself.

Finding specific evidence for this division of traditional employer functions in practice is rather challenging: there is little, if any, detailed qualitative research on the

63. PriceWaterhouseCoopers, *PE and VC Performance Measurement Survey* (BVCA 2008) 12.
64. PriceWaterhouseCoopers, *Private Equity and Venture Capital Report on Investment Activity 2008* (BVCA 2008).
65. BVCA, *February Briefing* (2010) 26.
66. PriceWaterhouseCoopers, *Private Equity and Venture Capital Report on Investment Activity 2012* (BVCA 2013) 4.
67. PriceWaterhouseCoopers, *Private Equity and Venture Capital Report on Investment Activity 2012* (n. 66) 3.
68. A Berle and G Means, *The Modern Corporation and Private Property* (Macmillan 1939).
69. A Alchian and H Demsetz, 'Production, Information Costs, and Economic Organization' (1972) 62 The American Economic Review 777; W Meckling and M Jensen, 'A Theory of the Firm: Managerial Behavior, Agency Costs and Ownership Structure' (1976) 3 Journal of Financial Economics 4.
70. M Jensen, 'The Eclipse of the Public Corporation' (1989) 67 Harvard Business Review 61, 64; 1997 revision 18.
71. J Gilligan and M Wright, *Private Equity Demystified: An Explanatory Guide* (2nd edn., ICAEW Corporate Finance Faculty 2010) 84.
72. G Akerlof, 'The Market for "Lemons": Qualitative Uncertainty and the Market Mechanism' (1970) 84 Quarterly Journal of Economics 488.
73. P Gompers and J Lerner, *The Venture Capital Cycle* (MIT Press 2004) 70.

actual modes of interaction between funds and their investee companies. In order to obtain the relevant information, several case studies were therefore conducted amongst London-based Private Equity funds.[74]

[a] Inception and Termination of the Contract of Employment

Most PE management companies maintain rosters of executives specialising on specific management tasks, from divisional restructuring to supply chain reorganisation. If a portfolio company decides to hire employees in any of these fields, the fund will 'assist' its efforts by selecting an executive from its database, or sometimes even propose one of its own senior partners as an appropriate (temporary) manager.[75] These candidates will normally be interviewed and selected directly by the PE management company team, who are also often tasked with negotiating further particulars of employment. Other funds maintain a much smaller stock of experienced executives, but nevertheless retain the power to direct the investee company's hiring choices.[76]

The right to terminate employment relationships is equally shared between both *loci* of control. Portfolio company management and investing funds can usually initiate redundancies, albeit through different processes. The former will retain the formal power to terminate most employment contracts, subject to key personnel clauses. Nonetheless, even minor terminations are usually discussed in informal phone calls between the PE operations team and the company's Chief Executive Officer (CEO) or Head of Human Resources.[77] If analysts within the Private Equity management company have identified potential redundancies, the next steps will depend on the fund's investment strategy: while some firms only initiate 'general conceptual discussions' with management,[78] others will provide detailed instructions on where and how changes to the workforce are to take place.[79]

[b] Managing the Enterprise-Internal Market

Control over the enterprise-internal market is not shared in the sense expounded, for example, in the first function. Rather, the same sets of functions are in fact exercised at different levels in the PE context: the investing fund will traditionally focus on business plans and development, leaving more detailed execution to the company's executives.

In nearly all investment agreements, there is a clear list that sets out which strategic matters can only be initiated and in some cases even executed by the PE firm. This will cover decisions on senior management, group structures and financing, from

74. Fieldwork approved by the Oxford University Social Sciences and Humanities Inter-Divisional Research Ethics Committee (IDREC) on 20 January 2010: SSD/CUREC1/10-285.
75. Telephone Interview with Senior PE Operations Executive (15 February 2010).
76. Interview with PE Business Development Partner (London 19 February 2010).
77. Interview with former Investee Company CEO (Oxford 23 February 2010).
78. Telephone Interview with Senior PE Operations Executive (15 February 2010).
79. Interview with PE Partner (London 10 March 2010).

repayment priorities to additional loans.[80] Whilst strategic change is often addressed at formal board meetings, there are other, more opaque, methods of communication between the two *loci* of control: the investors can, for example, request mere attendance rights at board meetings, with the minutes clearly reflecting that all decisions were made by the executive directors alone. In other scenarios, particularly when it comes to reductions in employment levels, information is conveyed as informally as possible, from telephone calls to lunch conversations.[81] Other funds take an even more active approach to managing the enterprise-internal market. The employment of operating partners as senior management has already been discussed; another frequently used technique is a direct secondment of junior analysts at all levels of the target company,[82] for example as chief of staff to key executives, in order to get 'very close to the operations' and deliver the strategic changes decided by the fund.[83]

[3] The Rise of Crowdwork

A final phenomenon which should be mentioned briefly is crowdwork,[84] a still-emerging model of employment relationships also known as crowdsourcing of labour or crowd employment. Crowdwork refers to the digital organisation of the outsourcing of tasks to a large pool of workers. The work (ranging from transportation services and cleaning to digital transcription or programming tasks) is referred to in a variety of ways, including 'gigs', 'rides', or 'tasks', and is offered to a large number of people (the 'crowd') by means of an internet-based 'crowdsourcing platform'.[85] This organisational model forms part of a larger set of processes known as 'crowdsourcing';[86] with customers (or indeed employers) referred to as 'crowdsourcers'. The resulting contractual relationships are manifold and complex: whilst the work is usually managed through an intermediary (the crowdsourcing platform), some will insist on direct contractual relationships between crowdsourcer clients and crowdworkers, whereas others will opt for tripartite contractual structures, akin to traditional models of agency work and labour outsourcing.[87]

Just as the two previous arrangements, crowdwork thus brings the contradictions inherent in the concept of the employing entity to the fore: the assumption that only a

80. Interview with PE Partner (London 10 March 2010).
81. Interview with PE Partner (London 10 March 2010).
82. Interview with PE fund General Counsel (London 11 March 2010).
83. Telephone Interview with Senior PE Operations Executive (15 February 2010).
84. *See* further J Prassl and M Risak, 'Rethinking The Legal Analysis Of Crowdwork: Platforms As Employers?' (2016) Comparative Labour Law & Policy Journal (forthcoming).
85. For the best-known, Amazon's Mechanical Turk (www.mturk.com) *see* Strube, 'Vom Outsourcing zum Crowdsourcing', in CristianeBenner (ed), *Crowdwork – zurück in die Zukunft* (Bund Verlag 2014) 75 ff.
86. A term derived from a combination of the words 'outsourcing' and 'crowd', and was used by Jeff Howe for the first time, cf. Jeff Howe, 'The Rise of Crowdsourcing' (*Wired Mag*, 14 June 2006).
87. Cf. AniketKittur et al., *The Future of Crowd Work.*, Paper presented at 16th ACM Conference on Computer Supported Cooperative Work, <www.lri.fr/~mbl/ENS/CSCW/2012/papers/Kittur-CSCW13.pdf>, accessed 13 January 2016; Jan Marco Leimeister, Shkodran Zogaj and Ivo Blohm, 'Crowdwork – digitale Wertschöpfung in der Wolke', in Walter Brenner and Thomas Hess (eds), *Wirtschaftsinformatik in Wissenschaft und Praxis* (Springer Verlag 2014) 51-64.

single entity, the counterparty to the contract of employment, can exercise employer functions is incongruent with their continuous joint exercise by two *loci* of control in the contexts surveyed. It is to the tension's practical implications for employment law coverage to which a second subsection now turns.

[B] Implications for the Scope of Employment Law Coverage

The tension characterising the concept of the employer makes employment law coverage fragile in multi-entity employment scenarios: it becomes unclear, incoherent and open to easy manipulation. This is because the identification of the employer is driven by two conflicting strands with the potential to point in different directions. In multilateral employment relationships, the multi-functional aspect of the concept instinctively points towards the identification of several relevant entities, whereas various elements identified as parts of the unitary strand in Chapter 1 insist on a single entity conceptualisation. As a direct consequence of the concept's underlying tension, no employer may be identified in the temporary agency work scenario; in the Private Equity scenario, identification is limited to a small subset, which may frequently be an inappropriate counterparty, or only one of several relevant entities.

[1] Breakd-Down of Employment Law Coverage

The joint exercise of employer functions is a clear illustration of the 'profound difficulties' posed by complex triangular or multilateral employment relationships:[88] it challenges the very existence of a contract of employment, thus leaving individual workers without recourse to the majority of domestic employment protective legislation. The complete breakdown of employment law coverage is a consequence of 'contractual arrangements that split, on the one hand, day-to-day control of work processes and, on the other hand, day-to-day securing and paying of people to work, [thus] prima facie prevent[ing] those working from being legally classified as anyone's "employees"':[89] neither the relationship with the agency nor with the end user is characterised as one of employment.

As regards the former, it is unlikely 'that many agency contracts will turn out to be contracts of employment [even if] the possibility should not be overlooked'.[90] Instead, while a contract with the agency will be found, it will usually be characterised as one of service. In *Wickens*,[91] for example, it was held that the claimant could not bring an unfair dismissal claim, as temporary agency workers were not engaged under contracts of employment, and that the relevant business size threshold had therefore

88. Freedland (n. 17) 36 ff.
89. L Barmes, 'Learning from Case Law Accounts of Marginalised Working' in J Fudge, S McCrystal and K Sankaran (eds), *Challenging the Legal Boundaries of Work Regulation* (Oñati International Series in Law and Society, Hart 2012) 308.
90. HMRC, *Employment Status Manual*, ESM 2002, <www.hmrc.gov.uk/manuals/esmmanual/ESM2002.htm> 1 September 2012.
91. *Wickens v. Champion Employment* [1984] ICR 365 (EAT).

not been met. Despite exceptions on the facts of specific cases[92] or in the practice of individual agencies that explicitly 'employ' their temporary workers,[93] temporary workers thus fall outside the protective scope of a contract of employment with their agency.

The situation as against end users is similar, if not even more difficult. There is generally no direct contractual arrangement in place between the parties, although factual exceptions are again possible.[94] A potential solution on the basis of implied contracts of employment proved to be rather short-lived. In *Dacas v. Brook Street Bureau*,[95] a Court of Appeal led by Mummery LJ picked up earlier foundations in cases such as *Franks v. Reuters*[96] and developed the use of implied contracts in triangular work scenarios. Upon a review of the existing case law on employment relations in triangular setups,[97] it was made clear that the threshold for implication was a high one: as the council's exercise of employer functions over Ms James could be explained by the parties' 'respective contracts with the employment agency, [...] it was not necessary to imply the existence of another contract in order to give business reality to the relationship between the parties.'[98] As a result, it is increasingly unlikely that a contract of employment would readily be implied between an agency worker and the end user of the agency's services.

[2] Incomplete and Incoherent Coverage

Even where there is a contract of employment between an individual worker and his or her immediate employer, however, the tension inherent in the concept of the employer may lead to incomplete or incoherent employment law coverage – most notably in the context of complex corporate setups, including PE firms, where internal management structures dividing up employer functions are liable to render employment law obligations nominal. A recent example can be found in the context of employers' duty to consult with employee representatives in the case of collective redundancies, derived from the (EU's) Collective Redundancies Directive 98/59/EC.[99] Where more than twenty employees are to be made redundant at an establishment within a period of ninety days, the employer has to commence negotiations, with a view to reaching

92. *McMeechan v. Secretary of State for Employment* [1996] EWCA Civ 1166, [1997] IRLR 353.
93. C Forde and G Slater, *The Role of Employment Agencies in Pay Setting* (ACAS Research Paper 05/2011) 14; K Ward, 'Making Manchester "Flexible": Competition and Change in the Temporary Staffing Industry' (2005) 36 Geoforum 223.
94. *Dacas* (n. 10): contract with client; *Motorola Ltd v. Davidson* [2001] IRLR 4 (EAT): very high level of end user control, including training and sanctions; worker is employee.
95. n. 10.
96. *Franks v. Reuters* [2003] EWCA Civ 417, [2003] ICR 1166.
97. James (n. 10) [46]-[52]. Agency worker cases at the tribunal stage had been stayed in anticipation of the decision.
98. *Ibid.* [42].
99. Council Directive (EC) 59/1998 of 20 July 1998 on the approximation of the laws of the Member States relating to Collective Redundancies [1998] OJ L 225/16.

agreement, on ways of avoiding the dismissals, reducing the numbers of employees to be dismissed, and mitigating the consequences of the dismissals.[100]

The issue of external influence is clearly addressed in the Directive's preamble, where the Community institutions note that:

> it is necessary to ensure that employers' obligations as regards information, consultation and notification apply independently of whether the decision on collective redundancies emanates from the employer or from an undertaking which controls that employer.[101]

In practice, however, this is not the case. In *Fujitsu Siemens*,[102] management control over manufacturing plants in Kilo, Finland and various locations in Germany was exercised by a Dutch Holding company. The executive team of the parent entity had resolved to propose the disengagement from the local plant to its board; the latter supported the proposal on 14 December 1999. Local management in Kilo consulted with employee representatives from 20 December to 31 January 2010, before ceasing activity on 1 February and terminating the employment of 350 workers from 8 February onwards. The trade unions representing the claimants alleged that these steps meant that Fujitsu Siemens had failed to comply with the Directive's obligations, as the real decisions had been taken by entities other than the undertaking's management, and prior to consultation with employee representatives.

In the resulting litigation, several questions were referred to the ECJ, including whether consultation needed to be finalised before the parent took general commercial or strategic specific decisions that might lead to redundancies, or only before the need for dismissals was certain. In following AG Mengozzi's line of reasoning,[103] the Court affirmed that the Directive's obligations were squarely based on the 'employer, in other words a natural or legal person who stands in an employment relationship with the workers who may be made redundant'. An undertaking, even if capable of controlling the employer through binding decisions, did not have that status.[104] The Directive was not to restrict the commercial freedom of corporate groups to choose their organisations' management structures, and none of its provisions could be interpreted as imposing any obligations on the controller.[105]

In situations of employer functions split across multiple corporations, this reasoning leads to an inability to identify the appropriate employing entity or combination of entities subject to the relevant obligations. In the context of redundancy consultations, such wrong identification places obligations on parties other than those who are contemplating dismissals and will eventually take the relevant decisions. If consultative obligations are placed on an investee company alone, for example, the scope of consultation would become vastly under-inclusive in the Private Equity

100. Implemented in the United Kingdom by the Trade Union and Labour Relations (Consolidation) Act 1992, Part IV, Ch. II: Procedure, s. 188-198.
101. Collective Redundancies Directive (n. 99) [11].
102. Case C-44/2008 Akavan Erityisalojen Keskusliitto AEK ry and Others v. Fujitsu Siemens Computers Oy [2009] ECR I-8163 (ECJ), AG[50].
103. *Ibid.* AG[35].
104. *Ibid.* [57] et seq.
105. *Ibid.* [59], [68].

context: it is at, or more precisely in the run-up to, the decision-making stage that consultation will be at its most effective, by making a broad range of information available to the decision maker. The PE analyst team preparing the redundancy decision will frequently not have access to information beyond the company's financial and strategic data. Its decision may therefore be inefficient, both in terms of its impact on employees and the financial performance of the fund, as there was no obligation to consult with worker representatives, who 'would be presented with a *fait accompli*, and the provision would be deprived of any practical effect.'[106]

§4.04 LEGISLATIVE AND JUDICIAL RESPONSES

In broad terms, English law's response to fissurised work has already been seen in the final subsection immediately above: employee-protective norms have failed to address many of the challenges arising from the fragmentation of employment across multiple entities. This should not be taken as a suggestion, however, that there are no measures in place to protect workers by going beyond the boundary of the legal entity. The following section sets out a series of examples from individual employment law, both at statute as well as the Common Law, before looking at the collective dimension.

[A] Individual Employment Law

Potential solutions to the problems arising from fragmented work in the individual domain can be found both at statute and common law. In preparation for discussion in the following section, it is important to note at the outset that whilst the models to be discussed all embody a functional approach to defining the employer at least to some extent, we cannot (yet) think of it as a coherent concept. The idea of looking to existing material for inspiration as to how a functional reconceptualisation might operate in practice, on the other hand, is not new. In 1990, Collins examined a range of piecemeal statutory interventions in search of a functional approach;[107] Fudge similarly found existing techniques in a number of statutory devices, notably those lifting corporate veils and ignoring privity for specific purposes in particular contexts,[108] as did Davies and Freedland.[109]

106. Case C-188/03 *Junk v. Kühnel* [2005] ECR I-885AG[60].
107. H Collins, 'Ascription of Legal Responsibility to Groups in Complex Patterns of Economic Integration' (1990) 53 The Modern Law Review 731, 738 ff.
108. J Fudge, 'The Legal Boundaries of the Employer, Precarious Workers, and Labour Protection' in G Davidov and B Langile (eds), *Boundaries and Frontiers of Labour Law* (Hart Publishing, Oxford 2006) 305.
109. P Davies and M Freedland, 'The Complexities of the Employing Enterprise' in G Davidov and B Langile (eds), *Boundaries and Frontiers of Labour Law* (Hart Publishing 2006).

[1] Statutory Avenues

A first statutory model can be found in the enforcement model of the National Minimum Wage Act 1998, section 34 of which is designed to ensure the protection of 'agency workers who are not otherwise "workers"'. Subsection two provides that:

> where this section applies, the other provisions of this Act shall have effect as if there were a worker's contract for the doing of the work by the agency worker made between the agency worker and—
>
> (a) whichever of the agent and the principal is responsible for paying the agency worker in respect of the work; or
> (b) if neither the agent nor the principal is so responsible, whichever of them pays the agency worker in respect of the work.

A tiered, functional approach is clearly visible in this provision: whoever is responsible for the exercise of the relevant employer function (providing pay), is under the primary obligation pursuant to subsection (2)(a). In the absence of clear responsibility, subsection 2(b) places responsibility on whichever entity actually effected the payments. It is furthermore not the only example of such regulation: a substantially identical approach applies in the working time provisions.[110]

A second potential solution can be found in the Health and Safety at Work Act 1957. This Act imposes a wide range of general duties on 'every employer to ensure, so far as is reasonably practicable, the health, safety and welfare at work of all his employees'.[111] Furthermore (and crucially for present purposes), employers are to 'conduct [their] undertaking[s] in such a way as to ensure, so far as is reasonably practicable, that persons not in [their] employment who may be affected thereby are not thereby exposed to risks to their health or safety'.[112] On the one hand, this approach evidently still differentiates between employees defined in a narrow sense as working under a contract of employment,[113] thus reinforcing formalistic distinctions. On the other, it also includes within its scope all those 'doing work', a category defined to include the self-employed.[114] For present purposes, the provisions can however be treated as identical: as Howes suggests, the sections impose the same kind of 'basic duty ... upon the defendant company to make sure that their business (undertaking) is operated (conducted) in such a way that employees and other people are not exposed to risk.'[115]

110. Working Time Regulations 1998, SI 1998/1833, reg 36.
111. Health and Safety at Work Act 1974 (HSWA), s. 2(1).
112. HSWA 1974, s. 3(1).
113. HSWA 1974, s. 53.
114. HSWA 1974, s. 52.
115. V Howes, 'Commentary: Duties and Liabilities under the Health and Safety at Work Act 1974: A Step Forward?' (2009) 38 Industrial Law Journal 306, 307; citing *R v. Gateway Foodmarkets Ltd* [1997] IRLR 189 (CA) and *R v. British Steel* [1995] IRLR 310 (CA).

[2] *Common Law Developments*

Judicial interpretation of the common law has similarly attempted to develop a number of interpretative responses to protect workers in multi-layered contractual relationships, albeit with varying degrees of success. Traces of a functional approach can be found, for example, in contract law, notably in the idea of implied contracts as already discussed in section §4.03[B][1], above. After the Court of Appeal's ruling in *James*,[116] however, leading commentators were quick to pronounce 'the end of the road for the implied contract' as a device to protect workers in multilateral employment scenarios.[117] Upon closer inspection, however, it is suggested that the *Aramis* enquiry could also be understood as a functional one,[118] insofar as it looks at the reality of the parties' actions, rather than the formal structure of their relationships.

Another avenue is the possibility of dual or joint and several liability in a multi-employer context, as discussed in *Viasystems v. Thermal Transfer*.[119] There, the claimant had contracted for the installation of air conditioning in his factory; the work was done by a range of subcontractors. When a negligent fitter's mate of one such subcontractor caused a flooding of the premises while under the supervision of another subcontractor's employee, the question as to the identity of his employer or employers arose for the purposes of vicarious liability. The Court of Appeal was clearly aware that it was operating in novel territory; after a detailed survey of the authorities, it found that traditional arguments in favour of single-entity liability were primarily based on unchallenged assumptions.[120] It therefore went explicitly on to embrace a functional approach, giving 'precedence to function over form',[121] in order to avoid 'an artificial choice required by an inflexible rule of law'.[122] On the facts, it was found that the relationships yielded dual control, i.e., that both the second and third subcontractors had exercised regulated employer functions.[123] Responsibility (in the sense of vicarious liability) fell in line with that: both employers were found to be liable for half the damage caused.

[B] Collective Labour Law

The concept of the employer can have an equally significant impact in that dimension of labour law, whether in the field of collective bargaining or in the course of industrial

116. James (n. 10).
117. E Brown, 'Protecting Agency Workers: Implied Contract or Legislation?' (2008) 37 Industrial Law Journal 178. M Wynn and P Leighton, 'Agency Workers, Employment Rights and the Ebb and Flow of Freedom of Contract' (2009) 72 The Modern Law Review 91.
118. *The Aramis* [1989] 1 Lloyd's Rep 213 (CA).
119. *Viasystems (Tyneside) Ltd v. Thermal Transfer (Northern) Ltd* [2005] EWCA Civ 1151, [2006] QB 510.
120. *Viasystems* (n. 119) [76] (Rix LJ); [12], [46] (May LJ).
121. *Viasystems* (n. 119) [55]; cf. also the references to function and purpose of the doctrine more broadly, e.g., [77]; R Stevens, 'A Servant of Two Masters' (2006) 122 LQR 201.
122. *Viasystems* (n. 119) [19].
123. *Viasystems* (n. 119) [79]–[80]. Rix LJ is somewhat more sceptical whether control is the only criterion, considering also the possibility of 'practical and structural considerations'.

disputes. The correct identification of the employer, for example, is an important criterion when determining the lawfulness of a strike. Under what is known colloquially as the 'Golden Formula',[124] any such action will only be protected if it is done 'in contemplation or furtherance of a trade dispute'.[125] This notably means that any strike can only be directed by workers against their immediate employer[126] – a provision which the courts have continuously interpreted in a narrow fashion clearly reminiscent of the received unitary concept of the employer.[127]

This approach to the concept of the employer was discussed in the European Court of Human Rights' recent scrutiny of the UK's ban on secondary action,[128] where the Strasbourg Court explicitly referred to the fact that the narrow single-entity focus embodied in current legislation:

> could make it easy for employers to exploit the law to their advantage through resort to various legal stratagems, such as de-localising work-centres, outsourcing work to other companies and adopting complex corporate structures in order to transfer work to separate legal entities or to hive off companies ... [as a result of which] trade unions could find themselves severely hampered in the performance of their legitimate, normal activities in protecting their members' interests.[129]

This, together with an earlier citation of the European Committee on Social Rights' concern that English law could prevent 'a union from taking action against the *de facto* employer if this was not the immediate employer',[130] provides a stark reminder that the concept of the employer continues to raise equally difficult question in the collective dimension.

§4.05 EVALUATION AND FUTURE PROSPECTS

As I have argued in *The Concept of the Employer*, in order to restore congruence to the application of employment law norms, that very concept must be reconceptualised as a more openly functional one. This section briefly sketches the contours of such a concept.

[A] Towards a Functional Concept of the Employer

Our conceptualisation of the concept of the employer needs to move from the current rigidly formalistic approach to a flexible, *functional* concept. In more concrete terms,

124. Wedderburn, *The Worker and the Law* (3rd edn., Penguin 1986) 520; B Simpson, 'A Not So Golden Formula: In Contemplation or Furtherance of a Trade Dispute After 1982' (1983) 46 The Modern Law Review 463, 476.
125. TULRCA s. 219(1).
126. TULRCA s. 244(1).
127. *Dimbleby v. NUJ* [1984] IRLR 161; *UCL NHS Trust v. UNISON* [1999] IRLR 31.
128. *National Union of Rail, Maritime and Transport Workers v. United Kingdom* (Application No. 31045/10) [2014] IRLR 467; for convincing criticism *see* A Bogg and K Ewing, 'The Implications of the *RMT* Case' (2014) 43 ILJ 221, 235ff.
129. *RMT v. UK* (n. 128) [98].
130. *RMT v. UK* (n. 128) [37].

the following working definition is offered in order to draw together a range of specific aspects to be discussed, below. It is suggested that employer should come to mean:

> the entity, or combination of entities, playing a decisive role in the exercise of relational employing functions, and regulated or controlled as such in each particular domain of employment law.

The account of functionalism proposed for purposes of identifying and defining the employer builds on the sociological concept of functional typologies, relying on the exercise of particular functions to determine the status of potential counterparties. A full exploration of the relevant sociological literature is beyond the scope of this article; the focus will instead be on Luca Nogler's writing in a very closely related area, applying different typological models to the determination of employee status.[131]

The key idea of this *functional approach* is to focus on the specific role different elements play in the relevant context, instead of looking at the mere absence or presence of predetermined factors.[132] The presence of a contract of employment (or other contract) can thus be an important indicator in particular fields (e.g., the obligation to pay wages), but it is by no means the only one. To adopt Nogler's language to the present proposal, a functional concept of the employer is one where the employing entity or entities are defined not via the absence or presence of a particular factor, but via the exercise of specific functions.[133] This exercise of specific functions extends to include a decisive role in their exercise, in order to take account of the judicial recognition in existing cases that as regards employer functions the right to play a decisive role in a particular function is as relevant as the actual exercise thereof.

The working definition suggests that the concept of the employer should be understood as the entity, or combination of entities, playing a decisive role in the exercise of relational employing functions, and regulated or controlled as such in each particular domain of employment law. There are several steps in putting this abstract conceptualisation into practice. First is the recognition that for each employee, a functional approach to different models of inter-entity relationships will lead to an *array* of potential employing entities, from which one or several may emerge as employers. Being within this array of potential counterparties does not automatically bring any specific set of employment law obligations with it, even less so responsibility for the full domain of labour regulation. It is only as a consequence of the exercise of a particular regulated function that employer responsibilities are triggered; limited, however, to the relevant domain or domains.

The array of those with a decisive role in management, particularly as regards the exercise of employer functions, will vary depending on the context in which the employing enterprises are organised. In triangular employment relationships, for example, it includes both agency and end user, despite their difference in organisational integration or economic interest alignment. In a Private Equity setting, both the 'immediate' employer (i.e., the portfolio company) and the PE management company

131. Nogler (n. 16). The following paragraphs draw extensively on this article and related work.
132. *Ibid.* pt 3.
133. *Ibid.* 463.

will find themselves within the array. It may also extend further, including for example a franchisor with very tight control over the operations of a particular franchisee.[134] Under the traditional approach, privity (or at most a specific statutory extension) would select the employer from this array of entities potentially able to exercise employer functions. In the reconceptualised concept of the employer, this role is replaced by the exercise of various functions. As a result, different employers may bear (or share) a range of obligations, depending always on their specific roles.

§4.06 CONCLUSION: RESTORING COHERENCE IN A FISSURED WORLD

In conclusion, at least three observations should be made on the basis of the foregoing examples of a reconceptualised concept of the employer in action: first, that employment law obligations may be spread across multiple legal entities. This is the core of the reconceptualisation's challenge to received concepts of the employer as a single entity. Second, as the functions of the employer can be subdivided into distinct groups, the employer is no longer exclusively defined as an entity exercising a single and simple function comprising all elements identified: exercising a particular subset of employer functions may suffice to trigger responsibility in that regard. Which of the functions are relevant depends on the particular area of legal regulation: the third implication of the functional approach proposed is that the attribution of responsibility will differ across distinct domains within employment law.

At first glance, it might be thought that a fundamental reconceptualisation of the concept of the employer would require significant innovation in both statutory design and the courts' adjudication. As section §4.04 has demonstrated, however, that is not necessarily the case. Indeed, it is hoped that there is relatively little, if any, need for radical innovation or departure from existing frameworks to achieve the functional outcome proposed. Many if not all of the required techniques can already be found in various pockets of case law, driven by seeds of the functional approach just described. Depending on fact patterns and the purpose of the relevant area of employment legislation, a combination of techniques already found in the law of the contract of employment and the many statutory extensions to it could be developed to give employment law scope functional flexibility in complex multilateral of fissured employment scenarios.

134. D Weil, *Fissured Employment* (Presentation given at the 2011 ISA Meetings, Pittsburgh, PA, May 2011).

APPENDIX: FURTHER READING IN *THE CONCEPT OF THE EMPLOYER*

Elements of this Report	Corresponding Passages
2: Identifying the Employer	
(i) A Unitary Strand	Chapter 1, section 1
(ii) A Multi-Functional Strand	Chapter 1, section 2
3. Fissurised Work in the United Kingdom Today	
(i) Agency Work	Chapter 2, section 1
(ii) Private Equity	Chapter 2, section 2
B. Implications for the Scope of Employment Law Coverage	
(i) Breakdown of Employment Law Coverage	Chapter 3, section 1 Chapter 3, section 2
(ii) Incomplete and Incoherent Coverage	
4. Legislative and Judicial Responses	
(i) Statutory Avenues	Chapter 5, section 2B
(ii) Common Law Developments	Chapter 5, section 2A
5. Evaluation and Future Prospects	
A. Towards a Functional Concept of the Employer	Chapter 5, section 1

CHAPTER 5

Reconsidering the Notion of 'Employer' in the Era of the Fissured Workplace in Germany: Should Labour Law Responsibilities Exceed the Boundaries of the Legal Entity?

Bernd Waas[*]

§5.01 INTRODUCTION

In his book '*The Fissured Workplace*', the author *David Weil* makes the case that large corporations in the United States (US) have shed their role as direct employers of the people responsible for their products, in favour of outsourcing work to small companies that often compete fiercely with one another resulting in an erosion of terms and conditions of work. This chapter will discuss to what extent such fissurisation also has been taking place in Germany and what the responses of the legislator and the courts are.

§5.02 EMPLOYEE AND EMPLOYER: BASIC INFORMATION AND RECENT DEVELOPMENTS

[A] The Notion of 'Employee'

[1] Basic Elements

In Germany, no statutory definition of the term 'contract of employment' (*Arbeitsvertrag*) exists. It is basically undisputed, however, that a contract of

* Goethe University of Frankfurt.

employment is a sub-category of the so-called service contract (*Dienstvertrag*).[1] A 'service contract', as legally defined in section 611(1) of the Civil Code (*Bürgerliches-Gesetzbuch*), is a contract on the basis of which 'a person is obliged to perform work [sub-ordinated or not] in exchange for remuneration owed to him by another person'. What makes a contract of employment a specific case, is the fact that there is personal subordination (*persönliche Abhängigkeit*) between the service provider and the other party to the contract in the sense that an employee in the performance of his or her duties is directed by another person, the employer. According to the Federal Labour Court, it is this very personal dependence that formed 'one of the essential reasons for the development and strengthening of labour law'.[2] In 'measuring' whether a person is sufficiently subordinated to justify the relationship with another person to be qualified as an employment relationship, the Federal Labour Court employs the so-called typological method. This means that an 'evaluating general assessment' (*wertendeGesamtbetrachtung*) forms the basis of legally qualifying the contract: the courts in deciding individual cases, take a 'holistic view' on whether a person qualifies as an 'employee'.[3] What is required when determining personal subordination varies from one case to the other. When determining the legal nature of a contract, the courts in any event apply the principle of 'primacy of facts'. The courts ask, in other words, what the 'true nature' of the contract is, irrespective of its 'labelling' by the parties.[4] In the view of the Federal Labour Court, it would harm the basic idea of employment law as an instrument of protecting employees from the (regularly economically more powerful) employer, if the latter could set aside this protection by simply using contractual language that points into the direction of, for instance, a 'free service contract' (*freierDienstvertrag*), that is a 'service contract' not leading to subordination. The only thing that matters therefore is the 'real content' of the contract to be derived from its practical implementation.[5] It is worth noting from the start that the principle of 'primacy of facts' not only applies to determining whether there is an employment relationship between two parties but the principle also applies if the courts examine the question whether employees of a subcontractor who work on the premises of an entrepreneur are vicarious agents of that subcontractor or temporary agency workers. To put it into the words of the Federal Labour Court: 'Legal qualification of a contract as a contract to temporarily assign workers (...) is dependent on its real business content. If practical implementation of the contracts differs from the contractual language, the former will prevail (...).'[6]

1. Critical, however, *Greiner*, Erfolgsbezogene Vergütungenim Arbeitsverhältnis – oder: der Arbeitsvertragalsspezieller Werkvertrag?, in: Recht der Arbeit 2015, p. 218 pointing to the fact that agreements on performance-related remuneration may render contracts of employments rather specific cases of so-called contracts to produce a work within the meaning of s. 631(1) of the Civil Code.
2. Federal Labour Court of 15.03.1978 – 5 AZR 819/76, explicitly referring to the labour law scholar *Alfred Hueck*.
3. Federal Labour Court of 23.04.1980 – 5 AZR 426/794.
4. *See*, for instance, Federal Labour Court of 19.11.1997 – 5 AZR 653/96.
5. Federal Labour Court of 19.11.1997 – 5 AZR 653/96.
6. Federal Labour Court of 27.01.1993– 7 AZR 476/92.

[2] Recent Developments

For quite a while, trade unions, in particular, claim that employers in Germany have increasingly been making use of 'ordinary civil law contracts' in order to avoid the application of labour law.[7] On an abstract level, it is relatively easy to identify a contract of employment, since these contracts are characterised by subordination or control. If there is a lack of that, the contract is a so-called free service contract. At first sight, it is even easier to differentiate between a contract of employment and a so-called contract to produce a work (*Werkvertrag*), since (only) the latter is 'result-oriented'. According to the legal definition in section 631(1) of the Civil Code, 'by a contract to produce a work, a contractor is obliged to produce the promised work and the customer is obliged to pay the agreed remuneration'.[8] A closer look reveals, however, that the differentiation issue is a tricky one.[9] The reasons for this are twofold: First, almost every duty to provide a service can, at least in theory, be 'translated' into a duty to provide a work (within the meaning of section 631(1) of the Civil Code). Second, the parties to the contract can considerably diminish the need for establishing control by fixing the tasks of the provider of a service in much detail in the contract itself.[10] Apart from that, there are practical problems when having to demonstrate that one person is subordinated to another in the course of his or her contractual performance. Specific problems arise in this regard if a line has to be drawn between temporary agency work on the one hand and a civil law contract concluded between two companies with the obligations of the debtor being fulfilled by his or her staff:[11] If work is performed in a given establishment by workers employed by another company, it will often be doubtful whether these workers are mere auxiliary persons of that company in fulfilling its contractual duties, or temporary agency workers assigned to the company running the establishment.

7. According to a survey of the metal workers' union IG Metall, 70 p.c. of all companies surveyed use civil law contracts; *see also Bonin/Zierahn*, MachbarkeitsstudiezurErfassung der Verbreitung und Problemlagen der Nutzung von Werkverträgen (BundesministeriumfürArbeit und Soziales), Mannheim, 2012. The use of 'ordinary civil law contracts' may also have been prompted by recent restrictions of temporary agency work as the result of some legislative reforms and court decisions; *see Hamann/Rudnik*: ScheinwerkvertragmitÜberlassungserlaubnis – Ein probates MittelzurVermeidungillegalerArbeitnehmerüberlassung?, in: NeueZeitschriftfürArbeitsrecht 2015, p. 449. However, some authors are hesitant in acknowledging an increased use of civil law contracts; *see*, in particular, *Henssler*, Überregulierung statt Rechtssicherheit – der Referentenentwurf des BMAS zur Reglementierung von Leiharbeit und Werkverträgen, in: Recht der Arbeit 2016, p. 18.
8. Section 631(2) adds that the 'subject matter of a contract to produce a work may be either the production or alteration of a thing or another result to be achieved by work or by a service'.
9. *See* for a more detailed discussion *Waas*, Werkvertrag, freierDienstvertrag und Arbeitsvertrag: Abgrenzung und IdentifikationimdeutschenRecht und in ausländischenRechtsordnungen, 2012: http://www.boeckler.de/pdf_fof/S-2011-477-3-1.pdf.
10. If the content of the service is fixed in detail in the contract between the parties and thus no instructions are needed to substantiate it, then no employment contract may exist; *see* Federal Labour Court of 30.10.1991 - 7 ABR 19/91, highly critical *Preis*, in: ErfurterKommentarzumArbeitsrecht, 16th ed., 2016, § 611 BGB note 52.
11. *See Hamann*, in Schüren/Hamann (ed.), Arbeitnehmerüberlassungsgesetz, 4th ed., 2010, § 1 AÜG notes 107 et seqq.; *Waas*, in: Thüsing (ed), Arbeitnehmerüberlassungsgesetz, 3rd ed., 2012, notes 59 et seqq.

The problem of differentiation between employment contracts and ordinary civil law contracts forms the subject of a fierce debate among legal scholars.[12] The courts have been struggling with the issue, too.[13] In November 2015, the competent Ministry put forward a Draft Act that aims to prevent a possible misuse of contracts to produce a work by employers. For the first time, indicators would have been introduced into statutory labour law to be used by the courts when determining the existence of an employment relationship.[14] According to the draft, it points to an employment relationship if: a person (a) is not allowed to decide on his or her working time, the owed services or his or her workplace; (b) a person predominantly renders his or her services at the premises of others; (c) regularly uses the resources of third parties for rendering owed services; (d) renders his or her services together with others who are deployed or charged by a another party; (e) works exclusively or predominantly for another party; (f) does not own an operational organisation to render the owed services; (g) renders his or her services without these services aiming at manufacturing or reaching a specific work product or a specific work result; (h) does not guarantee the result of his work. However, in January 2016, the Ministry withdrew its Draft amid protests from business, in particular.[15] Instead of fixing indicators, the present Draft does no more than repeat the general definition of a contract of employment as developed by the Courts. A consensus on this Draft was reached within the ruling Coalition government in May.

[B] Notion of 'Employer'

[1] Basic Elements

While German legal doctrine is rich with regard to the notion of 'employee', the legal concept of 'employer' has been somewhat neglected. As is the case with the term 'employee', there is no statutory definition of the term 'employer'. The courts derive the content of the term indirectly from the term 'employee', stressing that the legal concept of employment law is basically devised from the perspective of the employee.[16] According to the Federal Labour Court, 'an employer is a person who employs at least

12. *See*, for instance, *Brors/Schüren*, NeuegesetzlicheRahmenbedingungenfür den Fremdpersonaleinsatz, in: NeueZeitschriftfürArbeitsrecht, 2014, p. 569; *Deinert*, Kernbelegschaften - Randbelegschaften - Fremdbelegschaften, in: Recht der Arbeit 2014, p. 65.
13. *See*, for instance, Federal Labour Court of 18.01.2012– 7 AZR 723/10 (temporary agency work and contract of service); Federal Labour Court of 15.04.2014 - 3 AZR 395/11 (temporary agency work and contract of service/contract to produce a work); Federal Labour Court of 25.09.2013 - 10 AZR 282/12 (employment contract and contract to produce a work).
14. In social security law, many years ago, a presumption (s. 7(4) of Social Code IV) was introduced by the legislator based on similar indicators to be quickly abolished amid protests, however.
15. Critical too, for instance, *Baeck/Winzer/Kramer*, NeuereEntwicklungenimArbeitsrecht, in: NeueZeitschriftfürGesellschaftsrecht 2016, p. 20; *Schüren/Fasholz*: Inhouse-Outsourcing und der Diskussionsentwurfzum AÜG - EinDiskussionsbeitrag, in: NeueZeitschriftfürArbeitsrecht 2015, p. 1473 (the latter with specific regard to the position of temporary agency workers); *Henssler*, Überregulierung statt Rechtssicherheit - der Referentenentwurf des BMAS zur Reglementierung von Leiharbeit und Werkverträgen, in: Recht der Arbeit 2016, p. 18.
16. Federal Labour Court of 21.011999 - 2 AZR 648/97.

one employee'.[17] Every (natural or legal person) can qualify as an employer. On the other hand, a group of companies as such cannot be the employer since it lacks the quality of a legal entity.[18]

Employees often have more than one employer. This is certainly true in Germany, since so-called mini-jobs where by the employee earns no more than EUR 450 per month are widespread.[19] These situations do not pose major problems as different employment relationships can easily exist 'in parallel'. A case in point is employment with one employer and (lawful) secondary employment with another, the latter often taking the form of a mini-job. As opposed to this situation, there are cases where a true 'multi-employer' set-up exists in the sense that one employee with regard to his or her single employment relationship faces more than one employer.[20] In that case, there will often be joint and several liability[21] as well as joint and several creditorship on the part of employers.[22] In this context, the question can arise, for instance, who enjoys the right to direct the employee. If the parties to the contract did not clearly assign this power to one single person, then every employer is presumed to be able to make use of it. The employee then complies with his or her obligation to work by following the instructions of this particular person.[23]

[2] Recent Developments

The notion of 'employer' has always been dependent on the notion of 'employee'. This being the case, uncertainties as to the qualification as 'employee' necessarily impact on whether the partner to the contract qualifies as employer. Recently, the notion of 'employer' became further blurred, because of developments that could be referred to as fissurisation of the workplace. These developments will now be discussed in more detail.

17. Federal Labour Court of 21.01.1999 – 2 AZR 648/9; *see also* Federal Labour Court of 09.09.1982 – 2 AZR 253/80, stating that 'employer is the other party to the employment relationship, thus he who can demand work from the employee under the employment contract (...)'.
18. *See Richardi*, in Richardi al. (ed.), MünchenerHandbuchzumArbeitsrecht, vol. 1, 3rd ed., 2009, § 23 note 1.
19. The system of mini-jobs was developed to allow companies to hire *staff without heavy social insurance obligations*, making it easier for part-time workers to take on another side job.
20. It should be noted that there is no such 'multi-employer'-set-up if a person is employed by a partnership under civil (*GesellschaftbürgerlichenRechts*), since such partnership is regarded by the courts as enjoying a limited legal capacity; *see* Federal Civil Court of 29.01.2001 – II ZR 331/00.
21. *See* s. 427 of the Civil Code: 'If more than one person jointly binds himself by a contract to render divisible performance then, in case of doubt, they are liable as joint and several debtors.'
22. *See* s. 428 of the Civil Code: 'If more than one person is entitled to demand performance in such a way that each may demand the entire performance but the obligor is only obliged to effect the performance once (joint and several creditors), the obligor may at his discretion effect performance to each of the obligees. This also applies if one of the obligees has already sued for performance.'
23. *See Lange*, Mehrfacharbeitsverhältnisse – NichtnurFabelwesen, in: NeueZeitschriftfürArbeitsrecht, 2012, p. 1121 (1122).

§5.03 CURRENT SITUATION OF FISSURISATION

[A] Groups of Companies

'Fissurisation' of the workplace has taken different forms in Germany. A relatively old phenomenon is employment of workers within a group of companies. The legal problems that come with such employment have recently become even more accentuated since companies have increasingly been using so-called matrix-structures. In a matrix, certain corporate functions are concentrated at one group company, while they are reduced or even completely abolished in other group companies. Moreover, there is a group-wide breakdown by function and production areas. As a result, reporting lines and the rights to issue functional instructions are assigned due to economic realities overriding classic business structures as well as contractual arrangements.[24] But then again, the right to issue instructions other than functional ones remains largely with the contractual employer. This includes, for instance, granting of holiday and giving warnings or notice. In other words, the power to direct, which for its part is the defining element of an employment relationship, is split (between the contractual employer and the functional employer).

Matrix organisations offer a couple of advantages. Among them are shorter lines of communication, more flexibility for management, more focused leadership (with less burden on the top of management) and priority of substance-specific competence without regard for hierarchical levels. There are also drawbacks. This is particularly true from the point of employees, as they may often find themselves in a position of being responsible towards a company that is not their employer.

[B] Contracting-Out

As has already been said, there are claims that companies recently have been making increasing use of 'ordinary' civil law contracts instead of contracts of employment. Civil law contracts are mostly used in the context of subcontracting. Such subcontracting can take the form of a contract concluded between the parties and involving only these parties. Such situation then leads to the question whether the contract, on the basis of the application of the principle of 'primacy of facts', qualifies as a contract of employment. It seems that quite a few employers entered into such contracts with former employees[25] – a problem often referred to as 'new self-employment' (*neueSelbständigkeit*) in Germany.[26] More often subcontracting will take the form of one

24. This, for instance, can lead to problems when it comes to a possible transfer of undertakings as it will often be difficult to determine whether a certain worker belongs to the entity that is being transferred; ***see*** *Mückl*, Betriebsübergang und Matrix-Struktur – Welche Arbeitnehmer sind erfasst?, in: Der Betrieb 2015, p. 2695.
25. According to Federal Labour Court of 13.03.2008 – 2 AZR 1037/06, the entrepreneurial decision to outsource certain tasks that were formerly performed by employees can form the basis of a lawful redundancy.
26. For instance, in many slaughterhouses, one would find high numbers of so-called stand-alone self-employed persons (*Soloselbständige*) instead of employees.

company concluding a business contract with another company with the obligations of that company actually being performed by its employees. If a company outsources some (subsidiary) facilities to another, the issue arises whether the courts will acknowledge the existence of a business contract. As the principle of 'primacy of facts' also applies in these situations, the 'real nature' of the contract must be determined. The question is this: Is the contract in question a business contract, whose obligations are fulfilled by vicarious agents, or is it 'in reality' a contract that obliges the other company to provide employees? If the latter is true, the workers qualify as agency workers temporarily assigned to another company.

The first type of contracting-out may be motivated by an attempt of employers to escape the application of the rules of labour law. Considerations of tax and social security may also play a role. The second type of contracting-out will often be the result of 'genuine business considerations', for instance, an effort to focus on the particular strength in one field and to make the most of the strengths of other companies in areas that do not form part of the core business. However, labour law considerations may also be relevant, since contracting-out does offer an opportunity to escape duties arising from the position of 'employer'. Moreover, contracting-out offers the prospect of getting better conditions with regard to collective agreements. A case in point is contract logistics: In the more recent past, companies, for instance in the car industry, have increasingly moved work to logistic providers. At the same time, these companies are often not limited to providing mere logistics services anymore, but have extended their offerings to plant preassembly and subsequent 'plug-in status delivery'. The cost advantages involved are huge as, for instance, the minimum hourly wage in the metal and electronics industry (within the competence of the industry-sector-wide trade union *IG Metall*) is above EUR 14, while the medium hourly wage in the logistics industry (in the realm of the service-sector trade union *VERDI*) is above EUR 12. From this point of view, it must be noted that the two trade unions recently entered into a cooperation agreement setting out criteria for demarcation. According to this agreement, in the future IG Metall will, for instance, be competent if at least 75 p.c. of the activities of a logistics provider aim at an end customer that falls into the original organisational area of this trade union.[27]

[C] Supply Chains

Supply chains are a common feature of modern economies. Improving work conditions in global supply chains, in particular, has become one of the most important challenges in both national and international labour law.[28] These supply chains are permanently influx. For instance, car manufacturers who in the past used to dominate the suppliers of components, face the prospect of being forced into collaborating with the likes of

27. *See*: https://www.igmetall.de/kontraktlogistik-18244.htm.
28. *See*, for instance, the G7 efforts in addressing the root causes in global supply chains by creating the multi-donor 'Vision Zero Fund' for action in producing countries.

Google and Apple in the future.[29] There are undoubtedly many reasons for the wide use of supply chains. Even if it is not (primarily) motivated by labour law considerations, problems do arise in this regard, as for instance there is concern that employees' rights may be diminished by 'spreading' tasks over a long chain of different companies.

[D] Franchising

In Germany, franchising is widespread.[30] There are two major forms to be distinguished: subordination franchise on the one hand and cooperative franchise on the other. The latter is a relationship of partnership and cooperation. The former is characterised by a relationship of subordination between franchisor and franchisee. In that case, the franchise basically is an instrument within the marketing strategy of the franchisor.[31] The distinction between the two forms is often rather a matter of degree. In practice, subordination franchise seems to be the main form in Germany in any event.[32]

§5.04 RESPONSES BY THE LEGISLATOR AND THE COURTS

[A] Groups of Companies

Specific problems arise if an employee is employed by a company that belongs to a group of companies. What constitutes a 'group of companies' (*Konzern*) is defined in the Stock Corporation Act (*Aktiengesetz*).[33] This company law term also applies in

---

29. *See Weisser/Färber*: RechtlicheRahmenbedingungenbei Connected Car – Überblicküber die Rechtsprobleme der automobilenZukunft, in: MultiMedia und Recht 2015, p. 506.
30. Though *Commission Regulation (EEC) No 4087/88 of 30.11.1988 on the application of cartel law to categories of franchise agreements is not in force anymore, its definition of a 'franchise' is still widely regarded as useful.* According to Article 1(3) lit. a) '"franchise" means a package of industrial or intellectual property rights relating to trade marks, trade names, shop signs, utility models, designs, copyrights, know-how or patents, to be exploited for the resale of goods or the provision of services to end users'. According to Article 1(3) lit. b) '"franchise agreement" means an agreement whereby one undertaking, the franchisor, grants the other, the franchisee, in exchange for direct or indirect financial consideration, the right to exploit a franchise for the purposes of marketing specified types of goods and/or services; it includes at least obligations relating to: the use of a common name or shop sign and a uniform presentation of contract premises and/or means of transport, the communication by the franchisor to the franchisee of know-how, the continuing provision by the franchisor to the franchisee of commercial or technical assistance during the life of the agreement'.
31. *See*, for instance *Martinek/Habermeier*, in: Martinek/Semler/Habermeier/Flohr, Vertriebsrecht (ed.), 3rd ed., 2010, § 26 note 21.
32. *Graf von Westphalen*, in: Westphalen (ed.), Vertragsrecht und AGB-Klauselwerke, 2015, Teil 'Klauselwerke' note 4.
33. Section 18 of the Stock Corporation Act (*Aktiengesetz*) on 'Groups and Members of Groups' reads as follows:

    (1) If a controlling and one or more controlled enterprises are subject to the common direction of the controlling enterprise, such enterprises shall constitute a group and the individual enterprises shall constitute members of such group. If enterprises are parties to a control agreement (section 291) or if one enterprise has been integrated into the

labour law. The starting point of the legal assessment is the recognition that the group as such is not the employer. As has already been pointed out, an employer-position is generally considered out of the question, since the group as such has no legal personality and, accordingly, cannot be a party to a contract. However, the fact that the employer belongs to a group of companies and, consequently, that a contract of employment a group company is a party to, in one way or another relates to the group, will often influence its content. The best example of this are clauses often included in such contracts that allow the employer to either temporarily second the worker to another group company, or to temporarily send him or her to another group company, or to hire him or her out to such company. During such secondment, posting or hiring-out, the employment relationship with the hiring company remains fully valid. No (parallel or even exclusive) employment relationship with the other company is presumed to exist. Even so, a third party obviously becomes involved in the employment relationship. Accordingly, secondment, posting or hiring-out are only allowed, if there is a sound basis in the contract of employment. In principle, this is only the case, if either the worker was hired to perform his or her duties within the group from the outset, or if the employer has reserved the right to make the worker available for other group companies, or if the parties to the employment contract consented to amend the contract accordingly. And regardless of the contractual basis, the concrete decision of the employer to make the worker available for another company must meet the standards of good faith and is subject to judicial review.[34]

Another question is whether and to what extent the law takes a possible 'group dimension' of the employment relationship into account. A more detailed legal analysis shows that this is only partly the case. Take, for instance, application of the so-called employment law principle of equal treatment (*arbeitsrechtlicher Gleichbehandlungsgrundsatz*): As in many other jurisdictions, German law provides for an obligation of the employer not to discriminate workers without objective reason. The legal basis is the principle of equal treatment that has been developed by the courts and is generally considered to form customary law.[35] Originally, the Federal Labour Court assumed that

other (section 319), such enterprises shall be deemed to be subject to common management. A controlled enterprise and its controlling enterprise shall be presumed to constitute a group. (2) If legally separate enterprises are subject to common direction, although none of such enterprises controls the other, such enterprises shall constitute a group and the individual enterprises shall constitute members of such group.

34. *See* s. 315(1) of the Civil Code (*BürgerlichesGesetzbuch*): '(1) Where performance is to be specified by one of the parties to the contract, then in case of doubt it is to be assumed that the specification is to be made at the reasonably exercised discretion of the party making it.'
35. In substance, it is closely related to the constitutional principle of equality as laid down in Article 3(1) of the Basic Law, the German Constitution. Article 3(1) of the German Constitution (*Grundgesetz*): 'All persons shall be equal before the law'. As all other fundamental rights, except Article 9(3) enshrining freedom of association, Article 3(1) of the Constitution is not 'horizontally' applicable which means that it needs to be specifically 'implemented' in order to be applied to private law relationships like employment relationships; *see*, for instance, Federal Labour Court of 22.12.2009 - 3 AZR 136/08 (note 39): 'The employment law principle of equal treatment is the private law expression of the principle of equality as set forth in Art. 3(1) of the Constitution.'

such duty was limited to workers in a given undertaking. This was justified by the Court by pointing to a specific 'closeness' of workers belonging to a single establishment.[36] Later, the Court modified its position and held that employers had in principle to treat all employees in the company equally.[37] A 'group-related' obligation on the part of the employer, however, is in principle rejected by the Court. In support, the Court points to the fact that companies belonging to the same group form different legal entities, and that the employment law principle of equal treatment serves only the purpose of ensuring equal treatment of workers by their joint employer.[38] Accordingly, a 'group-related' obligation of equal treatment can exist in exceptional cases only.[39]

As for dismissal protection, the position is similar. Under German law, a compulsory redundancy is inadmissible if the workers could be further employed, either in the same establishment or in another which belongs to the same company. Section 1(2) of the Act on Dismissal Protection (*Kündigungsschutzgesetz*) expressly provides that the protection against dismissal is 'company-related', that is to say that it is not restricted to the establishment concerned. Alternative employment opportunities within the group, in contrast, are in principle irrelevant.[40] However, in exceptional cases it may be different. For instance, a 'group-related' obligation of further employment may exist if a company that belongs to the same group explicitly offers the opportunity of further employment or if an obligation to transfer the worker either directly arises from the contract of employment (or another agreement), or if the employer has made a promise to this effect.[41] In any event, it is required that the employer is in a position to ensure further employment with the other company. The decision, to offer further employment may in other words not be one solely for the other company to take.[42] Recently, the Federal Labour Court stressed again that 'an obligation of the employer to try to ensure further employment with another group company, before giving notice' does exist in 'exceptional cases' only. Moreover, the

36. Federal Labour Court of 26.04.1966 – 1 AZR 242/65.
37. Federal Labour Court of 17.11.1998 – 1 AZR 147/98, Federal Labour Court of 03.12.2008 – 5 AZR 74/08.
38. Federal Labour Court of 20.08.1986 – 4 AZR 272/85.
39. If, for instance, the mother company takes responsibility for granting certain benefits and instructs the group companies accordingly, then a 'group-wide' duty of equal treatment may apply; *see Preis*, in: ErfurterKommentarzumArbeitsrecht, 16th ed., 2016, § 611 BGB note 199. A 'piercing of the corporate veil' can take place if certain requirements are met; *see*, for instance, Federal Labour Court of 15.03.2011 –1 ABR 87/09. The Federal Labour Court in this regard follows the rules that have been developed by the Federal Civil Court; *see Müller-Glöge*, in: MünchenerKommentarzum BGB, 6th ed. 2012, § 611 BGB VertragstypischePflichtenbe-imDienstvertragnote 248.
40. *See* Federal Labour Court of 23.11.2004 – 2 AZR 24/04: 'Dismissal protection, in principle, is related to the establishment and, as far as the possibility of further employment is concerned, to the company. (...). The possibility of further employment, in principle, is not related to groups of companies.'
41. According to the Federal Labour Court, an obligation to offer further employment with another company may also be derived from past practice; *see* Federal Labour Court of 23.04.2008 – 2 AZR 1110/06.
42. Federal Labour Court of 23.11.2004 – 2 AZR 24/04.

burden of proving that there is a possibility of further employment is essentially on the employee.[43]

As already mentioned, so-called matrix-structures have been on the rise recently among groups of companies. Labour lawyers are still struggling with the problems posed by them.[44] While it is beyond doubt, that employers are free to establish these structures, there is dissent on how far the position of employees affected by these structures must be protected. Some authors, for instance, argue that the law in any event prevents the employer from transferring his or her power to direct without the consent of the employee.[45] Others are of the opinion that no change of 'ownership' of the power to direct is required as the other company could simply be authorised (*Ermächtigung*) by the contractual employer to make use of it. In the past, the Federal Labour Court, in any event, imposed relatively low requirements for a transfer of the power to direct.[46] It is doubtful, however, whether that is still true. Practically speaking, it is recommendable for employers to address the issue by making explicit provision for a (partial) transfer to another company. Another question is whether and to what extent the 'functional employer' is bound by provisions of labour law. Again, the legal position is far from clear. It is argued, however, that the (functional) power to direct, if 'transferred' to another company, must come with according obligations so as to ensuring that the interests of the worker subjected to that power are taken into proper consideration when making use of it.[47]

Specific problems arise if workers are hired out within a group of companies. In group settings section 1(2) no. 2 of the Act on Temporary Agency Work (*Arbeitnehmerüberlassungsgesetz*), the so-called intra-group exemption, is relevant. According to this provision, the Act basically does not apply to a hiring-out between group companies if the worker has not been taken into employment with the exclusive aim of later being hired-out. The Act does apply, on the other hand, if workers are hired by one group company whose exclusive business purpose is to act as a 'group temporary agency' (*reinePersonalführungsgesellschaft*).[48] Whether and to what extent the Act is

---

43. If such employee refers to a relocation clause, it is in principle up to him/her to show at which company and at which workplace further employment would be possible; *see* Federal Labour Court of 24.05.2012 – 2 AZR 62/11.
44. *See*, for instance, *Henssler*, 1. DeutscherArbeitsrechtstag – Generalbericht, in: NeueZeitschrift fürArbeitsrecht-Beilage (Supplement) 2014, p. 95.
45. In this context, s. 613 sentence 2 of the Civil Code is often referred to. This provision reads as follows: 'The party under a duty of service must in case of doubt render the services in person. The claim to services is, in case of doubt, not transferable.'
46. Federal Labour Court of 10.03.1998 – 1 AZR 658/97.
47. *See*, in particular, *Henssler*, 1. DeutscherArbeitsrechtstag – Generalbericht, in: NeueZeitschriftfürArbeitsrecht-Beilage (Supplement) 2014, p. 95 (101). Our discussion of matrix organisations is limited to questions of individual labour law. As regards matters belonging to the works constitution *see*, for instance, *Kort*, Matrix-Strukturen und Betriebsverfassungsrecht, in: NeueZeitschriftfürArbeitsrecht 2013, p. 1318. It is subject to debate, in any event, whether and to what extent current rules can cope with an increasing decentralisation of management decisions within matrix organisations or otherwise; *see*, *Rieble*, Mitbestimmung in komplexenBetriebs- und Unternehmensstrukturen, in: NeueZeitschriftfürArbeitsrecht-Beilage (Supplement) 2014, p. 28.
48. *See*, for instance, *Wank*, in: Dietericha.o., ErfurterKommentarzum, Arbeitsrecht, 16th ed., 2016, § 1 AÜG notes 31, 34a and 57a.

applicable in other group settings, is far from clear, however. This is all the more so since some authors argue that the 'intra-group exemption' as such does not conform with EU law and should have been completely abolished when the German legislator implemented the underlying EU Directive.[49]

[B] Contracting-Out

Whether or not certain tasks should be contracted-out, is for management to decide. The right to conclude business contracts with other companies is part of freedom of contract as well as part of freedom of entrepreneurship. As the German Constitution protects both,[50] the right to conclude business contracts with others can in principle not be limited.

Without directly limiting this power, the legislator has responded to contracting-out in two ways: by fixing a secondary liability of contractors with regard to certain labour law obligations and by enlarging the rights of works councils. Secondary liability can arise on two occasions. First, such liability arises under the Act on Posting of Workers (*Arbeitnehmerentsendegesetz*) which permits the state to declare collective agreements generally binding. According to section 14 sentence 1 of the Act, an entrepreneur who commissioned another entrepreneur with the provision of work or services, is liable for payment of the minimum wage to employees by a contractor, a subcontractor or a lender commissioned by the contractor or a subcontractor as a guarantor.[51] The purpose of section 14 of the Act is to ensure that companies commissioned by an entrepreneur actually pay the minimum wage. The provision applies to all companies belonging to the entrepreneurial chain. This means that an entrepreneur is also liable for any subcontractor of his or her direct sub-contractor.[52] The Federal Constitutional Court has held that section 14 is in conformity with the Constitution even though liability does not depend on fault or negligence. Though section 14 of the Act impacts on freedom of entrepreneurship as enshrined in Article 12 of the Basic Law, it conforms with the Constitution, since protection of workers is a legitimate aim, especially in light of Article 20 of the Constitution which contains the

49. *See*, for instance, *Böhm*, Umsetzung der EU-Leiharbeitsrichtlinie – mit *Fragezeichen*?!, in: Der Betrieb 2011, p. 473; *Wank*, in: Dietericha.o., ErfurterKommentarzum, Arbeitsrecht, 16th ed., 2016, § 1 AÜG note 57 (with further references). *See* in this context also ECJ of 21.10.2010 – Case C-242/09 (Albron Catering BV) according to which in the event of a transfer within the meaning of Council Directive 2001/23/EC of 12 March 2001, it is also possible to regard as a 'transferor', within the meaning of Article 2(1)(a) of that directive, the group company to which the employees were assigned on a permanent basis without however being linked to the latter by a contract of employment, even though there exists within that group an undertaking with which the employees concerned were linked by such a contract of employment.
50. Articles 2(1) and 12(2) of the Basic Law.
51. *See* in this regard also *Yorens* et al., Study on the protection of workers' rights in subcontracting processes in the European Union, 2012, pp. 47 and 52. Apart from that the Act imposes sanctions in cases of failing to grant minimum working conditions by either the principal contractor or subcontractor, even if this did not happen deliberately but negligently; *see*, in particular s. 23 in conjunction with s. 8 of,the Act on Posting of Workers.
52. *See* Federal Labour Court of 17.08.2011 – 5 AZR 490/10 (note 17).

so-called social state-principle (*Sozialstaatsprinzip*).[53] As from 1 January 2015, a general statutory minimum wage applies in Germany. Section 13 of the Act of the Minimum Wage Act (*Mindestlohngesetz*), by referring to section 14 of the Act on Posting of Workers, establishes the same secondary liability with regard to general minimum pay as that already existing with regard to minimum pay that is due under generally binding collective agreements. It was the explicit intention of the legislator to make sure that the same rules apply.[54] In both cases, entrepreneurs who depend on subcontractors are encouraged to adopt appropriate measures in order to reduce the risk of employees of contractors or subcontractors bringing claims against them. Apart from carefully selecting their contractor, entrepreneurs will try to ensure that if subcontractors are commissioned, these subcontractors will commit themselves to pay the minimum wage and, in case the subcontractor commissions further subcontractors, to include such obligation in their respective contracts as well.

The second response to contracting-out has been to enlarge the rights of works councils. In the very Draft Act that was already mentioned, the Federal Government included provisions amending the Works Constitution Act (*Betriebsverfassungsgesetz*) by adding information on the use of civil law contracts to the existing information rights of works councils. According to section 80(2) sentence 1 of the Works Constitution Act, the employer 'shall supply comprehensive information to the works council in good time to enable it to discharge its duties under this Act; such information shall also refer to the employment of persons who have not entered into a contract of employment with the employer'. The Draft adds to this that the information provided must include information on the duration of the job, the place of work and its content. According to section 80(2) sentence 2 of the Works Constitution Act, the works council 'shall, if it so requests, be granted access at any time to any documentation it may require for the discharge of its duties; in this connection, the works council committee or a committee set up in pursuance of section 28[55] shall be entitled to inspect the payroll showing the gross wages and salaries of the employees'. The Draft supplements this by adding a new sentence 3, according to which the works council has the right to examine the contracts on which the work of the employees of 'third companies' is based.[56] The purpose of this information right is to ensure that the works council can assess independently whether employment of staff 'in reality' is temporary agency work.[57] According to section 92(1) sentence 1 of the Works Constitution Act, the employer 'shall inform the works council comprehensively and in good time of matters

53. Federal Constitutional Court of 20.03.2007 – 1 BvR 1047/05; *see also* Federal Labour Court of 06.11.2002 – 5 AZR 617/01 (A). Moreover, it is in line with EU-law; *see* ECJ of 12.10.2004 – C-60/03 (Wolff & Müller GmbH & Co. KG / José Filipe Pereira Félix).
54. *See* German Parliament Printing Matter 18/2010, p. 23.
55. The works committee deals with the day-to-day business of the works council (s. 27(2) sentence 1 of the Act). Apart from that, committees can be set up to deal with specific tasks (s. 28(1) sentence 1 of the Act).
56. The Draft does not add much in substance but rather enshrines in statutory law what has already been developed by the courts; *see*, in particular, Federal Labour Court of 31.01.1989 – 1 ABR 72/87.
57. *See Karthaus/Klebe*: Betriebsratsrechte bei Werkverträgen, in: Neue Zeitschrift für Arbeitsrecht 2012, 417 (419).

relating to manpower planning including in particular present and future manpower needs and the resulting staffing and vocational training measures and supply the relevant documentation'. The Draft adds to this that 'staffing measures' encompass plans as to employ persons who are not in an employment relationship with the employer.[58]

The closest thing to what is the question of 'joint employers' under the National Labor Relations Act in the US might be whether more than one company can be regarded as 'owning' an establishment within the meaning of the Works Constitution Act. Section 1 of the Act indeed provides for the setting-up of works councils in establishments of several companies. According to section 1(1) sentence 1 of the Act, works councils shall be elected in all establishments that normally have five or more permanent employees. According to section 1(1) sentence 2 of the Act, the same shall apply to joint establishments of several companies. Section 1(2) holds a legal definition of a 'joint establishment'. A joint establishment of several companies is presumed to exist, in particular, 'if the companies employ the equipment and workers jointly in order to pursue their working objectives'.[59] This means that cooperation between different companies is not sufficient. What is required is joint operational management in the sense that essential employer functions in the area of human resources and social affairs are shared between two (or more) companies and concentrated in a common management team (which then constitutes a partner for the works council to deal with). The important question to ask is whether manpower is used across employers in the ordinary course of business.[60] In any event, however, joint operational management must derive from an explicit or tacit agreement between the companies.[61] Mere cooperation is not sufficient even if a control agreement exists between the companies. The same applies if, in the case of just-in-time production, one company exerts external control over another.[62]

[C] Supply Chains

So far, supply chains, at least in terms of 'fissurization' of the workplace, have not come into the focus of the legislator. This, however, could possibly change in the future. For instance, the Federation of German Trade Unions (*DGB*) demands to ensure that companies will bear greater responsibility for work conditions at companies in global supply chains. In particular, there are demands to oblige companies to publicly

58. *See* in this regard also Federal Labour Court of 31.01.1989 – 1 ABR 72/87 (on s. 92(2) of the Act): Works councils can suggest the use of regular staff instead of employees of contractors.
59. Section 1(2) no. 1 of the Act.
60. Federal Labour Court of 13.02.2013 – 7 ABR 36/11 (note 28).
61. *See*, for instance, Federal Labour Court of 20.02.2014 – 2 AZR 859/11.
62. *See Richardi*, in: Richard (ed.), Betriebsverfassungsgesetz, 15th ed., 2016, § 1 note 67. Mere cooperation of employers in an establishment within the framework of a matrix organisation might not be sufficient either; *see Witschen*, Matrixorganisationen und Betriebsverfassung, in: Recht der Arbeit 2016, 38 (44).

report on supply chains and to involve trade union representatives, works councils and workers' representatives in supervisory boards in this reporting.[63]

[D] Franchising

With regard to labour law, it is often difficult to draw a line between a (subordination) franchise on the one hand and an employment relationship on the other. As the franchisee under a subordination franchise undertakes to promote sales according to guidelines and instructions of the franchisor, there is a need to distinguish this kind of subordination from the one that arises from an employment relationship.[64] According to the courts, there is regularly no employment relationship, in any event, if the franchisee has the right to fulfil his or her contractual obligations with the help of other persons and if the franchisee for factual reasons depends on the support provided by others.[65] However, German law acknowledges a category of workers, so-called semi-dependent workers (*Arbeitnehmerähnliche*), in-between employees and self-employed persons. 'Semi-dependent workers' are persons who, though not being subordinated, are economically dependent on another person and, compared to employees, in equal need of legal protection.[66] There are cases where courts indeed have found that franchisees qualify as 'semi-dependent workers' in that sense.[67]

As the courts may consider whether a franchisee must be qualified as a 'semi-dependent worker' (or even an employee), there is at present (almost) no discussion on whether a franchisor may have to be qualified as the (co-) employer of persons employed by the franchisee. The reason for that might lie in the fact that, though the obligations arising for franchisees from agreement with franchisors may

63. *See Pütz/Giertz/Thannisch*: Compliance ausgewerkschaftlicherSicht, in: Corporate Compliance 2015, p. 19. This must be seen in the context of implementing Directive of the European Parliament and of the Council of 22 October 2014 amending Directive 2013/34/EU as regards disclosure of non-financial and diversity information by certain large undertakings and groups into national law. *See* recital 7 of this Directive:

> As regards social and employee-related matters, the information provided in the statement may concern the actions taken to ensure gender equality, implementation of fundamental conventions of the International Labour Organisation, working conditions, social dialogue, respect for the right of workers to be informed and consulted, respect for trade union rights, health and safety at work and the dialogue with local communities, and/or the actions taken to ensure the protection and the development of those communities.

See also the Proposal for a Directive amending Directive 2013/34/EU of 12.04.2016, COM(2016) 198 final.

64. *See* Federal Labour Court of 16.07.1997 – 5 AZB 29/96 according to which franchisees can perfectly qualify as employees.
65. *See*, for instance, Federal Civil Court of 27.01.2000 – III ZB 67/99 and State Labour Court Düsseldorf of 27.08.2010 – 10 Sa 90/10; *Preis*, in ErfurterKommentar, 16th ed., 2016, § 611 BGB note 30.
66. A statutory definition can be found in s. 12 a of the Act on Collective Bargaining Agreements (*Tarifvertragsgesetz*). According to this provision, there is 'economic dependence' in that sense if a person receives from a single other person on average more than half of his or her total income from his or her profession.
67. *See*, for instance, State Labour Court Saarbruck of 11.04.2011 – 5 W 71/11.

often be numerous as well as onerous,[68] they are rather not regarded as limiting the rights and powers which are derived from the legal position of 'employer'. While German law, at least at the moment, seems to be ill-prepared to treat franchisors as (co-) employers,[69] there is mounting political pressure. For instance, three Italian consumer organisations recently filed a complaint with the European Commission. Though they primarily allege McDonalds is abusing its franchises in Europe through restrictive contracts and property rental arrangements, they also blame the company for driving down wages for workers. Recently, these organisations received support for their complaint from the US labour union SEIU, which has already stirred up protests demanding higher wages for McDonald's workers.[70]

§5.05 EVALUATION AND FUTURE PROSPECTS

As the notion of 'employee' has been extensively discussed, the notion of the 'employer' has so far attracted much less interest in Germany. Similarly, it is rarely asked whether and to what extent obligations that 'normally' would depend on being the 'contractual employer' could (partly and possibly cumulatively) be assigned to a mere 'functional employer'. And while the possibility of 'co-employership' is generally acknowledged, there is also a consensus that such 'co-employership' must, in principle, be based on being one of the parties to an employment contract.

Against this background, it may be useful to distinguish two situations: First, the situation that the position of employer is split in the sense that another person than the contractual employer exerts the power to direct. This situation may lead to application of the rules on temporary agency work. Second, the situation that it in one way or another 'an employer behind the employer' exists. This latter situation is far less clear-cut than the former both in terms of requirements and in terms of legal consequences.

[A] The 'Functional Employer' in the Case of Temporary Agency Work

Temporary agency work is regulated in the Act on Temporary Agency Work (*Arbeitnehmerüberlassungsgesetz*) which also implements Directive 2008/104/EC on temporary agency work.[71] Temporary agency work constitutes a trilateral relationship: First, there is a contract of employment between the temporary agency worker and the temporary work agency. Second, there is a contract between the temporary work agency and the user-enterprise according to which the latter may make use of the manpower of the worker during an assignment. Third, there is a (non-contractual)

68. *See Graf von Westphalen*, in: Westphalen (ed.), Vertragsrecht und AGB-Klauselwerke, 2015, Teil 'Klauselwerke', note 10 who, however, mentions both the broad spectrum of rights and obligations and the fact that in terms of content they are subject to a dynamic development.
69. *See also* State Labour Court Mecklenburg-Vorpommern of 30.09.2014 – 2 Sa 77/14 (employer position of franchisor considered but quickly discarded).
70. Euroactiv.com: 'McDonalds' most dedicated opponents find allies in Europe', 13.01.2016.
71. Directive 2008/104/EC of the European Parliament and of the Council of 19.11.2008 on temporary agency work, Official Journal of the European Union of 05.12.2009, L 327/9.

legal relationship between the worker and the user-enterprise. A contract of employment exists only between the temporary work agency and the temporary worker. Only the temporary work agency is the employer. There is no double employment contract.[72] However, the contract of employment between the temporary work agency and the temporary agency worker will regularly form a so-called contract for the benefit of third parties (*Vertrag zugunsten Dritter*) within the meaning of section 328 of the Civil Code under which 'the third party acquires the right to demand the performance directly' (section 328(1) of the Civil Code).[73] While the relationship between the temporary agency worker and the user-enterprise is no employment relationship, it nevertheless forms a legal relationship that gives rise to secondary obligations, in particular, duties to care and to protect the worker (*Schutz- und Fürsorgepflichten*).[74] Though there is a fundamental agreement on the existence of these obligations, their legal basis is doubtful. Some authors claim that they are based on a quasi-contractual relationship, which essentially results from the fact that one party has intense possibilities of harming rights of others.[75] Other authors point to the contract between the temporary agency and the user-enterprise which they regard as a so-called contract with protective effect for third parties (*VertragmitSchutzwirkungfürDritte*).[76] In that case, workers would directly benefit from the contract concluded between the temporary agency and the user-enterprise in the sense of enjoying (contractual) claims. As regards the legal position of the user-enterprise, the employment contract between the temporary agency and the (temporary agency) worker is regarded by some authors as also constituting a contract with protective effect for third parties. In case of being harmed by the worker, the user-enterprise then also would have a claim based on contractual obligations to care and to protect.[77]

As far as health and safety is concerned, section 11(6) of the Act on Temporary Agency Work applies. According to this provision, activities of the temporary agency worker are subject to the rules of public health and safety law; and obligations arising from public health and safety law on the part of the user-enterprise are independent of obligations on the part of the temporary work agency. Section 11(6) must be seen in the light of the fact that the worker performs his or her duties as part of the work

72. In the past, legal doctrine was indeed of the view that there was such double employment relationship. This position is not in conformity with the current law anymore; however, *see Schüren*, in Schüren/Hamann (ed.), Arbeitnehmerüberlassungsgesetz, 4th ed. 2010, Introduction note 107.
73. *See Schüren*, in Schüren/Hamann (ed.), Arbeitnehmerüberlassungsgesetz, 4th ed. 2010, Introduction note 312.
74. *Schüren*, in Schüren/Hamann (ed.), Arbeitnehmerüberlassungsgesetz, 4th ed. 2010, Introduction note 312 and note 117, in particular.
75. *See* in general *Canaris*, Ansprüchewegen 'positiverVertragsverletzung' und 'SchutzwirkungfürDritte' beinichtigen Verträgen, Juristenzeitschrift 1965, p. 475.
76. *See Markesinis/Unberath/Johnston*, The German Law of Contract – A Comparative Analysis, 2nd ed., 2006, p. 204 et seqq. There are basically three requirements that must be met: First, a particularly close relationship between the third party and the promisee (contractual creditor); second, the promisee must have some interest in protecting the third party/must be responsible for the third party 'for better or for worse'; third, the promisor must be able to foresee that the third party would suffer damage in the event that the promisor performed his obligation badly.
77. *See Schüren*, in Schüren/Hamann (ed.), Arbeitnehmerüberlassungsgesetz, 4th ed. 2010, Introduction notes 113 et seqq., 130.

organisation of the user-enterprise. There is consensus that section 11(6) is declaratory in nature as the provisions of public health and safety law, including the Act on Safety and Health Protection of *Workers* at Work (*Arbeitsschutzgesetz*), would apply to the user-enterprise anyway.[78]

The temporary agency is liable for social security contributions. This corresponds with its position as exclusive employer of the temporary worker. However, the user-enterprise has a subsidiary liability. According to section 28(2) sentence 1 of Social Code IV (*Sozialgesetzbuch IV*), user-enterprises shall be liable as absolute guarantor for contributions to sickness, care, pension and unemployment insurance as far as contributions are concerned that are due for times of assignment.[79]

Under certain circumstances, the law even provides for the user-enterprise becoming the (contractual) employer of the (temporary agency) worker. According to section 10(1) sentence 1 of the Act on Temporary Agency Work, if the temporary work agency lacks permission to hire out workers and the employment contract with the worker accordingly is ineffective (section 9 no. 1 in conjunction with section 1 of the Act), an employment relationship between the worker and the user-enterprise is deemed to exist.[80] Section 10(1) sentence 1 primarily aims at protecting the worker. Indirectly, it also ensures alertness on the part of the user-enterprise which may not wish to land itself in a position where it becomes the employer of the temporary agency worker. It is worth noting, that according to the Draft Act that was mentioned above, employment contracts between the temporary agency and the worker will also be ineffective if, in the contract between the temporary agency and the user-enterprise, the existence of temporary agency work is not explicitly mentioned. As a result, companies will run the risk of becoming employers if they enter into bogus civil law contracts. In the past, if courts qualified a contract as a contract to assign workers, the companies could refer to a licence to hire out workers that they kept in stock just in case.

As regards workers' codetermination, it should be noted that temporary agency workers even during their assignments belong to the establishment of the temporary work agency (section 14(1) of the Act on Temporary Agency Work). During assignments, however, they are also entitled to elect a works council at the user-enterprise if they have been working in the establishment for more than three months (section 7

78. *See Schüren*, in Schüren/Hamann (ed.), Arbeitnehmerüberlassungsgesetz, 4th ed. 2010, § 11 AÜG note 135.
79. According to s. 150(3) Social Code VII in conjunction with s. 28e(2) Social Code IV, the same applies with regard to accident insurance. Similarly, there is a liability for income tax purposes under s. 42 d(86) of the Income Tax Act (*Einkommensteuergesetz*).
80. Application of s. 10(1) sentence 1 is restricted to cases of lacking permission to hire out. Other violations of the law are not within the scope of this provision. If the temporary work agency, for instance, hires out a worker permanently, though assignments according to s. 1(1) sentence 2 must be 'temporary', there is no legal fiction of an employment relationship between the worker and the user-enterprise as long as the temporary work agency is in possession of a permission; *see* Federal Labour Court of 10.12.2013 – 9 AZR 51/13. The Court, explicitly, states (under note 34) that substitution of one employer by another would also be problematic from the point of view of constitutional law (freedom of occupation of the temporary agency worker).

sentence 2 of the Works Constitution Act).[81] In this context, it should also be mentioned that the Federal Labour Court recently abandoned its so-called two-components-doctrine according to which affiliation of a worker with a given establishment required both existence of a contract with its owner and actual integration in the work organisation. According to the Court, 'unlimited application (of this doctrine) would not lead to reasonable results if staff is deployed on other companies'.[82]

[B] 'Indirect Employment Relationship' or 'the Employer Behind the Employer'

A fairly old institution of German law is the so-called indirect employment relationship (*mittelbaresArbeitsverhältnis*).[83] According to the courts, such relationship exists if an employee is employed by another person (often called the 'intermediate master' or *Zwischenmeister*) who for his part is an employee of a third party (the entrepreneur) whereby the work is performed directly for the entrepreneur who is fully aware of this.[84] Assuming such 'indirect employment relationship' aims at establishing subsidiary liability of the entrepreneur with regard to payment of wages, in particular. The rationale is that an entrepreneur must be liable if he or she directly benefits from the work performed. According to the courts, the 'indirect employment relationship' forms an 'unwritten principle of law'.[85] It is clear that this legal institution is close to the principle of good faith.[86] On one occasion, the Federal Labour Court, for instance, held that it amounted to an 'abuse of the legal form of indirect employment and a circumvention of laws and collective agreements' if an employer instructed his maintenance men to hire cleaning ladies in their own name, though on account of him, instead of offering them direct employment. According to the court, that was the case in any event if the intermediaries were not allowed to reach their own business decisions and could not make a profit either.[87]

The Federal Labour Court has made it clear on various occasions that an 'indirect employment relationship' in that sense only can occur if the intermediary himself is an

81. On the other hand, according to s. 14(2) sentence 1 of the Act on Temporary Agency Work, they cannot be elected.
82. Federal Labour Court of 05.12.2012 – 7 ABR 48/11.
83. The practical importance so far has been limited; *see Preis*, in: Erfurter Kommentar zum Arbeitsrecht, 16th ed., 2016, § 611 BGB note 172.
84. This is the definition provided by Federal Labour Court of 09.04.1957 – 3 AZR 435/54.
85. Federal Labour Court of 09.04.1957 – 3 AZR 435/54.
86. *See* s. 242 of the Civil Code: 'An obligor has a duty to perform according to the requirements of good faith, taking customary practice into consideration.' The principle of good faith also prevents employers from cooperating in a collusive manner; *see*, for instance, Federal Labour Court of 24.06.2015 – 7 AZR 452/13 on such collusion aiming at escaping the application of legal provisions that limit the right of employers to fix the terms of employment contracts. *See also* Federal Labour Court of 23.09.2014 – 9 AZR 1025/12: If in the context of temporary agency work, the temporary work agency and the user-enterprise abuse their freedom of contract in order to escape the limits that apply to the fixing of the term of a contract of employment, such abuse leads to the fixing of the term being ineffective, while it does not lead to an employment relationship with the user-enterprise.
87. Federal Labour Court of 20.07.1982 – 3 AZR 446/80.

employee. According to the court, persons employed by an 'independent entrepreneur' do not need 'additional protection' (by providing them with a subsidiary debtor). Moreover, only if the intermediary himself is a mere employee, he is regularly lacking the resources needed to bear the risks that come with the status of employer.[88]

In legal literature, the position of the Federal Labour Court has been criticised by some authors. There have even been demands to abandon this supposed institution of law altogether.[89] Irrespective of whether the 'indirect employment relationship' had an added value in the past, it may serve a legitimate purpose in the future, however. It seems that this could be the case in particular, if the courts would not require anymore that the intermediary must be an employee. Moreover, the courts could consider putting more emphasis on the aspect that actively encouraging involvement of third parties, if motivated by the wish of entrepreneurs to escape labour law obligations, should be tackled by establishing (at least) subsidiary liability of these persons in their capacity as 'indirect employers'. If further developed by the courts in that sense, fissurisation of the workplace could bring a breeze of fresh air to a legal institution that was presumed by some as being almost dead.

§5.06 CONCLUSION

Fissurisation of the workplace is a global phenomenon.[90] Germany is no exception. Though German law may already hold some of the answers, the problems involved will have to be further addressed by the legislator as well as the courts.

§5.07 SUMMARY

(1) Differentiation between contracts of employment and 'ordinary civil law contracts' has become a major issue as there are claims that employers increasingly take advantage of the latter in order to evade labour law.

(2) While the notion of 'employee' has been fleshed out by the courts and legal theory, there is little discussion of the notion of 'employer'.

(3) Courts and academics have been struggling for quite a while with employment in so-called matrix-structures of groups of companies that are characterised by the employer functions being split between companies belonging to the same group.

(4) Contracting-out is widespread. Mostly, it takes the form of work subcontracted to other companies in which case there may often be temporary agency work in disguise.

88. Federal Labour Court of 09.04.1957 – 3 AZR 435/54.

89. *See*, in particular, *Waas*, Das sogenanntemittelbareArbeitsverhältnis, in: Recht der Arbeit 1993, p. 153.

90. *See also Weil*, Afterword: Learning from a fissured world – reflections on international essays regarding *the fissured workplace*, in: Comparative Labor Law & Policy Journal 2015, p. 209 (209).

(5) Supply chains and franchising are widespread as well.
(6) In principle, labour law aims at individual establishments or companies. In a few cases, however, the law takes into account that a company is part of a group.
(7) The legislator responded to contracting-out by establishing secondary liability of contractors with regard to certain labour law obligations and, more recently, by enlarging the rights of works councils (along the lines of jurisprudence).
(8) Labour law problems that arise in the context of supply chains and franchising so far received little attention.
(9) The 'functional employer' (as opposed to the 'contractual employer') is acknowledged to a certain extent in the law on temporary agency work, which could provide a basis for further developing the law in this regard.
(10) The legal institution of 'indirect employment' aims at what is called the 'shadow employer' (or 'the employer behind the employer'). The courts could possibly further develop it in order to cope with the problems posed by fissurisation.

CHAPTER 6

Reconsidering the Notion of 'Employer' in the Era of the Fissured Workplace: Responses to Fissuring in French Labour Law

Sylvaine Laulom[*]

§6.01 INTRODUCTION

For a long time in France, as in many other countries, the question of 'who is an employer?' has not been considered a very important issue, the main question continuing to be 'who is an employee?'

Traditionally, the concept of the 'employer' is defined in relation to the concept of the 'employee', the employer and the employee being the two parties to the employment contract. The main test used to identify the employer is ownership of the company, together with exercising the managerial powers of control, direction and coordination over the working activity (the 'subordination test'). Most case law dealing with the issue of employer has traditionally been about identifying the 'real' employer, hiding behind the apparent, contractual one.[1] Therefore, and beyond the scope of the supply of workers, if the legal entity which exercises the managerial power of control and direction over the working activity is different from the legal entity which is formally part of the employment contract, the latter will not be regarded as the employer insofar as employment protection is concerned. According to Corazza and Razzolini, this principle is rooted in the rules governing the interpretation of contracts based on the idea that content prevails over form. They also consider that:

* University Lumière Lyon 2.
1. *See* for example, a case dated 1978, Soc. 9 November 1978, n°77-13723.

in Continental European legal systems, the prohibition of separation between the formal employer, who bears the employment risk and liabilities, and the employer who effectively owns the firm and exercises control and direction over the working activities, derives from the traditional hostility toward any form of labour intermediation.[2]

However, in France as in other countries, the transformation of economic organisations has led lawyers, scholars and, sometimes, legislators to discuss and redefine the concept of employer. As early as 1981, a conference on 'the fragmented company' ('*L'entrepriseéclatée*') was organised in Paris.[3] Here, the starting point of the analysis is the company (the employer) and not the workforce. In this conference, perhaps for the first time in France, the reality of this fragmentation of the company and its consequences was discussed and the fragmentation of workers' collectivity was analysed. Articles published at that time described how this fragmentation can occur and how civil and commercial law could be used to organise firms in such a way to disempower the formal employer.[4] According to these articles, what was at stake was temporary agency work, the freedom to organise corporate groups and recognising separate subsidiaries, subcontracting and franchising thirty years later, a new conference on the same issue was organised, this time with a subtitle: 'The fragmented company, identifying the employer and assigning liability'.[5] At this event, the processes described were more numerous and more complex, and discussions took place on the legal solutions to this fragmentation, specifically on how to identify decision-makers in order to make them liable. In an article published in 2000, Supiot also described the 'new faces of subordination'[6] whereby the single employer model is fragmented because of new forms of decentralisation of power within companies. The network enterprise model is also described as the disbanding of large companies which, by 'focusing on their core trade', further reduce the boundaries of their 'hard core' and the resources associated with it. Within the network enterprise, the organisation of power is no longer hierarchical. Non-hierarchical coordination is established among the entities, which affects the distribution of employer liabilities and obligations.[7] The single employer model does not seem to be adapted to this decentralisation

2. L. Corazza, O. Razzolini, 'Who is an Employer?', WP CDSLE Massimo d'Antona, 110/2014.
3. L'entrepriseéclatée, SAF conference of 24 January 1981, report published in Droit Ouvrier, March-April 1981.
4. M. Jeantin, 'L'entreprise éclatée: intérêts d'une approche commercialiste du problème', Droit Ouvrier, March-April 1981, p. 118; M. Henry, 'Les conséquences de l'entériorisation pour les salariés et leurs institutions représentatives', Droit Ouvrier, March-April 1981, p. 122; A. Lyon-Caen, 'A propos de l'entreprise éclatée', Droit Ouvrier, March-April 1981, p. 127.
5. L'entreprise éclatée, Identifier l'employeur, attribuer les responsabilités, SAF conference of 8 December 2012, report published in Droit Ouvrier, mars 2013. B. Dondero, 'Entreprise et personnalité morale: l'approche du droit des sociétés', E. Peskine, 'La responsabilisation des sociétés mères', N. Micault, 'Construction des groupes: à la recherche du responsable', D. Métin, 'Mise à disposition et prêt de main d'oeuvre: la main d'oeuvre extérieure importée dans l'entreprise'; M. Kocher, 'A la recherche de la responsabilité du donneur d'ordre dans les relations de travail de sous-traitance: une quête impossible?', S. Ducrocq, 'Externalisation de l'activité ou sous-traitance des licenciements?', A. Lyon-Caen, 'Retrouver l'entreprise'.
6. A. Supiot, 'Groupe de sociétés et paradigme de l'entreprise', RTDC, 1985, p. 5. 'Les nouveaux visages de la subordination', Droit Social, 2000, p. 131.
7. E. Peskine, Réseaux d'entreprises et droit du travail, LGDJ, 2008.

and redistribution of powers. More recently, the digitalisation of the economy and the 'Uberization' of the employment relationship has also become a concern.

Therefore, there is some evidence that fissured work arrangements have become an issue for labour lawyers, particularly when dealing with groups of companies, outsourcing, externalisation of the employment relationship and supply-chains.

This chapter initially presents the current situation of fissurisation in France. It then presents some of the French legal responses to this fissurisation as regards individual labour relations and collective relations. These legal responses are themselves fragmented, partly because fissurisation itself is not a unique phenomenon and partly because the traditional conception of the employer makes it difficult to define a 'plural-employer' model, where two or more firms can share employers' responsibilities.

§6.02 CURRENT SITUATION OF FISSURISATION IN FRANCE

Weil's description of a fissured workplace may be applied to the French labour market, although it is difficult to really ascertain the extent of fragmented work forms. There has been a movement from centralised decision-making towards decentralised structures and production networks. In both the manufacturing and service sectors, vertical disintegration and outsourcing have enabled firms to make their operations leaner and more flexible. Outsourcing and subcontracting activities as market forms of governance which replace hierarchy have definitely increased.

Two recent reports published by the National Institute of Statistics provide some information on two forms of this fissurisation: subcontracting and groups of companies. The use of temporary agency workers also takes place.

According to the first report, published in 2014 by the French National Institute of Statistics (INSEE),[8] 18% of companies employing at least fifty employees subcontract some of their activities outside France, particularly to other countries in the European Union and 38% rely to subsidiaries located outside France in their production process. Subcontracting in France is widespread and 57% of companies employing at least fifty employees subcontract some of their activities, which is particularly significant for groups of companies (60%).

A second Insee report provides an indication of the importance of groups of companies in the French economy.[9] This report uses an economic concept of firms to give an overview of the way groups are organised in France. According to this report, the main innovation illustrates the clearer picture obtained when groups are considered in economic analysis:

> In France, enterprises have long been defined in purely legal terms. In statistics and in terms of the law, an enterprise was defined according to its legal status, the

8. Insee Premières, n°1518, October 2014, 'La sous-traitance internationale, une pratique fréquente', http://www.insee.fr/fr/ffc/ipweb/ip1518/ip1518.pdf, accessed 22 February 2016.
9. Insee References Collections, 'Enterprises in France', 2015, Press kit, http://www.insee.fr/fr/ppp/comm_presse/comm/Dossier%20de%20presse%20Les%20entreprises%20en%20France_EN.pdf, accessed 22 February 2016.

'legal unit', i.e. a sole proprietor or company carrying out a production function. In December 2008, for the first time, the Economic Modernisation Act (LME –'Loi de modernisation économique') provided enterprises with an economic definition. This new definition gives a better understanding of the way a group was organised. Indeed, when an enterprise was assimilated with a legal unit, this did not describe the true situation of companies that were owned by other companies within a group organisation, as they were likely to have little, if any, decision-making autonomy. With the aim of implementing this new definition, profiling consists in identifying among groups the relevant enterprise(s) as defined by the decree of 2008, and reconstructing their consolidated accounts. Now that an economic definition has been established, it provides a better overview of the country's economic fabric. Using this definition, the economic fabric can be seen to be more concentrated than it had seemed.

Industrial enterprises have often created separate subsidiaries to perform a commercial role. In addition, a large proportion of their shares are in holding companies or real estate companies, classed as being in the tertiary sector. When the switch was made from a legal unit approach to an enterprise approach in industry, the total balance sheet more than doubled. This gave a more realistic view of company performance, as all resources contributing to the company results were now taken into account. Using this approach, the exportation rate of the manufacturing industry increased by 4 points, labour productivity was revised upwards, and the margin rate increased slightly. The perception of the weight of each sector has also changed.

In 2011, across all non-farm and non-financial market sectors, there were about three million enterprises. Of these, 95% were micro-enterprises. They employed 2.5 million payroll workers, i.e. only 20% of the total, and produced 16% of turnover and 21% of value added. At the other end of the scale, 222 large enterprises employed 3.1 million payroll workers, or 25% of the total, achieving 31% of turnover and 30% of value added. In addition to this duality, there was another fairly well-balanced division: 136,000 non-microenterprise SMEs and 4,900 intermediate sized enterprises (ISE) employed 29% and 26% of all payroll workers respectively. They produced 22% and 31% of turnover respectively, and 26% and 23% of value added.

Legal units were always considered by workforce size when measuring economic concentration and especially the proportion of SMEs. In 2011, out of more than 3 million legal units in market activities in the non-farm and non-financial sectors, only a hundred or so exceeded the threshold of 5,000 employees that defines large enterprises: they employed 13% of all payroll workers. If the economic approach to enterprises is used, this concentration is far higher. Since they employ 25% of payroll workers in the scope of the coverage, the economic weight of the 222 large enterprises is now more than twice that of legal units of comparable workforce size. They produce 30% of value added of enterprises (or 15% of GDP), which is more than double that generated by legal units of similar workforce size.

The change in the definition of the unit of analysis also changes the breakdown across sectors. Manufacturing or construction enterprises that form a group contain many companies within their core business. However, they have often also set up separate affiliates whose main role is to perform commercial functions in France or for export, and to carry out support functions (holding companies, head office activities, transport, real estate, research, etc.). Thus for the manufacturing sector, the switch from using legal units to an enterprise approach increases the sector's share in the economy in terms of workforce. This refocusing on manufacturing is even more visible for some aggregates that were particularly affected by spin-offs to affiliates within groups, such as net assets.

Finally, regarding temporary work, between 1988 and 2015, the percentage of agency workers within the workforce increased from 0.7% to 3%, representing 586,200 temporary agency workers. These workers are predominantly employed in building and industry, and this may be one of the reasons why most the temporary agency workers are men.[10]

§6.03 CURRENT LEGISLATIVE AND INTERPRETATIVE RESPONSES: INDIVIDUAL LABOUR RELATIONS

The process of fissurisation of workplace can take various forms. Some are not so new, nor are the responses of the legislator. For example, temporary agency work relationships have been regulated in France since 1972. Corporate groups have also existed for a long time and have challenged some of traditional representations of labour law.

Measures to protect workers by going beyond the boundaries of the legal entity do exist. In order to present them, it is necessary to distinguish the type of fissurisation at stake, as the solutions are not uniform. Labour intermediation has justified the most complete organisation of shared responsibilities between the user company and the employer, the temporary agency. In groups of companies, it is initially the definition of the unit of representation which has led the boundaries of the legal concept of the 'employer' to be redrawn, by focusing on economic activity. Going beyond the legal concept of the 'employer' in groups of companies has had knock-on effects in employment legislation. In subcontracting, the share of responsibilities mainly concerns in relation to health and safety legislation. Finally, in franchising, an old article of the French labour code allows labour legislation, under certain conditions, to be applied to the franchisee.

[A] Temporary Employment Agencies and Other Forms of Supplying Workers

Traditionally in France, any profit-making operations, the sole purpose of which is the supply of employees, is forbidden (*see* Article L. 8241-1 of the French Labour Code). This provision does not apply to temporary employment agencies and other marginal forms of intermediation such as job-sharing employment agencies, model agencies and sports' associations. In a mirror provision, Article L. 8241-2 of the Labour Code authorises loans of employees for non-profit purposes.

Although hiring workers through temporary work agencies is not the only authorised form for supplying workers, the regulation of temporary work, and the distribution of responsibilities among the employers which it implies, is the most

10. *See* 'Temporary work at the end of 2015', Insee, http://dares.travail-emploi.gouv.fr/dares-etudes-et-statistiques/statistiques-de-a-a-z/article/l-emploi-interimaire-les-series-mensuelles-trimestrielles-et-annuelles, accessed 30 March 2016.

complete. In 2011, a law was adopted to define the notion of 'non-profit-making purposes' which essentially draws the boundaries between the legal and illegal supply of workers. At the same time, the law defines the legal framework governing of the temporary hiring of employees.

[1] Temporary Employment Agencies: A Complete Regulation of a Triangular Relationship with Shared Responsibilities

Hiring workers through temporary employment agencies has been extensively regulated in France since their recognition in 1972. The lucrative hiring-out of labour and labour-only subcontracting is forbidden unless conducted through temporary employment agencies. The French regulation is based on three aspects: the regulation of temporary employment agencies, a limited use of agency work and a definition of rights for agency workers. In this chapter, we will only present the distribution of rights and duties between the user firm and the temporary employment agency as organised by the French Labour Code.

To summarise, the French Labour Code splits the rights and duties of employers between the employment agency and the user firm, thus creating a hypothetical duality of employers:

> The characteristic of temporary agency work is to create for the worker a dualistic relationship, with the temporary work firm on the one side, with the user company on the other. The first company takes on the legal status of employer while the second constitutes only the user of the worker's labour force. Therefore, agency work develops a new kind of legal position, the user of the worker. Distinct from the familiar status of employer, the status of user appears more singular to labour law structures. Nevertheless, the distinction between the one who employs and the one who uses the worker is fundamental to the legal mechanism of temporary agency work. To the employer the worker is subordinated, to the user the worker is at the disposal. While in the past the criterion of subordination assimilated the employer to the user, it is not necessarily the case nowadays.[11]

Labour law defines the rights relating to the presence of the agency worker within the user company. First, agency workers must enjoy similar treatment to that given to employees of the user firm. Permanent workers within the user company serve as comparators for determining most employment rights of agency workers. Equality also extends to pay and all working conditions. Second, the user may be found liable for any damages suffered by the agency worker during the assignment. Despite the lack of any contractual link between the temporary agency worker and the user company, some rights and obligations exist between the two. The very fact that the agency worker performs his or her duties within the user company creates some legal obligations for this company. The French Labour code states that for the duration of the assignment, the user company is responsible for all working conditions. Thus, a general obligation to protect the agency worker is binding upon the user company. Any damages caused

11. *See* C. Vigneau, 'Temporary Agency Work in France', *Comparative Labor Law and Policy Journal*, Vol. 23, No 1, pp. 45-66, Fall 2001.

to the agency worker during the assignment may trigger the user company's criminal or civil liability. The user company is also liable for all damages caused by the temporary agency worker to third parties. In particular, the user company has a duty to ensure the safety of temporary agency workers. Finally, if the user company decides to hire the temporary worker at the end of his or her contract, the continuity of the relationship is recognised and his or her length of service will be calculated taking into account the temporary employment contract. Any violation of the rules regarding the duration, renewal and successive number of assignments exposes the user company to specific sanctions. In this case, French law establishes an open-ended contract between the user company and the agency worker.

In terms of the collective rights of agency workers, the French legislator has attempted to adjust employment legislation to the peculiar situation of agency workers. Their collective rights are organised within the agency firm, with some adjustments. The law includes agency workers within the calculation of the workforce in order to decide whether the number of employees of the temporary employment agencies goes beyond the threshold established for trade union representatives or elected working committees. Agency workers may vote in elections within the temporary employment agency when they can justify three months' service during the last twelve months preceding the drafting of the lists. In order to stand in the elections, they must have been employed by the temporary agency firm for at least six months out of the last eighteen months prior to the election. Moreover, the worker must have been an employee of the temporary employment agency when the lists were drawn up.

Agency workers do not participate in the election of workers' representatives in the user company. However, staff delegates in the user company also represent agency workers.

Sectoral collective agreements play an important role in the regulation of temporary agency work. Employers are represented by PRISME, which claims to cover 600 temporary work agencies representing 90% of the sector. For example, specific provisions adapted to the precarious situation of workers can be found regarding vocational training, access to loans, social protection, etc. A new agreement, signed in July 2013,[12] introduced a new, open-ended contract for temporary agency workers in order to fight the precariousness of their employment. However, it has not been hailed as a success, as agencies only propose this type of contract to workers who do not have any difficulties finding jobs and, for these workers, an open-ended contract could be less advantageous than a fixed-term contract. If this is the case, they receive a bonus (known as the '*prime de précarité*'), which they lose if they have an open-ended contract.

[2] The Loan of Employees for a Non-profit Purpose

Although the exclusive loan of employees for the purposes of profit is prohibited, it is possible to loan employees for non-profit-making purposes. To avoid being considered

12. Agreement of 10 July 2013 on securing the career paths of temporary workers.

as illegally supplying employees or subcontracting labour, which would expose the companies to criminal sanctions, loaning employees must, necessarily, be for non-profit-making reasons. This technique has been increasingly used among groups of companies, particularly as a human resources management tool. Outside groups of companies, it has been presented as a way for companies to adapt to difficult economic contexts. Under this scheme, a company agrees to lend an employee for a fixed-term period to a so-called user company that has a temporary need for labour.

Until 2011, defining the concept of 'non-profit-making purposes' fell within the confines of case law. In an important decision, the John Deere decision of 18 May 2011,[13] the *Cour de Cassation*, the French Supreme Court, redefined the concept of non-profit-making purposes, taking into account the user's perspective in the context of an intra-group loan of employees.

In this decision, the *Cour de Cassation* clarified and extended the concept of the illegal supply of employees as part of a loan of employees from a parent company to one of its subsidiaries. In this case, employees had been hired by the parent company in order to subsequently be loaned to a subsidiary. Salaries were paid by the parent company which re-invoiced the salary costs and related social security contributions to its subsidiary. The *Cour de Cassation* recalled that the prohibition on lending employees for profit-making purposes set out in Article L.8241-1 of the French Labour Code applies both to the lending company and the user company. Neither of them may derive a financial gain or advantage from the loan of employees.

The *Cour de Cassation* specified that the profit-making nature of the loan may result from increased flexibility in staff management and administration and savings in social security charges enjoyed by the user company. Having recalled this principle, the *Cour de Cassation* noted that the subsidiary had not incurred any staff management expenses, with the exception of the reimbursement of salaries and social security charges on a euro for euro basis. The situation therefore, constituted an illegal loan of employees.

Shortly after this decision, which was criticised by employers' organisations, the Law Cherpion was adopted on 28 July 2011[14] in order to redefine the concept of non-profit-making and, at the same time, regulate the loan of employees for non-profit-making purposes. A new paragraph was added to Article L. 8241-1 of the French Labour Code, stating that the loan of employees does not have a profit-making purpose when the lending company only bills the user company during the loan period for the wages paid to the employee, the associated social security charges and contributions, and the professional expenses repaid to the employee in connection with the loan.

13. Cass. Soc. 18 May 2011, n°09-69175.
14. LawN°2011-893 of 28 July 2011 'pour le développement de l'alternance et la sécurisation des parcours professionnels'. Indeed, an amendment has been added to the bill following discussion with Parliament on the development of work/study programmes and securing career paths. F. Favennec-Héry, 'Prêt de main-d'oeuvre à but non lucratif: un texte décevant', Dr. soc. 2011, p. 1200; F. Pelletier, 'Le prêt de main-d'oeuvre exclusive', JCP S 2011, 1397; A. Teissier, 'Prêt de main-d'oeuvre: un nouveau régime juridique', Sem. soc. Lamy 2011, n° 1503, p. 4; S. Tournaux, 'Libéralisation des groupements d'employeurs et statut embryonnaire de la mise à disposition', RDT 2011, p. 572. D. Métin, 'Mise à disposition et prêt de main d'oeuvre: la main d'oeuvre extérieure importée dans l'entreprise', Droit Ouvrier, March 2013, p. 173.

With this new definition, which aims at putting an end to court decisions around the concept of 'non-profit-making purposes', the bill also introduces new provisions in order to regulate the loan of employees. The employee's express consent is now required and the conclusion of an amendment signed by the employee is mandatory, even if there are no substantial modifications to the employee's working conditions. Article L. 8241-2 of the French Labour Code specifies that the employee may not be sanctioned, dismissed or subject to discriminatory measures if he or she refuses to be loaned. The amendment to the contract must specify the duration of the loan, the work to be performed within the user company, the place where such work is performed as well as the specific features of the job and the working hours of the employees. The amendment may also include a probationary period if the loan entails a change in one of the main elements of the employee's employment agreement. The employee also continues to benefit from all provisions set out in the collective agreements which would have been applicable if the employee had performed his or her work in the lending company. This new provision generates some uncertainties, as it is not clear whether the employee should be entitled, as previously, to claim for the application of the provisions set forth in the industry-wide collective agreement or company-level bargaining agreements applicable within the user company, even when such provisions are more beneficial to him or her. The law also recalls that the loaned employee may access the services (e.g., the company restaurant) and collective transportation means established by the user company.

At the end of the loan period, the employee is reinstated to his or her position in the lending company, with no impact upon his or her career evolution or remuneration as the result of the loan period (L. 8241-2 of the Labour Code). In a decision dated 7 December 2011,[15] the *Cour de Cassation* ruled that in the event of termination of the employment contract by the subsidiary, the employee must be reinstated in the parent company, even if he or she had never effectively worked there before.

The lending company must consult the works council prior to implementation of the loan of an employee and inform the works council of the signed loan agreement. Furthermore, when the position in the user company appears on the list of jobs that pose particular risks to the health or safety of employees, the Health and Safety Committee of the lending company must be informed. Within the user company, the works council and the health and safety committee must be informed and consulted prior to integrating a loaned employee.

[B] Groups of Companies: Some Incomplete and Fragmented Solutions

Groups of companies are not a new phenomenon in France, but their numbers have increased and they are becoming increasingly complex. In groups of companies, several companies, although formally separated, are managed under the unified management and coordination of the holding as a single economic entity. A multiplicity

15. Cass. Soc. 7 December 2011, n°09-67367.

of companies thus coexists within the unity of the group.[16] The issue here is to go beyond the limits of the legal entity and rebuild a unity that matches the economic organisation of the group. In France, this was first implemented for workers' representation rights and, more recently, in the context of dismissal for economic reasons.

[1] Groups of Companies and Workers' Representation

The definition of the unit of representation is an important point in the French system of workers' representation, and the law attempts to adapt the structure of works' councils to that of the company. Where possible, the structure of the works council follows the structure of the company and the corporate group. Thus, each decision-making level corresponds to a specific structure of representation: the company works' council, the central works' council, the group council and, now, the European works' council.

The representation unit was initially structured around the concept of the company as a legal autonomous entity. Case law has gradually adjusted this approach by recognising the notion of the '*Economic and Social Unit*' (*Unitééconomiqueetsocialeor UES*). This notion emerged in the 1970s[17] against a backdrop of fraud in response to the issue of employers with separate legal entities each with fewer than fifty workers, but which together exceed this threshold. The *Cour de Cassation* thus decided that, in terms of workers' representation, each company could not be considered as a separate entity. Soon after, the recognition of the economic and social unit became independent from the existence of a fraud. When the conditions of the economic and social unit are met, the judges recognise that a group of companies represents a single unit. In 1982, the concept was recognised by the law and introduced into the Labour Code.[18] However, the Labour Code does not provide any definition of the concept, and it has fallen to case law to provide a definition. An economic and social unit is recognised through collective agreement or, failing such agreement, through court order.

The Courts use several indicators in order to recognise an economic and social unit.[19] The idea is that, when several companies which are technically separate legal entities, have strong operational, human resources, economic and financial ties, they can be stated to be an Economic and Social unit. In this case, works' council elections occur within this broader framework and only one works' council will operate within the entity.

The unit should be Economic and Social in nature. Economically, a managerial unity should be identified (the managers or the board members are the same), companies have common goals and strategies, there is a joint-exercise of a unified economic activity. Judges also verify whether the assets are similar and if the activities of the companies are similar or complementary. In social terms, some other criteria are relevant: the same collective agreement, similar working conditions, etc. apply. An

16. *See*. L. Corazza and O. Razzolini, *supra*.
17. Cass. Crim. 23 April 1970, EtsHerriau, D. 1970. 444.
18. *See* Article L. 2322-4.
19. *See* for example, Cass. Soc. 18 July 2000, n° 99-60353.

economic and social unit does not need to encompass account of all the companies within a group, and a group can integrate more than one Economic and Social Unit. A holding company without any employees can also be integrated in an Economic and Social Unit.[20]

The Economic and Social Unit is mainly used to define a workers' unit of representation, and the social partners may also negotiate at that level. However, the Labour Code refers to this notion in two others areas: for defining the employer's obligation to establish a profit-sharing plan[21] and for defining the level at which health services should be established (group, company or Economic and Social Unit).[22] However, the consequences of the recognition of an Economic and Social Unit in the context of dismissal for economic reasons are far more important.

[2] Groups of Companies and Employment Responsibilities

When an employer is contemplating a collective dismissal (affecting at least ten employees) in companies with more than fifty employees, he or she must establish a social plan ('an employment preservation plan' or *plan de sauvegarde de l'emploi*, PSE),which includes a number of measures aimed at limiting the number of redundancies and encouraging the reassignment of workers who are laid off. The content of the social plan depends on the company's resources, and the measures should be proportional to these resources. Since 2002, the content of the social plan is evaluated not at the level of the company but at the level of the Economic and Social Unit if such a Unit has been recognised. Otherwise, judges may sometimes appear to be reluctant to extend the scope of application of this concept. For example, judges refuse to recognise the Economic and Social Unit as being the employer responsible for the dismissals on economic grounds.[23] The legal entity, the formal employer, remains responsible for such dismissals and for establishing the social plan, and it does not share these responsibilities with other companies within the group or the Economic and Social Unit.[24] However, the *Cour de Cassation* decided that if the decision to dismiss is taken at the level of the Economic and Social Unit, the collective nature of the dismissal should be recognised at that level.[25]

Without using the notion of Economic and Social Unit, corporate groups are also taken into account by judges to check the employer's economic reasons and to define the scope of the obligation to redeploy employees prior to any dismissal on economic grounds.

According to Article L.1233-3 of the Labour Code, as interpreted by the Supreme Court, dismissal on economic grounds can be justified by economic difficulties, technological changes or a reorganisation of the company which is necessary to

20. Cass. Soc. 21 January 1997, n° 95-60833, 95-60838, 95-60839, 95-60840.
21. According to Article L3322-2 of the Labour Code, the establishment of a profit sharing plan is mandatory in the companies or Economic and Social Unit employing at least fifty employees.
22. Article D. 4622-1.
23. Cass. Soc. 16 December 2008, n°070-43875.
24. Cass. Soc. 13 January 2010, n° 08-15776, Flodor.
25. Cass. Soc. 16 November 2010, n°09-69485, note E. Peskine, RDT 2011, p. 112.

safeguard its competitiveness. Where a company is part of a corporate group and proceeds with a redundancy, the economic grounds are, in principle, assessed at the group level and, more precisely, at the level of the group's business line to which the company proceeding with the redundancies belongs. There must be valid economic grounds either at group level (if the group only operates in only one line of business), or at the level of the business line in which the company operates (if the group operates several business lines of business). Therefore, it is not sufficient to have valid economic grounds on the company level, it is the situation of the group which matters and the situation of the group in its transnational organisation.[26] Thus, the economic situation of companies located outside France and belonging to the same group shall be taken into consideration.

Prior to any economic dismissal, the employer also has an obligation of redeployment. Under this obligation, before dismissing an employee on economic grounds, the employer is bound to verify whether it is possible to redeploy the worker within the economic organisation. The employer is obliged to seek any alternative job opportunities for the employees concerned and to offer them, if necessary, professional training. In the event of an employee working in a company belonging to a group, the redeployment obligation is extended to the group as a whole (included companies outside France, although the redeployment obligation differs when the job proposal is located outside France). Economic dismissal is considered as unfair if possibilities of redeployment in the holding or in the other subsidiaries have not been taken into account.

Finally, it is in the context of dismissal on economic grounds that judges have recognised the concept of the 'co-employer' (or 'joint-employers'). This concept is not new and was traditionally used to seek the liability of parent companies.[27] In 2011, the Supreme Court issued decisions[28] which appeared to extend the scope of this concept. The 2011 case brought before the French Supreme Court related to the following situation. In 2004, the French company MIC, which was indirectly controlled by the German company Jungheinrich AG (the 'grand-parent' company), closed down its activities in France and made all its employees redundant. The employees challenged the redundancies and claimed for damages against not only MIC but also Jungheinrich AG. The Court of Appeal in Caen ruled that the German company Jungheinrich AG was also an employer of the employees working for its subsidiary MIC. Jungheinrich AG challenged this decision before the *Cour de Cassation,* claiming that even though a holding company has a control on its subsidiary and takes decisions which may have an impact on the employees of the subsidiary, this is not sufficient to prove that the

26. A highly debated Bill is currently being discussed in Parliament. Among its numerous provisions, it proposes redefining 'economic grounds' in such a way that economic difficulties will only be assessed at the national level, and the transnational nature of the group of companies will no longer be taken into account (Article 30). However, it remains to be seen whether the text will be amended in Parliament and whether the Bill will be adopted.
27. Cass. Soc. 24 March 1969, Bull. civ. V, n° 209.
28. Cass. Soc. 18 January 2011, n° 09-69199, 1 February 2011, 10-30045, Cass. Soc. 22 June, n° 09-69021, 28 September 2011, n° 10-12278, notes G. Couturier, Droit Social, 2011, p. 379; F. Géa, Revue de Droit du travail, 2011, p. 168; P.-A. Antonmattéi, 'Groupe de sociétés: la menace du co-employeur se confirme', Semaine Sociale Lamy, 2011, n° 1484.

holding company is a co-employer of these employees. The French Supreme Court did not accept the arguments of the grand-parent company and instead ruled that there was a 'confusion of interests, activities and management' between both companies, because there was a common management between both companies, under the supervision of Jungheinrich AG. The decisions taken by Jungheinrich AG had deprived MIC of any industrial, commercial and administrative autonomy; Jungheinrich AG was the owner of all trademarks and patents of MIC; the strategic decisions were taken by Jungheinrich AG, which also dealt with human resources management and had decided upon closing down the activities of MIC; the managing director of MIC had no real power and was entirely subject to the instructions of Jungheinrich AG. Consequently, Jungheinrich AG was deemed to be a co-employer of the employees of its subsidiary and could be held directly responsible for the damages claimed by these employees for unfair dismissal because of a lack of economic grounds.

With this decision, the *Cour de Cassation* appears to want to extend the scope of the concept of 'co-employer'. Taken in its widest sense, this concept could be used to redefine the boundaries of employment protection and admit a multiple-employer model where the responsibilities of employer could be shared by a number of companies belonging to the same group. However, in 2014,[29] the Supreme Court fell short of these expectations and confirmed that the concept of co-employer should be understood in its narrow sense. It is only when an 'abnormal' relationship between a parent company and a subsidiary is identified that a judge would be willing to infringe the formal separation between the corporations.

Judges will consider that a company is a co-employer (very often between a subsidiary and its parent company) only if there is a confusion of activity, interests and management at such a point and a level as to determine a contractual confusion and a mixed and indistinct use of the workforce within the group. Judges will assess, on a case-by-case basis, whether the subsidiary is autonomous or not. They will examine a series of elements in order to appraise the level of dependency of the subsidiary. These elements are, for example, the identity of the managers, the determination of the subsidiary's strategy, pricing policy, economic and labour related choices made unilaterally by the parent company, the existence of a centralised human resource and employment-related management system, full or quasi-full ownership of the capital, financial control, lack of autonomy in terms of operational and administrative management, and complete dependency of the subsidiary's economic activity upon the group to which it belongs. When an autonomous economic entity is, in practice, a mere establishment deprived of any decision-making authority and management powers and where it does not have any autonomy, a co-employer will be recognised. However, mere economic dominance over another company is not sufficient for the status as co-employer to be established.

The consequence is that a co-employer is subject to the same obligations and exposed to the same liabilities as an employer.

29. Cass. Soc. 8 July 2014, n°13-15573.

The concepts of the Economic and Social Unit and of co-employer could limit the fissurisation of employment created by corporate groups. However, the solutions which have largely been defined by case law are not general in scope and a general application of these concepts in order to establish shared responsibility among the various entity of a corporate group is lacking.

[C] Contracting-Out and Subcontracting Processes

There are two sets of rules to protect workers in subcontracting processes. The first relates to the fight against undeclared and illegal work and the second relates to health and safety regulations.

[1] The Responsibility of the Client or the Principal Contractor

The aim of the legislation, first adopted in 1975, is to prevent the use of illegal work in subcontracting processes. The contractor's responsibility reflects his or her 'dominant position' in the subcontracting process and is mainly a tool to combat illegal employment.

According to Article L.8222-1 of the Labour Code, any recipient of services which amounts to more than EUR 3,000 must require from its co-contractor documents to ensure that its co-contractor does not employ undeclared or illegal workers. The list of documents that the client must request was extended by Decree n°2011-672. The client shall ask and the provider of service must provide, upon the execution and every six months thereafter, proof of its registration (if any) and a certificate issued by the French body responsible for collecting social security contributions, proving that social security declarations have been made and social security contributions have been paid by the co-contracting party, dated within the past six months. The certificate must state the company's identification number, number of employees and total wages paid. The client is obliged to check with the relevant body that the certificate is genuine. In the event of failure to comply with these provisions, the recipient of the services may be sentenced to paying the social security charges which the service provider had failed to pay by not declaring its employees to the French government. A new law, No. 2014790 of 10 July 2014, was also adopted in order to counter unfair social competition or social dumping in relation to the posting of workers. The law institutes a system of joint financial liability designed to encourage contractors to make sure that posted workers are treated in line with the law. Here again, we can find a limited recognition of a form of dual employer.

[2] Health and Safety at Work in Subcontracting

The 1989 European Framework Directive (89/391), implemented in France, lays down certain obligations when several undertakings share a workplace. This is an interesting example, where a real share of responsibilities is organised among various employers even though each of them remains responsible for their own employees. An original cooperation agreement is established between the companies participating in the same production process. The Labour Code lays down the obligation of the various employers to cooperate in implementing safety and health provisions and coordinating their actions in relation to the protection of workers and the prevention of occupational risks, where several undertakings share a workplace.[30] The client must carry out a risk assessment, and contractors must assess the risks to their own workers. Both parties must cooperate and exchange information on the effects of interaction between the workers and the tasks of both parties and assess the possible risks arising from such interaction. The client or host company is responsible for this coordination. A specific inter-enterprise health and safety committee is also recognised in 'Seveso' facilities and in the building sector (*see* Articles L. 4523-11 and L. 4532-10).

This sharing of responsibility is limited to health and safety issues, although it would be possible to share other areas of responsibilities of the client company regarding employment, for example.[31]

[D] Franchising Systems

French legislation contains a specific regime dedicated to branch managers ('*gérant de succursale*', Article L. 7321-1 of the Labour Code). This article of the Labour Code was introduced just after the Second World War and is regularly applied in franchising situation.[32] It appears that this article began being discussed just after the *Cour de Cassation* refused to use the criteria of economic dependence to define the contract of employment.[33]

In the absence of a subordination relationship, the regime, defined by Article L. 7321-1 of the Labour Code, extends application of parts of labour legislation to this category of managers (who can also themselves be the employer of other employees). According to Article L. 7321-2, this is possible under four cumulative conditions. This regime applies when: (i) the franchisee sells goods (ii) exclusively or quasi-exclusively through a sole company (iii) in a locale attributed or agreed to by the company, (iv) under the conditions and prices imposed by the company. For example, the manager of an 'Yves Rocher' beauty centre used this legal technique. Her activity essentially consisted of selling 'Yves Rocher' branded products, but the brand imposed prices and conditions upon her exercising the activity. The *Cour de Cassation* decided that the manager should be considered as a branch manager, and that French Labour law and all its benefits should apply to the former franchisee.[34] French Labour law applies as soon as the conditions provided by Article L. 7321-2 are met, regardless of the provisions in the contract, although no subordination relationship is identified. Cases in different sectors of activity such as gas stations, hotels, telephony, transport,

30. Articles R. 4511-4, R. 4512-2 and following of the Labour Code.
31. *See* article by M. Kocher, 'A la recherche de la responsabilité du donneur d'ordre dans les relations de travail de sous-traitance: une quête impossible?', Droit Ouvrier, March 2013, p. 180.
32. R. Pihery, 'L'appréhension des accords de réseau par le droit social: pour une reconnaissance des spécificités de la franchise', AJ Contrats d'affaires, 2016, p. 11.
33. Cass. 6 July 1931, Bardou.
34. Cour de Cassation, 9 May 2011, n° 09-42901.

clothing or food retailing regularly apply this article. However, this article does not have any effect on the employees of the franchisee and, for them, only one employer is recognised, although their employer can ask for the Labour Code to be applied.

§6.04 CURRENT LEGISLATIVE RESPONSES AND INTERPRETATIONS: COLLECTIVE LABOUR RELATIONS

Different mechanisms exist which provide some responses to the fissurisation of workplace. A first mechanism is old but remains important in France. Collective bargaining at sectoral level is a traditional level of collective bargaining and, although a decentralisation of collective bargaining can be seen in France, as in many other countries, this level of bargaining plays an important role and small and medium enterprises are usually attached to this level. If companies belonging to a group or a chain of supply belong to the same sector, collective agreements at sectoral level can unify some of the working conditions of the workers.

As stated above, the French system of workers' representation and the law attempts to adapt the structure of works' councils to that of the company. Where possible, the structure of the works' council follows the structure of the company and the corporate group. Thus, each level of decision-making corresponds to a specific structure of representation: the establishment works' council, the central works council, when necessary, an Economic and Social Unit will be defined for the establishment of a works council. Collective agreements can be concluded at each level. Another level of representation exists. Established by the 1982 Auroux laws, group councils are set up within groups consisting of a controlling company and controlled companies. A group council must be created within each group composed of a parent company having its registered office in France, its subsidiaries and all affiliated entities (Article L. 2331-1 of the Labour Code). However, this is subject to the condition that the parent company directly or indirectly controls the subsidiary and/or affiliates. The group council is not a substitute for the works council. Its purpose is to provide the representatives of each company with more comprehensive information concerning the activity of the group as a whole. The group council meets at least once a year and must be informed on matters such as the group's businesses, its financial situation, changes in employment issues, employment forecasts on an annual or multi-annual basis, possible preventative actions, and the group's economic prospects for the year to come. The group council does not have a consultative function. A group council consists, on one hand, of the controlling company manager and, on the other, representatives of staff within the group. Staff representatives are appointed by the representative trade unions from the members of the various works councils of all of the group companies and on the basis of the results of the latest elections. Finally, Directive 94/45 of 22 September 1994 was transposed into French law, and European works' councils must be set up on the conditions defined by the Directive.

If we look at the competencies of works' councils, they have to be informed and consulted on the structure of the company to which they belong. There is also an obligation to inform and consult the works' councils at least once a year on the use of temporary work and subcontracting (Article L 2323-8 and L2323-10).

Finally, the collective rights of loaned employees are also organised. Employees loaned to a company are taken into account in the calculation of the workforce – in proportion to their presence within the company during the last twelve months – insofar as they are effectively present in the company's premises and have worked there for at least a year. Loaned employees, such as cleaning or security staff, are also entitled to vote in the elections of workers' representatives after twelve months of uninterrupted presence within the company. They are entitled to stand for election as a staff representative after twenty-four months of uninterrupted presence within the company, but are not entitled to stand for election to become members of the Works Councils.

Finally, it is possible for such employees to cast their vote and stand for election in their own company or in the company to which they have been loaned.

§6.05 CONCLUSIONS

France's responses to workplace fissurisation are extremely fragmented. Certainly, what is missing is a general reflection on who the employer is and how responsibilities can be shared when the employer is dual or plural. Indeed, it is difficult to overcome the single employer model and some legal solutions, like the Economic and Social Unit, simply tend to bring together several companies in a single economic entity.

However, some solutions defined in one specific context could be extended: this is the case, for example, of the Economic and Social Unit whose scope is mainly limited to workers' representation. The sharing of responsibilities on health and safety issues in subcontracting could also be extended. It is possible to argue 'that the best protection for workers derives from splitting the employment risk and costs among different employing entities'.[35] However, organisation of the business remains that of the main managerial power. Until now, the law has respected this power and the recognition of a plurality of employers has been limited and fragmented. In France, the economic and political context does not seem to be favourable to extending and generalising some of the responses given to specific issues, on the contrary. A significant reform of French labour law is currently being discussed and its main aim seems to give more flexibility to companies. Not only does the Bill fail to address the problem of fissured workplaces, but also some of the proposals could contribute further to this fissurisation. The bill aims at decentralising collective bargaining and if it is adopted could then contribute to weakening collective agreements at sectoral level. This level could contribute to the definition of a floor of rights for companies belonging to the same sector. Furthermore, in terms of collective dismissals, the transnational dimension of companies will no longer be taken into account in order to assess the economic difficulties allowing the company to proceed with redundancies.

35. L. Corazza, O. Razzolini.

CHAPTER 7

Labor Law and "Atomization of Work": Legal Responses to the "Fissured Workplace" in Spain

Diego Álvarez Alonso[*]

§7.01 INTRODUCTION

Work has changed. We still tend to think of workers and workplaces according to the archetypes smartly captured in Chaplin's great film *Modern Times*. But modern times are already the past. The old black and white picture of a numerous bunch of industrial workers employed together in the fordist-taylorist manufacturing chain of a big industrial plant is blurring. The new (smartphone?) pictures of work offer a much more complex and diversified panorama of employees, employers and workplaces. The classic patterns of salaried work have mutated in the context of the post-fordist version of capitalism developed since the late 1970s'.[1] As an indirect result of the 1973 crisis and with support in new technologic developments, traditional companies and new entrepreneurs started to follow new management orientations in business organization, as "flexible specialization" or focusing in "core competencies," and strategies like externalization of activities, outsourcing or offshoring, with the aims of, among other things, increasing adaptability, reducing risks and responsibilities and cutting costs, according to the new ideal of "lean management" and "lean production."[2] These trends have been causing profound transformations in the characterization of work, workers,

* University of Oviedo.

1. PIORE, M./ SABEL, C., *La segunda ruptura industrial,* Alianza, 1990, pp. 1-456.
2. RIFKIN, J., *El fin del trabajo. Nuevas tecnologías contra puestos de trabajo: el nacimiento de una nueva era*, Paidós, 2003, pp. 119-136; CASTELLS, M., *La era de la información. Vol. I: La sociedad red,* Alianza, 2005, pp. 111-205; LETAMENDÍA, F., *Estructura política del mundo del trabajo: fordismo y posfordismo,* Tecnos, 2009, pp. 123-135.

workplaces and employers, which is gradually moving away from the originals that we used to bear in mind. The former paradigm of large industrial companies managing the whole production and distribution processes and acting as single employer for all the legion of workers involved in such activities is being "fissured" or "atomized" into interconnected multi-layered business networks composed of a multiplicity of "daughter"/ "sister" companies, contractors, subcontractors, suppliers, franchisees and even other types of entities, each of them carrying out lesser piecemeal parts of the outsourced economic activity, as legally independent employers in charge of their own respective employees in minor-size workplaces.[3] To summarize, this process and its outcomes could be referred to as "atomization of work" or "the fissured workplace," graphically outlining the fact that it has served to major companies and leading brands to shed jobs and inherent employer's responsibilities that were once held inside, and which are now externally appointed to those other smaller units nonetheless integrated in a somehow coordinated business system.[4]

Labor Law was originally conceived on the basis of those earlier schemes of work that are now in withdrawal, addressing employment as a quite simplistic bilateral relationship of each single employer vis-à-vis the employees actually belonging to her staff, within the context of a "pre-fissured" workplace. Therefore, the new complexity of the world of work entails significant tensions and challenges for the application and enforcement of that legal system, which suffers from lack of adaptation to the renewed economic patterns.[5] The spreading of employment into complicated business networks entails increased risks of blurring of responsibilities or circumvention of law in regard to employers' obligations and employees' rights. It is a matter of fact that lack of compliance with labor standards has become more likely and harder to tackle in the context of "the fissured workplace." But even leaving apart pathologic cases, the problem is that some of the classic institutions and regulatory orientations of Labor Law might be quite outdated and do not fit properly to the new shapes of business and workplaces.[6] On the other hand, employment relationships in the lower levels of subcontracting and supply chains or franchising arrangements are usually managed by small and weak employers subject to fierce competitive pressure from the markets and though requirements imposed by the leading business, being consequently trapped in a difficult position that pushes them to lowering labor costs and even to "social dumping." As a combined result of those and other factors inherent to atomization of

3. VALDÉS DAL- RÉ, F., "La descentralización productiva y la formación de un nuevo paradigma de empresa", *Relaciones laborales: Revista crítica de teoría y práctica*, n. 18, 2001, pp. 1-8; CASTELLS, M., *supra*, pp. 201-249; LETAMENDÍA, F., *supra*, pp. 133-155.
4. WEIL, D., *The Fissured Workplace: Why Work Became So Bad for So Many and What Can Be Done to Improve It*, Harvard University Press, 2014, pp. 7-27.
5. SUPIOT, A. et al., *Beyond Employment: Changes in Work and the Future of Labour Law in Europe*, Oxford University Press, 2001, pp. 1-57.
6. BARREIRO FERNÁNDEZ, G., "Notas sobre la descentralización productiva en la empresa y su escisión interna", *Revista española de derecho del trabajo*, n. 94, 1999, pp. 165-186; VALDÉS DAL-RÉ, F., "Descentralización productiva y desorganización del Derecho del Trabajo", *Relaciones laborales: Revista crítica de teoría y práctica*, n. 20, 2001, pp. 1-10; RIVERO LAMAS, J., "Proyecciones de la descentralización productiva: instrumentación jurídico laboral", RIVERO LAMAS, J./ DE VAL TENA, A. L. (Eds.), *Descentralización productiva y responsabilidades empresariales. El "outsourcing"*, Thomson-Aranzadi, 2003, pp. 23-62.

work, the moves towards "the fissured workplace" tend to result in decrease of wages, poorer working conditions and, in general, more precarious work.[7]

Hence, it is urgent for Labor Law to adopt appropriate legal responses to the new challenges arising from the "atomization" processes leading to a "fissured workplace," in order to face its worst consequences, or even to accomplish a global resetting for a better adaptation to the new paradigms of work. This effort should acknowledge that, while "atomization" of work has enabled the leading companies and brands to reduce the responsibilities, costs and risks of being the employer by shedding employment to smaller units considered as legally autonomous undertakings, those upper-level stakeholders continue nevertheless to control the whole economic ensemble, by means of shareholding or imposing targets and rigorous standards to the lower levels of business-groups, subcontracting networks, supplier chains and franchising arrangements. In such circumstances, employees' work within those networks is somewhat run from beyond the entities that have formally entered the employment contract, as these can often be considered as "subordinated employers," or even as just the contractual connection to a complex "diffuse employer."[8] Thus, even if the starting point is to consider that these daughter companies, contractors, subcontractors, suppliers and franchisees are independent employers that should fully bear their commitments as such before their own respective employees, there could be a basis to justify somehow extending responsibilities to other upper or parallel levels of the business network, going through the boundaries of the legal entity to declare joint liabilities of client or leading businesses, or even considering these as joint employer according to a reconceptualization on the matter. This chapter explores to what extent Spanish Labor Law has established regulations with that aim, addressing the already existing provisions on several different forms of "the fissured workplace." According to the comparative purposes of this publication, it adopts therefore a national perspective, although it should be acknowledged that the "atomization of work" is a global phenomenon that would surely require supranational responses, so the study of different domestic legal regulations in each country is to be considered just a – nevertheless valuable – starting point for building a wider-scope approach in the future.[9]

§7.02 THE CONTEMPORARY PICTURE OF "THE FISSURED WORKPLACE" IN SPAIN

The phenomenon referred to as "atomization of work" or "the fissured workplace" is not entirely new in Spain. In fact, some of its most typical outcomes have been well known for decades. Subcontracting has for a long time been very common in the construction sector, and it has expanded very quickly to the industrial sector since the

7. WEIL, D., *supra*, pp. 93-177.
8. OJEDA AVILÉS, A., *La deconstrucción del Derecho del Trabajo,* La Ley, 2010, pp. 117-347.
9. For a comparative view on "the fissured workplace" from the standpoint of Labor Law, *see* the other contributions in this Volume and those included in *Comparative Labour Law & Policy Journal*, Vol. 37 (1), 2015.

late 1970s. The most recent development is its rapidly raising diffusion through other sectors in which it was not so frequent, as services (i.e., banking or transport) and retailing activities. The underlying reason is probably the growing popularity of outsourcing strategies among business managers, as a useful mechanism for cost-cutting and shedding responsibilities and, at the same time, increasing profitability and operational flexibility. Besides, supply chains as such have always existed, but they have been increasingly used as a resource in the context of the plans for externalization of business over the last thirty years. On the other hand, contracting-out mere workforce supply was previously forbidden, but it has been widely used since the legalization of temporary work agencies in 1994, probably due to the importance of some activities of a temporary nature in the Spanish economic structure (i.e., construction and tourism sectors) and to an entrepreneurial culture excessively oriented to prefer fixed-term employment rather than indefinite-term contracts.

Business-groups are becoming a quite usual form of organizing activities, especially amongst the Spanish major companies or leading brands, and in the context of multinational corporations. This is the result of different factors: some traditionally large entities have transformed their structures into groups of smaller undertakings for operational reasons and following the aforementioned trends in business organization; at the same time, some previously independent businesses have merged into business-groups, maintaining their legally independent status under a coordinated economic management, as a result of shareholding arrangements and other movements for concentration of capital and strengthening positions in the market; finally, some former big-size public companies have been frequently divided into smaller pieces prior to their privatizing, nevertheless maintaining some interconnections, and they have afterwards tended to increasingly organize their functioning as business-groups (i.e., Telefonica-Movistar, Iberia or the electric companies).

Conversely, franchising could be considered a rather contemporary feature from the outlook of "the fissured workplace." Certainly, this is a kind of contractual relationship between independent businesses that has been for long admitted under Commercial Law. But its role in fissuring of work began to be important only as a result of the arrival to Spain of some well-known franchised brands as McDonald's or Burger King, by the 1980s. In recent years, this form of arranging business is quite generalized either for either fast food or other different types of restaurants, and it is becoming very popular in other sectors too, from grocery and bakery to retailing or janitorial activities.[10] Moreover, it is currently being used not only by leading brands, but also by more modest entrepreneurs and start-ups. In this area, the use of franchising with the aim or effect of blurring employment responsibilities emerges as a raising problem. On the other hand, a relevant factor that, among others, could be underlying the rapid development of franchising is connected to the increasing customers' demand for

10. In fact, Spain is probably the European country in which franchising is most widespread, following USA, Canada and China in the world ranking. In 2014, there were 1.199 operating brands and 4.4619 franchised branches in Spain, and 296 Spanish brands operating 19.874 franchised branches in 132 other countries (AFE, "La franquicia en España. Informe 2015", Madrid, 2015; AFE, "La franquicia Española en el mundo. Informe 2015", Madrid, 2015).

"low-cost" products and services, frequently delivered through franchises or similar schemes.

The topic of "the fissured workplace" is not unacknowledged in Spanish Labor Law, as there have been a number of academic, statutory and case law contributions on the matter in the last decades, mainly from the standpoint of the consequences of outsourcing over employees' rights and industrial relations.[11] In particular, subcontracting has been regulated for long, as it is the most visible and traditional outcome of the phenomenon. These rules follow different aims, like serving as a deterrent to negligent behavior of the actors in a subcontracting chain, tackling bogus/fraudulent subcontracting practices, or fighting against non-payment and abuse of workers in the context of domestic subcontracting practices. Responsibilities in cases of subcontracting were provided for the first time in Law 16/1976, April 8, of Industrial Relations, and further regulated in detail by Decree 3677/1970, December 17, establishing rules to prevent and punish fraudulent activities in the recruitment and employment of workers. These regulatory patterns were afterwards adopted by the Workers' Statute since its first version of 1980(Law 8/1980, March 10), where Article 42 contained provisions about subcontracting that are very similar to the ones in force today, although they were initially limited to declare joint liability of the client/owner for the debts on wages and Social Security obligations of the contractor or subcontractor concerning their employees. These provisions were transferred to the later versions of the Workers' Statute, including that of 2015 (Legislative Decree 2/2015, October 23), currently in force. The regulatory basic scheme has therefore remained the same, although there have been several partial amendments tending to reinforce the specific framework of rights and obligations in subcontracting.[12] In contrast, other forms of fissuring the workplace have not been considered as attentively as subcontracting. Temporary work agencies are consistently regulated since their legalization in 1994, with several slight amendments, namely in the context of the latest major labor market reforms.[13] Conversely, other features of the "fissured workplace" as business-groups and franchising are only addressed by quite poor and isolated piecemeal provisions or some case law approaches, of unequal relevance and success, as it will be explained below.

11. For an early and profound overall view, CRUZ VILLALÓN, J., "Descentralización productiva y sistema de relaciones laborales", *Revista de trabajo y Seguridad Social*, n. 13, 1994, pp. 7-33.
12. The first relevant modification of Article 42 of the Workers' Statute (Law 12/2001, July 9) incorporated information rights for workers and their representatives in regard to subcontracting processes. Another update was introduced by Law 43/2006, December 29, with the purpose of reducing workplace accidents in the context of subcontracting. To that aim, that legal piece established specific requirements for coordination among all the undertakings operating in the same workplace, responding to the concern of the social partners for the numerous accidents that had occurred in cases related to subcontracting. Finally, a later reform by Law 13/2012, December 26, extended the deadline for enforceability of the client/owner's liability related to Social Security obligations in regard to the employees of the contractors or subcontractors. On the other hand, going beyond the general regulation of the Workers' Statute, Law 32/2006, October 18, established a special set of rules for subcontracting in the construction sector, with the main aim of reducing workplace accidents in cases of subcontracted construction works.
13. Law 35/2010, September 17, on Urgent Measures for Labor Market Reform, and Law 3/2012, July 6, on Urgent Measures for Labor Market Reform.

§7.03 PROTECTION OF EMPLOYEES IN SUBCONTRACTING PROCESSES

Within the Spanish legal system, the most outstanding measures aiming the protection of workers in the context of the "fissured workplace" are those related to the employees' rights in the context of contracting-out or subcontracting processes, all of them often broadly named "subcontracting,"[14] which are submitted to a framework of joint obligations and liabilities of the diverse involved undertakings that clearly implies going beyond the boundaries of the legal entity of the primary employer.[15] In general, outsourcing by means of external contractors and subcontractors is a lawful way of organizing economic activities in Spain, and limitations to this formula are very few, since Article 38 of the Constitution recognizes freedom to conduct a business, this including the free adoption of the preferred model for carrying out production and selling of goods and services. Nevertheless, as subcontracting causes a shift in corporate responsibility that can affect workers, Labor Law establishes protective rules for employees involved in these situations.[16] The substantial general rules on employees' protection in contracting-out and subcontracting chains are contained mainly in Article 42 of Workers' Statute,[17] Article 168 of the Social Security Law,[18] and Article 24 of Law on Health and Safety at Work,[19] all of them applicable to every economic sector. In addition, there are special rules for subcontracting in the construction sector.[20]

14. Spanish legislation does not provide clear definitions of the different actors and facts involved in subcontracting schemes. Anyhow, judges and experts on Labor Law frequently use some key terms and definitions that should be explained here for better understanding. The client or owner is any person or legal entity, of public or private nature, ordering and/or paying for the works/services or goods provided by other person or entity. The principal contractor is the person or legal entity to whom the client hires the work/service. This contractor can execute the work/service with means and personnel of her own. But the contractor can hire another contractor to execute total or partially the work/service hired by the client. The subcontractor is the person or legal entity hired by the principal contractor or other contractors to execute the work/service. Nevertheless, it is quite usual to refer as subcontractors to all the undertakings involved in contracting-out processes, including the principal contractor. If the contractors/subcontractors successively hire the execution of the works/services to a third party, then a subcontracting chain is created.
15. CRUZ VILLALÓN, J., "Descentralización productiva y responsabilidad laboral por contratas y subcontratas", *Relaciones laborales: Revista crítica de teoría y práctica*, Vol. 1, 1992, pp. 114-162; DE VAL TENA, A. L., "La responsabilidad empresarial en contratas y subcontratas: del supuesto de hecho a la diversidad de regímenes", RIVERO LAMAS, J./ DE VAL TENA, A. L. (Eds.), *Descentralización productiva y responsabilidades empresariales. El "outsourcing"*, Thomson-Aranzadi, 2003, pp. 83-123; GARCÍA MURCIA, J., "Contratas y subcontratas", *Revista del Ministerio de Trabajo e Inmigración*, n. 48, 2004, pp. 13-38.
16. For a general comparative perspective on the diverse European regulations on the matter, JORENS, Y./ PETERS, S./ HOWERZIJL, M., "Study on the protection of workers' rights in subcontracting processes in the European Union", European Commission, DG EMPL/B2-VC/2011/0015, pp. 5-192.
17. Royal Legislative Decree 2/2015, October 23.
18. Royal Legislative Decree 8/2015, October 30.
19. Law 31/1995, November 8, on Health and Safety at Work.
20. Law 32/2006, October 18, on Subcontracting in the Construction Sector.

[A] Joint and Several Liabilities and Other Legal Obligations Concerning Subcontracting of Works and Services

Article 42 of the Workers' Statute, entitled "subcontracting of works and services," establishes a large range of obligations and responsibilities for the different undertakings involved within subcontracting schemes, trying to prevent or to compensate the tendency to circumvention of labor standards that is often underlying in these situations.[21] However, Article 42 of the Workers' Statute is not applicable to all types of contracting-out or subcontracting processes. Indeed, it applies to every economic sector, but only when contracting-out or subcontracting affects the so called "own activity" of the client or "leading business." Therefore, the concept of "own activity" involves an important limitation for the scope of application of these regulations. As a consequence, contracting and subcontracting concerning works and services that are outside of the concept of the "own activity" of the client fall apart of that framework of legal responsibilities and obligations, which covers only the area of contractors and subcontractors directly involved in the core tasks for production of the goods or rendering of the services which are the final product of the whole chain.

That key concept of the "own activity" has been quite controversial in the past. Some academic opinions considered the "own activity" equivalent to all the activity which is "necessary" or "indispensable" for the client, in order to carry out her business properly. Other authors, however, preferred to limit the "own activity" to the accomplishments that are "inherent" to the client's production cycle, a more strict interpretation that would only be referred to those tasks that are a part of the process to develop the final product (good or service), and which, in the absence of contracting-out, would have to be carried out by the leading business itself with its own staff. Finally, the case law of the Spanish Supreme Court of Justice decided to support this second interpretation, therefore narrowing the area of action of the regulations on subcontracting established in Article 42 of the Workers' Statute.[22] Consequently, according to the legal concept of "own activity" (as interpreted by the case law of the Supreme Court), contracting-out and subcontracting of auxiliary, instrumental or accessorial activities, not withstanding how necessary they are for the company that hires them, is excluded from the application of the obligations and responsibilities contained in Article 42 of the Workers' Statute. So it is, for instance, with regard to building of infrastructure, repairing and maintenance of company's facilities or machinery, to the promotion, marketing, distribution and transport tasks, or to surveillance and security, janitorial, canteen and cafeteria services. Of course, all those contractors whose activity is limited to supplying of materials and resources and that are not directly involved in tasks "inherent to the production circle" of the client are outside of the scope of application of Article 42 of the Workers' Statute too. In addition, it must be pointed that Article 42 explicitly indicates that there will be no liability of the client for the acts of the contractor when the contracted activity relates exclusively to

21. Among others, BARREIRO FERNÁNDEZ, G., "Responsabilidad empresarial en contratas y subcontratas (Article 42)", *Revista española de derecho del trabajo*, n. 100 (1), 2000, pp. 889-902.
22. Supreme Court 3-10-2008, app. 1675/2007.

the construction or repairing of a family home, or when the client does not hire it because of a business activity. Therefore, Article 42 of the Workers' Statute contains a quite complex set of rules on prevention of fraud, joint liability and information rights, but focusing exclusively in contracting and subcontracting related to the "own activity" of the client or leading business, as explained, and consequently not being applicable to other forms of contracting-out. On the other hand, Article 42 of Workers' Statute is applicable in the public sector too, and specifically in regard to administrative concessions involving the indirect management of a public service.[23] But there are some peculiarities, according to Public Administrative Law on public sector contracts, and to specific provisions referred to public sector contracts in the fields of defense and security. Besides, Article 42 also applies to the so-called contract for posting of disabled employees concluded between a "special disabled-employment center" and an ordinary company for temporary employment of those workers.[24]

Article 42 of the Workers' Statute establishes checking obligations for the client or owner for which the contractors or subcontractors provide works or services. It obliges the client, owner (or any of the contractors in regard to their own subcontractors) to check, using the appropriate request to the Social Security Treasure, if the contractor or subcontractor is up to date in Social Security related payments. If the General Treasury of the Social Security certifies that there are no debts, or if there is no answer within thirty days, the client/owner is then relieved of liability concerning Social Security obligations of the contractor/subcontractor in regard to her workers. This certification must be requested every month during the period of time along which the relationship between the client/owner and the contractor/subcontractor extends. Otherwise, if the client/owner does not accomplish this previous checking obligation, or if subcontracting goes ahead while the Treasury of Social Security has assessed a lack of payment, the client/owner will be held responsible for the Social Security obligations of the contractor/subcontractor in regard to her staff, during all the period not covered by certificates on the absence of debts.[25]

Accordingly, along with the checking and information obligations strongly connected to them, Article 42(2) of the Workers' Statute establishes a rule on joint and several liability of the client/owner and the contractor/subcontractor concerning Social Security payments referred to the employees of the last, shared responsibilities that can be nevertheless avoided by the client/owner through the aforementioned mechanism of the certification issued by the General Treasury of the Social Security. This joint and several liability is exclusively referred to Social Security debts arising during the period in which contracting or subcontracting was being executed, but it can be enforced within three years after the termination of the relationship between both undertakings. These provisions refer not only to Social Security contributions and charges for outdated accomplishment, but also to payment of social benefits in some cases in

23. Supreme Court 24-06-2008, app. 345/2007.
24. Article 1(4) Royal Decree 290/2004, February 20, on Promoting Employment of Disabled Workers.
25. Supreme Court (3rd Chamber) 12-7-1994, app. 9559/1990.Supreme Court (3rd Chamber) 30-7-1996, app. 755/1991.Supreme Court (3rd Chamber) 4-3-1997, app. 329/1991.

which the employer may be obliged to directly afford them, so the arising responsibilities are quite serious and could reach large amounts of money. Besides, Article 42(2) of the Workers' Statute imposes joint and several liability of the client/owner concerning wages owed by the contractor/subcontractor to her employees. This liability is established in regard to debts arising during the execution of the contracted works or services, being enforceable within a year since the termination of the subcontracting relationship. On the other hand, conversely to what has been explained for Social Security obligations, there is no possibility for the client/owner to avoid the application of this joint and several liability on wages by means of previous checking proceedings, so it covers the whole contracting-out or subcontracting process in every case. This liability includes unpaid salaries in a strict sense, including remuneration due for holidays not taken at the time of termination of the employment relationship, but excluding any other economic concepts or perceptions that do not have that wage nature, as for instance severance payments or compensations related to unlawful dismissal.[26]

Thus, these regulations, both in the areas of Social Security obligations and wages, provide that all the contracting-out undertakings are joint and several liable regarding wages owed by the contractors and subcontractors to their employees and debts for Social Security payments during the term of the subcontracting relationship. Furthermore, as they have been interpreted by the Supreme Court, these responsibilities are applied as "chain liability," being therefore claimable against every undertaking participating in any of the upper links of a subcontracting chain, from the lower level subcontractor to the leading business on the top, and through all the range of intermediate level contractors.[27] On the other hand, creditors (the workers of the contractor or subcontractor who are owed wages, or the Social Security Treasury) can claim against any of the two (or more) undertakings responsible for the payment of the debt, and even against them all simultaneously. When the employees have claimed the debt to one of the responsible entities and this has not made the payment of that debt in full, the workers may claim to any of the other stakeholders of the subcontracting chain for the amounts remaining.

Article 42 of the Workers' Statute also includes the obligation of the involved undertakings to inform their workers about the circumstances of subcontracting. Again, these obligations only apply to the subcontracting processes related to the "own activity" of the client, as explained above. The employees of the contractor or subcontractor must be informed in written by their employer of the identity of the client for which they are serving at the time. This information must be provided before the start of the works or services to be performed for another undertaking, and it must contain the name and address of the client/owner/principal contractor, and her registered office and tax identification number. Along with those individual information rights, Article 42 establishes collective information rights in regard to the workers' representatives of the staff of both the client and contractor/subcontractor too, as it will be explained below in the section dedicated to collective rights. Also, the contractor or

26. Supreme Court 23-12-2003, app. 4525/2003.
27. Supreme Court 9-7-2002, app. 2175/2001.

subcontractor shall report the identity of the client to the General Treasury of the Social Security. In addition, when the client and the contractors or subcontractors continuously share the same workplace, the client must have a registry book in which information in regard to all the various undertakings involved in subcontracting on the premises of the leading business must be recorded.[28]

Anyhow, Article 42 of the Workers' Statute is not the only provision focusing on subcontracting. From August 1, 2011, undertakings which contract out works or services of their "own activity," or to be performed continuously in the workplace of their property, have an additional obligation to previously check that the workers to be involved in such subcontracting processes are adequately registered into the Social Security system.[29] Besides, Article 168 of the Social Security Law establishes secondary liability for the client regarding the Social Security debts of contractors and subcontractors arising during the term of subcontracting. Conversely to the regulation of Article 42 of the Workers' Statute, this responsibility applies to all forms of subcontracting, not only to those related to the core "own activity" of the client. On the other hand, it covers not only Social Security contributions, but also the direct payment of benefits by the employer in the cases in which she has been held responsible to do so. When the employer fails to fulfill Social Security obligations regarding register, affiliation and contribution in regard to her employees, she is considered obliged to direct payment of Social Security benefits at her own cost.[30] In this case, the client/principal/contractors can be declared liable for such direct payment. However, in relation to both contributions and direct payment of benefits, this is a secondary or subsidiary liability that can only be claimed against the client/owner if the principal debtor (contractor/subcontractor) has been previously declared totally or partially insolvent.

[B] Health and Safety at Work Within Subcontracting Schemes

Law 31/1995, November 8, on Health and Safety at Work, establishes a number of obligations in case of subcontracting, especially when the activities of workers belonging to the staff of different undertakings are developed in the same workplace.[31] These are mainly obligations to report, to cooperate and to coordinate between

28. The registry book shall contain the following information in regard to each contractor or subcontractor: (1) name or business-name, address and tax identification number of the contractor or subcontractor; (2) purpose and duration of the contract; (3) place of execution of the contract; (4) number of workers to be occupied by the contracts or subcontracts in the workplace of the client undertaking, and (5) measures envisaged for coordination of activities from the standpoint of health and safety at work.
29. Article 5 Royal Decree Law 5/2011, April 29, on Measures for the Regulation and Control of Undeclared Employment and Promoting Rehabilitation of Home Buildings. Failure to comply is punishable as a serious infringement, according to Article 22(12) Royal Legislative Decree 5/2000, August 4, on Infringements and Penalties in the Social Order.
30. Article 167 Royal Legislative Decree 8/2015, October 30, General Social Security Law.
31. DE VAL ARNAL, J. J., "Deberes de seguridad y salud laboral y externalización de actividades empresariales: la coordinación", RIVERO LAMAS, J./ DE VAL TENA, A. L. (Eds.), *Descentralización productiva y responsabilidades empresariales. El "outsourcing"*, Thomson-Aranzadi, 2003, pp. 163-186.

employers, and for the adoption of various prevention measures, as in regard to individual means and resources for protection against risks and hazards. These duties have been extended not only to any kind of employment relationships, but to self-employed people working in such shared workplaces too. In addition, undertakings (the client) that contract out their "own activity" are required to verify that contractors or subcontractors adequately comply with the rules on health and safety at work.[32] The duty of care in the area of health and safety requires the client to ensure that contractors and subcontractors fulfill their obligations regarding the prevention of occupational hazards while working in the workplace of the client/owner, during the term of the contract and in the work related to the "own activity" of the client. In executing this duty of care, Royal Decree 171/2004, January 30, imposes instrumental obligations to the client, such as the following: requiring contractors and subcontractors, before the start of the activity in the workplace, to evidence in written that they have made the necessary risk assessment and planning of preventive measures concerning the engaged activity, and that they have fulfilled the information and training obligations for workers there posted; checking that contractors and subcontractors have established the necessary measures for coordination among them; finally, having a registry which reflects all the circumstances of the contracting or subcontracting process, including the measures for coordination from the point of view of health and safety at work.

All these obligations on health and safety at work are enforced by means of the regulation on infringements and penalties contained in Royal Legislative Decree 5/2000, August 4. In the case of a breach, all the undertakings involved in the subcontracting process (including the client business) might be considered responsible, as joint and several liability is applied in this field too. Furthermore, any agreement that they may subscribe in order to avoid joint liability in circumvention of law shall be considered void and null, and should be punished as very serious offence against social legislation.[33] From another point of view, when an accident at work has occurred or its consequences have been aggravated as a result of a failure in prevention of occupational hazards, Article 164 of Social Security Law establishes that the employer will be responsible to pay the employee an additional amount, ranging between supplementary 30%-50%, of the Social Security benefits to which that injured worker might be entitled. This additional amount is called "benefit surcharge" due to lack of adequate health and safety measures. In this regard, when the client and the contractors/subcontractors share the same workplace, the client/owner is likely to be held responsible for the default in complying with the obligations in relation to health and safety at work, as she is the one who has the full capacity available to implement prevention measures within the physical environment in which the accident occurs, and the one that ultimately benefits from the products or results of work. Therefore, the main contractor may also be responsible for that "benefit surcharge," and this cannot

32. Article 24(3) Law 31/1995, 8 November, on Health and Safety at Work.
33. Articles 13(14) and 42(3) Royal Legislative Decree 5/2000, August 4, on Infringements and Penalties in the Social Order.

be excluded by means of agreements between the engaged undertakings, which should be considered void and null.

[C] Specific Provisions for the Construction Sector

Law 32/2006, October 18, on Subcontracting in the Construction Sector, contains special provisions for subcontracting in this specific economic activity.[34] Most of these rules aim to adequately ensure health and safety of the employees of contractors and subcontractors, as they were approved in line with a great concern of trade unions related to the frequency and seriousness of accidents in the context of subcontracted works within the construction sector. Anyhow, this regulation also seeks to improve job security and working conditions for the workers employed on those premises, in broader terms. For this purposes, this act provides a number of special limitations on subcontracting in this sector, which are to be applied additionally to the general legal framework explained before. First, this legislation explicitly prohibits contracting-out when the subcontractor's role is limited to providing workforce, that is, when only hand tools, including those portable or motorized, are needed to perform the relevant contracted work. Second, these special regulations establish restrictions to the number of undertakings that can be involved in construction works through contracting-out, therefore blocking the indefinite extension of the subcontracting sequence. While in other activities there are no limits regarding the number of participants in subcontracting schemes, in the construction sector the chain is circumscribed to three levels as a general rule. The law does not allow subcontracting the activity for the self-employed people, nor for the third subcontractor.[35] As an exception, Law 32/2006 allows a fourth level of subcontracting in some special situations, when it can be justified on grounds related to the high level of specialization of the work, technical difficulties or unexpected events.[36] This possibility is not supported, however, neither for self-employed or for undertakings that do not use more than hand tools, except in cases of force majeure.

Additionally, Law 32/2006 requires the contractors and subcontractors involved in construction works to monitor the compliance by subcontractors and self-employed workers of a wide range of legal obligations. Among other things, in order to participate in subcontracting of construction works, the contractors and subcontractors need to be in possession of an accreditation certifying that they are adequately equipped and that their staff has the necessary training on prevention of risks and hazards, being consequently listed in the public registry of certified undertakings. So, the client/owner/contractors need to check that contractors/subcontractors meet these requirements prior to hiring them. Subcontracting with companies that have failed to

34. For a deeper analysis on this specific act, MERCADER UGUINA, J. R. (Coord.), *Contratas y subcontratas en el sector de la construcción*, Lex Nova, 2008; GARCÍA BLASCO, J. (Dir.)/ DE VAL TENA, A. L. (Coord.), *La subcontratación en el sector de la construcción,* Thomson-Aranzadi, 2009.
35. Article 5 of Law 32/2006, October 18, on Subcontracting in the Construction Sector.
36. Article 5(2f)(3) of Law 32/2006, October 18, on Subcontracting in the Construction Sector.

comply with accreditation and registration obligations, as subcontracting in breach of the aforementioned limits of Law 32/2006, involves joint and several liability in relation to Labor Law and Social Security obligations of contractors and subcontractors. This responsibility is broader than that covered by Article 42(2) of the Workers' Statute for the following reasons: (a) it is applicable not only to subcontracting referred to the "own activity" of the client, but in any case; (b) it does not include temporary restrictions relating to the deadline to enforce it; finally, (c) it refers to all Labor Law responsibilities, not strictly to wages, so it may reach other perceptions such as severance payments or voluntary improvements of Social Security benefits.

[D] Evaluation and Future Prospect

The rules on joint and several liability of the client/owner and contractors/ subcontractors, including chain liability, are powerful and surely useful in order to ensure payment of wages to contractor's or subcontractor's employees, along with adequate compliance with Social Security obligations, and they seem to be properly serving in practice. It is to remark that they create a strong incentive for contracting-out companies to carefully select only solvent contractors and subcontractors that adequately comply with wage payment and Social Security obligations. However, these regulations contained in Article 42 of the Workers' Statute are attached to a limited scope of application according to the narrow definition of subcontracting of the "own activity" of the client, therefore not being applicable to all kinds of subcontracting. Furthermore, that definition has been built on the basis of a quite old-fashioned image of contracting-out in traditional manufacturing processes, with the fordist-taylorist paradigm as background, therefore leaving out other new forms of outsourcing that might deserve a similar treatment.[37] It could be arguable, but there should be at least some debate on updating that conception and somehow extending the area covered by these provisions. Besides, joint and several liabilities in subcontracting arising from Article 42 of the Workers Statute refer only to Social Security obligations and wages, but it might be convenient to extend joint or subsidiary liability to other employer's responsibilities, as dismissals or working time issues. Beyond Article 42, other regulations addressing subcontracting, as the specific ones for the construction sector or those on health and safety matters, seem to be even more complete and penetrating, but it must be said that lack of adequate compliance is not rare in practice.[38]

37. VALDÉS DAL- RÉ, F., "Descentralización productiva y desorganización del Derecho del Trabajo", *supra*, p. 4.; ESTEVE SEGARRA, A., *Externalización laboral en empresas multiservicios y redes de empresas de servicios auxiliares*, Tirant lo Blanch, 2016, pp. 116-120.

38. In regard to the already existing academic discussions and proposals for the amendment and update of the provisions on subcontracting, GARCÍA MURCIA, J., "La dispersa regulación de las contratas y subcontratas: propuestas de cambio", *Documentación laboral*, n. 68, 2, 2003, pp. 129-145; DE VAL TENA, A. L., *supra*, pp. 120-123.

§7.04 CONTRACTING-OUT WORKFORCE SUPPLY: GENERAL PROHIBITION AND CONSTRAINED ADMISSION OF TEMPORARY AGENCY WORK

Whereas subcontracting is considered a lawful way of organizing business activities, the loan of workers is considered unlawful in Spain as a general rule, with the exception of assignment of employees by means of legally authorized temporary work agencies according to their specific legal framework, and few other particular situations (business-groups, special regulations for professional sports, seaport dockers and protected employment of disabled persons). This means that contracting-out or subcontracting exclusively referred to workforce supply, with no other input by the contractor/subcontractor apart from assignment of employees, is rigorously forbidden, unless in the aforementioned cases in which it is explicitly allowed under strict legal conditions, as it will be immediately explained in detail.

[A] Illegal Assignment of Workers

As the pure and simple loan of workers is in general considered fully illegal, Spanish legislation provides rules aiming to prevent companies and other undertakings shedding their responsibilities as employers by means of contracting-out mere workforce supply. In particular, these regulations seek to tackle those situations where the client companies try to circumvent Labor Law by using a bogus appearance of subcontracting that, indeed, just hides behind a plain loan of workers. These regulations are contained mainly in Article 43 of the Workers' Statute, entitled "Illegal assignment of workers." Its first section establishes the general prohibition of loan of workers, in the already explained terms. Besides, the second section addresses the core legal issue of defining what illegal assignment of workers is, and how to distinguish between illicit trafficking of employees and, on the other hand, lawful subcontracting, what might be difficult in practice. In this sense, Article 43(2) of the Workers' Statute provides that there is no subcontracting, but illegal assignment of workers, whenever any of the following circumstances are met: (a) the object of the service contracts between the involved undertakings is solely limited to a mere provision of workers; (b) the contractor or subcontractor does not have a differentiated economic activity or its own and stable organization, or does not have the means and resources to carry out a business on its own, or (c) the contractor or subcontractor does not effectively perform the functions inherent to being a true employer (as, for instance, managerial powers, setting of payment, monitoring of workers or deciding about new hires and dismissals).

These criteria for assessing illegal assignment of workers, now made explicit in statutory law, were previously developed by the labor courts, providing an important background for legal interpretation on the matter. According to this case law, there is illegal assignment of workers when the contractor/subcontractor is just an empty nutshell used for shedding employees, under the false appearance of subcontracting between different undertakings. But even if the contractor/subcontractor is an undertaking with a consistent structure and a real business activity, illegal assignment could be assessed too, relaying on the key criterion lastly outlined by Article 43(2) of the Workers' Statute: who is effectively behaving as the real employer of the employees? That is to say, for instance, who is really giving orders and instructions to workers? Who supplies working tools, resources or even uniforms? Who is checking the correct performance of work and how? Do the supervisors of work belong to the staff of the contractor/subcontractor or to that of the client? If the answers point to the contractor/subcontractor, that is lawful subcontracting, while if they point to the client, the situation should be considered as illegal assignment of workers.

Illegal assignment of workers leads to joint and several liability of all the involved undertakings, both the workforce providers and the user undertakings.[39] These shared responsibilities include absolutely all Labor Law and Social Security obligations in regard to the illegally assigned employees (wages, severance payments and other economic compensations for dismissals, health and safety at work, Social Security contributions, direct payment of social benefits, among others), covering thus a much wider scope than in the case of lawful subcontracting. In addition, the workers engaged in these unlawful practices have the right to claim the consideration as permanent employees either of the workforce provider or of the user undertaking, with the same working conditions than any other similar worker in those employers' staff, and seniority counting since the beginning of the illegal assignment situation.[40] On the other hand, illegal workforce supply is considered a very serious infringement punishable with an administrative penalty, consisting in fines that may reach quite high amounts.[41] Joint and several liability applies to providers and users also in regard to these responsibilities.[42] In the most serious cases, this behavior can be punished even with a penalty of imprisonment from two to five years and fine from six to twelve months under Criminal Law.

[B] Temporary Work Agencies

The loan of workers, in general forbidden as it has been explained, is however admitted in Spanish legislation when it is carried out by temporary work agencies according to their specific legal framework.[43] These provisions follow the model of allowing this particular form of outsourcing, but only to a limited extent, under a quite strict administrative control and abiding respect to a wide range of conditions and responsibilities. To begin, temporary work agencies can operate as such only under an administrative authorization by the Labor Administration.[44] The issuing (and the maintenance) of this entitlement requires the fulfillment of some complex organizational requisites in regard to the solvency and functioning of the company. Among

39. Article 43(3) of Workers' Statute.
40. Article 43(4) of Workers' Statute.
41. Articles 8(2) and 40(1)(c) of Legislative Decree 5/2000.
42. Article 42(1) of Legislative Decree 5/2000 in connection to Article 43 of Workers' Statute.
43. This regulation is contained in Law 14/1994, June 1, on Temporary Work Agencies, and Decree 417/2015, a national regulation on the matter that is also in accordance to EU Directive 2008/104 (and Directive 91/383/CEE in regard to health and safety at work).
44. Article 2 of Law 14/1994.

other things, the temporary work agency shall institute a financial guarantee, an economic deposit that needs to be fixed in order to ensure payment of workers' wages and Social Security obligations, reaching a considerable amount (twenty-five times minimum wage in the beginning and as a total minimum, and 10% of total salaries when the company has already started to operate).[45] Other obligations refer to maintaining a minimum permanent staff and compulsory investment in occupational training of workers.[46]

The hiring of workers through temporary work agencies is only allowed in some specific cases in which the temporary character of the workforce needs is clearly evidenced, therefore not being lawful to use this mechanism to recruit employees in regard to activities of a permanent or indefinite-term nature. So, the assignment of workers from temporary work agencies to user undertakings is subject to the prerequisite of existing temporary hiring grounds, and to maximum duration limits, both aspects matching to the regulations established for individual fixed-term contracts.[47] If these requirements are not met, the situation should be qualified as "illegal assignment of workers," with the consequences above explained according to Article 43 of the Workers' Statute: joint and several liability of the agency and the user undertaking in regard to all Labor Law and Social Security obligations, and possibility for the workers to claim declaration as permanent employees of the staff of either of the involved entities. The workers may also claim the declaration as permanent employees of the user undertaking if they continue to perform work on its premises exceeding the maximum period of duration established for the temporary assignment of workers.[48] Besides, assignment of workers through temporary work agencies is explicitly forbidden in regard to some especially dangerous jobs, for substitution of workers on strike, for covering positions previously suppressed by the user due to economic or organizational reasons, or for assignment of employees through another temporary work agency.[49]

Temporary workers hired through an agency are entitled to the same labor rights that they would have enjoyed if they had been directly recruited by the user undertaking, at least in regard to "essential working conditions."[50] That consideration as "essential" is given in regard to the following matters: remuneration, workday and maximum working time, overtime working, rest and breaks, holidays and night work. The same rule shall be applied in regard to protection of young employees and pregnant workers, or in relation to equal treatment and non-discrimination principles. On the other hand, when the temporary contract is terminated, the employees are entitled to a severance payment, equivalent to twelve days of salary for each year of service.[51] However, in the context of temporary work agencies, subsidiary liability is imposed to the user undertaking concerning wages, Social Security obligations and compensations

45. Article 3 of Law 14/1994.
46. Article 2 of Law 14/1994.
47. Articles 6 and 7 of Law 14/1994, in connection to Article 15 of the Workers' Statute.
48. Article 7 of Law 14/1994.
49. Article 8 and additional provision two of Law 14/1994.
50. Article 11(1) of Law 14/1994.
51. Article 11(1) of Law 14/1994.

for the termination of the contract in regard to the posted workers, being applicable as a secondary responsibility in the case of insolvency of the temporary work agency, and all along the duration of the workforce supplying contract between the involved entities.[52] However, this turns into joint and several liability if the workforce supplying contract has been arranged violating the already explained legal requirements established in Law 14/1994 in regard to grounds and conditions for agency work.

Finally, the special legal framework on agency work establishes a specific scheme on employer's responsibilities of the different involved entities. The temporary work agency is the formal employer and, as such, it is in charge of most employer's functions and responsibilities (i.e., payment of wages and social security contributions or dismissals). But the user undertaking is the one entitled for direct management and monitoring of work performance, and it is also mainly responsible in the field of health and safety protection for temporary workers, and regarding the aforementioned Social Security "benefit surcharge."[53] The same liability regime is applicable respectively in connection to administrative penalties (fines) for ordinary infringements on wages and health and safety.[54] On the other hand, contraventions related to prohibitions, terms and conditions or preventive measures regulated in Law 14/1994 can be punished by means of administrative penalties specifically foreseen for temporary agency work in Legislative Decree 5/2000: Article 18 lists minor, serious and very serious punishable infringements of temporary work agencies (e.g., unlawful arrangement of workforce supplying contracts, or lack of actualization of the legally required financial guarantee for wages and Social Security payments); besides, Article 19 contains minor, serious and very serious infringements of user undertakings (e.g., unlawful arrangement of workforce supplying contracts, and lack of information, formation or preventive measures regarding occupational risks for temporary workers). In all these cases, fines can reach important amounts, depending on the grade of guiltiness and seriousness of the infringement, and increasable in the case of reiteration.[55]

[C] Evaluation and Future Prospect

Article 43 of the Workers Statute on illegal assignment of workers is a potent instrument in order to tackle trafficking of employees or abuse in contracting-out workforce supply, as it imposes joint and several liabilities to every undertaking involved in such practices in regard to all Labor Law and Social Security obligations. In other words, what this provision does is going beyond the boundaries of the legal entities to declare them as joint employers, being therefore the most ambitious regulation of Spanish legislation in that sense. It is frequently applied by the courts in practice, playing a key role in regard to those cases in which a formal appearance of lawful subcontracting hides behind pure and simple shedding of employment. Accordingly, contracting-out of workforce supply is quite effectively limited to the action of

52. Article 16(3) of Law 14/1994.
53. Article 16(2) of Law 14/1994.
54. Article 42(2 and 3) of Legislative Decree 5/2000.
55. According to Articles 40 and 41 of Royal Legislative Decree 5/2000.

temporary work agencies, which are at the same time subject to a very strict legal framework. The rules on the matter adequately ensure the basic labor rights of the temporary employees, as namely the payment of wages, backed by a financial guarantee and subsidiary liability of the user undertaking.

From another perspective, it is important to outline how these legal rules establish Labor Law responsibilities beyond the formal employer: Article 43 of the Workers' Statute allows to declare illegal assignment of workers and consequent joint liabilities when it is not the person or entity that has actually signed the employment contract, but the one behind, who performs "the functions inherent to being a true employer"; on the other hand, the legal framework on agency work establishes a distribution of responsibilities between the temporary agency and the user undertaking, according to a separate consideration of different areas of employer's functions. Hence, these regulations somewhat point to a "functional concept of the employer," an approach that has been suggested as a meaningful response to the phenomenon of the "fissured workplace,"[56] and that might be useful to explore more deeply in the future, maybe taking these provisions as starting point for a surely convenient update of the definition of the employer within Spanish Labor Law.[57]

§7.05 OTHER OUTCOMES OF "THE FISSURED WORKPLACE": PIECEMEAL REGULATIONS AND LEGAL RESPONSES "UNDER CONSTRUCTION"

Subcontracting and contracting-out workforce supply are the most obvious forms of workplace "fissurization," but not the only ones. Other formulas of economic cooperation among businesses and companies as supply chains, business-groups and franchising have played an important role in deconstructing the workplace from the old picture of the large industrial factory to the new one of the business network. However, Spanish Labor Law focuses almost exclusively in those more evident types of outsourcing, while it provides very few and quite poor legal responses regarding these other more subtle ways of externalization. These consist of rather isolated legal provisions and some deeper case law interpretations developed to fill-in an area in which there is still little to tell, and much to do. Besides, the widespread trend of shifting from traditional salaried employment to (sometimes pretended) independent self-employed contractors -frequently involved in subcontracting, supply-chain or franchising schemes under the control of a leading business- is another key element underlying "atomization of work," which involves an increasing tendency to "escape" from the

56. In regard to the idea of a functional concept of the employer, DEAKIN, S., "The Changing Concept of the 'Employer' in Labour Law", *Industrial Law Journal*, Vol. 30, n. 1, 2001, pp. 79-84; PRASSL, J., *The Concept of the Employer*, Oxford University Press, 2015, pp. 149-231.

57. MOLERO MARAÑÓN, M.L, "Sobre la inminente necesidad de revisar el concepto de empresario en su dimensión jurídico-laboral", *Relaciones laborales: Revista crítica de teoría y práctica*, Vol. 1, 2001, pp. 561-594.

application of labor standards,[58] in spite of some legal instruments and judiciary decisions trying to counteract against it.

[A] Supply Chains: Can They Be Subsumed Within the Current Legal Framework?

Supply chains in the strict sense (this is, providing material resources to client businesses) are not explicitly regulated as such in Spanish Labor Law. Therefore, the client business and the suppliers are to be seen in general as independent legal entities, each one with its own staff and separate Labor Law and Social Security responsibilities in regard to their respective employees. However, depending on the precise circumstances in which the supply relationship is performed, the situation may fall under the scope of application of the provisions on subcontracting or assignment of workers, in the terms explained in the above sections. For instance, if the object of the supply relationship is hiring and lending of workforce (and provided that it is done out of the legal framework of temporary work agencies), that should be qualified as illegal assignment of workers under Article 43 of the Workers' Statute, consequently leading to going beyond the boundaries of the legal entities by means of the already-mentioned rules on joint and several liability, and compulsory integration of the employees into the permanent staff of either of the engaged undertakings at their choice.

Besides, Labor Law regulations on subcontracting might be applied to supply chains if the engagement between the client and the supplier is too close, going further than a simple selling-buying of goods and services, a renting contract or other purely commercial relationships between fully independent legal entities. If the activities carried out by the supplier are totally integrated into the production process leaded by the client, as a core part inherently belonging to it, that could be qualified as subcontracting of the "own activity" of the client, therefore being applicable the above-described rules set in Article 42 of the Workers' Statute, including those about joint and several liability on wages and Social Security obligations. Nevertheless, this requires clearly evidencing that the situation is a true case of externalization rather than a mere external supply of resources, and this might entail difficult interpretation issues in practice. However, these could be addressed by assessing some relevant circumstances: does the supplied good or service have a separate economic utility itself, or does it only make sense on the premises of the client as leading business? Is the supplier free to supply the same goods and services openly in the market for other clients, or is she working on that exclusively for a leading business? Is the supplier allowed to freely manage the production process herself, or is this necessarily carried out according to strict standards previously given by the client? The aforementioned regulations on subcontracting of the "own activity" could only be applied when the answers to these or other similar questions point to a really strong outsourcing link

58. RODRÍGUEZ-PIÑERO, M., "La huída del Derecho del Trabajo", *Relaciones Laborales*, n. 12, 1992, pp. 1-8.

between the involved undertakings. If that is not the case, supplier and client are to be considered as independent businesses with fully separate Labor Law responsibilities.

[B] Business-Groups: Isolated Statutory Provisions and "Piercing the Corporate Veil"

Business-groups and corporate groups, in the different various forms of holding, trust, crossed shareholding and other types of coordination of economic activities, are a rising phenomenon in the economy of the whole world, and Spain is not an exception. However, Spanish Labor Law provides very few statutory provisions explicitly addressing it, as the scope of application of regulations continues to be based mainly on a classical and quite formal concept of employer referred separately to each legal entity that directly hires its own staff.[59] The employment relationship within business-groups is expressly considered as such only in regard to a pair of specific cases: high-level managers, who can be promoted from ordinary work in a company to managing tasks in the same or another entity belonging to the same business-group;[60] on the other hand, the regulation on posting of workers for transnational rendering of services is applicable when the employees of any kind are posted to a workplace of their employer or of "another undertaking belonging to the same business-group."[61] Besides, some other provisions that will be mentioned later take business-groups into consideration from the perspective of collective Labor Law and information rights of the workers' representatives.

With that quite poor background as starting point, the courts have developed some creative solutions to deal with some Labor Law related issues arising from business-group relationships in practice, as the problems of identification of the real employer, the risk of circumvention of responsibilities and the situations of employees' mobility between the different companies of a group, among others.[62] The milestone in this regard has been the application of the doctrine on "piercing the veil," this meaning trespassing the formal legal outlook to check what the external appearance of independent entities hides behind in reality.[63] As a result, the judges have sometimes identified as true employer a company that pretended to avoid the consideration as such, imposed joint and several liabilities among different companies of a group, or even declared different and apparently separate business as joint employer, using as underlying legal basis the analogic application of the shared responsibilities established in Article 42 (subcontracting), 43 (illegal assignment of workers) and 44 (change in ownership of business or workplace) of the Workers' Statute.

59. Article 1(2) of the Workers' Statute.
60. According to Article 9 of Royal Decree 1382/1985, August 1, on Special Employment Relationship of Managers.
61. Article 2 of Law 45/1999, November 19, on Temporary Posting of Workers in the Framework of Transnational Rendering of Services.
62. OJEDA AVILÉS, A., *supra*, pp. 231-233.
63. Supreme Court 18-5-1998, app. 3310/1997; 9-7-2001, app. 4378/1999; 26-9-2001, app. 558/2001, and 6-3-2002, app. 1666/2001.

Although the concept of employer outlined in Article 1(2) of the Workers' Statute refers to a natural person, entity or joint-ownership with a separate legal status, the courts have said that different formally independent bodies can be considered as joint employers being part of the same employment relationship with an employee if some circumstances are met. When the employee has been performing work equally and simultaneously or successively for different undertakings belonging to the same economic group, being difficult to identify a single employer, some judgments tend to consider all of them as joint employer, especially if this situation has extended for a long period of time.[64] On the other hand, those cases of simultaneous or successive working for different undertakings within a same business-group have been considered lawful posting of employees, excluding the application of the rules on illegal assignment of workers of Article 43 of the Workers' Statute. Besides, several decisions specifically outline that the computation of seniority in such circumstances should totalize the periods of services successively rendered on behalf of all of the entities. On the other hand, the temporary association of companies for specific works or projects has been usually considered as a particular case of joint-ownership acting as a single employer.[65]

Finally, even if the different undertakings of a group are to be considered as legally independent employers, each one with its own separate staff, "piercing the veil" could lead to declare joint and several liability concerning some specific Labor Law responsibilities, for instance, in regard to dismissals or wages. Nevertheless, case law requires some special circumstances in order to do so, in a doctrine which is summarized in three leading cases: Supreme Court 3-5-1990, systemizing the characteristics that justify "piercing the veil"; Supreme Court 26-1-1998, app. 2365/1997, clarifying cases in which "piercing the veil" is not to be applied; finally, Supreme Court 27-5-2013, app. 78/2012, offering a more recent overall consideration. Accordingly, joint and several liability of the different undertakings of a group should be declared in the following situations: (a) when there is an "integrated or unified functioning of work organization amongst the different companies of the group"; (b) when work is performed equally or ambiguously for different undertakings at the same time; (c) when the business network has been created with the purpose of blurring or circumventing Labor Law responsibilities.[66] The mixing of financial resources, credits, buildings, facilities or services of various entities can also be a relevant element to take into account.[67] Of course, the existence of an economic coordinated action, a unified management or other business-group link between the companies is a prerequisite, but not enough basis by itself for "piercing the veil," unless any of the already mentioned further requirements come across.[68]

64. Supreme Court 6-5-1981; 7-12-1987; 17-5-1990; 31-1-1991, app. 780/90; 18-5-1998, app. 3310/1997, and 23-1-2007, app. 641/20.
65. Supreme Court 29-9-1989.
66. Supreme Court 3-5-1990, and 27-5-2013, app. 78/2012.
67. Supreme Court 18-5-1998, app. 3310/1997, and 6-3-2002, app. 1666/2001.
68. Supreme Court 26-1-1998, app. 2365/1997; 30-4-1999, app. 4003/1998; 21-12-2000, app. 4383/1999; 26-12-2001, app. 139/2001, and 20-1-2003, app. 1524/2002.

[C] Franchising and Other Forms of Business Cooperation: A Pending Gap

Franchising and other similar relationships of close business cooperation between legally independent undertakings are allowed and already quite widespread in Spain. However, Labor Law does not address them explicitly.[69] In general, they are seen as contractual relationships between autonomous entities, each of these considered as different single employers in regard to their respective staff. This outlook is firmly supported on elements of the legal background that might seriously block the attempt to shift to another viewpoint: the classic concept of employer established in Article 1(2) of the Workers' Statute on the basis of the separate legal status of the natural person or legal entity that hires the employee within the employment contract and, on the other hand, the legal coverage of franchising and analogous business arrangements as merely contractual relationships according to both traditional and modern categories of contracts between independent entities, as admitted under Civil and Commercial Law (franchising itself, and also works or services contracts, hiring of industry or commercial licensing, among others). However, as it has been accurately pointed, franchising can imply a deep involvement of the franchisor in the production process of the franchisees and in regard to management of their activities, by means of delivering detailed "know-how" guidelines and strict standards and instructions, along with setting sophisticate methods for monitoring compliance.[70] Moreover, those demands and controls of the franchisor might sometimes affect work performance of the franchisee's employees very strongly and directly, despite not being their formal employer.[71] Let's think of the workers of a fast food restaurant whose diary activities are driven – even to the minute – by the rulings of a franchis or requesting, for instance, to fully clean the grill every half an hour. One could even wonder if the subordination inherent to the employment relationship is here really in regard to the actual employer or to someone beyond in fact.

In regard to these cases of particularly penetrating involvement of the franchisor in production and working management of the (only) theoretically independent franchisee, it could perhaps be conceivable to legally discuss the possibility of establishing joint and several liabilities, by means of applying the regulations of subcontracting set in Article 42 of the Workers' Statute, or through the doctrine on "piercing the veil."[72] However, according to what has already been explained, the application of Article 42 would require to clearly evidence that the relationship amongst the franchisor (potentially client or owner) and the franchisee (potentially contractor/subcontractor) is indeed a subcontracting process related to the "own activity" of the first, by means of which an inherent part of the integrated production process globally governed by the client is contracted-out to be externally handled by

69. For an early overview, *see* GONZÁLEZ BIEDMA, E., "Aspectos jurídico-laborales de las franquicias", *Revista española de derecho del trabajo*, n. 97, 1999, pp. 657-680.
70. WEIL, D., *supra*, pp. 122-158.
71. WEIL, D., *supra*, pp. 12-14 and 195-201.
72. OLMO GASCÓN, A. M., *La franquicia. Un procedimiento de descentralización productiva desregulado laboralmente*, Tirant lo Blanch, 2004, pp. 86-168.

the contractor. But this is quite difficult to assess concerning franchising, as this kind of business arrangements usually do not involve deconstruction of a unique production cycle, but simply spreading the different and somehow autonomous production tasks and economic activities (i.e., marketing, production, retailing) of the whole business. In fact, franchisees are frequently in charge only of final retailing or serving, not participating at all in the core of the production process as such, therefore not being applicable to the current regulation on subcontracting to these situations that, as said before, tend to be regarded under the traditional legal culture as mere contractual links between independent businesses, according to Commercial Law categories such as hiring of industry or trade licensing for retailers. On the other hand, the use of the solutions based in "piercing the veil" requires assessing the above-mentioned "special circumstances" outlined by case law, which are not so often met in regard to the most usual forms of franchising, so this seems to be a difficult path to follow that remains somehow unexplored to the date.

Moreover, even if there is not consistent and fully unified case law on the matter, one should outline that the attempts to claim joint Labor Law responsibilities of the franchisor before the courts tend to end in failure.[73] The application of Article 42 on joint and several liabilities in subcontracting processes has been rejected, for instance, in the case of a gas station managed by the actual employer under the brand of a big petrol company.[74] Also, claims of employees of the franchisee for joint and several liabilities of the franchisor according to Article 43 on illegal assignment of workers do often fail.[75] Besides, the declaration of the franchisor as joint employer has been denied in regard to a telephone service and smartphone retailing office integrated in the large franchising network used for that purpose by one of the major telephone companies, Vodafone.[76] Similarly, a judgment related to urgent post services was reluctant to consider the franchisor as true employer of the franchisee's staff.[77] The use of the doctrine on business-groups and "piercing the veil" has been refused in the case of franchised dentistry and ophthalmology clinics,[78] and concerning franchises for language learning centers too.[79] Finally, in the outstanding example of Burger King's and McDonald's fast food restaurants, the claims for joint liability of the franchisor have not been successful to the date.[80] Conversely, a grocery store franchisor has been considered as real employer and jointly responsible for unlawful dismissal of an employee of the franchisee, provided that the first was strongly involved in the ordinary activity of the last.[81] In a case linked to the international brand Coverall, specialized in franchising of janitorial services, "piercing the veil" has actually led to imposing joint and several

73. OJEDA AVILÉS, A., *supra*, pp. 259-268.
74. Catalonia Higher Court 1391/2003, February 26.
75. Castilla y León Higher Court, 167/2007, February 28; Madrid Higher Court 68/2010, February 2, and 373/2012, May 28.
76. Andalucía Higher Court 457/2014, March 13, and 464/2014, March 13.
77. Galicia Higher Court 4395/2015, July 9.
78. Andalucía Higher Court 2654/2005, October 19; Galicia Higher Court 1362/2012, March 5, and 1370/2012, March 6.
79. Galicia Higher Court 11-3-2004; Catalonia Higher Court 260/2005, January 14.
80. Andalucía Higher Court, 194/2000, January 25, and 1928/2000, November 10.
81. Catalonia Higher Court 1105/1993, February 26.

liability.[82] Finally, the business-groups and "piercing the veil" doctrine was applied to declare the franchisor jointly responsible for the void dismissal of a pregnant employee of a franchised hairdressing salon, considering the deep involvement of the leading business in recruitment, training and managing of the staff of the franchisees.[83] Therefore, looking at the overall scenery, one could say that, in regard to franchising, it is quite unlikely to expect going beyond the boundaries of the formal employer under the current legal framework, although it is not absolutely impossible. There might be a window to do so, but it is still to be fully opened.

[D] "Independent" Contractors: "Economically Dependent Autonomous Workers" and "Bogus Self-Employment"

In the "new economy" developed after the 1970s, the archetype of the salaried employee arising from the first industrial revolution and the employment contract have been somewhat in withdrawal as a consequence of emerging "alternative forms of contracting work" as, in particular, the engagement of independent contractors through other diverse kinds of commercial or professional contracts placed - at least initially – outside the boundaries of Labor Law.[84] Furthermore, it is already a quite common business strategy for slimming company structures and staff, and consequently avoiding risks and responsibilities, to replace direct recruitment of employees by shedding tasks - maybe formerly performed inside – to an external multiplicity of individual "self-employed" contractors or "freelance workers," with the aim or the effect of escaping from employment law (and collective bargaining), and sometimes even undermining working conditions. By means of contracting and subcontracting, supply arrangements, franchising schemes or other various types of relationships, these persons are integrated into business networks, formally as autonomous contractors, but frequently under a strict control by the leading company or brand indeed, and probably as the weakest link of the chain. However, notwithstanding that strong linkage and a high level of economic dependency from the leading business, this one cannot be claimed against concerning employer's responsibilities, as these workers are legally independent contractors that fall apart from the application of Labor Law standards referred to salaried work, even if they are often in a very precarious situation that might deserve a somewhat similar protective regulation.

Somehow in accordance to these last considerations, a statutory act entitled "Statute of Autonomous Work" provided a general legal framework on self-employment and, specially, some particular regulations explicitly aiming protection of those most vulnerable self-employed persons, called "economically dependent autonomous workers."[85] These are defined as self-employed workers whose income depends

82. Catalonia Higher Court 5152/1994, September 30.
83. Madrid Higher Court 366/2002, May 21.
84. CASTRO ARGUELLES, M. A., *Formas alternativas de contratación del trabajo: de los contratos de actividad a la descentralización productiva*, Thomson-Aranzadi, 2007, pp. 13-220.
85. Law 20/2007, July 11, "Statute of Autonomous Work", particularly Articles 3-22.

mainly (at least 75%) of one same client business, provided that some other requirements are met too (business structure, equipment and resources of their own; separate performance of work, not merging with the staff of the client; organizational autonomy; last but not least, not being employers of other workers).[86] On that basis, this Law establishes some specific rights for such economically dependent self-employed workers, which someway look like "labor rights," although they are not recognized with the same extent and consistency: among others, non-discrimination, maximum working time and rest periods, right to interruption of the activity (on the grounds of illness, family reasons or imminent risk for health and safety) and holidays.[87] On the other hand, this regulation proclaims some collective rights, and even supports a kind of "collective bargaining" that enables the adoption of "professional interest agreements" for the regulation of the conditions of execution of the working activity.[88]

Anyhow, shedding employment to independent contractors can in many cases be considered as a problem of misclassification of workers as "self-employed," while the true underlying nature of the situation perfectly fits in fact to a salaried employment relationship. The scope of application of Labor Law is mandatorily defined in Spain in regard to the legal concept of the employee ("workers who voluntarily provide paid services on behalf of someone else, within the management and organization area of another natural person or legal entity called employer"[89]), and the essential characteristics of the employment relationship that can be accordingly inferred (voluntary/subordinated/paid work on behalf/at risk of other). Hence, Labor Law shall be applicable if the basic elements of the definition of salaried employment (paid subordinated work on behalf of another person or entity) are met in fact, regardless of the external appearance and the formal characterization (*nomen iuris*) agreed by the parties of the contract, in accordance to the principle of primacy of facts. Thus, misclassification of employees as independent contractors is an unlawful situation of bogus self-employment that could be claimed against by either the workers or the Labor Inspection, and subsequently reverted into a declaration on the dependent employment real status corresponding to the relationship, and on the applicability of labor standards. This final statement should be adopted by the labor courts through assessing the presence of the characteristics of salaried employment in the concrete circumstances of the case. Besides, in uncertain cases, the judges tend to decide relying in a legal presumption in favor of the existence of an employment contract, which has been deduced from Article 8.1 of the Workers' Statute.

There is already a consistent and noteworthy case law doctrine on the matter, and the true employment nature of the relationship underlying other pretended legal cover (i.e., works or services contracts, hiring of business, retailing distribution agreements

86. Law 20/2007, July 11, "Statute of Autonomous Work", Article 11.
87. Law 20/2007, July 11, "Statute of Autonomous Work", Articles 6, 14 and 16.
88. Law 20/2007, July 11, "Statute of Autonomous Work", Article 13. ROQUETA BUJ, R., "Los derechos colectivos de los trabajadores autónomos. Los acuerdos de interés profesional", *Temas Laborales*, n. 114, 2012, pp. 13-30.
89. Workers' Statute, Article 1(1).

or supply contracts) has been asserted in a large number of judgments.[90] So, this approach could be used to reveal the existence of an employment relationship, and consequently to affirm the applicability of Labor Law, when franchising or other similar features are simply hiding behind misclassified employees under a false appearance of independent self-employed contractors, provided that the characteristics of salaried work are met in practice.[91] For instance, the Supreme Court stated that the individuals managing telephone box offices of the Spanish major telephonic brand, supposedly under services contracts, were indeed employees of the Telefonica Company.[92] Similarly, in several cases related to franchised dentistry clinics, the dentists working on the basis of fake works contracts, allegedly outside the boundaries of Labor Law, were finally considered as dependent employees of the franchisee.[93] However, the courts missed that good chance for going a step ahead, examining from this perspective the relationship between the franchisee's employees (and even the franchisee herself) and, on the other hand, the franchisor as possible employer of them all. Therefore, assessing franchising as a matter of bogus self-employment and misclassification of employees might be conceivable, but this possibility has not been fully explored to the date.

[E] Evaluation and Future Prospect

Spanish Labor Law offers just very few provisions about employment relationships in business-groups, although these are a raising feature within the Spanish economy. Therefore, a more exhaustive and systematical legislation on the matter would undoubtedly be desirable. Nevertheless, the lack of statutory regulation has been counterbalanced to some extent by means of creative solutions developed by the labor courts, which have often dealt with practical problems in regard to business-groups. The probably most outstanding among those case law responses is the "piercing the veil" doctrine, which, in some circumstances, allows to claim for Labor Law responsibilities beyond the boundaries of the formal employer, declaring the "mother" entities of the group, or the whole group as such, jointly responsible in regard to the labor rights of the employees belonging to the staff of the "daughter" (or "sister") entities. This is a powerful tool for the reconstruction of the previously deconstructed employer's responsibilities in fissured structures, and points to an interesting path to follow in future legislation. However, the application of this mechanism by the courts is very cautious, as very strict requirements need to be met. Indeed, they tend to apply it only to "pathologic" cases of business-groups in which the exclusively formal separation of the entities is in contrast with the real situation of merged finance and management, or when the group structure has been deliberately used with the aim of

90. Among others, Supreme Court 20-9-1995, app. 1463/1994; 29-12-1999, app. 1093/1999; 29-11-2010, app. 253/2010, and 25-3-2013, app. 1564/2012.
91. OJEDA AVILÉS, A., *supra*, pp. 248-251.
92. Supreme Court 20-7-1999, app. 4040/1998.
93. Supreme Court 19-6-2007, app. 4883/2005; 12-2-2008, app. 5018/2005; 18-3-2009, app. 1709/2007, and 9-3-2010, app. 1443/2009.

blurring responsibilities or circumventing Law.[94] It would be appropriate to adopt a broader legal discipline on labor rights and responsibilities in business-groups in general, regardless of the fact of being "pathologic" or not, although this is a quite controversial issue in which further developments should probably be expected not from judges, but from legislators, including a more precise and detailed approach and taking into account the actual differences between the diverse types of company networks.[95]

On the other hand, the legal responses to other outcomes of the fissured workplace as supply chains and franchising are even poorer. In some cases, they might be addressed by applying the current legal provisions on subcontracting and illegal assignment of workers, or by using the case law doctrine on business-groups and "piercing the veil." However, that has been attempted in several claims before the courts, and most of them have failed, as there are many obstacles that hinder a wide-ranging extension of employer's responsibilities on the aforementioned premises, as, among others, the narrow conception of "own activity" in which subcontracting regulations are based, or the self-restraint of the courts in the use of "piercing the veil'" Though, concretely in regard to franchising, it should be acknowledged that it often involves a high level of implication of the franchisor in production processes issues, work organization schemes and staff management decisions that the franchisee is supposed to accomplish as independent employer, but which are indeed strongly controlled by the first. This invites to reflect on to whom the employees of the franchisee are subordinated in reality, and consequently to discuss a new and different legal approach to the problem, going beyond the current silence of statutory legislation and the quite superficial responses given by the courts to the date.[96] Finally, concerning the issue of "independent" contractors, the Spanish legal system offers two different sorts of approach: the extension of some protective regulations to economically dependent autonomous workers, and tackling bogus self-employment and misclassification of employees by means of a mandatory definition of the scope of application of Labor Law applied with the noteworthy support of the legal presumption in favor of the existence of an employment relationship. But these seem to be quite weak and incomplete remedies against the flow of the so-called escape from Labor Law.

§7.06 COLLECTIVE LABOR LAW AND LABOR RELATIONS IN "THE FISSURED WORKPLACE"

Spanish collective Labor Law does not intensively deal with the issues arising from the "atomization" of work. It provides only a few isolated regulations concerning some of the most outstanding features of "the fissured workplace," as subcontracting and

94. OJEDA AVILÉS,A., *supra*, pp. 218-226.
95. In regard to academic debate and proposals on the matter, among others, MONEREO PÉREZ, J. L./ MOLINA NAVARRETE, C., *El modelo de regulación jurídico-laboral de los grupos de empresas. Una propuesta de reforma*, Comares, 2002, pp. 1-181; RIVERO LAMAS, J., *supra*, pp. 49-60.; OJEDA AVILÉS,A., *supra*, pp. 215-235.
96. For interesting proposals on the matter, *see* GONZÁLEZ BIEDMA, E., *supra*, pp. 657-680.

business-groups. On the other hand, workers' representatives and trade unions could be expected to be important actors in this field, and they certainly are to some extent. However, equally to legislation, they seem to focus their scope of action on the most obvious outcomes of the phenomenon, while its deeper consequences do not seem to be properly assessed, even if these are actually undermining the strength of their representation, bargaining and conflict functions and means. Anyhow, this is just a general outlook that should be more precisely addressed in the following lines, by means of a more detailed insight throughout different areas within collective Labor Law and labor relations.

[A] Workers' Representation and Information and Consultation Rights in Subcontracting Schemes

Employees' elective representation bodies (works councils or workers' delegates, depending on the size of the workplace) play a very significant role in enforcement and monitoring related to the rules on subcontracting. The client/owner or any undertaking that contracts-out a part of its "own activity" has the obligation to inform workers' representatives about the following issues: name, commercial and taxation identification data and address of domiciliation of contractors or subcontractors; purpose and duration of contracting or subcontracting agreements; place for the execution of the contract; number of employees of the contractor or subcontractor expected to perform their activity within the workplace of the client; finally, measures foreseen for coordination regarding prevention of occupational risks.[97] Besides, the contractor/subcontractor has the obligation to inform workers' representatives about the identity of the client undertaking (including name, commercial and taxation identification data and address of domiciliation); purpose and duration of the contract or subcontract; place for the execution of the contract; number of employees expected to perform their activity within the workplace of the client; finally, measures foreseen for coordination regarding prevention of occupational risks.[98] Additionally, workers' representatives have the right of free access to the obligatory subcontracting book in which the several different undertakings sharing the same workplace should be registered, as said before.[99] Further ahead, the Workers' Statute establishes a broad information right of works councils (or delegates) on subcontracting processes,[100] and a general entitlement for monitoring compliance with all Labor Law, Social Security Law and Health and Safety legal standards, which can of course be used regarding this specific matter.[101] In addition, trade unions could also be relevant actors concerning application or enforcement of the rules on protection of workers' rights in subcontracting processes, in particular by means of trade union representatives at the workplace,

97. Article 42(4) of Workers' Statute.
98. Article 42(5) of Workers' Statute.
99. Article 42(4) of Workers' Statute.
100. Article 64(2) of Workers' Statute.
101. Article 64(7)(a) of Workers' Statute.

who have also general information rights that can be used regarding this subject.[102] However, they usually act in this field through their presence among works councils and workers' delegates, as far as these take profit of the particular framework of specific rules hereby described.

Each undertaking of the subcontracting chain is independent, and must have its own workers' representatives, if the legal requirements on the matter are met. But Article 42 of the Workers' Statute provides possibilities for coordinated action. When the employees of the contractors and subcontractors do not have legal representation, they have the right to bring questions and claims to the representatives of the client about working conditions while sharing the same workplace. If both the client and the subcontractor have representatives, they have a right to celebrate coordination meetings or assemblies among them in connection to the execution of activities in the shared workplace.[103] Accordingly, workers' representatives of contractors and subcontractors that share continuously the same workplace at the owner's site have the right to use the places or premises available in that location for representative functions, even if they are property not of their employer but of the client, nonetheless in terms and conditions that have to be previously agreed.[104] On the other hand, when the employees of the contractors and subcontractors sharing location do not have their own works councils or delegates, they have the right to bring questions and claims before the representatives of the shared workplace of the client, concerning issues related to the execution of their activity in the context of subcontracting.[105] Violations of all this wide range of collective rights could involve important penalties.[106]

[B] Workers' Representation and Information and Consultation Rights in Business-Groups

In the field of business-groups, Spanish Collective Labor Law is currently lacking a global systematic approach, but it offers nonetheless several regulations on some specific issues. Most of them refer to employees' representation bodies and information and consultation rights of workers' representatives. Within this area, there are some

102. Articles 8 and 10 of Law 11/1985, August 2, on Trade Union Freedom of Association.
103. Article 42(7) of Workers' Statute.
104. Articles 42(7) and 81 of Workers' Statute.
105. Article 42(6) of Workers' Statute.
106. Royal Legislative Decree 5/2000 establishes administrative penalties for violations of the described information duties of the employer [Article 7(7,11) of Legislative Decree 5/2000 in connection to Articles 42(3), 42(4,5) and 64(2)(c) of Workers' Statute], in regard to the requirement of having a fully updated register book for contractors and subcontractors which perform their activities in the same location [Article 7(12) of Legislative Decree 5/2000 in connection to Article 42(4) of Workers' Statute], and also related to the obligation of allowing reunions between workers' representatives from the different undertakings (client and contractors) sharing a common workplace [Article 8(5) of Legislative Decree 5/2000 in connection to Article 42(7) of Workers' Statute]. Joint and several and chain liability is applicable in the context of these penalties to the client and the contractors, in the terms of Article 42 of Workers Statute, [Article 42(1) of Legislative Decree 5/2000]. The amounts of the fines depend on the grade of culpability and seriousness of the infringement, and are increasable in the case of reiteration (according to Articles 40 and 41 of Legislative Decree 5/2000).

provisions aiming to safeguard those information and consultation rights of the representatives in "daughter" or subsidiary businesses in regard to key management decisions, even if these are adopted by a parent or holding company beyond the boundaries of the actual employer. Concretely, as to changes in the ownership of the employer entity and collective dismissals, it is explicitly outlined that information and documents on the matter should be provided in those situations to the employees' representatives of the concerned workplaces, regardless of the fact that the managerial decisions have been adopted either by the direct employer or by another entity exercising control from an upper level, excluding justification of non-compliance based on the fact that the leading business has not delivered the relevant elements underlying its decision.[107] Moreover, according to statutory regulation, the previous information and consultation proceedings required in order to adopt collective dismissals should take part at the company or workplace-level, as a general rule.[108] However, although it was not legally foreseen, case law has admitted that business-groups as such can directly initiate collective dismissals in regard to the several different entities gathered inside, and that information and consultation proceedings with the workers' representatives in these cases could be accomplished jointly in the whole group-scale, instead of in the lower level of the diverse undertakings and workplaces.[109] This is surely a very adequate solution from the standpoint of the workers and their representatives, and in the interest of the employers too, as it combines better chances for effectively organizing collective action of the employees and simplification of procedures for the business-group managers.

On the other hand, business-groups are directly addressed in legislation on workers' consultation and information rights in multinational European-scale undertakings, according to the common EU Law framework on the matter. Law 10/1997, April 24, contains the national transposition of EU Directive 2009/38/EC, May 6, on the establishment of a European Works Council or a procedure in Community-scale undertakings and Community-scale groups of undertakings for the purposes of informing and consulting employees (which involves modification and recast of the previous Directive 94/45/CE). Accordingly, those undertakings and business-groups are obliged to negotiate the creation of a European-level representation body, or an alternative information and consultation procedure, and, in case that there is not an agreement, these regulations provide subsidiary rules for compulsory setting of a European Works Council. Similarly, European-scale joint stock companies and cooperatives ought to negotiate the establishment of a system for the involvement of the employees, according to Law 31/2006, October 18, which is national transposition of EU Directive 2001/86/EC, October 8, on supplementing the Statute for a European company with regard to the involvement of employees, and Directive 2003/72/EC, July 22, on supplementing the Statute for a European Cooperative Society with regard to the

107. Articles 44(10) and 51(8) of Workers' Statute.
108. Articles 51(2) and 41(4) of the Workers' Statute.
109. Supreme Court 25-6-2014, app. 165/2013.

involvement of employees.[110] In practice, many Spanish-based multinational corporate groups have already established European-scale information and consultation bodies in accordance to this legal framework.

[C] Collective Bargaining

From a different perspective, business-groups are somewhat considered by the legal regulations on collective bargaining agreements. In the past, these rules used to focus on sector and company-level agreements, not foreseeing collective bargaining in business-groups. This became however quite widespread in practice, although the legal framework presented some lack of adaptation on the matter, bringing up some problems, especially in regard to the statutory rules on legitimate representations entitled to negotiate such business-group agreements. The courts gave some case law responses expressly enabling collective bargaining in business-groups, and solving the difficulties concerning legitimate actors by combined analogical application, as appropriate, of rules either on sector and company-level negotiations. Through a reform enacted by Decree-Law 7/2011, June 10, these case law solutions have been afterwards incorporated into statutory legislation, which now explicitly allows collective bargaining agreements for business-groups and for other situations of multiplicity of undertakings with organizational or production-related links. The legitimate representation of workers in this regard is now unambiguously conferred to trade unions under the same requirements requested for sector-level bargaining.[111]

Leaving business-group agreements apart, as said already frequent, collective bargaining does not envisage the issues connected to the topic of "the fissured workplace" very deeply in practice. Collective agreements could regulate on the matter whenever to improve workers' rights and minimum standards given by statutory Law. In that sense, it is very common for collective agreements to contain references to subcontracting, while addressing other forms of "fissurization" is quite rare. However, these regulations are often limited to repeat the legal provisions, and do not introduce real original contents. Most sector agreements contain clauses about subcontracting, although with very little innovation. Some collective agreements provide a wider range of responsibilities compared to those established in Article 42 of Workers' Statute, reaching, for example, voluntary improvements in social security benefits (i.e., collective agreement for the construction sector). Conversely, it is not usual to find rules in this field in company-level agreements. In fact, the greatest contribution of collective bargaining is, in some sectors such as cleaning or hospitality, to establish the duty of a new contractor or subcontractor to continue to maintain the contracts of workers who were carrying out their activities for the previous contractor or subcontractor. Also, the great concern for health and safety at work explains that in some

110. Respectively linked to Regulation 2157/200, October 8, on the Statute for a European company, and Regulation 1435/2003, July 22, on the Statute for a European Cooperative Society.
111. Article 87(1, 2) of Workers' Statute.

sectors collective agreements have developed preventive guidelines and measures to avoid accidents, as in the construction sector and in the chemical industry.[112]

[D] Trade Union Action and the Right to Strike

In regard to the workers' collective action and the rights to trade union freedom of association/action and to strike, both proclaimed as constitutional fundamental rights in the Spanish Constitution [Article 28(1, 2)], there is not a statutory regulation specifically addressing the outcomes of "the fissured workplace" in that ground. However, the case law of the Constitutional Court has already dealt with the problem of violations of workers' constitutional rights (including the right to strike) caused not directly by their actual employer, but as a consequence of decisions or instructions adopted beyond, by the client for whom the first acts as a contractor or subcontractor.[113] The facts concretely examined by the Constitutional Court refer to a subcontracting case, where the client decided to cancel the relationship with the contractor, as a retaliation reaction against claims and a strike carried out by the contractor's employees, with the final result of these being dismissed as a consequence of the loss of the service contract. The Constitutional Court declared that the client is liable for the violation of fundamental rights (to judiciary action and to strike) in such circumstances, although the nature and distribution of liability among both involved undertakings was not clearly established. This case law has been very welcome by some commentators and sharply criticized by some other voices, including the attached dissenting opinions of some magistrates.[114] Employers' associations clearly dislike its orientation, and show a great concern on its possible further consequences, pointing that it creates uncertainty for business relations. However, from a less biased standpoint, the orientation of the commented judgment seems to be interesting in order to prevent using outsourcing as an instrument for directly undermining collective rights.

Another outstanding case refers to collective dismissals and the right to strike in "Coca Cola Iberian Partners," the business-group currently operating production and distribution of the world famous drink in Spain and Portugal under the well-known international brand. The beverage used to be produced and stocked in various plants and facilities belonging to different companies, each of them fabricating and serving for different parts of the Spanish territory. After shareholding movements, not for fissuring but for concentrating control by the parent undertaking "CC Iberian Partners," this new managing company decided a restructuring process leading to the prospect of closing some plants, the dismissal of an important number of employees and the reallocation

112. MENÉNDEZ CALVO, R., *Negociación colectiva y descentralización productiva*, CES, 2009, pp. 102-136; PÉREZ DE LOS COBOS ORIHUEL, F. (Dir.), *Contratación temporal, empresas de trabajo temporal y subcontratación en la negociación colectiva*, CCNCC, 2010, pp. 199-313.
113. Constitutional Court Judgments 75/2010, 76/2010, and 98 to 112/2010.
114. ESCRIBANO GUTIÉRREZ, J., "El derecho de huelga en el marco de la descentralización empresarial", *Temas Laborales*, n. 110, 2011, pp. 195-206.

of others. The previous consultation on restructuring measures and collective dismissals with the workers' representation, which is compulsory according to Labor Law,[115] was held at the group-level, not in the company or workplace-level as it is legally required as a general rule.[116] This was nevertheless accepted by the courts,[117] which seem to be adequately flexible to admit joint bargaining of these procedures for the whole business-group, as said before.[118] However, the Judgments of both the National Appeal Court and the Supreme Court declared these collective dismissals void and null for other reasons, and especially due to assessing a very particular form of violation of the right to strike in terms that are necessarily to be remarked here.[119] During the process for adopting collective dismissals, the employees of some - not all – of the plants, located in Madrid, initiated a strike against the business-group managers' intentions. Of course, the purpose of the strikers was to leave the capital city and the whole region with little Coca Cola to drink. However, the managers quite succeeded to avoid the effects of the strike by operating on the basis of logistics and decisions delivered to other companies within the holding: they just made the drinks come to Madrid from other companies and facilities belonging to the group and located in nearby regions, but which had never produced and distributed Coca Cola for that geographical area before. This was judiciary examined bearing in mind the prohibition of substitution of striker workers, a behavior considered a violation of the fundamental right to strike [Article 28(2) of Constitution], and explicitly forbidden in statutory legislation too.[120] Even if there was not a physical replacement of the striker employees by recruiting other workers in the terms of the statutory ban, the courts assessed that there was an abnormal use of the managerial powers and of the resources belonging to other companies of the group with the purpose of neutralizing the effects of the strike in the workplaces located in Madrid, and this brought to declare a violation of the fundamental right of Article 28 of the Constitution, and consequently that the collective dismissal was void and null.

[E] Beyond Legal Issues: Trade Unions and Labor Relations in the "Fissured World"

Anyhow, going beyond the strictly legal issues, the deepest outcome of "fissurization," and probably the most difficult to acknowledge at the same time, is its serious impact in the core of trade unions, workers' representation schemes and, in general, the classic features of collective labor relations. To begin, the "atomization" of companies and workplaces and the replacement of the former big fordist factory by the post-fordist business networks of smaller size and formally and physically separated legal entities involves obstacles for contact and collective organization among increasingly disperse

115. Articles 51 and 64 of Workers' Statute.
116. Articles 51(2) and 41(4) of Workers' Statute.
117. National Appeal Court 108/2014, June 14.
118. Supreme Court 25-6-2014, app. 165/2013.
119. National Appeal Court 108/2014, June 14, and Supreme Court 20-4-2015, app. 354/2014.
120. Article 6(5) Decree-Law 17/1977, March 4.

workers, therefore rising "invisible barriers" to workers' movement, which is suffering the consequences of profound changes in its traditional context and premises.[121] Additionally, the "new economy," innovative business strategies, globalization and other circumstances have fissured not only the workplace, but also the working class itself. Its old internal homogeneity according to the archetypical factory worker is now being broken into a multiplicity of different types of employees, of a highly diverse nature and often with diverging or even opposed interests: blue collar/ white collar/ silicon collar workers; qualified/ not qualified workers; permanent/ temporary/ "precarious" workers in a segmented labor market; typical/ "atypical" workers; nationals/ immigrant workers; well-paid/ middle-paid/ low-wage/ underpaid workers; last but not least, employees/ self-employed/ economically dependent self-employed/ workers misclassified as self-employed. Obviously, this tendency inherently involves a massive loss of class consciousness. On the other hand, this rising fragmentation is also a problem in regard to the usefulness and real effectiveness of the traditional institutions of industrial relations. Both collective bargaining and strike were conceived on the basis of the adequateness of "mass contracting" and "mass conflict" for handling industrial relations in the context of quite unified interests of workers, but these premises are also fissuring at present, according to what has already been said.

Besides, the position of collective bargaining in regard to setting of wages and other working conditions has been significantly undermined as a consequence of "fissurization." As it has been smartly pointed, the move from the traditional model of large companies in charge of the whole business to a chain of formally independent contractors, subcontractors and suppliers entails a really important change in wage determination, shifting from a staff management and industrial relations issue to a matter of fixing tariffs in highly competitive markets.[122] Formerly, the big employer had to negotiate (usually through collective bargaining) vis-à-vis her employees, who could put pressure on the first by means of trade unions, strike and collective action supported by a numerous bunch of employees belonging to the staff. But now, smaller-size contractors, subcontractors and suppliers have to contend amongst them in a much more open competition to gain a "little piece of the pie" that the leading companies are contracting-out, and obviously only those offering lower prices to the client business succeed. In order to decrease the fees, this competition necessarily requires dropping costs as much as possible and an inherent pressure to reduce wages, with no real opposition of workers due to different circumstances: (a) if wages are not adjusted to drop the prices offered to the client business, this will probably choose a cheaper contractor or supplier and there will be no jobs for the workers, so they are likely to accept; (b) contractors may use temporary workers, who will only be recruited if they accept the low wages fixed according to the prices agreed with the client, and (c) on the premises of small-size contractors, subcontractors or franchisees, generally,

121. VALDÉS DAL- RÉ, F., "La externalización de actividades laborales: un fenómeno complejo", PEDRAJAS MORENO, A. (Dir.), *La externalización de actividades laborales (outsourcing): una visión interdisciplinar*, Lex Nova, 2002, pp. 42-44.
122. WEIL, D., *supra*, pp. 76-92.

there is not collective representation of workers nor collective bargaining or action possible in order to push up salaries. Of course, collective bargaining in the sector level could be a remedy against this panorama, as it allows fixing standardized salaries and other working conditions equally applicable to the whole economic segment, including all the contractors, subcontractors and other undertakings, thus stopping to some extent the wage-cut competition and limiting social dumping. However, sector collective bargaining does not cover all the economic areas, and it has been constantly in withdrawal in recent years. In Spain, the number of employers and employees covered by sector-level collective bargaining has significantly decreased, and the area of coverage is generally referred to the most traditional economic activities, while the newest ones - perhaps more likely to fissure – tend to be left out. In addition, the latest Labor Law reforms[123] stand for the decentralization of collective bargaining, through broadly enabling the employers to derogate from sector-level agreements and, besides, giving absolute priority to the application of company-level agreements. This is contributing significantly to weakening sector-level collective bargaining and consequently reducing wages. On the other hand, the situation seems to be difficult to revert, as the direction of this legal orientation has been drawn up by the institutions of the European Union as a core part of the particular policies imposed to some Member States in the context of the economic and financial crisis.

Possibly, trade unions have not perceived all the above-mentioned changes and emerging challenges in full, and surely they have not succeeded to adapt to them. As a combined result of this lack of comprehension and adaptation and the new "invisible barriers" to collective action, they are currently suffering a deep intrinsic crisis, undoubtedly worsened in the adverse economic scenery subsequent to the great economic crash of 2008. Trade unions seem to remain attached to their old structures and strategies conceived in regard to the classic paradigms of work arising from the first and second industrial revolutions, focusing primarily on the traditional industrial sector, on the large workplaces and manufacturing plants according to the fordist-taylorist model, and on "blue collar" factory workers or "white collar" bureaucratic employees. Therefore, there is a loss of connection to other more recently developed economic activities and jobs, and consequently a "representation short-circuit" concerning the actual situation of, for instance, "silicon-collar workers," "precarious workers," new forms of employment linked to information and communication technologies, false or economically dependent self-employed, and, in general, "fissured workplace" employees. At the same time, these new categories of workers perceive that, while they generally bear poorer living and working conditions, trade unions concentrate their attention on their traditional and well-known areas, so those are increasingly developing rejection feelings that result in a vicious feedback circle which is enlarging the mutual distance.

What is more, current legislation on workers' representation and trade unions does not help much. It has also been designed in regard to the old models, focusing on big or middle-size workplaces. Workers' elective representation is established mainly

123. Decree-Law 7/2011, June 10; Decree-Law 3/2012, February 10; finally, Law 3/2012, July 6.

taking each workplace as reference, instead of the entity as a whole, consequently complicating the designation of representatives in big businesses divided into small units, as it is usual in practice. Besides, only workplaces of at least fifty employees can elect works councils, while those between 10 and 49 (or from 6, if decided by a majority of workers) can elect staff delegates, and those of five or less employees shall not have any representation scheme.[124] So, the existence of representation in smaller-size entities is not favored by statutory legislation, even if small and micro-size businesses are currently predominant in the Spanish economy. Accordingly, "fissuring the workplace" into small pieces can be a way of avoiding the creation of representative bodies too. Moreover, trade unions' representativeness, in order to the attribution of relevant functions and stronger means for action, is measured proportionally to the results obtained by the candidates of each union in the elections for delegates and works councils. As only large workplaces provide important election results in this regard, this system creates an incentive for unions to focus mainly in those big sites, usually located in traditional sectors. Therefore, the legal regulation itself discourages paying attention to small entities and fragmented sectors, consequently aggravating the already explained tendency of unions to withdrawal into their classic areas of action, leaving emerging sectors and "fissured workplaces" almost unattended.

[F] Evaluation and Future Prospect

Collective Labor Law is probably the area providing poorer and less adequate regulations to deal with "the fissured workplace." Certainly, there are a few interesting provisions on workers' representation and their information and consultation rights in the context of some forms of multi-layered organization of work. Namely, this matter has been carefully and properly regulated in regard to subcontracting, both from a general perspective and specifically in regard to health and safety, by establishing a wide range of information rights and correlative duties for the different involved undertakings, along with inspired solutions for coordinating and co-involving workers' representation structures beyond the boundaries of their respective employers (i.e., right to coordination between representatives belonging to different entities, joint assembly, right of subcontractor's employees to issue claims to the representatives of the client's shared workplace). In the area of business-groups, paradoxically, there are significant regulations on works councils and information rights in European-scale grouped undertakings, while there are only some isolated provisions for national-scale structures, fortunately counterbalanced by some case law approaches on the matter and group collective agreements. But, leaving apart those piecemeal regulations and judiciary or collective bargaining developments, the Spanish legal framework on workers' elective representation remains devoted in general to very classic schemes predominantly attached to big-size and middle-size workplaces as basic reference, therefore tending to obstruct the building of representation mechanisms in multi-layered business structures deconstructed into small-size units. Besides, a parallel

124. Articles 62 and 63 of Workers' Statute.

situation could be assessed in regard to trade unions, as both statutory law and their internal organization and strategies seem to be based primarily in the old fordist-taylorist paradigms of work, employees and employers, being consequently immersed in a crisis closely related to a lack of adaptation to the current context of "the fissured workplace" in post-fordist capitalism. Adequate comprehension of this phenomenon by the unions themselves and by legislation on the matter is crucial and urgent, in order to slow down a dynamic which is increasingly weakening the position of trade unions and creating a serious imbalance in the industrial relations system.

Collective bargaining is also being somehow destabilized as a consequence of the fragmentation of work. The deconstruction of production into a multi-level network of contractors, subcontractors and suppliers dilutes the former position of collective bargaining concerning setting of wages and other working conditions, which are now pre-determined in a highly strong market competition amongst contractors and subcontractors. A rearrangement of the framework and the structure of collective bargaining are subsequently needed. The support given to business-group-level collective bargaining by the courts and a later legal reform is a good step in this regard. Conversely, the aforementioned Labor Law reforms aiming decentralization of collective bargaining go in the wrong direction, weakening the position of sector-level agreements and favoring wage competition and social dumping, so they should be reverted. This is however unlikely, as these modifications have been introduced with strong political support from the European Union, the International Monetary Fund and business organizations. Finally, the "atomization" of work into multi-layered business structures involves new threats for the right to strike too. Among other things, the different forms of cooperation and interaction between legally separate entities allow employers to adopt innovative strategies to prevent strike, to block its effects or to retaliate against striker workers. Some judgments are adopting innovative approaches and noteworthy solutions on the matter, but unions and workers' representatives should develop their own strategies to face these arising challenges by themselves.

§7.07 CONCLUSION

The classic patterns of salaried work have intensively changed in the context of the evolution of the economic structures since the late 1970s. They have been increasingly moving from the former paradigm of large industrial companies managing all the crowd of workers involved in the production process in big-size plants to the "atomized" or "fissured workplace," deconstructed into a multi-layered business network composed of an interconnected multiplicity of smaller-size "daughter"/ "sister" companies, contractors, subcontractors, suppliers and other entities, each of them carrying out small parts of the outsourced economic activity, as legally independent employers in charge of their own respective employees. As Labor Law was primarily conceived and built on the basis of the traditional model, this phenomenon is leading to increasingly emerging challenges and concerns on its appropriate application and enforcement. Among other things, the renewed business structures in the fissured context entail blurring of responsibilities, increased risks of circumvention of law, and, more broadly, a general trend towards lowering of labor standards and undermining the efficacy of legal and collective bargaining regulations.

Certainly, the "atomization" or "fissuring" of work has not been completely unnoticed for Spanish Labor Law. In fact, many issues related to this matter have been already addressed by different statutory provisions since the 1980s. However, the regulation does not provide a systematical and fully complete regulation of the phenomenon, and the responses given to its diverse outcomes are somehow unequal. While subcontracting and temporary assignment of workers are quite intensively regulated, there are just very few and quite isolated rules in regard to business-groups and other more innovative forms of fissuring. These are starting to be dealt with by means of some interesting case law solutions, which are nevertheless still incomplete and can be considered "under construction." Further ahead, some challenging problems – as those arising from franchising schemes – remain somewhat unexplored or even misjudged, and the topic of "the fissured workplace" has not been considered from a global perspective, as it would be surely desirable. From a different point of view, the features in the field of individual Labor Law and Social Security seem to be more consistent than those in the area of collective labor relations.

Anyhow, in those fields in which it provides at least a piecemeal approach, Spanish Labor Law offers some interesting contributions to be remarked, as the already well-known and broadly applied mechanisms of joint and several liabilities, the creation of crossed workers' representation structures and information rights exceeding the landmarks of each independent employer and the "piercing the veil doctrine." All these tools are interesting inputs that might be further considered by the Spanish legal system (and even exported or shared with other systems), in the direction of (at least partially) going beyond the strict boundaries of the formal legal entity of the employer. However, this is still a path to follow in the future, which should probably be walked bearing in mind a deeper reconsideration of the concept of the employer, the notion of subordination and other basic founding institutions of Labor Law, adapting them to the new shaping of work in the era of post-fordist capitalism.

CHAPTER 8

Regulating the Fissured Workplace: The Notion of the 'Employer' in Chinese Labour Law

Mimi Zou[*]

§8.01 INTRODUCTION

The 'fissured workplace' is a term used by David Weil to describe fundamental changes in firms' competitive strategies that have reshaped the organisation of employment in the twenty-first century. According to Weil, the fissured workplace represents 'both a form of employment (e.g., temporary agency employment; independent contracting) and a *relationship* between different business enterprises (subcontracting, franchising)'.[1] Larger firms have devolved significant risk and responsibility for their workers to a myriad of complicated networks of smaller, lower-level business units through business practices, mechanisms, and organisational forms such as subcontracting, outsourcing, franchising, and supply-chain logistics. As Weil puts it, '[w]age setting and supervision shift from core businesses to a myriad of organizations, each operating under the rigorous standards of lead businesses but facing fierce competitive pressures'.[2] These pressures from the top translate into precarious jobs and deteriorating wages and working conditions for workers at the bottom and periphery of complex, multi-layered contractual chains.

In the context of a fissured workplace, there is a need to re-examine the notion of 'the employer' in labour law, which has traditionally imposed various obligations on a

* The Chinese University of Hong Kong.
1. David Weil, The *Fissured Workplace: Why Work Became So Bad for So Many and What Can Be Done to Improve It* (Harvard University Press 2014) 270 [italics in original].
2. *Ibid*. 8-9.

particular employing entity towards its employees in the context of a direct employment relationship. In a fissured workplace that may have multiple legal entities intertwined in a range of complex contractual relationships and indirect employment relationships, the notion of the 'employer' and thus the question of who should bear the legal responsibilities of employer become extremely problematic.

The phenomenon of the fissured work place in China and the regulatory dynamics of Chinese labour law in addressing the challenges of fissurisation have occurred against the backdrop of dramatic social and economic changes over the past three decades. It may be argued that what Weil describes as the 'pre-fissured world' in the Chinese context is a bygone era under a centrally planned economy whereby the state, as the only 'employer' under this system, directly provided urban employees with cradle-to-grave employment and social benefits – the so-called iron rice bowl.[3]

Since the 1980s, China's economic and social reforms in its rapid industrialisation and urbanisation have fundamentally altered the relationship between the state, labour, and capital. As the country quickly became the 'factory of the world' at an unprecedented pace and scale, its role as a key player in global production chains brought about a flexible labour market with an 'army' of hundreds of millions of rural migrant workers. The status of Chinese workers was transformed overnight from 'masters of the socialist state' into individual subjects of contractual relationships in a market economy with 'Chinese characteristics'. Employment relations have become incredibly complex and segmented, with enormous variations across localities, economic sectors, ownership structure, enterprise size, and workforce structures.

A multifaceted web of labour laws and institutions has been created, developed, and reformed to respond to China's rapidly evolving labour market dynamics and challenges. A deregulatory agenda in labour law making and enforcement in the 1990s saw the proliferation of temporary and fixed-term employment contracts and informal employment whereby many workers did not have a signed labour contract. The explosion of worker grievances and labour disputes arising from this period saw the introduction of new pieces of legislation from 2007 onwards that sought to bolster workers' rights under written labour contracts, enhance employment security, and extend social insurance protections.

The building of 'harmonious labour relations' has become the widely espoused policy goal underpinning the evolution of Chinese labour law. Yet, as this chapter examines, policymakers' attempts to address the socially destabilising effects of the fissured workplace have had unintended consequences. In response to more worker-protective laws, firms have devised new organisational strategies and employment practices to sidestep 'employer' obligations. In the current phase of China's economic downturn, accelerating trends of fissurisation have brought to the forefront some major challenges for policymakers arising from the broader social consequences of fissured workplaces. A large number of labour disputes in 2015 have been concerned with

3. Mimi Zou, 'The Evolution of Collective Labour Law with "Chinese Characteristics": Crossing the River by Feeling the Stones?' in Roger Blanpain, Ulla Liukkunen and Yifeng Chen, *Law and Fair Work in China* (Kluwer International 2013) 55-72.

violations of basic labour rights and laws such as non-payment of wages and social security payments arising from firms' downsizing, outsourcing, and closures.

This chapter is structured as follows. Section §8.02 analyses the extent to which fissurisation has emerged in China, which requires an understanding of the evolution of its labour relations from the 'pre-fissured' era to the present. In section §8.03, the notion of the 'employer' in the current labour law framework is examined. I further analyse how Chinese labour law in recent years has sought to regulate the use of labour dispatch (*laowuqianpai*) as the most prevalent manifestation of fissurisation in China. Part IV concludes with an overall evaluation of the current and future challenges for regulating an increasingly fissured workplace.

§8.02 THE EVOLUTION OF THE FISSURED WORKPLACE

The fissured workplace that has emerged in contemporary China cannot be separated from the analysis of labour market policies and laws over the past three decades.

[A] The 'Three Old Irons'

The 'iron rice bowl' has been widely evoked to capture the characteristics of labour relations for the urban workers of China under the former planned economy. Some have referred to an expanded notion of the 'three old irons': the 'iron rice bowl' of lifetime employment and cradle-to-grave social welfare provided by the state (*tie fanwan*); the 'iron wage' of centrally administered and fixed wages that sought to minimise disparities within and across workplaces (*tie gongzi*); and the 'iron chair' of state-controlled appointments and promotion of managers, generally based on the worker's tenure of employment and political orientation (*tie jiaoyi*).[4]

Almost all enterprises under the centrally planned system were state-owned, and a dual system of Party and management control became the basis of enterprise leadership. The basic institutional structure at the enterprise level consisted of the Party committee, the trade union and the workers' congress which was led by the trade union. The general manager often served as the Party Secretary and union secretary of the enterprise. All unions belonged to the sole Party-state sanctioned union body, the All-China Federation of Trade Union (ACFTU). With a role as the 'transmission belt' between the Party and workers, trade unions at the workplace were responsible for 'educating' workers and dealing with their grievances. The 'work unit' ('*danwei*') represented the basic-level organisation that linked workers to the Party, and enabled the Party to directly exert political control over workplaces.[5]

Due to the absence of an actual labour market prior to 1978, the regulatory framework could be better described as a labour administration system. Efforts to introduce labour laws were short-lived during this period. For example, the operation

4. Daniel Ding & Malcolm Warner, 'China's Labour-Management System Reforms: Breaking the "Three Old Irons"', (2001)18 Asia Pacific Journal of Management 315.
5. Simon Clarke, Chang Hee Lee & Qi Li, 'Consultative Consultation and Industrial Relations in China' (2004) 42 British Journal of Industrial Relations 235.

of the Labour Union Law 1950 and several labour regulations concerning state-owned enterprises came to an end in 1956. This was apparently due to ideological reasons within the Party – since the interests of workers and those of the enterprise were theoretically aligned in a socialist society, labour disputes would not be an issue.[6] Furthermore, there was a general breakdown in China's legal system during the Cultural Revolution, with the courts and legislative systems entirely abolished.

[B] Towards a Flexible Labour Market

As Deng's proposals for a 'socialist market economy with Chinese characteristics' became cemented in official policy, China's integration into global capitalism fuelled its unprecedented economic growth over the next two decades. The shift to a market-based economy entailed the decentralisation of state-owned enterprises (SOEs) in their personnel management, along with reforms to break the 'three old irons' that were seen to be associated with low flexibility and productivity. New policies were introduced largely to promote economic reform and efficiency, with the aim of making labour less rigid to facilitate China's participation in global competition – thereby meeting 'a key demand of the foreign capital that led China's post-reform economic development'.[7]

This period of economic reform also saw the dismantling of official barriers to urban labour market access by the rural population. At the heart of China's rapid industrialisation and urbanisation has been a labour force of hundreds of millions of rural migrant workers who have moved to the fast-growing coastal cities for employment in the burgeoning private sector. A salient feature of this rural-to-urban migration is the household registration ('*hukou*') system. Without a local urban *hukou*, these workers and their families are not entitled to reside permanently in those cities. Importantly they could not access, in law and in practice, a range of social benefits that their urban counterparts enjoyed.

A handful of China's coastal cities were turned into export hubs as foreign investment poured into the 'factory of the world', staffed by a seemingly abundant supply of low-cost labour. The labour market policy emphasis on job creation in the private sector generated new problems for labour relations as private employers gain increased autonomy in the workplace. While the economic transformation brought about an increasingly flexible labour market, the pre-reform institutions became ineffectual in governing new labour relations that weighed heavily in favour of capital. The tension between the pursuit of economic reform and the need to address the issues of an emerging labour market made it difficult for Chinese policymakers to reach consensus on new labour legislation.

The Labour Law 1994 was a significant breakthrough as the first national law of its kind in China. The Law established the system of labour contracts as the primary

6. Yun Zhao, 'China's New Labor Dispute Resolution Law: a Catalyst for the Establishment of Harmonious Labor Relationship?' (2009) 30 Comparative Labor Law & Policy Journal 409.
7. Feng Xu, 'The Emergence of Temporary Agencies in China' (2009) 30 Comparative Labor Law & Policy Journal 431, 433.

means for regulating employment relationships. Its provisions covered a wide range of matters, including the conclusion, variation and termination of labour contracts, a framework for collective consultation, reasonable working hours, paid leave, anti-discrimination, equal pay and a dispute resolution framework among others.

However, the Labour Law also left out significant details. The law did not, for example, cover contract formation in any detail or distinguish employees from independent contractors. There was no restriction on the minimum length of fixed-term contracts, which provided employers considerable freedom in using short-term contracts. Importantly, there was the systemic failure by the state to enforce labour laws and regulate labour relations in a fair and balanced manner. Acute competition among localities to attract and retain investment often led to local authorities relaxing their enforcement of labour standards – some local officials did not consider the 'floating population' of rural migrant workers as warranting any legal protection.

[C] The Emergence of Fissurisation

Changes in the state's labour policy from the 1980s onwards resulted in the dramatic downsizing of SOE and the removal of the cradle-to-grave social welfare. The pace of such reforms accelerated during the 1990s in the lead-up to China's accession to the World Trade Organisation. The proportion of state enterprises (including SOEs, township and village enterprises, and collectives) declined from 25% of the labour force in 1996 to only 7% in 2003, with 30 million workers losing their jobs in the SOE sector during this period.[8] The establishment and formalisation of the labour contract system was a decisive step by the state in 'smashing the iron rice bowl' to facilitate and accelerate economic restructuring.[9] Not only did the 1994 Labour Law provide for the use of temporary labour contracts which was perceived as enhancing the efficiency of SOEs, it also legitimised the mass redundancies undertaken by SOEs. As Gallagher et al. have observed, 'the termination of employment at the end of the contract was done using the language of the law'.[10]

The mass layoffs of workers from the state-owned sector during this period also saw the emergence of labour dispatch arrangements. Labour dispatch, as it is referred to in Chinese labour law, is perhaps better known as temporary agency work, labour hire, or on-hire labour in other parts of the world. Labour dispatch became part of the Chinese state's active employment' policy as tens of millions of urban employees were laid-off during SOE restructuring and the adoption of the labour contract system. Labour dispatch became a common practice in the state-owned sector for SOEs to cut

8. Chang-Hee Lee, Industrial Relations and Collective Bargaining in China, 5 (ILO, Working Paper No.7, 2009).
9. Eli Friedman & Ching Kwan Lee, 'Remaking the World of Chinese Labour: A 30-Year Retrospective', (2005) 48 British Journal of Industrial Relations 507-533; Mary Gallagher, *Contagious Capitalism: Globalization and the Politics of Labor in China* (Princeton University Press 2005).
10. Mary Gallagher, Sarosh Kuruvilla & Ching Kwan Lee, 'Introduction and Argument' in Sarosh Kuruvilla, Ching Kwan Lee & Mary E. Gallagher, *From Iron Rice Bowl to Informalization: Markets, Workers, and the State in a Changing China* (Cornell University Press 2011) 5.

costs in the restructuring process and to re-engage former direct employees (who were under the 'three-old-irons' system) as fixed-term contract workers. These labour dispatch agencies often operated by the labour bureaus and personnel departments of local governments.

Private labour dispatch agencies also expanded from the 1990s onwards and played a key role in supplying the masses of rural migrant workers to meet the demands of China's rapid industrialisation. Some private agencies started to provide training and job-seeking services for university graduates, first-time labour market entrants, and vocational training school graduates. Many foreign-owned human resources and labour hire companies, including some well-known multinational agencies, also entered China's fast-growing labour dispatch market from the 1990s onwards.

Chinese workers' access to and enjoyment of employment and social rights and protections, in law and practice, became increasingly differentiated based on the type of labour contract or the absence of a formal written labour contract.[11] Rural migrant workers were commonly engaged in work without formal written contracts, which made it difficult to prove the existence of a labour relationship when the workers sought to claim wage arrears and other employment and social security protections.

[D] A Case Study of the Construction Sector

The above-mentioned problems experienced by rural migrant workers (in accessing basic labour protections) have been most acute in the construction sector, which has over 40 million workers employed at the bottom on complex, multi-layered subcontracting chains. Around one-third of rural migrant workers end up working in the construction sector.[12]

A multi-tier labour contracting system emerged from the state's restructuring of the construction industry during the 1980s and 1990s. For example, the highest executive organ of the state, the State Council, issued a Regulation that required general contractors or contracting companies to *not* directly employ their blue-collar workers, but instead engage labour subcontractors who were responsible for recruiting the workforce.[13] The fissurisation of *relationships* between different firms in the construction sector in China is illustrated in figure 8.1.[14]

11. *See* Sean Cooney, Sarah Biddulph and Ying Zhu, *Law and Fair Work in China* (Routledge 2014).
12. Sarah Swider, 'Building China: Precarious Employment Among Migrant Construction Workers' (2015) 29 Work, Employment and Society 41.
13. *See* Pun Ngai and Lu Huilin, 'A Culture of Violence: the Labor Subcontracting System and Collective Action by Construction Workers in Post-Socialist China' (2010) 64 The China Journal 143, 147.
14. *Ibid.*, 148.

Figure 8.1 A Typical Chain of Subcontracting in the Construction Sector in China

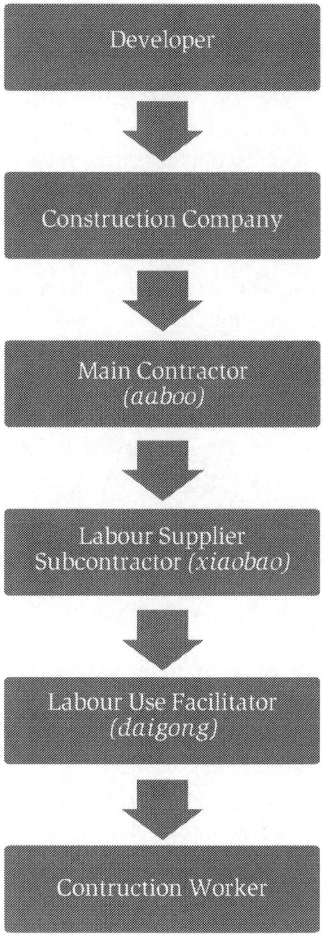

Figure 8.1 shows the multiple layers of contracting and subcontracting between:

- the property developer at the apex of the chain;
- the construction company with the bid that is responsible for the overall project management;
- the main general contractor that is responsible for providing raw materials and labour for the project;
- the labour-supply subcontractors that recruit the workers, manage the day-to-day work division and pay workers wages upon completion of project;
- the labour use facilitators who actually look for workers in their own village networks; and
- and the workers who perform the actual labour.

The most chronic and widespread labour violation in the construction sector has been the non-payment of wages to workers. The multi-layered chain obscures a readily identifiable employer to discharge this basic obligation of the employer under labour law. The subcontractors (most of whom have little capital themselves) usually have inadequate funds to pay workers wages until they are paid by the construction company and developer, usually when the project is completed.

Lower-tier subcontractors have very little bargaining power compared to the construction companies and property developers, which often have close ties with the local government. As Pun and Lu have observed, the local government commonly favours first-tier contractors over lower-tier contractors in construction disputes.[15] Lower-tier subcontractors are often owed payments from those higher up the chain. Therefore, the investment risks of the top-tier contractors are transferred down the chain to lower-tier subcontractors and ultimately, the workers who experience the non-payment of wages, social insurance, and work injuries payments.

Wage arrears in the constructor sector have become a common cause of labour disputes and collective worker protests throughout the 1990s and 2000s. Furthermore, there had been a very low rate of signed individual labour contracts in this sector, which rendered it difficult to resolve disputes over wage arrears where the existence of a formal employment relationship cannot be documented. The limited details on contract formation in the Labour Law 1994 and the broader labour law framework (prior to 2008) also did not help labour arbitrators and courts to deal with the particular problems for workers to prove the establishment of an employment relationship within a complex, multi-layered contractual chain.

Recognising the socially disruptive forces that arose from the large numbers and scale of labour disputes in the construction sector, state organs at national and local levels instigated a three-year 'clean up' campaign to deal with the problems of non-payment of construction funds and non-payment of wages. The State Council issued a Notice on Conscientiously Resolving the Problem of Delayed Payment of Construction Funds in the Construction Sector in November 2003 that instructed various state agencies to strengthen inspection and enforcement efforts and the severity of penalties for breaches. A Work Plan set out a timeline and concrete tasks for a range of actors including the local courts. The Ministry of Human Resources and Social Security (MHRSS) further issued a specific Provisional Measures on the Payment of Wages to Migrant Workers in the Construction Sector in September 2004.

The problems that have arisen from a highly fissured workplace in the construction sector had catapulted wage payment issues to the top of the regulatory agenda. As Biddulph and others have argued, the 'clean up' campaign of wage arrears in the construction sector and its associated regulatory measures had contributed to the drafting of the 2008 labour law reforms, not only in relation to the enactment of specific provisions on wage payments in the LCL, but also the production of considerable

15. *Ibid.*, 150.

information about the nature and causes of the problem to enable better monitoring and enforcement.[16]

[E] Reversing the Deregulatory Agenda

By the mid-2000s, what became apparent to policymakers were the major deficiencies in the legal framework for dealing with the detrimental effects of fissurisation that, to a considerable extent, emerged from the deregulatory wave of labour market reforms in the 1990s. The rapidly escalating trend of labour disputes over this period revealed significant discontent and frustration among workers over issues of wage arrears and violation of basic employment and social protections. In 1996, China's labour dispute arbitration committees handled 47,951 cases. The number of cases had increased to 350,182 in 2007.[17] While there are no reliable data on strikes, frequent incidences of wildcat strikes and collective workplace disturbances by 'unorganised' workers in the private sector have been on the rise over the past decade.

A wave of worker-protective labour law reforms in 2007 represented an endeavour by Chinese policymakers to 'reverse the deregulation agenda' of the 1990s and to 're-regulate' the labour market with the overarching goal of building harmonious labour relations.[18] The Labour Contract Law (LCL), together with the Labour Dispute Mediation and Arbitration Law (LDMA) and the Employment Promotion Law (EPL) came into effect in 2008. A key objective of the LCL was to regulate the widespread use of fixed-term labour contracts. Employees can now request an open-ended contract if they have been working continuously for the employer for ten or more years,[19] or if they have already been on two consecutive fixed-term contracts with the employer.[20] If the employer fails to sign a written contract within a year of employing the worker, an open-ended labour contract shall be deemed as concluded.[21] As shown in Table 8.1, strong enforcement efforts by the state and trade unions have resulted in the rapid expansion of signed labour contracts after the enactment of the LCL, especially with regards to rural migrant workers.

16. Sarah Biddulph, Sean Cooney, and Ying Zhu, 'Rule of Law with Chinese Characteristics: The Role of Campaigns in Lawmaking' (2012) 34 Law and Policy 373.
17. National Bureau of Statistics, 2007 Statistical Bulletin on Labour and Social Security, *China Labor and Social Security Yearbook* (China Labor and Social Security Publishers, 2009) 1272.
18. Chang-Hee Lee, William Brown, and Xiaoyi Wen, 'What Sort of Collective Bargaining is Emerging in China?' (2014) 54 British Journal of Industrial Relations 214.
19. Labour Law 1994 had a similar but weaker provision where the employee could 'request' to sign an open-ended contract with the employer after ten consecutive years of service.
20. LCL, Article 14(1).
21. LCL, Article 14(3).

Table 8.1 Proportion of Wage Workers with Signed Labour Contracts[22]

	Rural Migrant Workers			*Urban Local Workers*		
	Male	Female	**Total**	Male	Female	**Total**
2001	34.60	28.15	**31.97**	77.23	69.76	**74.06**
2005	39.15	33.19	**36.85**	76.37	68.90	**73.14**
2010	60.44	59.01	**59.76**	81.24	78.78	**80.20**

The LCL further introduced new obligations on employers to prevent the underpayment of wages, provisions for the transmission of employee entitlements during firm restructuring, and as will be discussed in greater detail later on, controls and restrictions over the use of labour dispatch. Meanwhile, the LDMA focused on improving the procedural aspects of settling labour disputes through the official channels of mediation, arbitration, and litigation. The EPL expanded the grounds of prohibited discrimination in the 1994 Labour Law to include discrimination against migrant workers based on their residential status. The new laws appeared to have raised workers' expectations about improvement of their wages and working conditions, along with better access to pursue their claims through mediation and arbitration. Within the first twelve months of the passage of these laws, official statistics reported a doubling of cases accepted by labour dispute arbitration committees from around 350,182 in 2007 to 693,465 in 2008.[23]

This period also saw the stepping up of regulatory efforts to develop collective labour law institutions against the backdrop of a persistent rise of collective labour disputes. In particular, there has been accelerated expansion of formal laws and institutions to promote collective bargaining as a key pillar of labour relations policy since the 2000s. The number and coverage of collective contracts at the enterprise level and increasingly at sector and regional levels to regulate wages, employment conditions, and other workplace issues has also increased considerably. Based on the statistics of the ACFTU, a total of 1.9 million enterprises signed 1.1 million collective contracts in 2008, covering 150 million workers (or 60.2% of workers) in the urban workforce. In 2011, these figures had increased to a total of 3.61 million enterprises and 223 million workers (or 62.1% of workers in the urban workforce) covered by 1.79 million collective contracts.[24] The extent to which collective contracts address the fissurisation of employment will be discussed later in the next part.

22. Mary E Gallagher, John Giles, Albert Park, and Meiyan Wang, China's 2008 Labor Contract Law: Implementation and Implications for China's Workers (World Bank Policy Research Working Paper 6542, 2013).
23. National Bureau of Statistics, *Labor Statistical Yearbook 2009*, 9.1 tbl.(China Statistics Press 2009).
24. ACFTU, *2011 GonghuiZhuzhi he Gonghui Gongzuo Fazhan Zhuangkuang Tongji Gongbao* [*2011 Statistical Communique of Trade Union Development and Trade Union Work*], http://stats.acftu.org; also *see Employmeht and Wages*, China Statistical Yearbook 2011, available at: <http://www.stats.gov.cn/tjsj/ndsj/2011/indexeh.htm≥ (accessed 1 February 2016).

§8.03 THE NOTION OF THE 'EMPLOYER'

[A] The Scope of the 'Labour Relationship'

The labour law framework applies where a 'labour relationship' has been formed inside China. It should be noted that Chinese labour law has tended to avoid the use of the Chinese terms for 'employment' (*guyong*), 'employer' (*guyongren*), and 'employee' (*shouguren*) for ideological purposes. Based on Marxist notions of labour relations, there is a distinction between a relationship of exploitative exchange under an 'employment contract' (*guyonghetong*) and a socially regulated industrial relationship of a 'labour contract' (*laodonghetong*).[25] The 'employer' is commonly referred to as the 'employing unit' or 'work unit' (*yongrendanwei*).

The actors of a 'labour relationship' are stipulated in Article 2 of Labour Law 1994:

> This Law applies to enterprises and individually-owned economic organisations(hereinafter referred to as 'employing units') and persons who engage in work ('labourers') who form a labour relationship with them within the boundary of the People's Republic of China. State departments, institutional organisations and social groups and labourers who form a labour contract relationship with them shall observe this Law.

Furthermore, Article 2 of the Labour Contract Law 2008 states that:

> This Law shall apply to the establishment of employment relationship between labourers and enterprises, individual economic organizations, private non-enterprise entities, or other organizations (hereinafter referred to as 'employing units'), and to the formation, implementation, amendment, dissolution, or termination of labour contracts. State organs, public institutions, social organizations, and the labourers with whom they have formed an employment relationship shall observe this Law in the formation, implementation, amendment, dissolution, or termination of labour contracts.

This definition of an 'employing unit' excludes individuals and households.[26] The Supreme People's Court has confirmed that disputes between individual or household and domestic workers are not deemed as labour disputes.[27] Besides domestic workers, other categories of workers who are not covered by Chinese labour laws include: agricultural workers (other than those engaged as employees in large agricultural enterprises), student interns undertaking work as part of their vocational training, some public sector and military workers, and post-retirement individuals who return or remain in the workforce. These categories are subject to contract and civil law or special public sector rules. Furthermore, the employing entity must be an enterprise or

25. Cooney, Biddulph and Zhu (n. 11) 53.
26. MOLSS, Opinion on Certain Questions during the Enforcement of the PRC Labour Law, 4 August 1995.
27. The Supreme People's Court of PRC, Interpretation on the Certain Issues on the Applicable Laws about Hearing of Cases of Labour Disputes, 1 October 2006.

economic organisation that is a formally registered legal entity. This has the effect of excluding workers that are engaged by unregistered organisations or individuals.

[B] A 'De Facto' Employment Relationship

The MHRSS issued the Notice on Relevant Matters related to the Establishment of Labour Relationships 2005 (No. 2) which laid out the criteria for determining whether a de facto labour relationship had been formed, even where there is no written or signed labour contract:

(1). The employer and employee meet the legal qualification in the relevant laws and regulations.;
(2). Workplace rules made by the employer in accordance with the law are being applied to the employee, and the employee is subject to the employer's control and management and carries out the paid work as assigned by the employer.;
(3). The labour provided by the employee is part of the business of the employer.

The courts have applied the above criteria to address employment-related responsibilities in multi-layered contractual relationships. In one case, the People's Court of Linmu County, Shandong Province, ruled that a de facto employment relationship existed between a construction company and a worker of a subcontractor who died on the construction company's project site.[28] In 2012, the construction company undertook a project as the general contractor. The construction company subcontracted the moulding and carpentry work of the project to an individual contractor, who then subcontracted the work to three other individuals. One of the three individuals further 'sub-subcontracted' some of the work to the worker in this case. In October 2012, this worker died on the project site. The construction company paid RMB 100,000 in funeral expenses to the workers' family. In December 2012, the deceased workers' family filed for labour arbitration, claiming the existence of a de facto employment relationship between the worker and the construction company. In March 2013, the labour arbitration committee ruled in favour of the workers' family. The construction company challenged the arbitration award in the local people's court and argued that since the worker was recruited, managed, and paid by the subcontractor, the company did not have an employment relationship.

The arbitration award was affirmed by the local people's court. The court decided that there was a de facto employment relationship between the worker and the construction company due to the company's subcontracting of construction work to individuals who were not licensed contractors. Neither the subcontractor nor the

28. Baker & McKenzie, 'Deceased Worker of Sub-contractor Held to Have De Facto Employment with Construction Company', *China Employment Law Update*, February 2014, http://www.bakermckenzie.com/files/Publication/4cc22b38-de52-4a8d-a08d-33c128479629/Presentation/PublicationAttachment/b9ef7f79-f2d0-4137-8f8c-42b59ffd62c0/NLChinaEmploymentLawUpdateFeb14.pdf (accessed 1 February 2016).

'sub-subcontractors' had the legal capacity to hire employees. Based on the MHRSS's Notice, the company must assume the responsibilities of an employer for any worker recruited by an unlicensed contractor (who may be an individual or organisation) to undertake the work.

[C] Employee Versus Independent Contractors

Although it is not the focus of this chapter, the distinction between employees and independent contractors who are engaged on a 'contract for services' (*laowuhetong*) has attracted growing regulatory attention in China. The question of 'who is an employee' has attracted considerable interest due to the expansion of the so-called gig economy, perhaps most visibly through the growth of online car-hire services such as Uber and a number of highly successful domestic Chinese competitors.

Two recent labour disputes before the local people's court in Beijing examined this issue arising from the claims of two former 'employees' of a Chinese Uber-style mobile ride hail service.[29] The plaintiffs in both cases unsuccessfully tried to prove the existence of an employment relationship with the defendant company and presented supporting evidence to the court, including bank statements with regular monthly payments from the company, a driver ID card with the company's name, the provision of a work uniform and a mobile phone, and an induction letter upon joining the company. The 'cooperation agreement' between the plaintiffs and defendant stated that the company would provide an information platform (via its mobile app) to its drivers regarding customer orders. Drivers can provide their services to customers and directly charge customers their fees (set by the company). Drivers must pay a monthly deposit to the company. The company deducts from that deposit a service fee for its information provision after the completion of each order by the driver.

In both cases, the court decided that the nature of the relationship between the two parties was not a labour relationship. Of primary consideration was that the plaintiffs could control their own working hours. When and where the plaintiffs worked or rested wholly depended on them. The court also determined that there was no direct payment of a monthly salary from the company and the company in fact charged a 20% information service fee from its drivers. The plaintiffs' arguments regarding joining the company via a formal process of recruitment, interview, and training, and their acceptance of the defendant's company rules in performing their work and the associated disciplinary measures did not seem to have persuaded the court in reaching its decision in both cases.

29. *Labour Dispute between Wang ZheShuan and Beijing YixinYixing Automotive Technology Development Services Ltd.* Beijing Shijingshan District People's Court Civil Judgment No. 367 (2014); *Labour Dispute between Sun Youliang and Beijing YixinYixing Automotive Technology Development Services Ltd.* Beijing First Intermediate People's Court Judgment No. 176 (2015).

[D] Regulating Labour Dispatch Arrangements

[1] Background

Perhaps the fastest-growing and most rampant manifestation of fissurisation in China, which has attracted the most regulatory attention in recent years, is the use of labour dispatch. Labour dispatch arrangements involve triangular contractual relationships whereby workers are hired by a dispatch agency (*laowupaiqiandanwei*) to provide services for a labour-using entity (*yongrendanwei*). The labour dispatch agency is deemed to be the 'employing unit' under Chinese labour law.[30] The labour-using entity does not have a direct employment relationship with dispatch workers and is not responsible for the payment of wages and benefits to the workers. Instead, it has a service agreement with the dispatch agency that includes remuneration for workers.[31]

As discussed in Part II, labour dispatch was used significantly by the state during the restructuring of SOEs in the 1990s as a means of 'smashing the iron rice bowl' and facilitating the introduction of a new labour contracts system. The growth of the labour dispatch industry in recent years, particularly the number of small and medium dispatch agencies, has been linked to the use of labour dispatch arrangements to sidestep the protections introduced by more worker-protective labour law reforms over the past decade.[32] Some have argued the LCL has had the unintended consequence of expanding informal work arrangements, as reflected by the substantial increase in the use of labour dispatch since its enactment.[33]

The ACFTU estimated that in 2011, there were approximately 37 million dispatched workers, representing around 13.1% of all employees in the urban workforce. This figure represents a substantial increase from the ACFTU's estimate of 25 million dispatched workers in 2006.[34] Based on these statistics, labour dispatch is primarily used by SOEs and foreign-invested enterprises that engage 16.2% and 14.2% of dispatched workers respectively. In some large cities such as Beijing and Shanghai, the use of labour dispatch is much higher. Rural migrant workers represent 52.6% of the dispatched workforce. Furthermore, it was found that 39.5% of dispatched workers surveyed had worked for the same labour-using firm for over six years.[35] Other studies have highlighted a general lack of labour protection as experienced by dispatch workers, including job insecurity, inferior wages and conditions than comparable direct or regular employees, and the common withholding and/or deduction of wages by dispatch agencies.[36]

30. LCL, Article 58.
31. LCL, Articles 59, 60.
32. Kuruvilla, Gallagher and Lee (n. 10), Ch. 1.
33. *Ibid.*
34. ACFTU, 'Dang Qian WoGuo Lao Wu Pai Qian Yong Gong Xian Zhuang Diao Cha' ['Survey of China's Current Labor Dispatch Situation'] (2012) 5 China Labor 23.
35. *Ibid.*
36. Feng Xu, 'Temporary Work in China: Precarity in an Emerging Labour Market' in Judge Fudge and Kendra Strauss, *Temporary Work, Agencies and Unfree Labour: Insecurity in the New World of Work* (Routledge 2014) 143-163; Juliana So, 'Exploring the Plight of Dispatch Workers in China and How to Improve their Conditions: a Preliminary Study' (2014) 17 The Journal of

[2] Dispatch Labour and the Labour Contract Law

The LCL contained numerous provisions to enhance the protection of labour dispatch workers. It attempts to delineate the various legal obligations of the dispatch agencies and labour-using firms.[37] The labour dispatch agency is deemed to be the 'employing unit' as defined in the LCL and shall perform the obligations of the employing unit for its employees.[38] The labour contract between the worker and the agency must specify matters such as the entity that the worker will be dispatched, the duration, and the role/position of the dispatch assignment. There is a minimum term of two years for the fixed-term contracts concluded between the dispatch agency and worker.[39] The dispatch agency must also pay workers their wages on a monthly basis. If there is no work during a particular period, the agency must pay the worker an amount equivalent to the minimum wage of the locality where the agency is located.[40] The agency must also inform dispatched workers of the content of the dispatch service agreement it had signed with the labour-using entity.[41] This agreement must included the following content: the positions which the workers are dispatched to, the number of dispatch workers, the duration of dispatch, the amount and terms of remuneration and social security payments, and liability for breach of the agreement.[42]

In regulating the practices of labour-using firms, the LCL places restrictions on the use of labour dispatch only for 'temporary, auxiliary, or substituting positions'.[43] A labour-using entity is prohibited from establishing its own labour dispatch service for the purpose of dispatching workers to itself and to its subsidiaries.[44] Furthermore, the LCL requires the labour-using entity to decide the length of using labour dispatch on the basis of actual organisational needs and not divide an assignment of a longer continuous period into several short-term dispatch agreements.[45] The labour-using entity must also provide labour dispatch workers with the labour rights and protections in accordance with national laws and regulations, overtime pay, performance-based bonuses and other benefits related to the job, regular wage increases, and essential on-the-job training based on the needs of the position.[46] The principle of 'equal pay for equal work' is also applicable to dispatch workers. An amendment to the LCL in 2013 clarified this principle as providing dispatch workers the right to enjoy the same remuneration rates paid to directly employed workers in a comparable position in the labour-using firm.[47]

Labor & Society 531; Ka Ni Li, 'Re-conceptualizing the Notion of "Employer": The Case of Labor Dispatch Workers in China' (2015) 40 Brooklyn Journal of International Law 619.

37. LCL, Article 58.
38. *Ibid.*
39. LCL, Article 58.
40. LCL, Article 58.
41. LCL, Article 60.
42. LCL, Article 59.
43. LCL, Article 66.
44. LCL, Article 67.
45. LCL, Article 59(2).
46. LCL, Article 62.
47. LCL, Article 63.

If a labour dispatch agency violates the provisions of the LCL, it will be subject to rectification orders by the labour administrative authorities, fines of RMB 1,000-5,000 per person, or/and revocation of business licence for serious offences.[48] This direct imposition of legal liability on the dispatch agency for violations of the LCL reflects its status as the 'employing unit'. There is no equivalent provision for the labour-using entity. However, if there is any damage caused to dispatch workers, the LCL stipulates that the dispatch agency and the labour-using entity are jointly and severally liable with respect to compensation.[49]

[3] Further Restrictions in 2013

The enhanced worker protections introduced by the LCL (such as the restrictions on the use of fixed-term contracts and dismissals) seem to have prompted greater use of labour dispatch by firms to avoid the heftier legal obligations. As Ho and Huang also claim, the 'explosion' of the labour dispatch industry in recent years has largely taken place 'in technical compliance with the LCL'.[50] The requirements to set up a dispatch agency were fairly minimal: a standard business registration and registered capital of RMB 500,000.[51] There was no need for any other special authorisation. Labour dispatch became an increasingly profitable sector that had few formal mechanisms of regulatory oversight.[52]

The response of policymakers to the perceived inadequacy of the LCL to address the problems with labour dispatch was to introduce further amendments to the LCL in 2013 and its implementing rules, the Interim Provisions on Labour Dispatch (IPLD) issued by MHRSS in 2014. The amended LCL clearly states that direct labour contract is the basic form of employment in enterprises and that labour dispatch is a supplementary form.[53] Other changes brought in by the amended LCL include: increasing the registered capital minimum for dispatch agencies to RMB 2 million and requiring agencies to obtain an administrative licence with the local labour bureau and register as a dispatch agency with the local industry and commerce office;[54] refining the equal pay principle for dispatched workers;[55] stipulating certain mandatory issues to be included in the dispatch agreement;[56] and requiring dispatch agencies to register and pay social insurance for dispatched workers in the locality of the labour-using firm.[57]

48. LCL, Article 92.
49. LCL, Article 92.
50. Virginia Harper Ho and Huang Qiaoyan, 'The Recursivity of Reform: China's Amended Labor Contract Law' (2014) 37 Fordham International Law Journal 973.
51. LCL, Article 57.
52. Ho and Huang (n 50).
53. LCL, Article 66(1).
54. The Ministry of Human Resources and Social Security Notice on the Effective Implementation of Labour Administrative Permit (promulgated 21 June 2013, effective 1 July 2013).
55. LCL, Article 63.
56. IPLD, Article 7.
57. IPLD, Articles 18 and 19.

The IPLD sets a 10% cap on the proportion of dispatched workers in the labour-using firm's workforce.[58] This is intended to give substance to Article 66 of the LCL, which requires the labour-using firm to control the number of dispatch workers. A company will not be allowed to engage new dispatch workers until it has reduced the existing number to the required proportion. Companies have been given two years from 1 March 2014 to comply with the new rules and to file an adjustment plan with the labour authority.[59]

The IPLD gives further substance to the requirement that labour dispatch is restricted to 'temporary, auxiliary or substitute' positions under the LCL.[60] The ambiguity of this provision under the original LCL provided firms with considerable scope to justify the 'need' for labour dispatch.[61] Under the IPLD, a 'temporary' position refers to a position of no more than six months. An 'auxiliary' position refers a 'non-major business position' that provides support or services to the business. Such positions require the employer to consult the employees' representative congress or all employees, and to negotiate with its trade union or employee representative. Finally, a 'substitute' position is where the original employee in that position is absent for a period of time due to study, leave or other reasons.

The IPLD also considers forms of 'sham' outsourcing and subcontracting that is disguised as labour dispatch to be covered under the Provisions.[62] However, it is still unclear what types of arrangements would fall within the ambit of this provision. The inclusion of the provision itself arguably reflects, to some degree, policymakers' concern that firms may attempt to sidestep the restrictions on the use of dispatch labour under the amended LCL with new forms of labour outsourcing and subcontracting practices that are subject to less or no legal regulation.

[4] Dispatch Labour and Occupational Health and Safety Issues

The obligations of labour dispatch agencies towards dispatch workers in the area of occupational disease and work injury have also been strengthened by the amended LCL and IPLD, with the aim of limiting the opportunities for contractual risk-shifting between the dispatch agency and labour-using firm. The labour dispatch agency has legal liability for providing workers with work injury insurance 'but may negotiate with the labour-using entity over the compensatory approach'.[63] Meanwhile, the labour-using entity has responsibility over the workers' diagnosis and assessment of occupational diseases, which is regulated by a separate legal regime.[64]

Major amendments to China's Work Safety Law in 2014 also recognised the particular occupational health and safety issues faced by dispatch workers. Dispatch workers are subject to the same rights and obligations under the Work Safety Law as

58. IPLD, Article 4.
59. IPLD, Article 28.
60. IPLD, Article 3.
61. Ho and Huang (n. 50) 101.
62. IPLD, Article 27.
63. IPLD, Article 10(1).
64. IPLD, Article 10(2).

direct employees of the labour-using entity.[65] The labour-using entity must also include dispatch workers in the overall work safety management system of the firm. Both the labour-using entity and the dispatch agency have work safety training and education obligations to the dispatch workers.[66] Failure of the labour-using entity to provide workplace training and education gives rise to legal liability such as fines and the suspension of the firms' production.[67]

[5] Collective Labour Relations and Dispatch Workers

Article 64 of the LCL provides for the right of dispatch workers to join the trade union of the labour dispatch agency or the labour-using entity or to organise such unions in accordance with the law, so as to protect their own lawful rights and interests. It may be argued that the policy rationale for providing dispatch workers with the choice of joining the union of the agency or labour-using entity, or to organise a union (within a legal framework that provides only for affiliation to the ACFTU) is to recognise the particular difficulties of union participation for this group of workers, such as frequent changes in workplaces and the dispersion of dispatch workers across different labour-using firms.

Dispatch labour has become a particular of concern for the ACFTU as labour disputes involving the labour dispatch workforce grew sharply over the past decade. The ACFTU and its local union federations used their political influence to push for the amendments to the LCL in 2013. There was extensive disagreement among different interest groups and policymakers in the lead-up to the amendments. The ACFTU had been pushing for more restrictive regulations on the use of labour dispatch. Enterprises, including many large central SOEs that used dispatch workers, had strongly opposed any legislative restrictions. The Ministry of Human Resource and Social Security highlighted the role of labour dispatch in job creation and labour flexibility, especially in the context of policy concerns over the Chinese economy in the aftermath of the 2008 global financial crisis. The ACFTU submitted to the National People's Congress in 2011 and 2012 two comprehensive reports on the widespread problems of dispatch labour and proposed legislative restrictions. The ACFTU particularly urged the inclusion of an objective cap on the use of labour dispatch during the drafting process of the 2013 amendments.[68]

Over the past fifteen years, there has also been an accelerated expansion of laws and institutions to promote 'collective negotiations' (collective bargaining)[69] as a central pillar of Chinese labour relations policy. While a vast majority of collective contracts are at the enterprise level, there has also been growing regulatory interest in relation to collective negotiations and collective contracts concluded in a certain sector

65. Law of the People's Republic of China on Work Safety 2002 (Work Safety Law), Article 58.
66. Work Safety Law, Article 25.
67. Work Safety Law, Article 94.
68. Lu Zhang, *Inside China's Automobile Factories* (Cambridge University Press 2015) 178-179.
69. The literal terms found in Chinese labour law refer to 'collective negotiations' or 'collective consultations', which are deemed to be less confrontational than 'collective bargaining'.

and/or within a set geographical region (usually up to municipal level) between trade unions and groups of employers in the same sector. Collective wage bargaining at the sector and regional levels has been developing in certain localities in recent years.[70]

The number and coverage of collective contracts at various levels to regulate wages, employment conditions, and a range of other workplace issues has also increased considerably. However, the focus has largely been on the quantity of signed collective contracts, with numerical targets set for local trade union federations and local governments. The quality of collective contracts in practice has generally been quite weak, as Chinese trade unions continue to face institutional and capacity challenges in its ability to represent workers.[71]

There has been the emergence of collective contracts specifically seeking to regulate the rights and interests of dispatch workers. One such example was a dispatch labour collective contract entered into by a dispatch agency and five labour-using entities in a county in Nanjing in 2008, which covered nearly 30,000 dispatch workers. The collective contract explicitly set out the responsibilities of the agency and labour-using firms in relation to protecting the various rights and interests of workers. The trade unions from the dispatch agency and the labour-using firms constituted the labour side for the negotiations.[72] However, it seems that collective negotiations on labour dispatch issues remain a contested agenda among the various actors. The final version of the recently enacted 2015 Guangdong Regulation on Collective Bargaining took out a reference to the protection of labour dispatch workers in an earlier draft of the Regulations. The original provision would have allowed for labour dispatch issues to be included in the content of collective agreements not only at the enterprise level, but also in sector-level and regional-level collective contracts.

[6] Other Legal and 'Soft Law' Measures

It should be further noted that China's tort liability regime recognises an expanded notion of the 'employer' in relation to the employer's vicarious liability for its workers' tortious acts that cause damage to third parties. According to the Tort Law 2012, if during a dispatch arrangement, the dispatched worker causes damage to a third party due to performance of working tasks, the entity accepting the dispatch arrangement shall be subject to tort liability.[73] This means that, from a vicarious liability perspective, labour-users are treated like employers and therefore bear corresponding risks for some workers who are not their direct employees.

In dealing with the deleterious consequences of fissured workplaces for worker protection, a relatively under-developed area of regulation has been the use of 'soft law' measures. There have been some innovative developments in recent years. One

70. Lee, Brown, and Wen (n. 18).
71. Zou (n. 3).
72. Wan Yi Caijing (Money.163.com) 'Can collective contracts resolve the dilemma of labour dispatch', 18 February 2008, http://money.163.com/08/0218/07/44VF2OCU00251RJ2.html (accessed 16 February 2016).
73. Tort Law 2010 (PRC), Article 34.

prominent example is the ILO's Sustaining Competitive and Responsible Enterprises (SCORE) programme for small and medium enterprises (SMEs). Around 99% of all private registered enterprises in China are SMEs.[74] In the context of fissured workplaces, SMEs have been on the receiving end of risk transfer associated with the fissurisation of employment by the large firms.[75] Many SMEs in China are embedded within global supply chains and face significant pressures to be competitive and productive in order to access market opportunities nationally and internationally.[76]

SCORE is a modular training programme aimed at developing cooperative labour relations in SMEs through training and capacity building activities for employers and workers in five areas: workplace cooperation, quality management, clean production, human resource management, and occupational health and safety. In Phase I of the programme (2009-2013), SCORE China worked with the official employers' association, China Enterprise Confederation (CEC), in several provinces across the country in the machinery manufacturing, auto parts, and garments sectors. Phase II of SCORE China (2013-2017) focuses on training local organisations to run ongoing SCORE training to SMEs, independent of the ILO and international donors.[77] To this end, the ILO has signed cooperation agreements with the CEC and the government agency responsible for work safety, the State Administration of Work Safety, to gradually take over the lead of SCORE training after 2016.[78] To date, SCORE China has trained 145 trainers, 120 enterprises, and more than 1,500 workers and managers.[79] A recent evaluation of the programme has shown encouraging results at the enterprise level, including 'improved working conditions, remarkable cost savings and greater efficiency through workplace dialogue and cooperation, workers' participation and collective actions and investment in training'.[80]

§8.04 CONCLUSION

As observed in other parts of the world, the emergence of the fissured work place in China has accompanied deregulatory policies associated with goals of increasing flexibility for enterprises (particularly SOEs) and facilitating job creation during

74. ILO, 'Sustaining Competitive and Responsible Enterprises (SCORE) Project Phase I' http://www.ilo.org/beijing/what-we-do/projects/WCMS_142938/lang--en/index.htm (accessed 16 February 2016).
75. Weil (n. 1).
76. ILO, Sustaining Competitive and Responsible Enterprises (SCORE) Project Phase I, http://www.ilo.org/beijing/what-we-do/projects/WCMS_142938/lang--en/index.htm (accessed 15 March 2016).
77. ILO, Sustaining Competitive and Responsible Enterprises (SCORE) Project Phase II, http://www.ilo.org/beijing/what-we-do/projects/WCMS_238771/lang--en/index.htm (accessed 15 March 2016).
78. ILO, 'ILO signs agreement with Consulting and Training Centre of China Enterprise Confederation for implementing Score project', Press Release, 1 April 2014; ILO, 'ILO signs agreement with the State Administration of Work Safety for implementing Score project', Press Release, 8 April 2014.
79. ILO, SCORE China Newsletter (No. 7), November 2015, http://us8.campaign-archive1.com/?u=5b3287fed6963b8cf74f149d2&id=2d253fc371&e=8443d219f1 (accessed 15 March 2016).
80. *Ibid.*

economic and labour market restructuring. The fissurisation of work in China has taken place in the context of the country's fundamental transition to a market-based economy with 'Chinese characteristics' over the past three decades. The conceptualisations of the 'employing unit' and the 'labour relationship' in the two main pieces of labour legislation in China (Labour Law 1994 and LCL 2008) have remained limited in their scope and coverage, with the effect of excluding certain groups of workers such as independent contractors and domestic workers. The threshold requirement of proving a labour relationship before one can pursue a formal claim for non-payment of wages and/or other rights violations becomes highly challenging in complex, multi-layered contracting chains such as those commonly found in the construction sector.

This chapter has focused on the use of labour dispatch as the fastest-growing and most prevalent manifestation of the fissured workplace in China today. Labour dispatch arrangements have destabilised labour relations by creating ambiguity around which entity has the responsibility for a range of 'employer' obligations under labour, social security, and health and safety laws. It was not until the LCL in 2008 that sought to regulate labour dispatch issues for the first time in Chinese labour law. Yet, the LCL's heightened standards of labour protections were associated with firms' (actual and/or perceived) increase of compliance burden and costs, which increased the demand for labour dispatch.

In addition to clarifying the obligations of the dispatch agency and labour-using firm, the amendments to LCL in 2013 seem to have facilitated litigation by dispatch workers to challenge illegal practices as well as stricter administrative oversight by local regulators.[81] Nevertheless, there remain significant gaps in Chinese labour law in relation to addressing 'sham' outsourcing or subcontracting and other forms of non-standard employment arising from fissurisation. Furthermore, there is still a long way to go in developing collective bargaining laws and institutions at the enterprise level and higher levels to effectively protect dispatch workers' rights and interests. The development of 'soft law' measures such as the ILO's SCORE training programme for SMEs offers some potential for filling some of these regulatory gaps.

In the midst of China's current economic downturn and industrial restructuring, many firms in certain sectors (such as the labour-intensive, lower-end manufacturing sector) are responding to competitive pressures and financial hardship through outsourcing, downsizing, restructuring, and other means of survival. The stakes are high for the ACFTU and the state in the attempt to build 'harmonious labour relations' in an increasingly fissured workplace, which brings with it ever greater possibilities for industrial conflict and social instability.

81. Ho and Huang (n. 50) 1017-1020.

CHAPTER 9

Realizing Workers' Rights Beyond Corporate Boundaries in South Korea

Aelim Yun[*]

§9.01 INTRODUCTION

In Korea, like many other countries, an 'employer' under labour regulations is the prime subject who is responsible for securing labour rights. For example, the Supreme Court held 'the term "employer" in individual labour relations means those who enter into an explicit or implicit employment contract, where they are provided labour with direction or supervision over the performance of an employee, and pay the corresponding wages to the employee'.[1]

The traditional notion of an employer has implied that four functions that Freedland identified are integrated in a single entity: (1) engaging workers and terminating employment; (2) remunerating and providing them with other benefits; (3) managing the employment relationship and the process of work; and (4) using workers' services in the process of production or service provisions (Freedland 2003).

While increasing precarious employment[2] challenge to this notion, the labour laws liability is still identified in terms of one-to-one relation. In triangular employment

* Teaching Professor at Korea National Open University, aelimyun@hotmail.com.
1. The Supreme Court, 12 July 1999, 99-ma-628.
2. Such terms as 'non-standard' or 'atypical' employment relationships that have often been referred to, take 'standard' employment relationships as a definitional starting point but without examining how that norm is deteriorating – what is standard today may be very much worse than what was standard two or three decades ago (Fudge, 2005). By way of contrast, Gerry Rodgers has suggested that there are several elements that make a particular form of employment precarious, including the degree of certainty of continuing work and the number and type of labour protections enjoyed by workers, either by law or as negotiated by a collective organization like a trade union (Rodgers, 1989). I refer to 'precarious workers' as those who are excluded from much labour protection, due to them having either different contractual arrangements or because they lack various institutional protections.

relationships such as agency work, for example, a user enterprise contracts out some or all those functions to different legal entities, retaining the right to control over the whole process. Nevertheless, many legal systems have not succeeded in capturing the changing concept of employer, therefore failed in providing effective labour protections. Some regard a 'provider' (employment agency) solely as an employer. Others allocate a little liability of employer to a 'user employer'. In other extreme cases, if the employer's control factors are not identified vis-à-vis a user as well as a provider respectively, neither a user nor a provider is regarded as an 'employer', and furthermore, it contributes to the denial of 'employee' status of agency workers (Davidov 2004).Weil describes the modern workplace as the 'fissured workplace', noting that the basic terms of employment are now the result of multiple organizations, and consequently responsibility for conditions has become blurred (Weil 2014: 7). To respond to this 'fissurization', we should note that the user's control over labour expands beyond corporate boundaries, while the employing entity is divided along the network of firms. To reconsider the concept of 'employer' in this changing world of work, this chapter first analyses the structure of employer's power and changing nature of subordinate relations with a case study of triangular employment relationships in Korea. Second, it reviews current legislative and interpretative responses to emerging fissurization of work. In conclusion, I argue that the fissurization of emerging work relationship is the outcome of a cost-and-risks transfer from capital to labour, and thus, the approach of reversing this transfer would be more effective and fair method for labour protection.

§9.02 CURRENT SITUATION OF FISSURIZATION

[A] Overview

In the Korean labour law system, triangular employment relationships were prohibited in principle, before 1998. In the principle of elimination of Intermediary exploitation, Article 9 of the *Labour Standards Act* (LSA) states that no person shall intervene in the employment of another person for making a profit or gain benefit as an intermediary, unless otherwise prescribed by any Act. The *Employment Security Act* (ESA) also restricts a 'labour supply business' (Article 33) with the exception where trade unions provided their members to users (Article 33 paragraph 3). Since 1998, however, triangular employment relationships have been legitimated under certain conditions by the *Act on Protections for Temporary Agency Workers (*APTAW).

The most contentious types of triangular employment relationship are as follows.

[1] Multi-Layered Subcontracting

Multi-layered subcontracting is conventional practices, in particular, in such industries as construction and freight road transport. The construction industry, for example, is characterized by a complex pyramid structure that is comprised, at any one site, of one main construction company ('main contractor') and several layers of subcontractors.

Under the *Framework Act on the Construction Industry* (FACI), subcontracting is permitted only in cases where a main contractor subcontracts some tasks to specialized subcontractors. Nevertheless, the predominant practice is multi-layered subcontracting, and construction firms directly employ only a few technicians and skilled workers, and use the bulk of workers via subcontractors or intermediaries, seeking a reduction in costs. Figure 9.1 describes this multi-layered industrial and employment structure in construction.

Figure 9.1 Industrial and Employment Structure in the Construction Industry

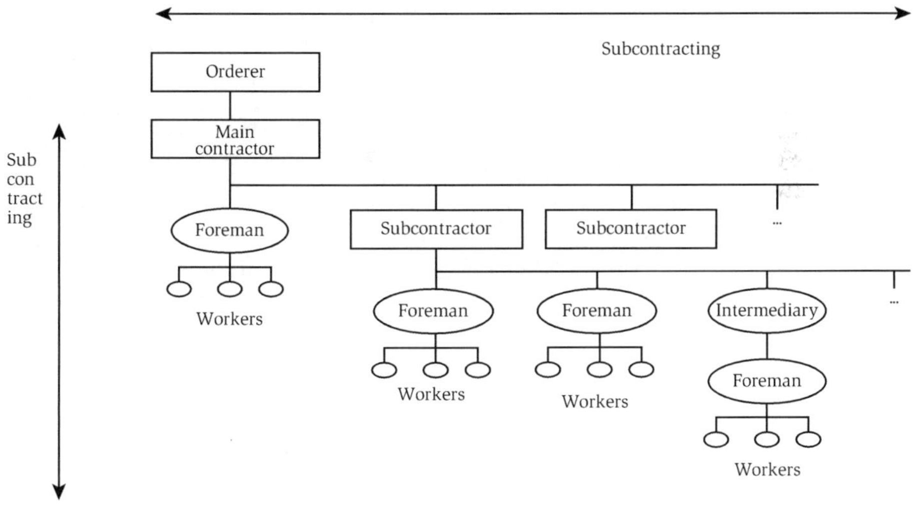

Source: Author's elaboration.

The multi-layered subcontracting has had various effects on the employment relationship in construction. First of all, the prevailing form of employment relationship is informal and indirect employment via intermediaries or foremen. The labour intermediary or foreman is often a skilled craftsman who operates as an independent manager-cum-worker. He/she receives a contract from a subcontractor or a sub-subcontractor and does the construction work by recruiting temporary workers through personal network. A recent survey revealed that over 70% of construction site workers got a job through foremen (Sim et al., 2013). Although foremen recruit and manage workers and distribute the remuneration, they cannot bear employer liability. Construction site workers work under the control of both the main contractor and the upper-level subcontractors who are provided workers via intermediaries or foremen.

Second, about 90% of construction site workers are employed on temporary and short terms 2008 (Ministry of Labour, 2008). Most construction workers are hired only for the period of a certain construction project, and therefore they suffer from repeated unemployment.

Third, the most significant changes in the employment relationship are a massive shedding of labour, particularly amongst construction equipment operators, by construction firms seeking cost-cuts, and an increase of independent workers and dependent self-employment since the late 1990s. For example, over 90% of concrete mixer truck drivers and dump truck drivers provide their labour as an 'independent contractor' without employing others (Sin, 2014).

[2] Agency Employment

As above mentioned, since 1998, just after Korean economic crisis occurred, temporary agency employment has been legitimated under certain conditions by the APTAW.

Temporary agency employment is allowed in 197 different job categories, including work requiring expert knowledge, technology and experience, for a maximum of two years. Otherwise, temporary agency employment is allowed only where a temporary need for workers arises due to pregnancy, disease or injury of employees, for a maximum of six months. Additionally, no temporary agency employment shall be conducted for jobs such as work performed at a construction site (Article 5 paragraph 3). Any person who intends to engage in temporary agency employment business shall obtain permission from the Minister of Employment and Labour (Article 7).

Under the APTAW, a temporary employment agency is party to the employment contract with a worker. However, it should be noted that most temporary employment agencies are, in practice, merely intermediaries, and are unable to take legal responsibility for workers' rights. For example, the wage of the worker is, in practice, decided by the contract between a temporary employment agency and a user employer. If a user employer demands that a certain worker of a temporary employment agency be replaced, the worker has no choice but to lose that job. According to information provided by the Ministry of Employment & Labour, approximately 80% of employment contracts with temporary employment agencies are only for the period that the worker works for a particular user employer (Yun, 2007:12). The APTAW has no regulation on this type of temporary employment contract between a temporary employment agency and a worker.

Under the APTAW, a user employer shall directly employ a temporary agency worker, where the worker has worked longer than two years or where the user employer uses the temporary agency worker in violation of provisions of the APTAW (Article 6-2). However, the APTAW does not have any equivalent provision in the case where a user employer switches one temporary agency worker for another worker before the two-year deadline. As a result, these protections can have a reverse effect. To avoid their legal responsibility, most user employers replace a temporary agency worker with another worker every two years. Moreover, most temporary employment agencies have an employment contract with a worker, only for the period that the worker works for a user employer, as mentioned above. Consequently, neither a user employer nor an agency holds responsibility for employment security, while a temporary agency worker suffers from periodical job insecurity.

[3] In-House Subcontracting

In the Korean manufacturing sector, the most common practice to use precarious employment is 'in-house subcontracting'. In that, a worker having an employment contract with a 'subcontractor' is provided for a 'subcontracting company' and the worker works under the control of both employers. With in-house subcontracting, the subcontracting companies use the excuse that they are not the user employers under the APTAW and thus do not hold themselves responsible for workers who in fact are working for them.

For instance, Hyundai Motor Company began to use this type of workers when the mass-production process was introduced in the early 1980s (Korean Metalworkers' Federation, 2003: 112). Subcontracted workers provide their labour at a subcontracting company's workplace under supervision of a subcontracting company as well as a subcontractor (Yun, 2011). Whereas both subcontracted workers and the regular employees of Hyundai Motor typically work for ten hours per day on a two-shift basis, in many cases the work intensity of subcontracted workers is much higher than that of regular employees (Korean Metal Workers Union, 2007: 51).

Nevertheless, working conditions of subcontracted workers are much inferior to those of regular employees. For example, it was reported the average monthly wage of subcontracted workers in Hyundai Motor was merely 60%-70% of that of regular employees of a same length of service (Korean Metal Workers Union, 2009: 55).

Subcontracted workers usually have an employment contract with a fixed term of three or six months. Normally the employment contract is repeatedly renewed, but subcontracted workers would be dismissed at any time when their jobs at a subcontracting company are reduced.

Another characteristic of in-house subcontracting exists in the power of a subcontracting company to decide business of subcontractors in practice. According to the result of a survey of in-house subcontracting at Hyundai Motor Company Ulsan plant in 2006, fifty-two of ninety-five subcontractors were the former management staffs of Hyundai Motor (Cho, 2006: 81). In-house subcontractors usually recruit workers only after making a contract with Hyundai, and they do no other business but providing and managing workforce for Hyundai exclusively. The most important criterion for selecting subcontractors is their ability in labour management, and Hyundai even limits the volume of personnel of each subcontractor to about seventy-five persons. While the period of a contract for subcontracting is usually six months, the contract would be repeatedly renewed if there would be no problem with labour management. In case one subcontractor is replaced by another subcontractor, normally workers of the former are rehired by the latter (En, 2008: 151).

[4] Procurement/Contracting-Out of Public Service

It is a noteworthy characteristic that Korean Government itself is a major employer who has abused precarious employment. Since the economic crisis in 1997, the Government has driven the public sectors to reduce personnel and to contract out their services to private enterprise. Particularly, the Government has forced this restructuring through budget mechanisms, that is, imposing financial penalties, when public organizations fail in implementing required restructuring. As a result, hundreds of thousands of public employees have been retrenched and precarious employment has been introduced, which in turn has made budget cuts possible.[3]

In accordance with a Government directive on restructuring, for example, the Korea National Railroad was converted to the Korea Railroad Corporation (KORAIL) in January 2005. At about same time, the management of the KORAIL restructured the labour force, including large-scale cut-backs in employee numbers, recruiting workers on precarious employment contracts and contracting out. For instance, the KORAIL has used 370 female attendants provided by its subsidiary (Korea Railroad Distribution) since it started a high-speed railway business (KTX) in 2004. Although female attendants are on fixed-term employment contracts with the Korea Railroad Distribution, they perform work under the instructions and control of the KORAIL. In contrast with male attendants who are directly employed by the KORAIL on permanent employment contracts, female attendants are all precarious workers.

Contracting-out of municipal service is another example. Since the late 1990s, most municipalities have contracted out public service such as street cleaning and garbage collection to private subcontractors. Nevertheless, local authorities can still control over wages and employment conditions via cost-plus arrangement with subcontractors. Moreover, it can unilaterally terminate the arrangement on the ground of complaints of local residents. As most subcontracted workers are employed only for the period of the arrangement between a local authority and a subcontractor, they suffer from constant insecurity of employment.

[5] Supply Chain

With the increasing cost of labour and competition in global market, Korean large conglomerates (*Chaebol*) increased foreign direct investment in the mid-1990s. For example, Samsung Electronics has moved its low value added products such as white goods to production lines in Southeast Asia and China, while high value added products such as semiconductors and core technology are kept in South Korea (Chang 2006).

The domestic production and supply for Samsung Electronics is made up of five layers. The first layer is composed of Samsung Group's subsidiaries, and the second layer is made up of transnational electronics component suppliers such as Qualcomm. The third and fourth layer comprises suppliers to which Samsung Electronics outsources parts production for cost or production capacity reasons. The final layer in the supply chain is composed of small and medium-sized suppliers located in industrial

3. The share of precarious work in public sector including education and health has increased from 37.6% in 2003, when the first survey on precarious work in public service sector was conducted, to 40.1% in 2007 (Korean Public Service Workers Union, 2008: 277-278).

complex. As these companies supply low-cost parts, Samsung Electronics frequently switches among them, exacerbating price competition (Han et al., 2013).

Although the top end of global value chains (GVCs) of Samsung Electronics has been produced in Korea, this does not mean that working conditions of the Korean workers are better off. The important basis of Samsung's management is a risks-and-cost transfer towards workers and the bottom of GVCs as well as its brutal and systematic 'No Union' policy.

At Seoul Digital Complex in the southern Seoul, for example, there are approximately 200,000 workers most of whom work for suppliers of Samsung Electronics, but the union density is less than 1%. As of 2009, the share of firms with four or less employees amounted to 46.4%, and that of firms of between five and nine employees was 25.6% (Future of Workers et al., 2011).

The result of survey conducted in 2011 by the campaign alliance for rights of workers at Seoul Digital Complex, called 'Future of Workers', revealed poor working conditions: over half of workers were precarious workers (52.0%), and the amount of average monthly wages was KRW 1,923,000, which was less than those of whole workers (2,026,000). The average working hours were 47.1 hours per week, and one in five workers worked for over fifty-two hours per week. The amount of average hourly wages was KRW 4,391, which was close to the statutory minimum wage in 2011 (KWN 4,320). Workers paid less than the minimum wage amounted to 13.8% (Future of Workers et al., 2011).

[6] Others

Private employment agencies are other types of labour intermediaries which compose a triangular employment relationship. Personal care workers in hospitals are such an example. Most of them provide their service to patients through a private employment agency under the supervision of a hospital. However, there are no contracts among them and therefore personal care workers have been regarded as an 'informal worker' or a 'domestic worker'.

Private employment agencies collect membership fee from job seekers and offer jobs to them. A private employment agency, which does not have an employment contract with a job seeker, is regarded as not a 'temporary employment agency' under the APTAW but a fee-charging job placement service agency under the ESA. In a case of personal care work, private employment agencies provide job seekers for hospitals, and care workers provide their service for patients under the supervision of a hospital. The arrangement between an agency and a hospital usually contains requirements of care worker, the standard of service fee, working hours, uniform and appearance rule, evaluation and sanctions upon care workers and so on. Nevertheless, courts have hardly regarded a hospital as an employer.[4]

4. The Supreme Court, 24 November 2009, 2009-du-18448.

[B] Motives and Backgrounds

[1] Trends and Size of Precarious Employment

According to the result of analysis by Yoo-Sun Kim (Korea Labour & Society Institute), precarious workers accounted for 45.0% of total wage workers in August 2015. Here, 'precarious workers' are defined as 'workers who are not expected to be employed constantly or those with fixed-term contracts', or 'workers with shorter contractual working time than normal employees' or 'workers with different forms of service from typical employment'.

Figure 9.2 shows that about half of total wage workers were precarious workers since 2000. The number of part-time workers and triangular employment workers has doubled.

Figure 9.2 The Share of Precarious, Part-Time and Triangular Employment Workers, 2001-2015

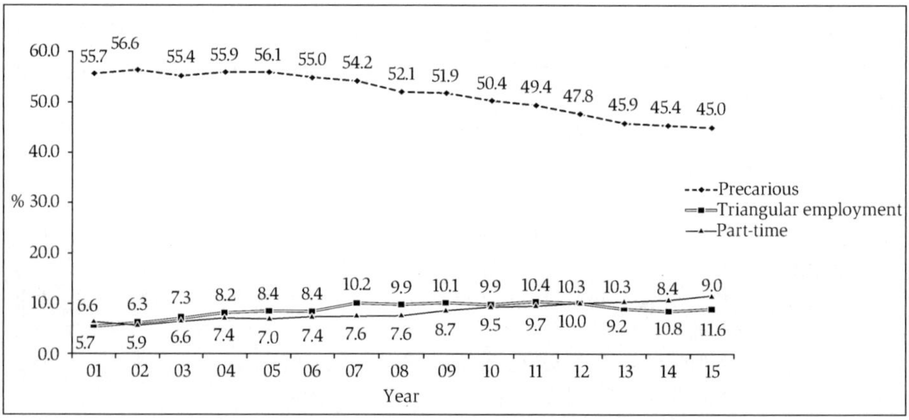

Source: Kim (2015).

It is noteworthy that triangular employment relationships have been underrepresented in the statistics. For example, in-house subcontracting is misclassified as regular employees, as they have a permanent employment contract with a subcontractor. According to a result of survey conducted by the Ministry of Labour in August 2010, the number of in-house subcontracted workers was 324,932, which amounted to 24.6% among workers at firms with 300 and more employees.

[2] Factors of the Growth of Precarious Employment

Since widespread labour protests in 1987, a new independent trade union movement with rank-and-file militancy has developed in South Korea, breaking the Government-controlled industrial relations system.[5] It weakened authoritarian industrial relations based on low-wage and barrack-like control (Koo 2000). Faced with mass resistance to low wages, employers of big enterprises began to pay relatively good wages to regular employees while increasing automation and labour flexibilization through the use of precarious employment.

The economic crisis of 1997 was a turning point; there occurred a significant change in the composition of labour market. After the economic crisis, employers have minimized the use of regular employees and replaced their jobs by precarious employment through redundancy, restructuring, outsourcing and so on. Since then, new jobs have been created mostly only in forms of precarious employment and precarious workers have become the core workforce.

In particular, *Chaebols* have reorganized production networks at home and abroad. *Chaebols* formed vertically integrated production networks with multi-layered subcontracting in South Korea. Samsung Electronics and Hyundai Motors, for example, moved abroad aggressively and integrated developing countries into their global production networks in the first half of 1990s.

The trends that large corporations have taken the lead in increasing triangular employment relationships are statistically verified; the result of public notice of employment types in 2015 showed that 32.9% workers of firms with 10,000 and more employees were in triangular employment relationships, while the ratio was 7.7% at firms with500 and less employees (Kim & Yun, 2015).

In particular, segmented system of collective bargaining is other factor with regard to the increasing triangular employment relationships. In Korea, enterprise-level industrial relations are still dominant and collective bargaining is limited to trade union members. While a large number of enterprise-level unions have been integrated into industrial unions since 2000, most collective bargaining is still done on an enterprise level. The Korean Metal Workers Union (KMWU), for example, has bargained collectively with an employers' organization in metal industry since 2003, but the actual working conditions including wage and employment rights are still dealt with on enterprise-level negotiations. Moreover, the major automakers, including Hyundai and Kia, that hire over 60% of trade unionists of the KMWU have not joined that industrial collective bargaining so far. This fragmented structure of collective bargaining has vulnerability to deal with triangular employment relationships. Both a subcontracting

5. After the military coup in 1961, the military dictatorship repressed labour movement and dominated trade unions via government-controlled confederation (Federation of Korean Trade Unions, FKTU). In 1987, the military dictator called a direct election of the president under the pressure of mass anti-government demonstrations. In this political democratization, workers resistance to inhumane working conditions also erupted. For example, the number of trade unions nearly doubled and the total number of workers who participated in collective actions was estimated to be 1.2 million, equivalent to approximately one-third of the regular employees in enterprises with ten or more workers (Koo, 2000).

company and an enterprise-level union are reluctant to deal with triangular employment workers' issues, regarding them as employees of 'other' companies.

On the other hand, the Government has driven forward deregulation of financial markets and corporate activities, and pursued labour market flexibilization. Government policy and regulations for facilitating greater labour flexibility have helped foster a significant increase in labour flexibility. Government legalized redundancy and temporary agency employment in 1998, and legislated law on the fixed-term employment contracts in 2006 (Yun, 2007).

The new *Act on Protections of Fixed-term and Part-time Workers* (APFPW) allows the free use of fixed-term employment for up to two years without any reasons, and creates broad exceptions where fixed-term contracts over two years would be allowed (Article 4, paragraph 1). The Government argued that this law would introduce some protective measures, such as converting fixed-term contracts to contracts of unlimited duration for those workers who have worked for more than two years (Article 4, paragraph 2). In reality, however, it is clear that employers do not hire fixed-term workers for more than two years and instead terminate contracts before the two-year deadline, or switch to another precarious worker such as a subcontracted worker. This reverse effect has already been shown in employers' practices since 2000 under the APTAW, as discussed earlier.

[C] Overview of the Labour Law Issues

[1] Individual Labour Relations

In principle, the scope of 'employer' in individual labour relations is same as that of an employer on an employment contract. In relation to triangular employment relationships, there are two exceptions. First, an 'implied contract of employment' could be established between a user employer and a worker of a supplier. The Supreme Court has found the existence of an implied contract of employment, where a statutory employer is no more than a nominal entity, since the employer lacks independency as a business owner and merely performs a function as a labour management department of a user employer, and; where the statutory employer's worker provides his/her labour for a user employer in a subordinate relation, and the user employer indeed offers remuneration to the worker.[6]

Second, under the APTAW, both an agency and a user employer take the employer's responsibility as to individual labour relation. A temporary employment agency takes responsibility for wages and social insurances contribution, while a user employer takes responsibility for working hours, holidays and occupational health and safety (Article 34 and 35). In particular, a user employer should directly employ an agency worker, in cases of using the worker in breach of regulations under the APTAW (Article 6-2).

6. The Supreme Court, 12 November 1999, 97-nu-19946.

The issue of whether or not the in-house subcontracting amounts to an illegal use of temporary agency employment is thus one of the major bones of contention between employers and the unions, and subcontracted workers and trade unions often demand that subcontracted workers be hired as direct employees of a user employer under the APTAW.

[2] Collective Labour Relations

The Constitution declares that workers shall have the right to association, collective bargaining and collective action (Article 33 paragraph 1). Under the Constitution and the Trade Union and Labour Relations Adjustment Act (TULRAA), an employer has the basic legal obligation to bargain with an eligible trade union, and should not conduct unfair labour practices.

The Supreme Court had decided that only an employer who entered into an employment relationship with an employee should take responsibility under the TULRAA until the mid-2000s. In other words, a user employer did not fall under an employer under the TULRAA.[7]

However, the working conditions of triangular employment workers cannot be improved unless a user employer enters into collective bargaining, since the real power in terms of finances and labour management in practice lies with the user employer. Even though unions and temporary employment agencies reach collective agreements about wages and union activity, these in effect cannot be implemented without a user employer's consent. That is the reason triangular employment workers' unions have demanded to bargain with user employers. Nevertheless, even if triangular employment workers form a trade union, the user employers refuse to bargain with the union on the basis that they are not the employer under the TULRAA.

When triangular employment workers form a trade union, in the majority of cases the user employer terminates the contract with the supplier who unionists belong to. The process of changing a supplier or a temporary employment agency involves the dismissal of the entire workforce followed by the arbitrary re-employment of some or most workers except unionists, with the enforcement of extremely poor working conditions as the basis of re-employment.

As triangular employment workers have attempted to form a union, and to bargain vis-a-vis with user employers since the early 2000s, the courts' view has gradually changed. In 2010, the Supreme Court held that a user employer also should take liability for unfair labour practices under the TULRAA, where the user employer would effectively and concretely control or decide the employment and working conditions of a supplier's worker.[8]

---

7. The Supreme Court, 22 December 1995, 95-nu-3565; The Supreme Court, 16 April 2004, 2004-du-1728 etc.
8. The Supreme Court, 25 March 2010, 2007-du-8881.

§9.03 CURRENT LEGISLATIVE AND INTERPRETATIVE RESPONSES

[A] Individual Labour Relations

[1] Implied Contract of Employment Theory

The LSA provides that the 'term "employment contract" means a contract which is entered into in order that a worker provides labour for which the employer pays its corresponding wages.' (Article 2 paragraph 1)

In determining the status of an employer, judicial precedents have consistently required the existence of a subordinate relation, holding that:

> the subordinate relation is determined by actual labour relations such as the existence of direction/ supervision relations, wages as a price for labour, the nature and content of labour between the employer and provider of labour regardless of the form of the labour supply contract, be it employment, contractual, delegation or anonymous, as long as there exists a user-subordinate relation between two parties.[9]

Therefore, an employment contract and labour relation will be recognized as long as a subordinate relation is acknowledged, regardless of the form of the contract.

As mentioned above, the Supreme Court developed the 'implied contract of employment' theory, in order to find who is an employer in triangular employment relationship. The most commonly used factors for determining whether the implied contract of employment exists between a user employer and a supplier's worker are as follows: who has the right to control or supervise concretely and directly the performance of work; who has the right to hire, deploy, discipline and dismiss the worker; who has the right to set wage rates and pays for the worker and so on.[10]

In determining whether the implied contract of employment exists, on one hand, the courts have emphasized whether or not a user employer solely exercises the power to instruct or supervise the performance of work, and determine the levels of remuneration. On the other hand, the courts have not recognized such an implied contract of employment between a user and a supplier's worker, where the supplier somewhat instructed or supervised the performance of work, even though the user employer share the right to control over the performance of work.[11]

In other words, the implied contract of employment theory is applied, only where a supplier is not substantial as an independent entity and merely functions just as the user employer's agent. In this respect, this theory has shortcomings as to providing triangular employment workers with effective protections.

9. The Supreme Court, 25 May 1993, 90-nu-1731.
10. The Supreme Court, 10 July 2008, 2005-da-75088.
11. The Supreme Court, 12 July 1999, 99-ma-628.

[2] The Standard for Establishing Temporary Agency Employment

Legalization of temporary agency employment, which legitimized the bifurcation between employment contracts and the subordinate relation, made the implied contract of employment theory outdated. The APTAW implies that an employment contract is no longer the sole legal basis of subordinate relation. Therefore, the main issue has moved to the standard for establishing temporary agency employment.

[a] Leading Case

As explained earlier, it became the hottest issue on triangular employment relationship, whether or not in-house subcontracting amounts to illegal temporary agency employment. Since the early 2000s, in particular, trade unions representing in-house subcontracted workers have filed a series of suits, demanding user employers must directly hire in-house subcontracted workers according to the APTAW.

On 22 July 2010, the Supreme Court decided that in-house subcontracting at Hyundai Motor Company (HMC) fell under the illegal temporary agency employment, thus employment relationship existed between HMC and subcontracted workers who had worked over two years.[12] The Supreme Court relied on the following factors in reaching such a conclusion:

- work done by subcontracted workers was conducted on conveyor belts at the workplace of HMC;
- subcontracted workers were positioned on the same assembly lines along with regular employees of HMC, and used production facilities, auto parts and supplies provided by HMC, and did work under detailed work directions made by HMC;
- HMC had the right to deploy and redeploy subcontracted workers in general, and decided workload, working methods and workflow;
- HMC gave subcontracted workers directions for the performance of work directly or through subcontractor's supervisors;
- HMC decided working time, break times, the need for overtime, operation of shift work and the pace of work of subcontracted workers;
- HMC ordered subcontracted workers to fill a vacancy on assembly lines; and
- HMC supervised personnel and performance standards of subcontracted workers through subcontractors.

This precedent left some questions such as what differences exist between standards for an implied contract of employment and for a temporary agency employment. In this case, nevertheless, the Supreme Court recognized that a user employer and a supplier could share the right to control over a supplier's worker, while the courts focused on whether or not a user employer solely possess the right to control over a supplier's worker in direct or detailed manner before this precedent. The Supreme

12. The Supreme Court, 22 July 2010, 2008-du-4367.

Court held that 'although subcontractors gave day-to-day directions for performance of work, it was nothing more than communicating directives of HMC, or being controlled by HMC.'

[b] New Precedent

After the *HMC* case, the courts maintained a view that in-house subcontracting in manufacturing fell under temporary agency employment.[13] However, In the *KTX* case,[14] the Supreme Court established the standard for temporary agency employment in a new and slightly different direction.

For the first time, the Supreme Court provided the following indicators in determining an existence of temporary agency employment:[15]

- the user employer directly or indirectly gives the subcontractor's worker binding directives as to performance of work itself;
- the subcontractor's worker was incorporated into the business of the user employer (e.g., the subcontractor's worker and the employee of the user employer form an integrated working unit, and work together);
- the subcontractor independently exercises the right to hire a worker, and/or decides the number of workers, training, working time and break times, vacation and performance standard etc.;
- the purpose of the contract between the user employer and the subcontractor is fixed for performance of a limited task; tasks of the subcontractor's workers are distinguished from those of the user employer's employees; and tasks of the subcontractor require expertise and skills; and
- the subcontractor possesses an independent business organization and the equipment for contract fulfilment.

---

13. The Supreme Court, 1 July 2011, 2011-du-6097 (*Kumho Tire* case); The Supreme Court, 23 February 2012, 2011-du-7076 (*HMC Ulsan plant* case); The Supreme Court, 28 February 2013, 2011-do-34 (*GM Korea* case) etc.
14. The Korea Railroad Corporation (KORAIL) used 370 female attendants provided by Korea Railroad Distribution since it started a high-speed railway business (KTX) in 2004. When female attendants joined in the Korean Railway Workers' Union in 2005, Korea Railroad Distribution refused to renew the contracts of union members and KORAIL terminated the contract with Korea Railroad Distribution. In response to these unfair labour practices, female attendant union members accused KORAIL of the use of illegal temporary agency work, and staged collective action including strike over four years.

    In September 2006, The Ministry of Labour ruled that the use of female attendants was not illegal temporary agency work but legitimate subcontracting, although it partly recognized the existence of a subordinate relation between KORAIL and the female attendants. Female attendants filed a series of suit, thereafter, demanding KORAIL must directly hire them. The Seoul High Court ruled that an implied contract of employment existed between KORAIL and female attendants (the Seoul High Court, 19 August 2011, 2010-na-90816), while in another case the Seoul High Court denied an existence of implied contract of employment as well as temporary agency employment between them (the Seoul High Court, 5 December 2012, 2011-na-78974).
15. The Supreme Court, 26 February 2015, 2012-da-96922.

The Supreme Court denied the existence of temporary agency employment between KORAIL and the female attendants on the grounds that KORAIL did not give KTX female attendants 'direct and detailed' directives, and their tasks could be distinguished from tasks of KORAIL's male attendants.

In the *KTX* case, the Seoul High Court had recognized that KORAIL had the right to control over the female attendants and supervised them through the subcontractor. Further, the Seoul High Court held that tasks of female attendants and that of male attendants could not be separated, and thus, it was impossible to contract out tasks of female attendants alone.

It is still controversial whether or not the Supreme Court provides different standards as to establishing temporary agency employment. Nevertheless, it seems that the Supreme Court again focused on the extent of direction and supervision of a user employer, and required its directives to be binding and detailed.

[c] Allocation of Employer Responsibility Etc.

The APTAW allocates employer responsibility, as shown in Table 9.1 (Articles 34 and 35).

Table 9.1 Allocation of Employer Responsibility

Supplier's responsibility	User employer's responsibility
- Clear statement of terms and conditions of employment - Restriction on dismissal, etc. - Advance notice of dismissal - Retirement allowance system - Settlement of payments - Certificate of employment - Payment of wages - Emergency payment - Shutdown allowances - Payment of overtime, night or holiday work - Annual paid leave - Accident compensation etc.	- Working hours - Restrictions on overtime work - Break times - Paid holidays - Monthly menstrual leave - Protection of pregnant women and nursing Mothers - Permission for time for medical examination of unborn child - Nursing hours etc.

In addition, the APTAW states that 'neither temporary work agency nor user company shall give discriminatory treatment to any temporary agency worker on the ground of his/her employment status compared with other workers engaged in the same or similar kind of duties at the business of the user company.' (Article 21 paragraph 1) Any temporary agency worker who has received discriminatory treatment may request a correction thereof to the Labour Relations Commission (Article 21 paragraph 2).

However, most triangular employment workers refrain from appealing to the Commission or courts, for fear of the reprisal of the employer. Use employers effectively decide whether or not a service contract lasts, and in turn, suppliers may easily terminate an employment contract with their worker on the basis of termination of the service contract.

On the other hand, the amended APTAW in 2006 weakened the provisions concerning the legal establishment of an employment relationship between an agency worker and their user employer in cases of illegal temporary agency employment (Article 6-2). Under the previous law, a temporary agency worker was regarded as being employed directly by a user enterprise where the worker has worked longer than two years. Although this provision had a reverse effect as discussed earlier, many trade unions demanded the application of this provision to temporary agency workers and in-house subcontracted workers who had worked for a user enterprise longer than two years. However, under the amended APTAW, an employment relationship between a user employer and a temporary agency worker is not established by law. Even if a user employer does not hire a temporary agency worker who has worked longer than two years, only fines of up to about KRW 30,000 could be imposed for reasons of breach of the APTAW.

[3] Multi-Layered Subcontracting

According to the FACI, subcontracting is permitted only in cases where a main contractor subcontracts some tasks to specialized contractors (Article 29). However, labour-only contractors might be allowed to take part in the construction work on the condition that they were supervised by the upper contractor with license. This provision was introduced for the purpose of bringing out into the open the foremen practice in 1996, but it in effect played a role in legitimizing the illegal multi-layered subcontracting. In particular, this was often used for contractors and subcontractors to evade the employer's responsibility by hiding behind intermediaries or foremen.

Since the Korean Federation of Construction Industry Trade Unions (KFCITU) demanded on the abolition of this for past ten years, this provision was repealed in 2007, and the contractor or the subcontractor may not use intermediaries or foremen as a nominal employer.

Further, the amended LSA in 2007 stipulates if a subcontractor who is not a 'constructor' under the FACI, fails to pay wages to a worker he/she has used, the direct upper-tier contractor shall take responsibility for paying wages to the worker of the subcontractor, jointly with the subcontractor (newly inserted Article 44-2). Also, according to the revised LSA, if the main contractor subcontracts the construction project to two or more tiers of contractors, the worker may demand the main contractor to directly pay an amount equivalent to wages the subcontractor should have paid to him or her (newly inserted Article 44-3 paragraph 2). Through this revision, it becomes clear in a legal term that a main contractor or a subcontractor under the FACI takes responsibility for paying wage to the worker hired by a labour-only contractor or a foreman.

Also, trade unions have struggled to eradicate wage arrears and delayed wages in the industry. For example, the Korean Construction Workers Union has demanded that local authorities take measures to secure wages in the construction project awarded by public organs. As a result, municipal ordinances have been enacted in three provinces and five cities up until 2011. According to municipal ordinances, local authorities should supervise contractors in public procurement to pay workers in a timely manner, and should secure wages in cases wherein contractors do not pay workers. In particular, these ordinances secure the wages of owner-operators as well as construction site workers.

In addition, social security laws have established the responsibility of a main contractor on behalf of construction workers hired by a subcontractor or an intermediary. In case construction work is subcontracted down several levels from a main contractor, the main contractor should pay into employment insurance and industrial accident compensation insurance fund (*Act on the Collection, etc. of Premiums for Employment Insurance and Industrial Accident Compensation Insurance*, Article 9 paragraph 1).

On the other hand, subcontracted workers' unions have fought in order that the main contractor should take responsibility for safety and health at its premises.[16]

The *Occupational Safety and Health Act* (OSHA) states that 'the owner of business specified by Presidential Decree, who conducts projects at the same place, shall take measures to prevent industrial accidents which may occur when those employed by him/her and those employed by his/her subcontractors work together at the same place.' (Article 29 paragraph 1)

Accordingly, a business owner should take such measures, including the establishment of safety and health facilities, when employees of his/her subcontractors work at a place with a risk of an industrial accident (Article 29 paragraph 3). Also, a business owner should conduct safety and health inspections at his/her job site regularly or occasionally, together with his/her employees, subcontractors, and employees of subcontractors (Article 29 paragraph 4). A person who outsources any project to another person should cooperate adequately with the subcontractor, such as providing the subcontractor with any place to install sanitary facilities or allowing the subcontractor's employees to use his/her sanitary facilities (Article 29 paragraph 9).

16. For example, in 2009, the Local Seoul & Gyeonggi of Korean Public Service Union ('*Seogyeongjibu*') launched an organizing campaign targeting subcontracted cleaners at university in Seoul, with various civic group including university student organizations. Cleaners had to bring their lunch and eat it (usually cold rice) in the toilet or the shed, because neither lunch nor an access to a staff lounge was provided for them. One of the campaign slogans, 'Right to Warm Lunch' disclosed this inhumane working conditions and demanded that a user employer (a building owner) should provide cleaners with an access to appropriate staff lounges and safety facilities at workplace. This has borne fruit as a revision of the *Occupational Safety and Health Act* in 2011, which obliges a contracting company (a user employer) to provide sanitary facilities for employees of a subcontractor.

[B] Collective Labour Relations

As mentioned above, the Supreme Court held that a user employer also should take liability for unfair labour practices under the TULRAA, where the user employer is in position to control or decide effectively and concretely essential terms and conditions of employment of the worker.[17]

It is notable that the courts have recognized a user employer who is not the party to an employment contract would be liable for unfair labour practices. Nevertheless, the Supreme Court decided that a user employer is an employer under the TULRAA, as he/she 'is in position to control or decide *so effectively and concretely that he/she seems to share the right and the responsibility as an employer*'.

Thus, it seems that the courts still hold a view that a user employer would take responsibility in collective labour relations exceptionally. Actually, the case of the Supreme Court decision in 2010 was such an exceptional case, as it could be arguable that an implied contract of employment existed between the user employer and the worker.[18]

Although the courts began to recognize the user employer's liability for unfair labour practice, it is still controversial issue to what extent the user employer must have a legal obligation to bargain with the union. In academic discussions, it is argued that the user employer should enter into collective bargaining to such an extent as he/she has the right to decide (i.e., working time, occupational health and safety). In other words, the user employer may refuse to bargain on subjects such as the level of remunerations and direct hiring.

This argument, however, does not fit into the reality of current industrial relation. As explained above, it is hardly possible to reach effective and meaningful collective agreements, unless the user employer enters into collective bargaining on essential terms and conditions of employment which he/she effectively controls. In practice, more and more collective agreements on those subjects are concluded between the user employer and the union representing triangular employment workers.

On the other hand, triangular employment workers are rarely allowed to conduct collective actions at the contracting company (user employer) workplace, even though this is the actual place of work. The courts, for example, have penalized union members who joined collective actions against a contracting company, ruling that such union activity is an 'obstruction of business' under criminal law statutes.[19] While a user company can exert the power to terminate a contract, which results in dismissal of workers, collective actions against the user company are often banned.

17. The Supreme Court, 25 March 2010, 2007-du-8881.
18. In-house subcontracted workers at Hyundai Heavy Industries Co. formed a trade union in August 2003. Shortly after the union was formed openly, all union members were dismissed and subcontractors employing union members closed down their business. Non-union subcontracted workers were rehired by other subcontractors thereafter. The union accused the Hyundai Heavy Industries Co. of unfair labour practices, arguing that the user enterprise had subcontractors closed down on the basis of union activities.
19. The Busan High Court, 22 July 2015, 2014-no-781; The Cheonan Branch Court, 21 September 2004, 2004-kahap-525 etc.

For example, since September 2003, the police and prosecuting authorities have begun a series of unjust investigations specifically targeting the organizing efforts of the KFCITU local unions. The police and prosecutors accused these trade union officials of: (i) using force and coercing construction site managers of main contractors to sign collective agreements; (ii) threatening to report Occupational Safety and Health violations if the main contractor did not sign these agreements; and (iii) extorting payments as a result of these collective agreements. Up to 2006, thirteen union organizers were arrested and fined or jailed.

Following a complaint by the KFCITU and international trade union bodies, the ILO Freedom of Association Committee requested the Korean government to recognize that the relevant construction industry trade union should also be able to request negotiations with the employer of its choice, including a main contractor, on a voluntary basis. Especially in cases such as this one, the Committee noted that it would be impossible to negotiate with each and every one of the subcontractors. Also it noted that the arrest of trade unionists may create an atmosphere of intimidation and fear prejudicial to the normal development of trade union activities, and this intimidating effect is likely to be even stronger in the case of precarious, and therefore particularly vulnerable, workers who had just recently exercised their right to organize and bargain collectively.[20]

Current regulations and the judicial precedents that limit industrial relations into corporate boundaries and associate an employee status with freedom of association have motivated employers to increase triangular employment relationship. In this respect, the ILO also requested that:

> the Government to develop, in consultation with the social partners concerned, appropriate mechanisms aimed at strengthening the protection of subcontracted workers' rights to freedom of association and collective bargaining, guaranteed to all workers by the TULRAA, and at preventing any abuse of subcontracting as a way to evade in practice the exercise by these workers of their fundamental rights.[21]

§9.04 EVALUATION AND FUTURE PROSPECT

By legalizing agency employment, Korean labour laws recognized the bifurcation between employment contracts and the subordinate relation. However, the courts and the Government still focus on whether or not a user enterprise *exercises* directions or control over the performance of work, in order to identify who is responsible for workers' rights.

The 'standard employment relationship' was historically formed in the internal labour market of the vertically integrated firms in the early twentieth century (Deakin 2002). In the vertically integrated firm, the most common method to control workers

20. Case no. 1865, Freedom of Association Committee, Report No. 340, 2006, paragraphs 775 and 778.
21. Case no. 2602. Freedom of Association Committee, Report No. 359, 2011, paragraph 270; Case no. 2602. Freedom of Association Committee, Report No.363, 2012, paragraph 467.

was instructing the performance of work 'directly'. Whereas, controlling the performance of work has become less and less important for employers, as technologies have developed and the forms of corporate organization have changed in the late twentieth century (Marchington et al., 2005).

More and more transnational corporations (TNCs), for example, build global value chains and contract out most process of production to other firms. Samsung Electronics, for example, can control workers of the suppliers as effectively as its own employees, through detailed guidelines for service, training, monitoring system and control of its suppliers. As such is the construction industry where subcontracting was traditionally used. A main contractor can secure workforce stably through labour intermediaries or subcontractors that recruit and manage workers.

When we see only individual entities separately, it is difficult to identify who should take responsibility for workers' rights, as a 'function' of the employer is performed by several firms. However, if we look into the whole value chains, it can be found that a lead company *retains* power to control over the whole chains. In this respect, contemporary forms of corporations are referred to 'vertically integrated networks' rather than 'vertically disintegrated firms' (Kim 2009).

Besides changing corporate forms, changing nature of control and dependency should be analysed at the same time, to understand precarious work. The courts normally held that a contracting company should take legal responsibility for workers' rights only where the company instruct or supervise the performance of work. Thus, the courts have seldom recognized the employer's responsibility of a contracting company, in cases where it made the subcontractor supervise the performance of work on behalf of the contracting company, or the worker had to obey service guidelines by which the contracting company instructed a standardized process of work.

However, the factor as to whether or not an employer exercises control over the details of work becomes less and less dispositive for identifying an employer and an employee. Instead, the power to decide the period of existence of the contract or the power to provide jobs (i.e., opportunities for remunerations) for workers has got a significant meaning. This would be more important to workers who do not have a permanent employment contract with a particular employer, thus who have to find several jobs to make a living. Likewise, an 'independent worker' who provides her labour to several users, does not always have independency. Rather it might imply that the worker has more precarious conditions like a day labourer. In this respect, even workers who are the most deviated from the standard single employment relationship are strongly dependent upon a user, and this should be evaluated as 'alienated dependence' rather than 'quasi-dependence', which must be viewed from the whole networked firms (Yun 2014).

On the employer's side, using labour in an indirect way might bring out difficulties in recruiting and managing workers. There are some practices to cope with this problem. One is using labour intermediaries such as private employment agencies and exerting control over the labour intermediaries as well as workers. Another is taking advantage of the external labour market with regard to a particular trade or occupation. The more prevalent are precarious forms of employment in the industries, the easier is to recruit experienced workers in the external labour market. The cost of recruiting and training is transferred onto individual worker, and the level of wages is standardized downward at minimum wages.

As such, the unbalanced distribution of cost and risks between employers and workers is ensured over the labour market, even though an employment relationship between individual employer and worker seems indistinct like a dotted line.

Many legal systems such as Korea have limited regulatory interventions into a boundary of separate entities, and this allowed the lead company to transfer their liabilities to others downwards value chains. Nevertheless, workers have attempted to face the one that retains the real power to control over their working conditions, as shown above. To secure labour law liabilities beyond the boundary of the legal entity, right to collective bargaining and collective actions should be secured to the level of the lead company across the whole value chains.

In order to realize this principle, industrial relations institutions need to be reconstructed as follows. Facilitating collective bargaining with the 'user enterprise' is the most effective way for resolving such questions as who is an employer and what responsibility the employer must take. While employment law could provide some regulatory answers to these questions, employers easily avoid those regulations by transforming the form of contract or corporation. On the other hand, collective bargaining could find tailored approach to improve working conditions and enhance rights at work without falling under a dogmatic boundary. Therefore, realizing right to collective representation and right to collective bargaining should be considered essential for responding to both questions, that is, 'who is a worker?' and 'who should take responsibility for the worker's rights?'

§9.05 BIBLIOGRAPHY

Chang, Dae-oup. 2006. 'Samsung Moves: Aportrait of Struggles', in: Chang, Dae-oup (ed.), *Labour in Globalising Asian Corporations: A Portrait of Struggle*. Hong Kong: Asia Monitor Resource Centre.

Cho, Sung-Jae. 2006. 'The Reality of in-Company Subcontracting and an Alternative', in: Park, Tae-Joo et al. (eds.), *A Review on the Industrial Relations of Hyundai Motor Company and an Alternative*. Seoul: Korean Labour Education Institute, pp. 77-105 (*in Korean*).

Eun, Su-Mi. 2008. 'Why Are Employers Preferring Indirect Hiring?:A Case Study of the Manufacturing Industry in Korea'. *Quarterly Journal of Labour Policy*. Vol. 8, No. 3. pp. 125-158 (*in Korean*).

Davidov, Guy. 2004. 'Joint Employer Status in Triangular Employment Relationships'. *British Journal of Industrial Relations*. Vol. 42, No. 4. pp. 727-746.

Deakin, Simon. 2002. 'The Many Futures of the Contract of Employment', in: J. Conaghan, R.M. Fischl and K. Klare (eds.), *Labour Law in an Era of Globalization*. Oxford: Oxford University Press.

Freedland, Mark. 2003. *The Personal Employment Contract*. Oxford: Oxford University Press.

Fudge, Judy. 2005. 'Beyond Vulnerable Workers?: Towards a New Standard Employment Relationship'. *Canadian Labour and Employment Law Journal*. Vol. 12, No.2. pp. 145-170.

Future of Workers et al. 2011. The Result of Survey on the Working Conditions at Seoul Digital Complex. Seoul. (*in Korean*)

Han, Ji-Won et al. 2013. 'In the Belly of the Beast: Samsung Electronics' Supply Chain and Workforce in Korea', in: Asia Monitor Resource Centre, *Labor Rights in High Tech Electronics: Case Studies of Workers' Struggles in Samsung Electronics and Its Asian Suppliers*, http://www.amrc.org.hk/content/labour-rights-high-tech-electronics-case-studies-workers-struggles-samsung-electronics-and-0.

Hong Kong: Asia Monitor Resource Centre. Kim, Cheolsik. 2009. *Commodity Chain Reorganization and the Change of Employment Systems: The Korean Automotive Industry*. Unpublished Ph.D. Dissertation, Seoul National University. (*in Korean*)

Kim, Yoo-Sun. 2015. *Size and the Employment Conditions of Precarious Workers: An Analysis of Supplement Survey of Economically Active Population*. KLSI Issue Paper No. 11. Seoul: Korea Labour& Society Institute. (*in Korean*)

Kim, Yoo-Sun & Ja-ho, Yun. 2015. *Size of Precarious Employment at Large Corporations: An Analysis of Public Notice of Employment Types*. KLSI Issue Paper. No.8. Seoul: Korea Labour& Society Institute. (*in Korean*)

Koo, Hae-Geun. 2000. 'The Dilemmas of Empowered Labor in Korea', *Asian Surveys*. Vol. XL, No. 2.

Korean Metalworkers' Federation. 2003. *Studies for Organizing Subcontracted Workers in Metal Industry*. Seoul. (*in Korean*)

Korean Metal Workers Union. 2007. *Studies on Labour Market and the Actual Conditions of Precarious Employment in Metal Industry*. Seoul. (*in Korean*)

Korean Metal Workers Union. 2009. *A Study on Wage Policy of Industrial Union*. Seoul. (*in Korean*)

Korean Public Service Workers Union. 2008. *Precarious Employment in Public Service Sector and Trade Unions' Response*. Seoul. (*in Korean*)

Marchington, Mick, Grimshaw, Damian Lubery, Jill & Willmott, Hugh (eds.). 2005. *Fragmenting Work: Blurring Organizational Boundaries and Disordering Hierarchies*. Oxford: Oxford University Press.

Ministry of Labour. 2008. The Second Framework Plan for the Improvement of Employment of Construction Workers. (*in Korean*)

Ministry of Employment & Labour. each year. Report of the Current State of Temporary Agency Employment. (*in Korean*) Rodgers, Gerry. 1989. 'Precarious Work in Western Europe: The State of the Debate'. in: Rodgers, Gerry. Rodgers, Janine (eds.). *Precarious Jobs in Labour Market Regulation: The Growth of Atypical Employment in Western Europe*. Geneva: International Institute for Labour Studies. pp. 1-16.

Sim, Kyu-Beom et al. 2013. *The Real Condition of Manpower Demand and Supply in Construction Industry*. Seoul: Construction and Economy Research Institute of Korea. (*in Korean*)

Sin, Young-Cheol. 2014. On the Remedial Measures to apply the Industrial Accident Compensation Insurance to Construction Equipment Operators. Seoul: Korean Construction Workers Union. (*in Korean*)

Weil, David. 2014. *The Fissured Workplace*. Harvard University Press.

Yun, Aelim. 2007. *The ILO Recommendation on the Employment Relationship and Its Relevance in the Republic of Korea*, GURN Discussion Paper No. 4, available at: http://www.ilo.org/public/libdoc/ilo/2007/107B09_95_engl.pdf.

Yun, Aelim. 2011. 'Building Collective Identity: Trade Union Representation of Precarious Workers in the South Korean Auto Company'. *Labour, Capital and Society*. Vol. 44, No. 1. pp. 154-178.

Yun, Aelim. 2014. 'Organizing Workers Beyond an Employment Relationship', in: Bhowmik (ed.), *The State of Labour*, Routledge.

CHAPTER 10

The Fissured Workplace and Predicaments and Breakthroughs in Taiwanese Labour Law

Shih-Hao Liu[*]

§10.01 INTRODUCTION

In Chapter 3 of his book *The Fissured Workplace,* David Weil writes:

> The large corporation of days of yore came with distinctive borders around its perimeter, with most employment located inside firm walls. The large business of today looks more like a small solar system, with a lead firm at its center and smaller workplaces orbiting around it. Some of those orbiting bodies have their own small moons moving about them. But as they move farther away from the leading organisation, the profit margins they can achieve diminish, with consequent impacts on their workforces.[1]

This poetic statement mirrors both the painful experiences[2] of Taiwan and the fruits of its economic growth.

Weil goes on to explain:

> During much of the twentieth century, the critical employment relationship was between large businesses and workers. ... However, most no longer directly employ legions of workers to make products or deliver services. Employment has

* Ming-Chuan University.

1. David Weil. *The Fissured Workplace: Why Work Became So Bad for So Many and What Can Be Done to Improve It,* Harvard University Press, 2014, p. 43.
2. The author gives an example of a painful experience: sex tourism in developing countries. *See* Chyong-Fang Ko and Han Pi Chang, 'Is the 21st Century World-Economy a Passport to Development or to Sexual Exploitation?' in *Emerging Issues in the 21st Century World-System,* edited by Wilma A. Dunaway, pp. 34-35 (2003).

> been actively shed by these market leaders and transferred to a complicated network of smaller business units. Lower-level businesses operate in more highly competitive markets than those of the firms that shifted employment to them.

This passage examines not only the case of the United States domestic market, but also production in the international market. Economic globalisation is defined as the increasing economic interdependence of national economies across the world through a rapid increase in cross-border movement of goods, service, technology, and capital. Labour law scholars have addressed 'fissured workplaces' within individual countries, but Immanuel Wallerstein's world systems theory[3] must also be discussed. He has rightly pointed out a major flaw in the world economy that international resolutions have not yet discussed in depth.

However, Taiwan is a special case in the world systems theory. Taiwan almost completely lacks important minerals and other raw materials, and must rely on a large amount of international trade with 'core' (developed) countries in order to maintain its economy and the livelihoods of its people. Fissured workplaces are not uncommon in Taiwan; most industries must maintain this state in order to cope with fierce competition in the international market. Taiwan has transitioned from the 'periphery' (developing countries) to the 'semi-periphery'in past decades, and currently plays an occasional role as a core country.[4] I mention this phenomenon not to provoke international controversy over the idea of worldwide socialism. I simply hope that readers understand why Taiwan has so many fissured workplaces. Please allow me to dispense with that tongue-twisting term in this chapter, because many developing countries function as large-scale fissured workplaces for developed countries, as described by David Weil in *The Large Business.*[5] I will discuss certain questions within a Taiwanese context, emphasising that its industrial structure is different from those of other countries.

§10.02 THE PHENOMENON OF FISSURED WORKPLACES IN TAIWAN

Many countries, such as the US, Japan, Germany, France, Korea, the UK, Spain, Hong Kong, and even Mainland China have powerful companies which have fissured their powerful and centralised business bodies into various forms, such as multi-layered

3. Immanuel Wallerstein wrote an article discussing world systems in the twenty-first century. *See* Wallerstein, 'Structural Crisis, or Why Capitalists May No Longer Find Capitalism Rewarding' in *Does Capitalism Have a Future?*, edited by Wallerstein, Collins, Mann, Derluguian, Calhoun, Oxford, 2013, pp. 9-10.
4. Chinese scholars have also considered the reorientation of China in the modern world system. For example: De-Ming Lu, *Development of China in the Modern World System*, Singapore, 2010, pp. 151-202. There are some interesting and persuasive arguments in this book, such as that with the international transfer of technical advancement, management learning and institutional evolution changed the economic position of Mainland China in the modern world system.
5. Weil, David. *The Fissured Workplace: Why Work Became So Bad for So Many and What Can Be Done to Improve It*, Harvard University Press, 2014, p. 43.

subcontracting, outsourcing, franchising, and supply chains.[6] By contrast, the Taiwanese economy was formerly supported by medium and small enterprises. Unfortunately, before 1980 most small business owners had relatively little knowledge of how to form effective supply chains, and did not even understand basic economics or management theories. However, they learned by doing. They inadvertently developed companies that operated similarly to fissured workplaces to cope with the drastic economic changes that occurred during the period of rapid globalisation in the 1990s.

[A] The Industrial Ecology of Small and Medium Enterprises

The Taiwanese Ministry of Economic Affairs, in its Standards for Identifying Small and Medium-sized Enterprises, establishes the following conditions for a business to qualify for this category:

> The enterprise has been established in the manufacturing, construction, mining or quarrying industry with either paid-in capital of NT$80 million or less, or has hired fewer than 200 regular employees.
>
> The enterprise has been established in an industry other than those mentioned in the previous paragraph and either had a sales revenue of NT$100 million or less in the previous year, or has hired fewer than 100 regular employees.

In 2014, there were 1,353,049 small and medium enterprises in Taiwan, respectively, accounting for 97.61% of entrepreneurs. Approximately 80% of these enterprises were in the service industry, nearly half (49.40%) were in the wholesale and retail trade, and 55.04% were involved in mining operations. Key characteristics of small and medium enterprises include their flexibility and ability to quickly cycle in and out of the market. The majority (50.67%) of small and medium enterprises operate for fewer than ten years.[7] Total employment in Taiwan is 110,719,000, with employment in small and medium enterprises accounting for 78.25%.[8]

The huge number of small and medium enterprises constitutes a powerful chain of industries. Some are able to function independently, filling both domestic and foreign orders, and others may ally themselves with leading companies such as Taiwan Semiconductor Manufacturing Co., Ltd (TSMC, one of the largest wafer manufacturers in the world), allowing for greater competitiveness in international markets. For example, a TSMC factory was severely damaged during a 6.5 earthquake on 6 February 2016 in Tainan, a city in southern Taiwan. TSMC organised its subsidiaries around the world to assist in emergency rescue operations, repatriating a total of 500 engineers who worked alongside employees from thirty allied small and medium enterprises.

6. Weil, David. *The Fissured Workplace: Why Work Became So Bad for So Many and What Can Be Done to Improve It*, Harvard University Press, 2014, pp. 10-11.
7. Ministry of Economic Affairs of Taiwan, 'White paper on small and medium enterprises in Taiwan', 2015, pp. 16-17.
8. Ministry of Economic Affairs of Taiwan, 'White paper on small and medium enterprises in Taiwan', 2015, p. 18.

After seven days of recovery efforts, TSMC was able to resume its regularly scheduled shipping to customers around the world.[9]

[B] The Popularity of Amoeba Organisations in Taiwan

'Amoeba organisations' are similar to fissured workplaces. Prof. Warren Bennis and Henry Mintzberg created academically the theory of 'Amoeba organisations'. This management theory were developed and put into practice by Inamori Kazuo, founder of the Kyocera Corporation, eventually earning him the moniker of the 'new Japanese god of business' (taking up the mantle of the 'old god of business', Konosuke Matsushita).[10] Many Taiwanese entrepreneurs believe strongly in Inamori's business philosophy.

Many Taiwanese enterprises of all sizes have cultivated flexible design approaches to adapt to environmental changes. In a globalised environment, enterprises must develop and adjust their organisational patterns to maintain and improve their competitiveness, and strive for innovation in addition to other aspects that contribute to success, such as manpower, equipment, processes, and marketing.

The amoeba organisational design possesses two forms. The first form involves the structure of the organisation itself, which consists of many groups operating independently or as units within task groups. They create competitive products according to the changing business environment, and are immediately reorganised after tasks are completed or if they cannot maintain competitiveness.

The second form involves mutually dependent alliances forged between organisations, which can create considerable profits. Once the business environment changes, however, they are rapidly dismantled and each enterprise forms new alliances. Because these alliances create organisations that do not physically exist, they are also known as virtual organisations.

[C] OEM-Based Businesses in Taiwan

Although Taiwan lacks its own major brands, numerous enterprises are involved in original equipment manufacturing (OEM),[11] and some are able to undertake more complex tasks as original design manufacturers (ODMs).[12] The IT company Foxconn and the wafer manufacturer TSMC are both internationally famous and are able to

9. A report from the Central News Agency, 12 February 2016, *see*: http://www.cna.com.tw/news/afe/201602120240-1.aspx.
10. Ishida, Hideki, 'Amoeba Management at Kyocera Corporation', *Human Systems Management*, vol. 13, No. 3, p. 183, 1994.
11. OEM (Original Equipment Manufacturing): a system where production is entrusted to the party that provides requests and authorisation, according to the specific conditions involved.
12. ODM (Original Design Manufacturer):an enterprise involved in product design and development activities, via high-performance product development and a competitive manufacturing performance to meet the needs of the buyer.

engage in OEM as ODMs. Foxconn made several attempts at becoming an OBM (Original Brand Manufacturer),[13] but its performance was not satisfactory.

Taiwanese companies entered the OEM footwear business almost forty years ago. The athletic footwear industry had a vertical division of labour, with international brands focused only on product design and brand marketing, and the other production processes outsourced to specialised factories. Adidas and Reebok originally structured their factories according to a vertically integrated model, but after continual attempts, they were unable to maintain it. Nike began as an importer for the Japanese company Onitsuka. Later, Nike began designing its own sneakers, but still received help in the production stage from Japanese trading companies which used a vertical division of labour. Adidas, Reebok, Converse, and Nike eventually transferred their production bases to Taiwan. The relationship between Taiwanese factories and multinational companies led to the formation of a huge supply chain involving many small and medium enterprises.[14] In 1994, research published by the MIT Sloan School of Management stated that major American businesses relied heavily on suppliers in Taiwan and Mainland China through strategic outsourcing and the retention of only essential technology. The report analysed Nike as an example of this strategic outsourcing from 1984 to 1993. During this period, Nike increased turnover and profit after tax by 20%.[15]

These supply chains were usually pyramid-shaped, with the main company located at the top and the employees of small enterprises at the bottom. Some of these employees worked at home rather than in factories or workshops. I remember helping my mother with a part-time job of this type when I was 15 years old. After 35 years, I still remember how to bind an insole to the inside of a sneaker.

Because Taiwan for the most part lacks its own international brands, numerous companies rely on OEM to stay competitive. Certain companies even integrate design orders; for example, the Pou-Chen Group is one of the most successful OEM and ODM sneaker companies in the world, and was responsible for the development of the NikeAir Jordan series. Many of these small and medium enterprises do not earn favourable or even adequate profits from these major multinational companies. Taiwanese small and medium business owners must therefore develop cost-saving production techniques. These enterprises use the amoeba management theory to maintain their existence and pay their employees relatively low wages. They generally do not outsource or use worker agencies, because these legal relationships are too complex for their purposes. If they aim to reduce labour costs, small and medium enterprises prefer to hire foreign or part-time workers. The alternative is to move their factories to Mainland China or Vietnam. By contrast, OEM factories that produce phones or computers receive large and unpredictable domestic and foreign orders.

13. OBM (Original Brand Manufacturer): an enterprise that develops its own corporate image and brand and then reaps the maximum economic benefits.
14. Zhen, Lu-Lin, *Taiwan: A Radical Quarterly in Social Studies*. Volume 35, 1 September 1999, p. 3-4.
15. Quinn, James Brian; Hilmer, Frederick G., *Sloan Management Review*, summer 1994, 15 July, 1994, p. 43.

Non-fixed term employment is a serious challenge for them, and for that reason they frequently employ agency workers.

§10.03 EXTENSION OF EMPLOYER RESPONSIBILITY IN THE FISSURED WORKPLACE

[A] Historical Background

The predecessor of the Taiwan Labour Standards Act is the Factory Act which was passed by the Nationalist government in 1939. The Factory Act had a narrow scope, and Taiwan did not have a truly comprehensive labour law until 1984. The Labour Standards Law of that year established minimum standards for working conditions, but its scope of application was limited to eight sectors. At that time, most enterprises were what would today be called micro-enterprises. The government even promoted an entrepreneurial slogan stating 'the living room is a factory'. Beginning in 1987 with the lifting of martial law, however, Taiwan has undergone gradual but substantial changes in its socioeconomic development. Workers began to gain rights consciousness, and in 1996, the Legislative Yuan decided to extend the application of the Labour Standards Law to all employees, with certain exceptions such as doctors[16] and teachers.[17] Overall, from 1988 onwards almost all workers were protected under the Labour Standards Law.

[B] Legal Sources of Basic Worker Protection Standards

[1] Employment Agreements and the Labour Standards Law

The primary legal source of the employer-employee relationship is the agreement concluded between both parties, as established by the Labour Standards Law (although some contracts avoid this law by using freelance workers, as I will explain later). In general, the employer and the employee are free to determine the provisions of their employment agreement. Yet in practice, these agreements merely supplement binding statutory law and collective agreements. For example, Article 21 of the Labour Standards Law states:

> A worker shall be paid such wages as determined through negotiations with the employer, provided, however, that such wages shall not fall below the basic wage. The basic wage referred to in the preceding paragraph shall be prescribed by the basic wage deliberation committee of the Central Competent Authority and submitted it to the Executive Yuan for approval.

16. *See* the executive order, Council of Labor Affairs, reference number:(87), word 1 of Lao- Dong No. 059 605. Paragraph 2, No. 7.
17. *See* the executive order, Council of Labor Affairs, reference number: (87), word 1 of Lao- Dong No. 059 605. Paragraph 2, No. 2.

The Labour Standards Law is the most important statutory law on working conditions in Taiwan. Whether the employer operates an independent enterprise or an amoeba organisation (such as fissured workplaces) affiliated with a large company, so long as an enterprise hires an employee directly, then the enterprise is the employer of the employee as defined in the Labour Standards Law.[18] The employer shall provide the worker with conditions that meet or exceed the standards of the Labour Standards Law.[19]

Furthermore, the Courts claim the right to review the content of an individual employment contract with respect to fairness, pursuant to Article 247-1 of the Civil Code. For this reason, and for the purpose of efficiency, employers often use standard employment contracts for all employees and only amend them as necessary, particularly in the case of higher-level employees. Article 247-1 of the Civil Code stipulates:

> If a contract has been constituted according to the provisions which were prepared by one of the parties for contracts of the same kind, the agreements which include the following agreements and are obviously unfair under that circumstance are void.
> (1) To release or to reduce the responsibility of the party who prepared the entries of the contract.
> (2) To increase the responsibility of the other party.
> (3) To make the other party waive his right or to restrict the exercise of his right.
> (4) Other matters gravely disadvantageous to the other party.'

Taiwanese courts have affirmed that an employment contract is a standard contract that shall be governed by the principle of equity restrictions, referring to the terms of the contract that one of the parties has prepared in advance. The other party can only be made to work in accordance with the terms of the contract, and the legal principle of equity should be applied to exclude unfair unilateral interest clauses that would economically disadvantage the non-contracting party. If the other party does not accept the terms of a vertical contract, it should be considered invalid and in violation of the principles of equity, equality, and mutual benefit.[20]

[2] Non-fixed Term Contracts and Unfair Dismissal

Employment contracts are divided into two categories: fixed-term contracts and non-fixed term contracts. Fixed-term contracts are appropriate for temporary, short-term, seasonal, or specific work, but not for continuous employment.[21]

Temporary, short-term, seasonal, and specific work are defined as follows:

(1) Temporary work shall mean work of an unexpected and non-continuous nature, and is not to exceed six months.

18. Article 3 of the Labor Standards Law.
19. Article 1 of the Labor Standards Law.
20. Taiwan High Court, Civil Judgment 2014, *Labour Affairs*, No. 6.
21. Article 9 of the Labor Standards Law.

(2) Short-term work shall mean work of a non-continuous nature that is expected to be completed within a short period of time and is not to exceed six months.
(3) Seasonal work shall mean work of a non-continuous nature which is influenced by seasonal raw materials, the sources of materials, or their sale in markets, and is not to exceed nine months.
(4) Specific work shall mean work of a non-continuous nature which can be completed within a specific period. If the length of work is to exceed one year, it should be reported to the competent authority for approval and inclusion in employment records.[22]

The Labour Standards Law requires that employers provide reasonable cause for the termination of an employment contract; otherwise, it would be considered an unfair dismissal and therefore invalid. Employers must also provide severance pay and notify the employee before their termination.

[3] Collective Agreement

Collective agreements are contracts concluded between a single employer or an employers' association on one side and a trade union on the other, according to Article 2 of the Collective Agreement Act. Collective agreements generally regulate a large number of key working conditions, such as working hours, remuneration, the notice period prior to termination, number of vacation days, and overtime bonuses. They have an immediate and binding effect on individual employment relationships, pursuant to Article 19, paragraph 1 of the Collective Agreement Act, if the employer is bound by the collective agreement and the employee is a member of the union which concluded the contract.[23] Although collective agreements have considerable power, there are few which are currently in effect.

In recent decades, no more than forty collective agreements have been concluded each year, and the number of collective agreements has diminished in tandem with the privatisation of nationalised businesses. The main reason for this is the lack of a mechanism to ensure bargaining in good faith.[24] As a result, employers often disregard requests from unions to engage in negotiations. Moreover, union bargaining is often in vain because labourers have difficulty launching collective industrial action. Consequently, the amendments to the Collective Agreement Act in 2011 attempted to promote good-faith practices. Article 6 stipulates: 'Both the labourer and the employer or employer's association shall proceed in good faith when bargaining for a collective agreement.' This provision clearly states that any party cannot reject the collective bargaining proposed by the other party without justifiable reasons; if employers pretend to bargain, prolong or boycott the bargaining process, or refuse to offer any

22. Article 6 of the Enforcement Rules of the Labor Standards Law.
23. Liu, Shih-Hao, 'An Analysis of the Amendment of the Collective Agreement Act', *Journal of New Perspectives on Law*, vol. 9, p. 18-20, 2009.
24. Huang, Yao-Zhan, 'The Research of the new Collective Agreement Act', *Taiwan Labor Quarterly*, No. 12 pp. 48-49, 2008.

necessary documents, those actions will be defined as an unjustifiable rejection. According to the Settlement of Labour-Management Disputes Act, employers who are determined to have unjustifiably rejected proposed collective bargaining will be subject to fines.[25] Beginning in 2012, the number of concluded collective agreements grew quickly. As of the third quarter last year, there are more than 300.[26]

[4] Working Rules

In practice, the most common legal tool with which business owners manage their employees are 'working rules':

> An employer hiring more than thirty workers shall set up working rules in accordance with the nature of the business, and shall publicly display the said rules after they have been submitted to the competent authorities for approval and record. The rules shall specify the following subject matters:
> 1. Working hours, recess, holidays, annual paid leave of absence and the rotation of shifts for continuous operations,
> 2. Standards, method of calculation and pay day of payable wages,
> 3. Length of overtime work,
> 4. Allowances and bonuses,
> 5. Disciplinary measures,
> 6. Rules for attendance, leave-taking, award and discipline, promotions and transfer,
> 7. Rules for recruitment, discharge, severance, termination and retirement,
> 8. Compensation and consolation payment for accident, injury or disease,
> 9. Welfare measures,
> 10. Safety and health regulations to be followed and observed both the employer and the worker,
> 11. Methods for communication of views and enhancement of cooperation between employer and worker, and
> 12. Miscellaneous matters.'

The Supreme Court regards the clauses of working rules as the contents of employment contract by default, if the employer has publicly displayed said rules after they have been submitted to the competent authorities for approval and record.[27] But the High Courts and District Courts regard the clauses of working rule as standard contracts; meaning that the courts can claim the right to review the clauses of working rules with respect to fairness, pursuant to Article 247-1 of the Civil Code.[28]

25. The decision system *see* Article 35 and Article 45 of the Settlement of Labor-Management Disputes Act.
26. The Statistics of Labor Affairs, the Ministry of Labor Affairs in Taiwan. *see*: http://statdb.mol.gov.tw/html/mon/23040.htm.
27. Wang, Neng-Gin, 'Working Rules', in Taiwan Labor Law Association, The Interpretation of the Labor Standards Law, 2009, pp. 407-409; Highest Court, in Civil Judgment, 1999, Tai Shag Zhi, No. 1696.
28. Taipei Court, in civil Judgment, 2002, Lao Shu Zhi, No. 6; Taipei Court, in civil Judgment, 2002, Lao Shu Zhi, No. 105; High Court, Civil Judgment, 2003, Lao Shu Zhi, No. 5.

[5] Laws Protecting Subcontracted Workers from Occupational Accidents

According to Article 62 of the Labour Standards Law, in the case of an:

> owner of a business entity who contracts his/her work to a subcontractor who subsequently subcontracts, the contractor, the subcontractor, and the last subcontractor shall be jointly and severally liable to pay the compensation prescribed in this Chapter for occupational accidents related to the work performed by the workers hired by the contractor and the subcontractor.
>
> When a business entity or contractor or subcontractor pays compensation for occupational accidents in accordance with the provisions of the preceding paragraph, each may claim reimbursement from the last subcontractor for the portion borne.
>
> Furthermore, where a contractor's or subcontractor's work site is located within the scope of work site of the original business entity or is provided for by the same, the said original business entity shall supervise the contractor or subcontractor to provide their hired workers with such labour conditions as prescribed in applicable statutes and administrative regulations.

In accordance with Article 63 of the Labour Standards Law, a business entity shall be jointly and severally liable with the contractor or subcontractor for the compensation of occupational accidents caused to workers hired by the contractor or subcontractor for having violated the provisions of the Labour Safety and Health Act pertaining to obligations which the contractor or subcontractor are required to perform.

[C] Reform of the Occupational Safety and Health Act

[1] Expanding the Scope of Protection to All Workers

The new Occupational Safety and Health Act requires employers to protect not only their employees but also other people in their workplaces who are directed or supervised by employees. These workers are described in Article 2, subparagraph 1 of the Occupational Safety and Health Act as those 'who have no employment relationship with the business entity, but engage in work or for the purpose of learning skills or receiving occupational training at such business entity's workplace'.

[2] Expanding the Scope of Protection to Entire Workplace

The Occupational Safety and Health Act expanded the scope of protection to the entire workplace. According to the Enforcement Rules of the Occupational Safety and Health Act, the workplace can be defined as any of the following places:

(1) For the duration of the labour contract, the place where the employer assigns labourers to carry out work services to fulfil the terms of the contract.
(2) The actual place where self-employed workers engage in work.

(3) The actual place where other people engaged in work and directed or supervised by supervisors engage in work.

[D] Reform of the Gender Equality in Employment Act

The Gender Equality in Employment Act was enacted to protect gender equality in the workplace, implement thoroughly the constitutional mandate to eliminate gender discrimination, and promote the spirit of gender equality. The 2014 Amendment expands the scope of protection to agency workers. According to Article 2 of this act, an 'employer means a person, a public or private entity or authority that hires an employee. A person who represents an employer to exercise managerial authority or who represents an employer in dealing with employee matters is deemed to be an employer.' Client entities employing agency workers are deemed to be employers that must prohibit gender discrimination and sexual harassment, as well as instituting preventive and corrective measures.

[E] Lack of Protection for Sspecial Wworkers

[1] Lack of Complete Protection for Agency Workers

Agency work is common but controversial in Taiwan, because although it is legal under the Civil Code and the Labour Standards Law,[29] there are no specific protections in place for labourers in this system.

Agency work is carried out within a triangle of contractual relationships involving the agency (agency employer), agency worker, and client. Thus, there are two contracts involved:

(1) A service contract between the agency and the client.
(2) An employment contract which regulates the employment relationship between the agency worker and the agency.

Article 9 of the Labour Standards Law requires that employers of agency workers hire them under non-fixed term employment contracts, even if the employer has not had any dispatch work from client businesses. However, authorities have difficulty regulating compliance with this aspect of the law, because there are no specific statutes governing this industry. Any company can run an agency-work business so long as it has registered with in the Ministry of Economic Affairs, and these businesses are increasing in number. As mentioned previously, cell phones or IT factories often receive large domestic and foreign orders on an irregular schedule, rendering non-fixed

29. *See* the Executive Order from 30 October 1997, Tai-Lao-Dong 1 Zhe, reference number No. 047 494 which categorises agency work as part of the manpower supply industry, according to industry standard classification (subclasses ID: 7901), and states that it falls under the purview of the Labor Standards Law.

term employment contracts a challenge to maintain. As a result, they frequently hire agency workers to avoid complying with the Labour Standards Act in areas such as contract termination procedures.

The Ministry of Labour has attempted to regulate agency work, but this legislation has been attacked by client businesses, agencies, and trade unions. After twenty years of unnecessary quarrelling, the Council of Labour Affairs finally put forward a draft. Some aspects of this draft deserve praise, such as the requirement that agency work is based on the principles of Equal Pay and Equal Treatment. According to these principles, agency workers are entitled to the same remuneration and benefits as comparable permanent employees of the client.[30] Also worth mentioning are the joint liabilities of agencies and clients in occupational accident compensation and wage arrears. As for limiting the proportion of agency workers to 3% of total employees, the draft completely ignores the reality of the Taiwanese business environment. Unfortunately, debates over this draft will likely drag on for years.

[2] Lack of Protections for Freelance Workers

Under Taiwanese law, the distinction between employees and freelance workers is of particular importance in determining the application of labour laws. A freelance worker performs services according to Articles 490, 492 Civil Code on an independent basis and assumes sole risk for their business. These services might include projects completed under a highly specific contract. Conversely employees, often have requirement to perform services under the directives of an employer.

The difference between employees and freelance workers is not only in employment law, as well as the payment of social security contributions and the obligations of employers to deduct income tax. For example, according to Article 6 Labour Insurance Act, an employee, who has a fixed employer, must be insured through their employer by the Labour Insurance Bureau. The employee pays only 20% of normal insurance premium. The employer must pay 70% of normal insurance premium and 100% occupational accident insurance premium for workers. Freelance can insure the labour insurance, but they shall pay 60% premiums by themselves, and the government pays 40% premiums for them.

On the other hand, if the relationships fall within the scope of employment law, greater protection is given to them than to freelance workers. In accordance with Articles 11, 12 of Labour Standard Law, the termination of an employment relationship must comply with restrictive employment law provisions which do not apply to a freelance relationship. They may be terminated at any time.

Central and local governments frequently hire freelance workers, because the Legislative Yuan and local councils control personnel budgets and staffing and often use laws or regulations to place strict limitations on the number of civil servants and governments. The reason behind this is that the central and local governments had formerly abused their personnel budgets to hire excess employees. However, this

30. *See* the legislative reasons and Articles 16-20, of the Draft of Protection of dispatched worker Act.

limitation would prevent the various levels of the Taiwanese government from providing adequate public services under recent laws mandating increased access. This problem is often managed by hiring freelance workers under the operational budget instead. Although freelance workers in central and local governments can receive higher pay, they are not extended the same legal protections as normal employees.

§10.04 CONCLUSION

Legal ambiguities involving freelance and agency workers are serious problems in Taiwan, but the government is unwilling to face these phenomena related to the concept of the fissured workplace. After the national elections this year, a new Legislative Yuan was called into session on 1 February, and the new executive government will be sworn in on 20 May. I predict that the new administration will continue to avoid addressing these topics.

A famous Taiwanese proverb states: 'It is a shame that the state allows the officials to set fire to houses, but prohibits the people to light a candle.' Who are the main employers of freelance workers? Who are the main employers of agency workers? Actually, the central government and local governments hires a lot of freelance workers and agency workers. We have another proverb: 'The people are not clumsy enough to drop stones on their own feet.'

The government and parliament cannot avoid this issue, because dispatch workers and the freelance workers lack special protection of the law, it is vulnerable to exploitation of workers. They shall revise the drafts of protection laws for agency and freelance workers so that they are at least acceptable to every party. This might be the only method of solving the underlying legal problems I present in this chapter.

BCLR - BULLETIN OF COMPARATIVE LABOUR RELATIONS

Vol. Author/Title/Year/ISBN

1. Roger Blanpain, *Individual Employment Contracts: Collective Agreements,* 1970.
2. Roger Blanpain, *Social Planning,* 1971 (ISBN 90-312-0018-2).
3. Roger Blanpain, *Guaranteed Income Funds,* 1972 (ISBN 90-312-0019-0).
4. Roger Blanpain, *Employee Participation at the Level of the Enterprise,* 1973 (ISBN 90-312-0020-4).
5. Roger Blanpain, *Vastheid van Betrekking: Staking en Bezetting,* 1974.
6. Roger Blanpain, *Labour Law and Industrial Relations (International Bibliography),* 1975 (ISBN 90-312-0023-9).
7. Roger Blanpain, *Multinational Enterprises,* 1976 (ISBN 90-312-0024-7).
8. Roger Blanpain, *Worker's Participation in the European Company,* 1977 (ISBN 90-312-0044-1).
9. Roger Blanpain, *Women and Labour,* 1978 (ISBN 90-312-0077-8).
10. Roger Blanpain, *European Conference on Labour Law and Industrial Relations: Multinational Enterprises,* 1979 (ISBN 90-312-0091-3).
11. Roger Blanpain, *Job Security and Industrial Relations,* 1980 (ISBN 90-312-0147-2).
12. Roger Blanpain, Greg Bamber & Russell Lansbury, *Technological Change and Industrial Relations: An International Symposium,* 1983 (ISBN 90-312-0205-3).
13. Roger Blanpain, James Janssen van Raay & A. Moulty, *Worker's Participation in the European Community: The Fifth Directive,* 1984 (ISBN 90-654-4187-5).
14. Roger Blanpain, *Equality and Prohibition of Discrimination in Employment,* 1985 (ISBN 90-654-4215-4).
15. Roger Blanpain, *Restructuring Labour in the Enterprise: Law and Practice in France, F.R. of Germany, Italy, Sweden and the United Kingdom,* 1986 (ISBN 90-654-4283-9).
16. Roger Blanpain & E. Kassalow, *Unions and Industrial Relations: Recent Trends and Prospect: A Comparative Treatment,* 1987 (ISBN 90-654-4294-4).
17. Roger Blanpain & Marco Biagi, *Trade Union Democracy and Industrial Relations,* 1988 (ISBN 90-654-4394-0).
18. Roger Blanpain & Jelle Visser, *In Search of Inclusive Unionism,* 1990 (ISBN 90-654-4439-4).
19. Roger Blanpain, *Flexibility and Wages: A Comparative Treatment,* 1990 (ISBN 90-654-4461-0).

20. Roger Blanpain, Stephen Frenkel & Oliver Clarke, *Economic Restructuring and Industrial Relations in Industrialised Countries,* 1990 (ISBN 90-654-4488-2).
21. Roger Blanpain & Friedrich Fürstenberg, *Structure and Strategy in Industrial Relations,* 1991 (ISBN 90-654-4559-5).
22. Roger Blanpain, Amira Galin & Ozer Carmi, *Flexible Work Patterns and Their Impact on Industrial Relations,* 1991 (ISBN 90-654-4572-2).
23. Roger Blanpain, *Workers' Participation: Influence on Management Decision-Making by Labour in the Private Sector,* 1992 (ISBN 90-654-4600-1).
24. Roger Blanpain, Brian Brooks & Chris Engels, *Employed or Self-Employed,* 1992 (ISBN 90-654-4613-3).
25. Roger Blanpain & Tiziano Treu, *Industrial Relations Developments in the Telecommunications Industry,* 1993 (ISBN 90-654-4642-7).
26. Roger Blanpain & Marco Biagi, *Industrial Relations in Small and Medium Sized Enterprises,* 1993 (ISBN 90-654-4696-6).
27. Roger Blanpain & Marco Biagi, *Participative Management and Industrial Relations in a Worldwide Perspective,* 1993 (ISBN 90-654-4769-5).
28. Roger Blanpain, Jacques Rojot & Hoyt N. Wheeler, *Employee Rights and Industrial Justice,* 1994 (ISBN 90-654-4804-7).
29. Roger Blanpain & Ruth Ben-Israel, *Strikes and Lock-Outs in Industrialized Market Economies,* 1994 (ISBN 90-654-4841-1).
30. Roger Blanpain, Kazuo Sugeno & Yasuo Suwa, *The Harmonization of Working Life and Family Life,* 1995 (ISBN 90-411-0064-4).
31. Roger Blanpain & Laszio Nagy, *Labour Law and Industrial Relations in Central and Eastern Europe,* 1996 (ISBN 90-411-0298-1).
32. Roger Blanpain, *Labour Law and Industrial Relations in the European Union,* 1997 (ISBN 90-411-0527-1).
33. Taco Van Peijpe, *Employment Protection under Strain,* 1998 (ISBN 90-411-0528-8).
34. Roger Blanpain, Takashi Araki & Ryuichi Yamakawa, *The Process of Industrialization and the Role of Labour Law in Asia,* 1999 (ISBN 9-041-1104-7-X).
35. Roger Blanpain & Marco Biagi, *Non-standard Work and Industrial Relations,* 1999 (ISBN 90-411-1117-4).
36. Roger Blanpain, *Private Employment Agencies: The Impact of ILO Convention 181 (1997) and the Judgment of the European Court of Justice of 11 December 1997,* 1999 (ISBN 90-411-1118-2).
37. Roger Blanpain, *Multinational Enterprises and the Social Challenges of the XXIst Century: The ILO Declaration on Fundamental* Principles *at Work, Public and Private Corporate Codes of Conduct,* 2000 (ISBN 90-411-1280-4).
38. Roger Blanpain, Ryuichi Yamakawa & Takashi Araki, *Deregulation and Labour Law: In Search of a Labour Concept for the 21st Century,* 2000 (ISBN 90-411-1370-3).
39. Roger Blanpain, *The Council of Europe and the Social Challenges of the XXIst Century,* 2001 (ISBN 90-411-1543-9).

40. Roger Blanpain, *On-Line Rights for Employees in the Information Society, Use & Monitoring of E-Mail & Internet at Work,* 2002 (ISBN 90-411-1626-5).
41. Roger Blanpain, *The Evolving Employment Relationship and the New Economy: The Role of Labour Law & Industrial Relations,* 2001 (ISBN 90-411-1691-5).
42. Roger Blanpain, *Involvement of Employees in the European Union, Works Councils, Company Statute, Information and Consultation Rights,* 2002 (ISBN 90-411-1760-1).
43. Michele Colucci, *The Impact of the Internet and New Technologies on the Workplace: A Legal Analysis from a Comparative Point of View,* 2002 (ISBN 90-411-1824-1).
44. Roger Blanpain, *White Paper on the Labour Market in Italy: The Quality of European Industrial Relations and Changing Industrial Relations,* 2002 (ISBN 90-411-1841-1).
45. Roger Blanpain, Russell D. Lansbury & Young-Bum Park, *Impact of Globalisation on Employment Relations: A Comparison of the Automobile and Banking Industries in Australia and Korea,* 2002 (ISBN 90-411-1850-0).
46. Roger Blanpain & Antoine Jacobs, *Employee Rights in Bankruptcy: A Comparative-Law Assessment,* 2002 (ISBN 90-411-1942-6).
47. Roger Blanpain, Takashi Araki & Shinya Ouchi, *Corporate Restructuring and the Role of Labour Law,* 2003 (ISBN 90-411-1949-3).
48. Roger Blanpain, *Collective Bargaining, Discrimination, Social Security and European Integration,* 2003 (ISBN 90-411-2010-6).
49. Roger Blanpain & Luis Aparicio-Valdez, *Labour Relations in the Asia- Pacific Countries,* 2004 (ISBN 90-411-2239-7).
50. Roger Blanpain & Ronnie Graham, *Temporary Agency Work and the Information Society,* 2004 (ISBN 90-411-2252-4).
51. Roger Blanpain, *The Actors of Collective Bargaining: A World Report,* 2004 (ISBN 90-411-2253-2).
52. Roger Blanpain & Michele Colucci, *The Globalisation of Labour Standards: The Soft Law Track,* 2004 (ISBN 90-411-2303-2).
53. Roger Blanpain, Takashi Araki & Shinya Ouchi, *Labour Law in Motion: Diversification of the Labour Force & Terms and Conditions of Employment,* 2005 (ISBN 90-411-2315-6).
54. Roger Blanpain, *Smoking and the Workplace,* 2005 (ISBN 90-411-2325-3).
55. Roger Blanpain, *Confronting Globalization: The Quest for a Social Agenda,* 2005 (ISBN 90-411-2381-4).
56. Roger Blanpain, Thomas Blanke & Edgar Rose, *Collective Bargaining Wages in Comparative Perspective: Germany, France, the Netherlands, Sweden and the United Kingdom,* 2005 (ISBN 90-411-2388-1).
57. Roger Blanpain & Anne Numhauser-Henning, *Women in Academia & Equality Law: Aiming High - Falling Short?,* 2006 (ISBN 978-90-411-2427-6).
58. Roger Blanpain, *Freedom of Services in the European Union: Labour and Social Security Law: The Bolkestein Initiative,* 2006 (ISBN 978-90-411-2453-5).
59. Roger Blanpain, Frans Pennings & Nurhan Sural, *Flexibilisation and Modernisation of the Turkish Labour Market,* 2006 (ISBN 978-90-411-2490-X).

60. Roger Blanpain & Boel Flodgren, *Corporate and Employment Perspectives in a Global Business Environment*, 2006 (ISBN 978-90-411-2537-X).
61. Roger Blanpain, Shinya Ouchi & Takashi Araki, *Decentralizing Industrial Relations and The Role of Labor Unions and Employee Representatives*, 2007 (ISBN 978-90-411-2583-3).
62. Roger Blanpain, *European Framework Agreements and Telework: Law and Practice: A European and Comparative Study*, 2007 (ISBN 978-90-411-2560-4).
63. Roger Blanpain, Jim Kitay, Leanne Cutcher & Nick Wailes, *Globalization and Employment Relations in Retail Banking*, 2007 (ISBN 978-90-411-2620-1).
64. Roger Blanpain, Russell Lansbury, Jim Kitay, Nick Wailes & Anja Kirsch, *Globalization and Employment Relations in the Auto Assembly Industry: A Study of Seven Countries*, 2008 (ISBN 978-90-411-2698-6).
65. Roger Blanpain & Michele Tiraboschi, *The Global Labour Market: From Globalization to Flexicurity*, 2008 (ISBN 978-90-411-2722-8).
66. Roger Blanpain, Michele Colucci & Frank Hendrickx, *The Future of Sport in the European Union: Beyond the EU Reform Treaty and the White Paper*, 2008 (ISBN 978-90-411-2761-7).
67. Roger Blanpain, Linda Dickens, *Challenges in European Employment Relations: Employment Regulation, Trade Union Organization, Equality, Flexicurity, Training and New Approaches to Pay*, 2008 (ISBN 978-90-411-2771-6).
68. Roger Blanpain, Hiroya Nakakubo & Takashi Araki, *New Developments in Employment Discrimination Law, 2008* (ISBN 978-90-411-2782-2).
69. Roger Blanpain, Andrzej Marian wiątkowski, *The Laval and Viking Cases: Freedom of Services and Establishment v. Industrial Conflict in the European Economic Area and Russia*, 2009 (ISBN 978-90-411-2850-8).
70. Roger Blanpain, William Bromwich, Olga Rymkevich, Silvia Spattini, *The Modernization of Labour Law and Industrial Relations in a Comparative Perspective*, 2009 (ISBN 978-90-411-2865-2).
71. Roger Blanpain, Juan Pablo Landa & Brian Langille, *Employment Policies and Multilevel Governance*, 2009 (ISBN 978-90-411-2866-9).
72. Roger Blanpain, European Works Councils; *The European Directive 2009/ 38/EC of 6 May 2009, 2009* (ISBN 978-90-411-3208-6).
73. Roger Blanpain, William Bromwich, Olga Rymkevich & Silvia Spattini, *Labour Productivity, Investment in Human Capital and Youth Employment: Comparative Developments and Global Responses*, 2010 (ISBN 978-90-411-3249-9).
74. Greg J. Bamber & Philippe Pochet, *Regulating Employment Relations, Work and Labour Laws: International Comparisons between Key Countries*, 2010 (ISBN 978-90-411-3199-7). General Editor: Roger Blanpain.
75. Roger Blanpain, Desislava Nikolaeva Dimitrova, *Seafarers' Rights in the Globalized Maritime Industry*, 2010 (ISBN 978-90-411-3349-6).
76. Roger Blanpain, Hiroya Nakakubo & Takashi Araki, *Regulation of Fixed- Term Employment Contracts*, 2010 (ISBN 978-90-411-3356-4).

77. Roger Blanpain, William Bromwich, Olga Rymkevich & Iacopo Senatori, *Rethinking Corporate Governance,* 2011 (ISBN 978-90-411-3450-9).
78. Roger Blanpain & Frank Hendrickx, *Labour Law between Change and Tradition: Liber Amicorum Antoine Jacobs,* 2011 (ISBN 978-90-411-3424-0).
79. Roger Blanpain, Thomas Klebe, Marlene Schmidt & Bernd Waas, *Trade Union Rights at the Workplace,* 2012 (ISBN 978-90-411-3460-8).
80. Roger Blanpain, William Bromwich, Olga Rymkevich & Iacopo Senatori, *Labour Markets, Industrial Relations and Human Resources Management: From Recession to Recovery,* 2012 (ISBN 978-90-411-4004-3).
81. Roger Blanpain, Hiroya Nakakubo & Takashi Araki, *Systems of Employee Representation at the Enterprise: A Comparative Study,* 2012 (ISBN 978-90-411-4080-7).
82. Roger Blanpain & Frank Hendrickx, *Temporary Agency Work in the European Union and the United States,* 2013 (ISBN 978-90-411-4769-1).
83. Roger Blanpain, Toker Dereli, Y. Pınar Soykut-Sarıca & Aslı en-Tabaı, *Emerging Patterns of Work and Turkish Labour Market Challenges under Globalization: Readings on Labour and Employment Relations,* 2014 (ISBN 978-90-411-4983-1).
84. Roger Blanpain, Pablo Arellano Ortiz, Marius Olivier & Gijsbert Vonk, *Social Security and Migrant Workers: Selected Studies of Cross-border Social Security Mechanisms,* 2014 (ISBN 978-90-411-4770-7).
85. Roger Blanpain & Nikita Lyutov, *Workers' Representation in Central and Eastern Europe: Challenges and Opportunities for the Works Councils' System,* 2014 (ISBN 978-90-411-4746-2).
86. Roger Blanpain, Ulla Liukkunen & Chen Yifeng, *China and ILO Fundamental Principles and Rights at Works,* 2014 (ISBN 978-90-411-4984-8).
87. Roger Blanpain, *The Use of Languages and Employment Relations,* 2014 (ISBN 978-90-411-5606-8).
88. Roger Blanpain, Hiroya Nakakubo & Takashi Araki, *Protection of Employees' Personal Information and Privacy,* 2014 (ISBN 978-90-411-5608-2).
89. Roger Blanpain, Jan Wouters, Glenn Rayp, Laura Beke & Axel Marx, *Protecting Labour Rights in a Multi-polar Supply Chain and Mobile Global Economy,* 2015 (ISBN 978-90-411-5662-4).
90. Roger Blanpain & Stefania Marassi, *Globalization and Transnational Collective Labour Relations: International and European Framework Agreements at Company Level,* 2015 (ISBN 978-90-411-4748-6).
91. Roger Blanpain, Frank Hendrickx & Petra Herzfeld Olsson, *National Effects of the Implementation of EU Directives on Labour Migration from Third Countries,* 2016 (ISBN 978-90-411-6257-1).
92. Roger Blanpain, Frank Hendrickx & D'Arcy du Toit, *Labour Law and Social Progress: Holding the Line or Shifting the Boundaries?* 2016 (ISBN 978-90-411-6747-7).

93. Roger Blanpain & Frank Hendrickx, *Reasonable Accommodation in the Modern Workplace: Potential and Limits of the Integrative Logics of Labour Law*, 2016 (ISBN 978-90-411-6258-8).
94. Roger Blanpain, Frank Hendrickx & Bernd Waas, *New Forms of Employment in Europe*, 2016 (ISBN 978-90-411-6239-7).
95. Roger Blanpain, Frank Hendrickx, Hiroya Nakakubo & Takashi Araki, *The Notion of Employer in the Era of the Fissured Workplace: Should Labour Law Responsibilities Exceed the Boundary of the Legal Entity?*, 2017 (ISBN 978-90-411-8470-2).

Made in United States
Orlando, FL
04 November 2026

90208069R00146